# "A FEW BLOODY NOSES"

# "A FEW BLOODY NOSES"

## The Realities and Mythologies of the American Revolution

## ROBERT HARVEY

THE OVERLOOK PRESS
Woodstock & New York

First published in paperback in the United States in 2003 by
The Overlook Press, Peter Mayer Publishers, Inc.
Woodstock & New York

WOODSTOCK:
One Overlook Drive
Woodstock, NY 12498
www.overlookpress.com
[for individual orders, bulk and special sales, contact our Woodstock office]

NEW YORK:
141 Wooster Street
New York, NY 10012

Library of Congress Cataloging-in-Publication Data

Harvey, Robert.
"A few bloody noses" : The realities and mythologies
of the American Revolution / Robert Harvey
p. cm.
Originally published: London : John Murray, 2001
Includes bibliographical references (p. ) and index.
1. United States—History—Revolution, 1775-1783. 2. United States—
History—Revolution, 1775-1783—Influence. I. Title
E208 .H376 2002    973.3—dc21    2002020619

Printed in the United States of America
ISBN 1-58567-414-1
1 3 5 7 9 8 6 4 2

*For Cherry, Andrew, Henrietta and Hugo*

# Contents

# Illustrations

*(between pages 232 and 233)*

The author and publishers would like to thank the following for permission to reproduce illustrations: Plate 1, The Art Archive/Musée de Versailles/Dagli Orti; 2, 3, 8, 11, 13, 16, 21, 22, 23, 29, 33 and 36, Mary Evans Picture Library; 4, 6, 9, 10, 12, 18, 24, 26, 27, 28, 31, 34, 35 and 37, AKG London; 5 and 32, Hulton Archive; 14, 15, 17, 20 and 25, Faces from the Past; 19, The Art Archive/Château de Blerancourt/Dagli Orti; 30, © Francis G. Mayer/CORBIS.

# Acknowledgements

I must declare a small family interest in the American War of Independence on both sides of the British argument: George Grenville, the prime minister whose Stamp Act was widely credited as having started the chain of events that led to the war, is a direct ancestor of mine, while his brother-in-law, William Pitt the Elder, Earl of Chatham, who passionately opposed British policy, was a collateral forebear, as was Thomas Grenville, who helped to initiate the peace moves that ended the war. Another prime minister before the war, the Marquess of Rockingham, who also ended it, is a direct ancestor through the Fitzwilliam family. I myself have always been fascinated by how the war divided British opinion, for and against: as with the Vietnam War, it was lost as much in the mother country and globally as in the actual theatre of hostilities.

I hope these connections do not predispose me to devote too much of this book to the British side; I have tried to be as balanced as possible in these pages. But having been brought up with the portraits and books of these men, I have always wanted to write on the subject, and have finally fulfilled my ambition.

There is, of course, a vast literature on the War of Independence. There are excellent general histories and a wealth of brilliant specialist scholarly studies which I have enjoyably worked my way through during three years to try to write my own version. Why add to them? As I undertook the research, I uncovered an enormous amount of material that seemed to challenge the conventional view of the war in almost every field – why it happened, who was winning when, the characters of the principal protagonists, the role of the Indians (as the native Americans were referred to then and so will be referred to here) and black slaves, the nature of the American Revolution, and so on.

I felt that this protracted, very bloody and epic conflict, full of colourful characters and events, which culminated in one of the formative events in world history, the founding of the United States of America, justified an attempt to synthesize the new scholarship into a narrative history that I have tried to make as compelling as possible. This is not so much historical revisionism as using modern scholarship (most of it American) to recast a perhaps outdated and even polemical common perception of what the war was really about.

All errors and judgements are, of course, mine alone; but I hope I have contributed to an understanding of what was, after all, arguably the world's only successful and enduring revolution (the seventeenth-century English Revolution having of course been reversed, and the 1688 Glorious Revolution having been more of a palace coup than the true thing). The result was, eventually, the creation of the most powerful country the world has ever known.

I am indebted to a great many people on both sides of the Atlantic who have given me freely of their time, suggesting avenues for inquiry as well as offering me their interpretation of events. This final version is, however, no one's responsibility but my own. Among those I owe are the Hon. Raymond Seitz, former US ambassador in London (and author of the best modern study of US–British relations); Gary McDowell, Professor of American Politics at London University; Professor Robert Rutland of Tulsa University; Professor Merrill Peterson of Virginia University; Professor James Horn of the Jefferson Memorial Foundation; the Rt Hon. Lord Ryder; the Hon. Johnny Grimond, foreign editor of *The Economist*; Brian Beedham, former foreign editor of *The Economist*; and Edmund Fawcett, former *Economist* bureau chief in Washington.

I am grateful to staff at the library of London University, several Oxford and Cambridge university libraries and the United States Information Service at the American Embassy in London for their help. I owe my brilliant and painstaking editor at John Murray, Grant McIntyre, a great debt for his cheerful encouragement and help, as well as Anne Boston, Gail Pirkis, Caroline Westmore and Stephanie Allen. I owe particular thanks to the advice and encouragement of Gillon Aitken and to the literary advice of Raleigh Trevelyan. I am enormously indebted to my assistant Jenny Thomas for her hard work and patience with my foibles, as well as her historian husband, Geoffrey. Many thanks also to Christine, Richard and Emma and all our friends in Meifod. I owe my warmest thanks to my mother, sister Antonella and brother-in-law Abdullah, and their family, and especially above all for the love and devotion of Jane and Oliver.

# Maps

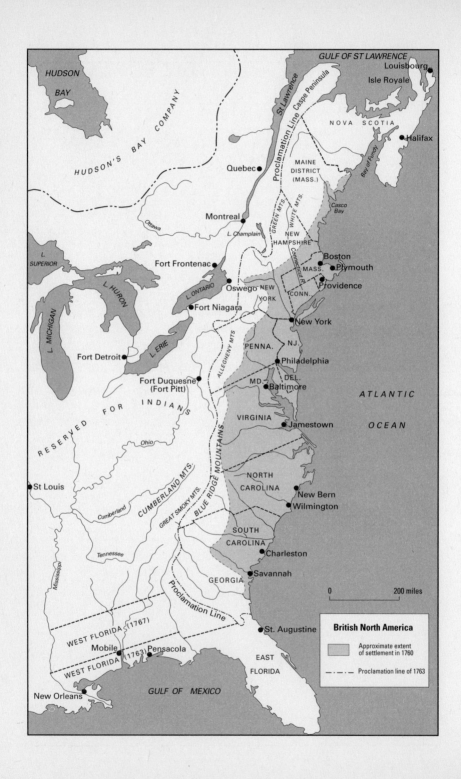

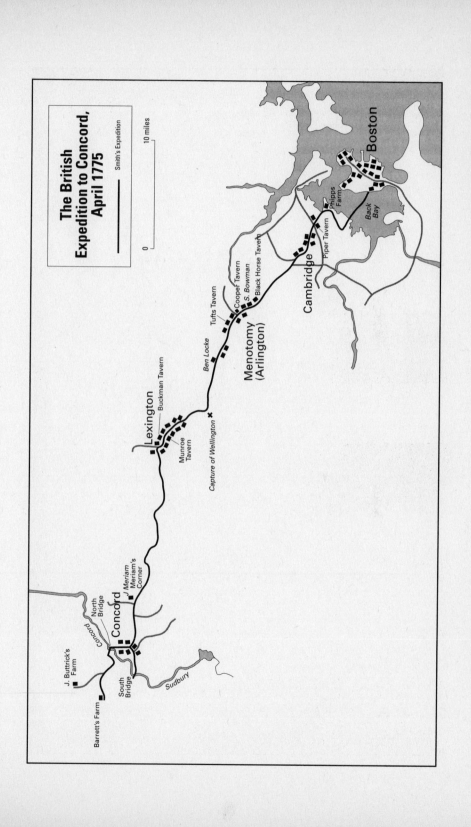

The British
Expedition to Concord,
April 1775

0     10 miles

—— Smith's Expedition

Boston

Phipps
Farm

Back
Bay

Piper Tavern

Cambridge

Black Horse Tavern

S. Bowman

Cooper Tavern

Menotomy
(Arlington)

Tufts Tavern

Ben Locke

Capture of Wellington

Buckman Tavern

Lexington

Munroe
Tavern

Meriam
Meriam's
Corner

Concord

North
Bridge

Concord

J. Buttrick's
Farm

South
Bridge

Sudbury

Barrett's Farm

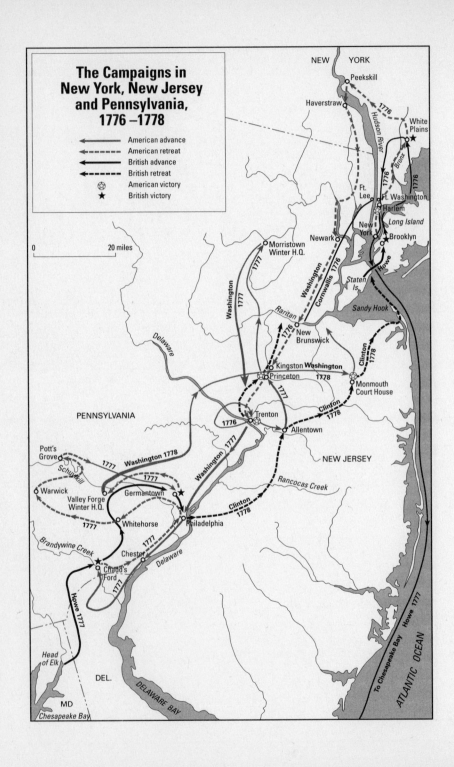

## The Campaigns in New York, New Jersey and Pennsylvania, 1776–1778

→ American advance
→ American retreat
→ British advance
→ British retreat
✿ American victory
★ British victory

0 — 20 miles

NEW YORK

Peekskill

Haverstraw

White Plains

Hudson River

1776

1776

Bronx

1776

Ft. Lee

Ft. Washington

Harlem

New York

Long Island

Newark

Brooklyn

Howe

Washington 1777

Morristown Winter H.Q.

1777

Washington 1777

Cornwallis 1776

Staten Is.

Sandy Hook

Raritan

1776

New Brunswick

Clinton 1778

Kingston  Washington

Princeton

1778

Monmouth Court House

PENNSYLVANIA

1777

Trenton

Clinton 1778

Allentown

NEW JERSEY

Delaware

Washington 1777

1776

Pott's Grove

1777

Washington 1778

Schuylkill

1777

Warwick

Valley Forge Winter H.Q.

Germantown

1777

Whitehorse

Philadelphia

Clinton 1778

Rancocas Creek

1777

Brandywine Creek

Chester

Delaware

Chadd's Ford

1777

Howe 1777

Head of Elk

DEL.

DELAWARE BAY

MD

Chesapeake Bay

To Chesapeake Bay  Howe 1777

ATLANTIC OCEAN

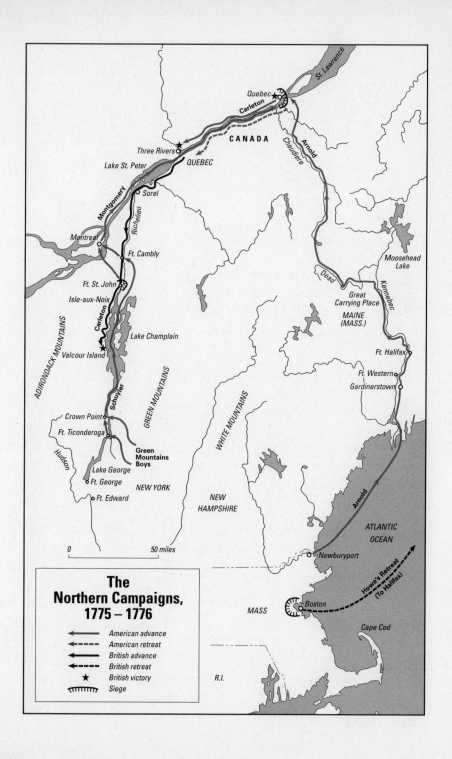

St. Lawrence

Quebec
Carleton
Quebec

CANADA

Arnold

Chaudiere

Three Rivers
Lake St. Peter
QUEBEC

Sorel

Montgomery

Montreal

Richelieu

Ft. Cambly

Moosehead
Lake

Dead

Ft. St. John

Isle-aux-Noix

Great
Carrying Place

Kennebec

Carleton

MAINE
(MASS.)

Lake Champlain

Valcour Island

Ft. Halifax

ADIRONDACK MOUNTAINS

Ft. Western
Gardinerstown

Schuyler

GREEN MOUNTAINS

WHITE MOUNTAINS

Crown Point

Ft. Ticonderoga

Green
Mountains
Boys

Hudson

Lake George
Ft. George

NEW YORK

NEW
HAMPSHIRE

Ft. Edward

ATLANTIC
OCEAN

Arnold

0          50 miles

Newburyport

Howe's Retreat
(To Halifax)

**The
Northern Campaigns,
1775 – 1776**

MASS

Boston

Cape Cod

⟵——— American advance
⟵- - - - American retreat
⟵——— British advance
⟵- - - - British retreat
★ British victory
⏡⏡⏡ Siege

R.I.

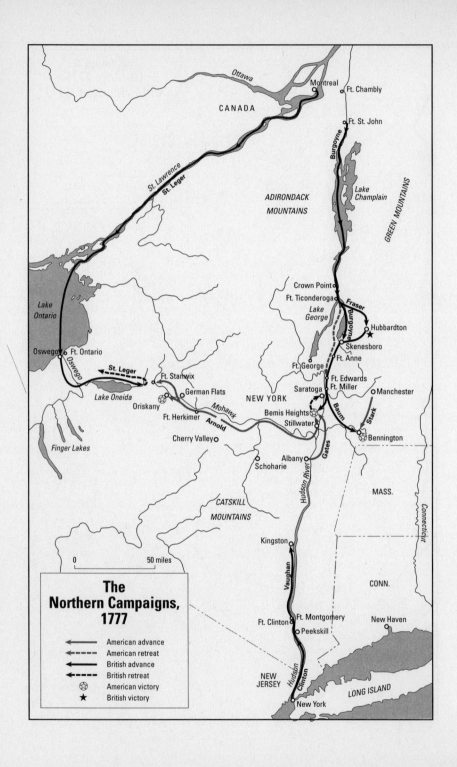

The
Northern Campaigns,
1777

→ American advance
⤍ American retreat
→ British advance
⤍ British retreat
✪ American victory
★ British victory

Ottawa
Montreal
Ft. Chambly
CANADA
Ft. St. John
St. Lawrence
St. Leger
Burgoyne
Lake Champlain
ADIRONDACK MOUNTAINS
GREEN MOUNTAINS
Crown Point
Ft. Ticonderoga
Fraser
Burgoyne
Hubbardton
Lake George
Skenesboro
Lake Ontario
Ft. Anne
Oswego
Ft. Ontario
Oswego
St. Leger
Ft. Stanwix
German Flats
Ft. George
Ft. Edwards
Ft. Miller
Manchester
Lake Oneida
Oriskany
Saratoga
Stark
Ft. Herkimer
Mohawk
Arnold
NEW YORK
Bemis Heights
Baum
Finger Lakes
Stillwater
Bennington
Cherry Valley
Gates
MASS.
Albany
Connecticut
Schoharie
CATSKILL
MOUNTAINS
Hudson River
Kingston
CONN.
Vaughan
Ft. Clinton
Ft. Montgomery
New Haven
Peekskill
NEW
JERSEY
Hudson
Clinton
LONG ISLAND
New York

0        50 miles

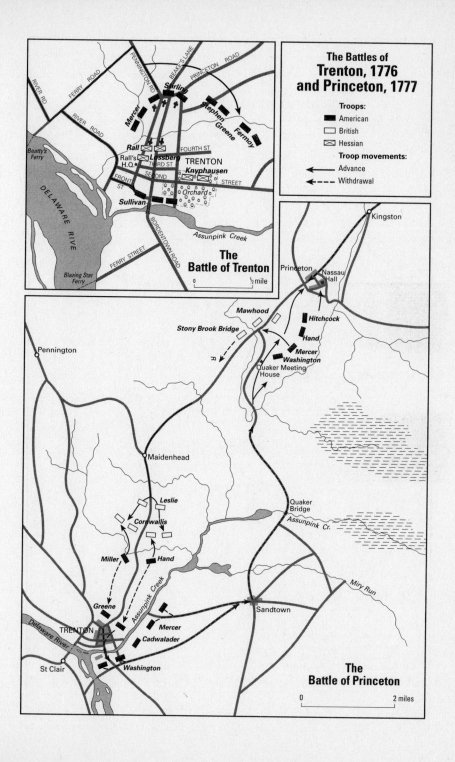

The Battles of
**Trenton, 1776
and Princeton, 1777**

Troops:

- ■ American
- □ British
- ⊠ Hessian

Troop movements:

- ← Advance
- ←--- Withdrawal

**The
Battle of Trenton**

0        ½ mile

**The
Battle of Princeton**

0        2 miles

*The Battle of Trenton labels:*

PENNINGTON RD
FERRY ROAD
BEAKE'S LANE
PRINCETON ROAD
RIVER RD
RIVER ROAD
Stirling
Mercer
Stephen
Greene
Fermoy
Rall
Lossberg
Rall's H.Q.
FOURTH ST
TRENTON
THIRD ST
Knyphausen
FRONT ST
SECOND
STREET
Beatty's Ferry
DELAWARE RIVER
Orchard
Sullivan
FERRY STREET
BORDENTOWN ROAD
Assunpink Creek
Blazing Star Ferry

*The Battle of Princeton labels:*

Kingston
Princeton
Nassau Hall
Mawhood
Hitchcock
Hand
Stony Brook Bridge
Mercer
Washington
Quaker Meeting House
Pennington
Maidenhead
Leslie
Cornwallis
Quaker Bridge
Assunpink Cr.
Miller
Hand
Miry Run
Greene
Assunpink Creek
TRENTON
Mercer
Cadwalader
Sandtown
Delaware River
St Clair
Washington

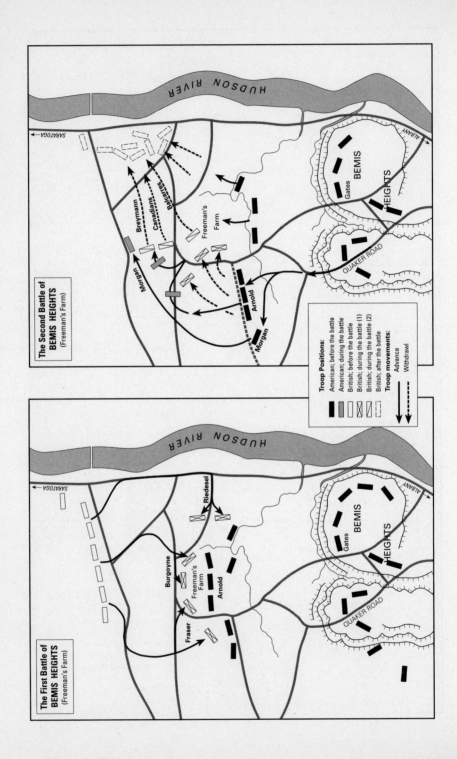

**The Second Battle of BEMIS HEIGHTS**
(Freeman's Farm)

HUDSON RIVER

SARATOGA →

BEMIS HEIGHTS

Gates

QUAKER ROAD

ALBANY

Breymann

Canadiens

Balcarres

Freeman's Farm

Morgan

Arnold

Morgan

**Troop Positions:**

American; before the battle
American; during the battle
British; before the battle
British; during the battle (1)
British; during the battle (2)
British; after the battle

**Troop movements:**

Advance
Withdrawl

**The First Battle of BEMIS HEIGHTS**
(Freeman's Farm)

HUDSON RIVER

SARATOGA →

BEMIS HEIGHTS

Gates

QUAKER ROAD

ALBANY

Riedesel

Burgoyne

Freeman's Farm

Arnold

Fraser

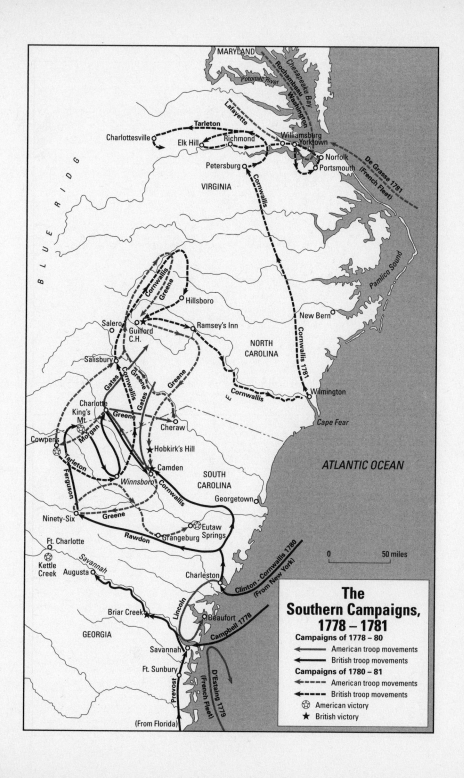

MARYLAND

Potomac River

Rochambeau
Washington

Chesapeake Bay

Lafayette

Tarleton

Charlottesville    Elk Hill    Richmond    Williamsburg    Yorktown

De Grasse 1781
(French Fleet)

Norfolk

Petersburg    Portsmouth

VIRGINIA

Cornwallis

B L U E   R I D G E

Pamlico Sound

Cornwallis    Greene

Hillsboro

Salero    Ramsey's Inn

New Bern

Guilford
C.H.

Salisbury    NORTH
CAROLINA

Cornwallis 1781

Greene    Gates

Greene

Cornwallis    Gates

Charlotte    Cornwallis    Wilmington

King's
Mt.    Greene    Cheraw

Cowpens    Morgan    Cape Fear

Tarleton    Hobkirk's Hill

ATLANTIC OCEAN

Ferguson    Winnsboro    Camden    SOUTH
CAROLINA    Cornwallis

Georgetown

Ninety-Six    Greene

Rawdon    Grangeburg    Eutaw
Springs

Ft. Charlotte

0          50 miles

Kettle
Creek    Augusta    Savannah

Charleston

Clinton - Cornwallis 1780
(From New York)

## The
## Southern Campaigns,
## 1778 – 1781

Briar Creek    Lincoln    Beaufort

Campbell 1778

**Campaigns of 1778 – 80**

⟵    American troop movements

⟵    British troop movements

**Campaigns of 1780 – 81**

◀╌╌    American troop movements

◀╌╌    British troop movements

⊛    American victory

★    British victory

GEORGIA

Savannah

Ft. Sunbury

Prevost
(From Florida)

D'Estaing 1779
(French Fleet)

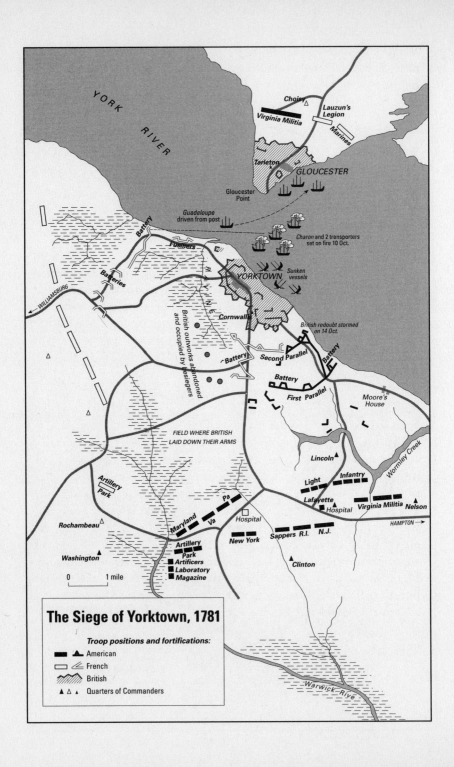

The Siege of Yorktown, 1781

We meant well to the Americans – just to punish them with a few bloody noses, and then to make laws for the happiness of both countries. But lack of discipline got into the army, lack of skill and energy in the navy, and lack of unity at home. We lost America.

George III

We have an old mother that peevish is grown,
She snubs us like children that scarce walk alone;
She forgets we're grown up and have sense of our own,
Which nobody can deny, deny, which nobody can deny.

Benjamin Franklin

The America that emerged from the War of Independence was a nation without prehistory in the traditional sense. Having won their independence, the rather loosely knit United States had to find myths and symbols to reinforce and give substance to that national unity which for the first eighty years was so precariously maintained. Myths had, perforce, to be created around the moment of birth. What Homer and the siege of Troy had been to the Greek states of the Periclean Age, George Washington and the campaigns of the Revolution were to nineteenth-century Americans. What Romulus and Remus and the Twelve Tables of the Law had been for Imperial Rome, the Founding Fathers and the Federal Constitution were for a United States searching in the midst of extraordinary social and economic transformations for unifying symbols.

The American Revolution has, thus, been encrusted with mythic elements and residues which have vastly complicated the task of the historian who wishes to state the truth of the events that took place in that era. The historian, being human and ineluctably partaking of the ideals and values of his own day, has been under the strongest pressure to make the events of the Revolution conform to the particular time and spirit of which he himself has been a self-conscious and articulate representative. He has been, therefore, not simply the enemy of the myths, as he would like to see himself, but quite as often the victim, in the sense that he has seldom escaped the temptation to make the Revolution prove something about his own society or about the society which he wishes to see evolve in the future ...

Page Smith, David Ramsay and the Causes of the<br>American Revolution, quoted in John Wahlke, ed.,<br>The Causes of the American Revolution, 1973

# "A FEW BLOODY NOSES"

# *Introduction*

Creation myths are the most enduring myths of all. The younger the country, the more potent and necessary the myth. The American Revolution and War of Independence arguably constituted the defining event in shaping the world as we know it. That Revolution, two and a quarter centuries ago, resulted in the birth of a nation which has had more impact upon the events of the last century than any other, and which has entered the new millennium in the unchallenged position of the sole global superpower, its armies and fleets bestriding the world, its businesses dominant wherever they impact, its culture popular and pervasive.

The Revolution not only created the mightiest nation in human experience: it set down, in a style virtually without parallel, the form and ethos of a government through a constitution which remains largely unaltered and reverentially respected to this day. The French revolutionary constitution has long since been discarded; the Russian formula lasted little more than seventy years; even the British constitution has steadily evolved. America's remains holy writ, and is still fully functional.

Most Americans grow up with a heroic view of the Revolution and the War of Independence that is starkly at odds with the reality exposed by more detailed study (much of it American). The relative dearth of British books on the subject is also surprising. It is as though both countries still feel the wounds after all these years: the Americans needing constantly to assert the rightness of the struggle and the courage with which they fought it, so that their nation can be said to have been forged in the fires of righteousness and valour, the British still too hurt and humiliated by their loss.

This book is an attempt to right the balance. Obviously it is liable to be criticized for its British perspective, and indeed I have consciously devoted more analysis to the motives and politics of the war on this side of the Atlantic than is usual in American studies. But, in developing my argument that the creation of the United States and its constitution was the defining act in modern world history, I have also tried to be as fair as possible to the remarkable determination and achievements of the rebellious colonists.

It does not, I believe, detract from greatness to show America's war for independence in its true light, 'warts and all'. Rather, that greatness is enhanced. *Pace* Tolstoy, exceptional human endeavour is the more remarkable in having been achieved by mortal men with all their weaknesses, suspicions, treacheries and greed. Few figures in modern history remain more godlike – and therefore unreal and unsympathetic – than those towering, all-knowing founding fathers of the United States: Washington, Samuel Adams, Franklin, Jefferson, Madison, Hamilton. Two and a quarter centuries is time enough for more shades of grey to be introduced into a picture that remains largely black and white to this day.

On the British side it is time to dispel the embarrassment of defeat and the caricature of incompetence that cloud the bitterly fought war in America. Stupidity there was – perhaps more so than on the American side – but there was also a string of victories, and acts of restraint, skill and intelligence. The causes of American victory and British defeat are a good deal more complex than the picture provided by received wisdom of determined, valiant Americans and bungling British oppressors.

Two factors, I believe, account for the remarkably enduring nature of the myths surrounding the Revolution. First, America remains a comparatively young country with a formidable patriotic sense that underlies much of its world success today: it is therefore vital to uphold the idealism and good intentions behind the country's creation. As one prominent American told me, 'America is a profoundly ideological country.' This may sound odd to those who consider it primarily a pragmatic and materialistic nation, but is nevertheless absolutely true, in that most of its people still believe in its founding ideals (in contrast to the widely discredited ideology of, for example, its old Communist opponent).

The second factor is that, as far back as the late eighteenth century, the Americans were strikingly adept at, in the modern phrase, 'spinning' their own version of events. Americans mastered the use of propaganda from the beginning: their ability to present their case in terms of impeccable righteousness, and to extract victories out of military defeat and exaggerate infrequent victories into Alexandrian triumphs, was second to none. This is not surprising given that, as the underdogs and rebels in one of the most fiercely fought and devastating wars of the eighteenth century (although rarely recognized as such), the colonists sometimes had only propaganda to fight with, and it was always an invaluable adjunct to the military effort. Exaggeration and misinformation were vital in order to boost support among the American people, frighten domestic enemies, and demoralize a British war effort that had only the half-hearted approval of public opinion at home.

In this, as in so many other respects, the ironic similarities between the American War of Independence and America's own experience two centuries later in Vietnam are striking. Britain in the eighteenth century was an over-extended, over-eager power with a young empire, imbued with deep conviction of its own rightness and the belief that it should extend its protection to the majority of Americans who were believed to embrace its values – a belief that also coincided with self-interest. Contrary to the widely held American view, but as with the Americans in Vietnam, its motives for resisting independence for the inhabitants of its colonies were idealistic as well as self-interested.

British public opinion – in a country where the small middle class had the vote and Parliament was now the ultimate arbiter of power, not the King, his servants or the nobility – was always divided or indifferent about the war. Many viewed the North American colonies as of little importance and certainly not worth the waste of young men's lives or large amounts of money. British armies could win most of the set-piece battles, but they faced an enemy that, like the Vietcong in Vietnam, could retreat at will into a vast hinterland, regroup and fight again, while waging a continual guerrilla war of attrition. While the British could not protect any but the key coastal enclaves they controlled, American guerrillas could roam, attack and intimidate almost at will throughout the countryside. They were also generally more single-minded in their methods, disregarding traditional rules of conduct – and sometimes their own word.

As in Vietnam, Great Power interests were sucked in on the side of the colonial power's enemies, rendering victory impossible. As in Vietnam, it was sheer exhaustion, the realization that decisive victory was impossible, and the growing hostility of public opinion to the continuing war, rather than military defeat, that caused the colonial power to withdraw. George III might have died with America written on his heart; very few other Britons thought the place was worth so much. (They were wrong, of course, as it turned out.)

What emerges from the fog of myth on the one side, and collective national amnesia towards a disagreeable topic on the other, is a fascinating epic bearing little relation to the popular version of events in either nation. Virtually every common assumption has to be substantially modified, if not rejected. It is generally believed that the Americans were being oppressed by a centuries-old British colonial yoke: on the contrary they were self-governing in all but name throughout most of the colonial period. British taxation, customs duties and regulations were said to be crushingly oppressive: in fact they were far lighter than in the mother country itself, and almost entirely unenforced, the great bulk of America's trade being contraband.

It is asserted that the fundamental motive for the war was an ideological love of liberty reacting against British military oppression. The motives were in fact much more complex – ranging from a love of liberty, certainly, to economic self-interest, and above all to the extraordinarily rapid transformation undergone by American society, both in numbers and in material wealth, over the preceding half-century. This resulted in a genuinely revolutionary society, in which the thrusting newcomers challenged the staid gentry of the old social order. It was in fact an internal American confrontation, to which the struggle with Britain was largely peripheral. The old order's most intelligent members sought to divert this irresistible pressure against themselves into a crusade against the British.

It is claimed that America was in deep economic trouble under British exactions before 1775; in fact the economy was booming. Much more significant than the issue of taxation (and more discreditable to the rebels) was the colonies' bitter resistance to the British 'Proclamation Line', which sought to prevent the seizure of Indian territory west of the Appalachians by land-hungry settlers. Meanwhile the rebels' pragmatic refusal to oppose slavery in their own country (to avoid losing the support of the south) made a mockery of high-flown expressions of freedom and the rights of man. As for British military oppression, the British army had intervened in strength only to defend the Americans against their French and Indian enemies during the Seven Years War, and thereafter it was barely visible until the rebellion gathered strength.

It is widely believed that Americans overwhelmingly rallied to the patriotic cause of resistance to the British. There is no evidence to support this. By the rebels' own admission, as many Americans may have been opposed to independence as in favour, and the vast majority were probably indifferent. The exodus after the end of the war of those opposed to independence numbered at least 8 per cent of the population – a staggeringly high proportion. Independence was a minority cause, support for which was whipped up by a group of committed political ideologues supported by sympathetic commercial interests.

It is widely believed that the Continental Congress summoned to consider action against the British in 1776 represented the American people. On the contrary, it was largely chosen by unrepresentative cliques (except in Massachusetts, where there was overwhelming popular support for independence – although not in Boston). The war was alleged to have started as a result of unprovoked British military aggression at Lexington and Concord; the evidence of close study is that the British blundered into a carefully organized, efficiently executed ambush. The Battle of Bunker Hill is usually considered an American triumph. In fact it was a British victory – although a costly one – and was fought on Breed's Hill.

British commanders in the war are generally portrayed as incompetent buffoons. This description applies with accuracy to only two admirals, Graves and Arbuthnot – not to the highly competent Richard, Lord Howe, or to the exceptional Rodney and Hood – and only one general, Burgoyne, the victim of his vanity and over-ambition. Admiral Howe's brother, General William Howe, was effective and audacious, if lazy and unconvinced by the rightness of Britain's cause; Clinton was competent, but overdefensive and introverted; while Cornwallis was a fearless tactician and leader in battle, but an appalling overall strategist.

Conversely, in the American pantheon, Washington ultimately displayed exactly that combination of qualities that establishes true greatness: patience and restraint, with lightning audacity when the moment is right. But his botched defence of New York and, thereafter, his headlong flight across New Jersey and – except for the brilliant guerrilla strikes at Trenton and Princeton – his crablike caution placed him under increasing pressure and criticism from Congress and his own generals, rendering him an always bitterly disputed commander-in-chief. (Indeed his chief quality at one stage seemed to be his ability to dispose of his rivals with consummate ruthlessness.)

As for the rest of the American high command, Generals Lee,

Conway, Gates, Lincoln and Arnold all fell from the stars to ignominious discredit with dizzying velocity. Only the spectacularly able, larger than life Henry Knox and Daniel Morgan emerged with their reputations intact, alongside such foreign supporters of America as Baron Johann de Kalb (killed at Camden), the Marquis de Lafayette and Baron Friedrich von Steuben. At the end of the war, Nathanael Greene, the brilliant commander in the south, emerged as a star that burned as brightly as Washington's, but he died tragically young immediately afterwards.

So the myths go on. Washington's crossing of the Delaware, immortalized in American iconography, was a brilliant and daring guerrilla raid, but had no real military impact (although a great effect on public opinion). His failure to defend Philadelphia was potentially disastrous for the American cause, but was redeemed by Gates's victory at Saratoga – which was almost a textbook example of how a single overambitious and overconfident British commander could sacrifice an entire British army.

Contrary to the received wisdom, Saragota was not militarily fatal to Britain, nor even the turning point except that it averted American defeat and provided a pretext for the French to declare war on Britain. In fact Saragota was not technically a British defeat at all, in that the British army was promised safe passage home. The cynical and unexpected American betrayal of this promise was what turned a setback into a disaster for the British. Even French entry into the war was not decisive: it merely ensured that the force of British power would be concentrated more on their Continental enemy than on the colonies: from that moment on, intervention by Britain in the numbers required to crush the American rebels was out of the question. However, to begin with, the French proved no more able to defeat the British in the colonies than the Americans alone.

British defeat after Saragota was very far from inevitable. Indeed, with the launching of Britain's campaign in the south and the successful capture of Savannah and Charleston, the initiative seemed to have returned to the mother country. The Indians and the blacks, whom the British sought to protect against their American overlords, were overwhelmingly on the British side. The darkest chapter in the war was the American massacre of the Indians and the seizure of their lands. Only as Cornwallis's small army tried to penetrate deep into guerrilla-held territory did the British effort in the south falter, although Britain won most of the battles. Cornwallis then made the epic strategic blunder of penetrating into Virginia and allowing his troops to be trapped on the Yorktown peninsula. Up to that point the Americans' own view was that they had probably lost the war.

But it was the French navy, momentarily in control of the sea, and French besiegers, supported by the Americans, that did the trapping. In most respects Yorktown was a classic French defeat of the British, with the Americans in a supporting role. It could not possibly have happened without the French. And even this defeat was not militarily disastrous – Britain still held New York and other enclaves, which could be reinforced. It was, however, decisive in its effect on British public opinion, which concluded that it had had enough. Britain decided to settle with the rebels, who then agreed to squeeze their French allies out of America – a settlement which pleased both English-speaking parties. The Americans also reneged on their treaty promise to compensate the tens of thousands of dispossessed and fleeing loyalists, many of them from the old gentry class. America was born of American valour, determination and ruthlessness, and British exhaustion.

The old order in America had been overthrown, and with the war's end the revolutionary forces that had surged forward to break the umbilical link with Britain were now in control. It took nearly four years, when the country came under threat of economic collapse, anarchy and disintegration, for the conservative forces in America to unite around Washington and impose order upon the American people, under threat of force, through an unelected assembly which imposed the (in some respects undemocratic) constitution that has endured until this day. There was nothing representative about that greatest of all assemblies. The 1787 constitutional convention represented not the apogee of the American Revolution, but its defeat – the crushing of the men who had overthrown the old gentry order, as well as the British. It imposed a measure of central control, taxation and military enforcement greater than any previously attempted by the British – while respecting British-style constitutional liberties.

That counter-revolutionary settlement has endured to this day, making America, despite its revolutionary credentials, one of the most conservative societies on earth, yet one wedded to the virtue of individual freedom. This formidable reconciliation of those old antagonists, freedom and order – a reconciliation that emerged during the twelve tumultuous years from 1775 to 1787 – lies at the heart of American success. It deserves far greater attention that it has received in Europe, and far more detached general analysis than it has received in the United States.

This book inadequately attempts to provide both. Along the way, the story of the War of Independence is an enthralling one of outstanding personalities, suffering soldiery and civilians, vivid battles, military verve and incompetence, clashing ideals, betrayal and villainy – and the indomitable tenacity with which a handful of brave and determined men took on a superpower. They did not win their independence alone – Britain gave up, and it was largely the French who inflicted the decisive defeat – but the outcome was the same, and the battle could not have been continued without their determination.

# PART 1

*A Fire in America*

# I

## *The Cauldron*

On the night of 19 April 1775, as the sun set beneath a horizon darkened with thunderclouds, hundreds of soberly attired men, and women in bustles and petticoats, were crowded along the wooden waterfront of Boston harbour, facing away from the open sea, gazing across the calm waters of the Charles estuary. Crimson flashes illuminated the dusk and the underbellies of the approaching storm clouds, but they were not lightning, nor were the detonations thunder. Then the flashes stopped and the rain came, followed by nature's own display of violence.

For three hours, until ten o'clock at night, the staid townspeople waited curiously and gravely for their first glimpse of men battered by their own kind. Altogether, around 2,000 were ferried over from the teardrop peninsula of Charlestown, just north of Boston itself. Many were horribly wounded, all were soaked to the skin, and most were suffering from the traumatized exhaustion of soldiers who had been fighting for their lives for eight long hours.

As the men were brought ashore to the inadequate attentions of eighteenth-century army doctors, and as the townspeople slowly dispersed to the warmth of their lodgings that crisp April night, few can have realized that they were witnessing the birth pains of the most powerful nation the globe has ever known, the beginning of the most enduring revolution in history – indeed the defining event in the shaping of the world as we now know it. Some may, however, have foreseen that they were witnessing the start of a vicious, long war, which was to exact a terrible death toll.

But surely the question on the lips of the British recruits, wretched and shivering with cold and shock as the boats pulled them across to safety, was, Why? Why had the colonists – their own kin, enjoying virtual self-government, British maritime protection and the commercial advantages of belonging to the greatest trade grouping on earth – chosen to unleash a war of attrition against the country of their common origin? Why were humble British boys killing and being killed by their American cousins? The answer was far more complex than is generally assumed.

Outside newly acquired Canada, British America in 1764, on the eve of the Revolution, consisted essentially of a long coastal strip penetrating at most some 300 miles inland, with a series of ports or cities as focal points. Only 21 million acres – 8 per cent of the occupied area – was cultivated. There was New Hampshire in the north, a long strip sandwiched between Massachusetts and its remote dependency of Maine. New Hampshire depended upon the former's port of Boston for its exports to the outside world. Prosperous, underpopulated, and a prime source of naval masts and timber, it was dominated by one Benning Wentworth as a personal fiefdom; his family and friends occupied most sinecures and were awarded the cream of grants of land and contracts, while the New Hampshire council ate out of his hand.

Next-door Massachusetts itself radiated from Boston – run down, economically depressed, a hotbed of political intrigue, whose factions strove for dominance under the usually helpless eye of the British-appointed governor. Further south was the small enclave of Rhode Island, with a reputation for contraband, quirkiness and eccentricity, and with a genuinely popularly elected legislature which dominated the state's few chafing 'Tory' grandees.

In neighbouring Connecticut religious factions held sway, while to the west the state of New York encompassed one of America's biggest ports and, along the Hudson valley, a vast backcountry of immensely prosperous landowners who presided over large numbers of tenants, of whom some were well off, most less so. The port of New York itself ran the state's politics, and was riven by arguments between quarrelling factions.

The great state of Pennsylvania was dominated by the descendants of William Penn, the Quaker leader, who were so incompetent and argumentative that in 1746 even Benjamin Franklin had petitioned the Crown to rule the state directly. Pennsylvania also provided a home to a large German settler population and an astonishing variety of their Churches. Maryland, Massachusetts and Delaware were also held by royal charter; Connecticut, like Rhode Island, actually elected its own government; and the rest of the states were Crown colonies with their government chosen in London.

Religion played a major role in more peaceful New Jersey's politics. Delaware was smaller and sleepier. Maryland, with its important port of Baltimore, was a country of great landowners and impoverished tenants. Virginia, the tobacco state, distinguished and wealthy, enjoyed tranquil politics centred around its staid House of Burgesses. Its greatest land-owner, Lord Fairfax, presided over an estate millions of acres in extent. North and South Carolina, and below that the little settlement of Georgia, with their ports of Wilmington, Charleston and Savannah and their slave-plantation societies, also home to great territorial magnates, enjoyed largely peaceful political existences.

Each state was parochial and independent of the others; although there were considerable cross-border commercial links, the states looked primarily to Britain for trade. Their political arrangements suited both sides. A British-appointed governor – usually a soldier or ex-soldier – presided over a locally chosen executive council and over the squabbling factions and interests in the local assembly to which – on a property qualification – representatives were elected by a considerable part of the male population (from as much as one half to as little as one-sixth in different places). The governor's appointment was often given to a local man of prominence and, provided that the colony paid lip service to the Crown, Britain barely interfered in how it was run. The colonies were distinct, yet surprisingly uniform in style of government and social patterns. They were quasi-independent.

To the mother country they were relatively insignificant. Far more important than Virginia's tobacco producers were the West Indian islands to the south, supplying the insatiable European demand for sugar and the global thirst for rum, distilled from molasses. Capital investment in the West Indian sugar industry was some £60 million in 1750 – around six times the total English stake in the North American colonies. By the 1770s there were reckoned to be some seventy MPs for the Caribbean plantation interest in the House of Commons, representing an absurdly backward and inefficient system of slash-and-burn production, worked by slaves on huge plantations draining the soil of its fertility. The sugar was grown for export, and then only through England.

The British sugar producers came increasingly under challenge from their French neighbours, who favoured more efficient smallholdings worked in rotation with different types of crop. John Dickinson, the prominent English-trained American lawyer, remarked ironically, 'By a very singular disposition of affairs, the colonies of an absolute monarchy [France] are settled on a republican principle; while those of a kingdom in many respects resembling a commonwealth [England] are cantoned out among a few lords vested with despotic power over myriads of vassals and supported in the pomp of Baggas by their slavery.'

For Britain, with this colossal trade in the West Indies under challenge from the French, with the hostile Spanish Empire to the south, and engaged in continuing Continental power struggles and expansionary commitments in India and the East, the North American colonies were something of a backwater.

Yet the thirteen colonies were changing fast. Nine-tenths of all Americans lived in the countryside – hence the political power of the rural magnates – and most were smallholders, tenants, or settlers. However, the towns exercised disproportionate influence in an overall population which had exploded from just 250,000 in 1700 to around 2,500,000 three-quarters of a century later – a rate of 3 per cent a year or roughly a third every decade. There was plenty of room: the country supported around three persons per square mile in 1775. Yet poor agricultural practices meant that average farms had diminished in size – for example, in New England, to around 100 acres in extent.

Modest little towns had become small cities during the thirty years before the Revolution: Philadelphia's population increased from 13,000 to 40,000, New York from 11,000 to 25,000, Charleston from about 7,000 to 12,000, Newport from 6,000 to 11,000. Boston had stagnated at about 16,000, losing its pre-eminence to Philadelphia and New York. Even so, compared with England, most American urban centres remained stiflingly provincial: for example, London had more than a million inhabitants, and more than fifty cities in England could boast a population of 10,000 or more.

The rapid growth in the American population was caused both by high birth rates and by immigration: most new arrivals were no longer high-minded zealots, some from gentrified backgrounds, but poor people driven in search of a better life. Two-thirds of non-native Americans were of British descent. The biggest non-British population consisted, of course, of black slaves: around 500,000, a fifth of the total population, had arrived by 1775. Although they were to play a far from negligible role in political events after that year, they were excluded politically, with no vote or voice, functioning only as labour to fuel the southern economy, occasionally inspiring the fear of revolt in their white overlords.

Another huge influx had come from Northern Ireland: tough-minded Scots-Irish Presbyterians bearing a grudge against the English for enticing them to move to Ireland and then discriminating against their produce and local religion there. The Scots-Irish settled the western frontier along the Connecticut river, southern New Hampshire, Maine and Worcester, then down towards the Delaware and the Susquehanna, Maryland, Virginia, the Carolinas and Georgia.

Some 100,000 Germans formed another major group. Mostly fleeing religious persecution, they were pious and hard-working, excelled as farmers, and settled in the Susquehanna valley and Pennsylvania, where they made up a third of the population. A smaller Lowland Scottish migration of 25,000, as well as several thousand Highlanders, came in search of a better life around 1750. Other nationalities to settle in significant numbers were the Dutch, Swedes, Finns, Welsh, Irish and French. In addition some 1,400 British convicts were transported to America every year.

These people had no loyalty to Britain; indeed, some were deeply hostile. The Scots, Welsh and Irish had no affection for the throne of Hanover, and the first had recently risen in rebellion against it. Yet their influence can be overstated. Comprising only around 15 per cent of the population they were divided and most were politically passive.

The Indian population in touch with the whites may have numbered as many as 250,000, with 150,000 being distributed within the states themselves, the rest along the western frontier. Around 50,000 whites lived west of the Appalachians. Mohawks and Delawares lived in the same villages as different white nationalities, while Catholic Indians with French names were common along the border. The relationship between Indians and whites was often close, but also complex and competitive, as a fine passage by Colin Calloway shows:

> Colonists from Europe, where hunting was a gentleman's sport, learned from Indians how to hunt for a living. Colonial hunters who operated in Indian country pulled on Indian leggings, breechclouts, and moccasins, dressed their long hair with bear grease, and sometimes donned war paint. Anglican preacher Charles Woodmason denounced settlers in the Carolina backcountry as being 'hardly one degree removed' from their Indian neighbours. General Thomas Gage reckoned backcountry settlers

on the Ohio River 'differ little from the Indians in their manner of life'. Missionary David McClure said that backcountry Virginians were 'generally white savages, and subsist by hunting, and live like the Indians'.

Whereas Indians in Canada took to wearing jackets and waistcoats like their French neighbours, Frenchmen travelling in Indian country 'generally dressed like the natives', exchanging their trousers for leggings and loincloths. Young men in backcountry Virginia were proud of their 'Indian-like dress', and even wore leggings and breechclouts to church, which apparently sparked the interest of young women in the congregation. When George Rogers Clark and his Virginians arrived at Kaskaskia in 1778, they were dressed Indian style, 'in hunting shirt and breech cloth'. Their appearance surprised the Spanish governor of Saint Louis but was not unusual for men accustomed to life in Indian country.

In the Mohawk Valley in the 1760s, Peter Warren Johnson met Europeans who tattooed their faces and chests like their Indian neighbours, 'which is done by pricking the skin with pins, till the blood comes, and then applying gunpowder to it, which will remain for ever'. French fur traders in Canada likewise tattooed their bodies. Cultural boundaries between Indians and Europeans, and between Indians and Africans (as between Indians and other Indians), were often fuzzy and porous.

The mixing of peoples and cultures did not erase differences or eradicate conflict. Surveying the inventory of things colonists borrowed from Indians, James Axtell reminds us that 'their goal was not to become Indian, nor did their selective and piecemeal adaptations of native techniques and technology make them so'. The same can be said of Indians who borrowed from European culture: they did not intend to, nor did they, become Europeans. In fact, conflict between Indian and European cultures was increasing steadily by the eve of the Revolution, as growing pressure on Indian lands eroded previous patterns of coexistence.

The significance of religion among the American settlers can be exaggerated. At first most of the colonies were dominated by the established Anglican Church – the unzealous agent of everything that was most orthodox about the religious establishment of the mother country. In New England, Protestantism continued to play as large a part as it always had in politics, divided though it was between the various reformed churches of the Congregationalists who formed the social Establishment. Anglicans, Baptists and Quakers were divided within themselves – the Baptists between 'separate' and 'royalist' branches, the New Lights, supporters of the fundamentalist 'Great Awakening' theory of possession by the Spirit, and the Old Lights, who opposed them.

In the middle colonies, the Quakers, who had helped to found Pennsylvania, had a disproportionate influence, as did the Presbyterians, split between the 'New Side' based in New York and the 'Old Side' based in Philadelphia. The German Reformed and Lutheran churches – the Mennonites, Dunkers and Moravians – fought between themselves for the allegiance of the remote farming communities of Pennsylvania, although many of these communities were not especially religious and lacked any place of worship.

It is hard to point to any organized religious opposition to British rule as such. The new Puritan churches were too divided and inward-looking. Rather, the various branches of Protestantism were marked by a dependency on secular devotion, a suspicion of the well-heeled Anglican religious establishment (which in America was far less respected than in Britain), and a devotion to the ethics of hard work and self-reliance that viewed government, religious establishments and impositions from abroad, or even outside their local communities, with equally deep suspicion.

Perhaps the Protestant churches' most important role was as informal natural rallying points for the disaffected against the sedate social order in the colonies. If the Anglican churches were seen as pillars of the some-times hugely wealthy Establishment, and even the Congregationalists became so in New England, the new Puritan churches became magnets for poorer immigrants such as the Scots-Irish who had no more love for the local territorial magnates and prosperous merchants than their equivalents in Britain. To attract the support of the poor, Baptists and Presbyterians moved into the stagnant southern colonies, where the Anglican churches held sway.

During the eighteenth century the thirteen colonies were undergoing a ferment of social change probably unparalleled anywhere else in the world – in the emergence of a thrusting, ambitious middle class, in the explosive growth of a poorer underclass that threatened the traditional domination of the landowners and rich merchants, in the new wave of hardy, impoverished immigrants and in the growth of anti-establish-ment religious sects. In just seventy years, sleepy, provincial colonies with a predominantly monoglot population had been transformed into a bubbling cauldron of social ferment. A new phalanx of settlers, previously condemned as no-hopers in stagnant European social structures, now found that with a little effort they could vastly improve their lives.

Either indifferent towards or resentful of the English, they had little reason to respect the British Crown.

Yet the monarchy was not the chief target of their hatred. Britain's pompous governors exerted virtually no power over elected local assemblies, and its aloof, even neglectful, attitude made the mother country remote from colonists whose frontiers were limited only by the immense American land mass. Their target was their own establishment, securely in place after some 200 years of settlement. The local social order, of which the Crown was no more than the symbolic peak, was a far more immediate cause of anger to the new colonial aspirants. As long as they could acquire land for cultivation relatively freely, and thus escape poverty, resentment against the class structure could be contained. But their scope for settling new land was soon to be threatened – specifically by Britain.

Meanwhile, few Americans felt affection or allegiance towards structures dominated by hugely wealthy American absentee landowners, monopolist merchants and traders in cahoots with corrupt political dynasties who shared the spoils and opportunities of development. A rapidly increasing population of the land-hungry resented the placid social order set up in the interests of those who had arrived before them. Beside this tension the largely titular rule extended by Britain from thousands of miles away was something of an irrelevance.

Under the pressure of tumultuous change, the social fabric in America itself began to buckle. From 1750 riots were staged against the great landowners of New York and New Jersey. In 1766 a tenants' revolt had to be suppressed by troops. In 1764 the 'Paxton Boys' arrived in Philadelphia demanding increased representation for the west in the local assembly. In 1768 the 'Regulator' movement of small western farmers rampaged against the gentry through South Carolina before being defeated by the authorities at the Battle of the Alamance.

When more enlightened members of the established order realized what was happening, they switched allegiance, placed themselves at the head of the revolutionary movement – making the British connection the scapegoat – and then in the interests of self-preservation furiously tried to channel and direct the flood. Had they not done so the American Revolution might have much more closely resembled the French one thirteen years later.

The classic economic-determinist view of the American Revolution holds that, after the Seven Years War with France (1756–63) the colonies plunged into an economic depression which sparked off deep resentment against British colonialist mercantilist 'exploitation'. Britain's own economic depression led the mother country and the colonists to engage in bitter warfare over a shrinking market, with Parliament passing a series of acts to raise taxation from the colonies and to restrict their trade. Inevitably, the resentful colonists exploded against their political and economic oppression, and American independence was born.

While there are elements of truth in this, its substance does not stand up to scrutiny. The post-war depression was in fact short-lived, and the colonists' chief problems before 1775 were ones of breakneck economic expansion, not contraction. In any case Britain's 'exploitative' measures barely worked, and were sometimes actually beneficial to trade. In particular, the undoubtedly ill-conceived and provocative attempt to impose taxation failed completely, so it could hardly be blamed for the harsh conditions the Americans supposedly laboured under.
The argument for the traditional view is set out by Louis Hacker:

> The mother country had bound the colonies to itself in an economic vassalage: opportunities for colonial enterprise were possible only in commercial agriculture (supported by land speculation) and in trade.
>
> But when the expanding commercial activities of northern merchant capitalists came into conflict with the great capitalist interest of British West Indian sugar and the related merchant and banking groups dependent upon it; when the southern tobacco and rice planters, in their role of land speculators, collided with English land speculators and the mighty fur interest; and when the colonial need to move into manufacturing and to develop adequate credit facilities for its growing enterprises threatened the very existence of English mercantile capitalism in all its ramifications: then repression, coercion, even the violence of economic extinction (as in the case of the Boston Port Bill) had to follow. There could be no accommodation possible when English statesmen were compelled to choose between supporting English mercantile capitalism and supporting colonial mercantile and planter capitalism.

Furthermore:

> The colonies had enjoyed a period of unprecedented prosperity during the years of the war with France. The expanding market in the West Indies, the great expenditures of the British quartermasters, the illegal and contraband trade with the enemy forces – all these had furnished steady employment for workers on the fleets and in the shipyards and ports as

well as lucrative outlets for the produce of small farmers. But with the end
of the war and the passage of the restrictive legislation of 1763 and after,
depression had set in to last until 1770.

Stringency and bankruptcy everywhere confronted the merchants and
big farmers. At the same time, seamen and labourers were thrown out of
work; small tradesmen were compelled to close their shops; and small
farmers faced ruin because of their expanded acreage, a diminished
market, and heavy fixed charges made particularly onerous as a result of
currency contraction. Into the bargain, escape into the frontier zones –
always the last refuge of the dispossessed – was shut off as a result of the
Proclamation of 1763 and the land policy of 1774. The lower middle
classes and workers of the towns in almost all the colonies, beginning in
1765, organized themselves into secret societies called the 'Sons of Liberty'
and demonstrated and moved against the colonial agents of the crown. In
these acts they were encouraged by the merchants and landlords.

It is worth looking more closely both at America's economy and at the
extent of British exploitation. The booming economy of the thirteen
colonies in the eighteenth century acted as a magnet for immigrants. In
1688 the colonies exported some 28 million pounds of tobacco to
Britain; in 1771, 105 million. Some eight times as much rice was being
shipped from South Carolina in 1774 as in 1725. Altogether exports to
the mother country increased sevenfold in seventy-five years. Trade in
bread, meat and fish increased exponentially. Imports also rose sharply,
although not quite as fast.

If British colonial restrictions were indeed oppressive to trade, they
must have been highly inefficient, since trade flowed despite that oppression. In fact the evidence suggests that the British colonial regime was
highly beneficial to business.

As late as 1774 lawyer John Dickinson, then an enthusiastic supporter
of the British connection, wrote:

> If an archangel had planned the connection between Great Britain and
> her colonies, he could not have fixed it on a more lasting and beneficial
> foundation, unless he could have changed human nature. A mighty naval
> power at the head of the whole – that power, a parent state with all the
> endearing sentiments attending to the relationship – that could never dis-
> oblige, but with design – the dependent states more apt to have feuds
> among themselves – she the umpire and controller – those states produc-
> ing every article necessary to her greatness – their interest, that she should
> continue free and flourishing – their ability to throw a considerable
> weight in the scale, should her government get unduly poised – she and

all those states Protestant – are some of the circumstances, that delineated by the masterly hand of a Beccaria, would exhibit a plan, vindicating the ways of heaven and demonstrating that humanity and policy are nearly related.

The first principal colonial economic restriction was the 1660 Navigation Act, which confined the carriage of trade to and from the colonies to British vessels. This in fact turned out to be hugely beneficial to New England, which produced much of the English fleet. By 1775 nearly a third of all English ships were being constructed in America. Some 4,000 ships docked at American ports and, far from inhibiting trade, the provision ensured that America had a large and dependable merchant fleet for its exports – essential for commodities such as tobacco, rice, sugar and indigo, which faced ruin if exports were interrupted or delayed. English dominance of the sea lanes ensured safe passage for American goods. There is no evidence that English freight rates were high compared to foreign ones.

A second alleged abuse of British colonial power was the system of 'enumeration' – a kind of quota system, defining levels of production and targeting them for British markets. The main American crops affected were tobacco, rice and indigo. The importance of the British market for tobacco was by any standards beneficial. Exports to Scotland alone, for example, rose from 12 million pounds in 1746 to an astonishing 48 million in 1771. Over the same period they rose from 26 million pounds in the London market to 45 million, while dropping from 13 million to 10 million in other markets. Scotland and London acted as entrepôts, exporting three-quarters of the crop elsewhere.

Could the crop have been more efficiently and profitably sold directly by the colonies to their ultimate markets rather than through Britain? A glance at what happened after America gained its independence gives the answer. After reaching a high of 100 million pounds in exports in 1775, the trade collapsed to just 51 million in 1814, when the Americans were selling directly, recovering only to 79 million in the 1820s. As a result of the Revolution, some $35 million in direct British investment in tobacco in the southern states was lost, and only some $2.6 million later recouped.

Thomas Jefferson, a wealthy tobacco planter from Virginia, came closer to the truth in describing his own self-interested resentment of the British for getting the planter 'more immersed in debt than he could pay without selling his land or slaves ... These debts had now become hereditary from father to son ... so that the planters were a species of property annexed to certain mercantile houses in London.'

Rice production from South Carolina was also growing apace before independence, jumping from 81,000 bales a year to 120,000 in the decade from 1760 to 1770. (Georgia's exports rose from 5,000 bales to 22,000 bales over the same period.) Of total American rice exports of 156,000 bales in 1782, 98,000 went to Britain. By the 1820s, American rice exports to Britain would slump from 469,000 to 217,000 hundred-weight; and to Europe from 484,000 to 367,000. Again the planters lost their prime source of investment capital.

American indigo exports in 1773 were running at around 1.4 million pounds, almost all of it to Britain, which also funded the plantations. By 1822 American indigo exports had dwindled to just 3,000 lb, and imports were up to 1.1 million.

However, compared with the gradual growth in the value of exports from America to Britain between 1769 and 1771 – from £1.2 million to £1.5 million – imports from the mother country rose dramatically – from £1.6 million to £4.5 million in the same period. The colonies were a captive market for manufactured and luxury goods such as hardware and furnishings, and had only rudimentary plants to produce textiles and finished iron goods. In those three years the colonies' trade deficit rose from around £500,000 to £3 million.

How was the gap bridged? Partly by capital investment from Britain – largely to the southern colonies; and more importantly, by the massive trade growth that the North American colonies experienced as the booming British West Indian sugar islands bought their lumber, flour and fish. The simple view is of North America as a dumping ground for expensive British products, exchanged for cheap commodities. In fact there was a three-way trade: the wealthy West Indian colonies absorbed North American products, while exporting their sugar to British markets and thence overseas, the British exported luxuries and bought commodities from North America, and the latter balanced its trade by supplying both markets.

In addition, the importance of the American colonies' thriving trade in piracy and smuggling cannot be overstated. Raiding Spanish ships was estimated to bring £100,000 a year to New York alone; the prize money of a single cargo could range from £50,000 to £200,000. At least £1 million a year flowed into North America from piracy compared with £40,000 a year taken in British tax revenues from the colonies.

Smuggling was a massively lucrative sideline, involving mainly embargoed goods supplied by North American producers to European markets. The Molasses Act, imposed in 1733, had aimed to provide a captive market for British West Indian sugar, rum and molasses: in fact it encouraged a colossal illicit trade in more efficiently produced sugar-based exports from the French West Indies, which were up to 40 per cent cheaper. This trade was so enormous, and British attempts to police it so ineffectual, that by the late 1750s only 2,500 hogsheads of the molasses reaching the smugglers' haven of Rhode Island came from British sources, while 11,500 were landed illegally from Britain's competitors. In Massachusetts alone there were no fewer than sixty-three illicit distilleries. Thus the colonies enjoyed a huge source of illegal income in the face of an act so often cited as a terrible British imposition, yet so ineffectual as to be almost irrelevant.

The British were justifiably charged with attempting to strangle the growth of local industries in the colonies so as to maintain their monopoly to export processed goods to America. The three most celebrated means were the Iron Act, the Woollens Act and the Hat Act. Forges and furnaces for the making of iron were prohibited; exports of woollens and hats from America were prohibited. But these measures were almost entirely ineffectual.

With only a shambolic militia barely loyal to the British, policing iron forges and furnaces – mostly small, local, backyard affairs – throughout the colonies was a farce. By 1775 more forges were estimated to be working in America than in Britain, and total output was reckoned to be greater. By 1764 the American Iron Company had even been set up with capital from London, while Pennsylvania was a heartland of small-scale iron production. There is no record of a single prosecution against an iron manufacturer. The Iron Act was totally ignored – almost certainly with impotent official connivance.

The Woollens Act was similarly ineffective. At the time of the Revolution, America enjoyed a thriving trade in wool based on cottage production, which largely clothed the people of the colonies: there were virtually no woollen imports into America. So the British had failed to find a captive market. Ironically, woollen imports were to account for around a third of all imports into America after 1821, though the colonies had previously been self-sufficient. Restrictions on the production of woollen goods were less onerous than in England itself. Hats, ludicrously, were also barred from export, but enjoyed a thriving trade in

America itself, where 842 hatters operated at the time of the Revolution, 532 in Pennsylvania alone.

Another much-touted example of British commercial 'exploitation' was the time-honoured practice of subsidization. Naval stores, lumber and indigo all attracted such subsidies, which were guaranteed for as long as twenty years and cost Britain around £37,000 a year in the early 1760s. They could hardly be said to discriminate against any but foreign producers: they directly benefited the American manufacturers of these goods, as well as providing a secure supply of products deemed necessary by the British government. The southern states where the bulk of these subsidies were paid were to be the most loyal to the Crown. Subsidies were indeed non-competitive interferences with the market, but such practices were common in most trading nations and most developing countries, and preferential tariffs benefited American producers.

Britain's strenuous efforts to restrict currency expansion in the colonies are cited as a further instance of skulduggery. The Americans produced 'community money', which the British refused to recognize in their contracts. The colonies tried to mint money, but the British prohibited mints in 1684. The Americans then tried to inflate the value of overseas coins and prevent any being exported. They printed paper money based on expected tax revenues, and issued money on the security of property alone. The Land and Manufacture Bank, set up in 1740, was promptly closed down by the authorities – ruining, among others, the father of the great revolutionary Samuel Adams.

The state of Massachusetts issued its first bills in 1690; by 1750 some £4.6 million had been printed, with its currency eventually backed at a level of 11 to 1 against sterling. In profligate New Hampshire and Rhode Island the ratio was 25 to 1. More modestly, Connecticut, and North and South Carolina had ratios of between 10 to 1 and 7 to 1. These represented staggering rates of inflation, deeply damaging to ordinary Americans who bought the paper and soon found its value plunging. Only New York and Pennsylvania maintained sound currencies, worth around a quarter of the value of sterling.

Alarmed at the issue of paper money and the resentment being aroused in the North American colonies, the British government in 1764 passed the Currency Act, which effectively prohibited the issuing of further currency. This had an immediate deflationary effect, and the colonial authorities – many of them benefiting from corrupt deals and windfalls made possible by the issuing of paper money – were furious.

Did the British act out of cynical motives of colonial repression designed to benefit their own traders? Certainly American attempts to trade in their own depreciated currency were troublesome for British merchants, most of whom refused to accept paper money which was considered valueless in Britain. Yet any government, however remote, would have viewed with alarm the pace of expansion of credit in the colonies. Britain could be said to be acting responsibly against the paper inflation which brought ruin to those on fixed incomes (although many of the poorest were outside the moneyed economy altogether). Britain can be faulted for not acting sooner rather than for taking action to curb credit, and the effects of its action were less deflationary than expected.

But the colonial elites were angry at this inhibition of their freedom to issue money. British policy created many enemies, of whom Sam Adams's father was typical, and ignited a great deal of ill-feeling among newly prosperous Americans. John Dickinson wrote in 1765:

> Trade is decaying and all credit is expiring. Money is becoming so extremely scarce that reputable freeholders find it impossible to pay debts which are trifling in comparison to their estates. If creditors sue, and take out executions, the lands and personal estates, as the sale must be for ready money, are sold for a small part of what they were worth when the debts were contracted. The debtors are ruined. The creditors get back but part of their debt and that ruins them. Thus the consumers break the shopkeepers; they break the merchants; and the shock must be felt as far as London.

Research by the economic historian Oliver Dickerson has shown that during the Seven Years War with France the colonies had incurred a debt of some £2.6 million, which by 1769 had slumped to just £777,000, a reduction of 20 per cent a year – a remarkable achievement. Nevertheless, America was growing fast economically, importing ever greater quantities of luxury goods, its wage rates among the highest in the world. As Dickerson observes:

> Conditions for the period as a whole must be considered. A country that was a mecca for immigrants; that was importing slaves in large numbers; that was rapidly expanding its settled area into the back country; that could order from overseas expensive marble statues of its favourite English politicians as did South Carolina and New York; that could squander large sums on the public funeral of a royal governor and bury him in a

sepulchre as elaborate as was accorded to royalty in England; that could find the funds for better church buildings than it ever had before in its history; that could sink public debts more rapidly than other countries; and whose population could live on a far better scale than similar classes in any other part of the world; was not suffering from economic ills that lead to permanent poverty.

North America in 1765 was an exciting, expanding, self-enriching, largely autonomous society, whose settled upper classes were being challenged by a new population of tough and ambitious immigrants. In colonies largely settled by the English these immigrants enjoyed the same rights as Englishmen, and if anything rather less control by their superiors than their equals in the mother country's older, more deferential, social structure.

Any yearning for liberty was thus not that of a slave seeking to be freed from his chains, but that of a vigorous young man hoping to escape the stuffy social order that was represented in theory by Britain, though in practice by the local establishment. The colonies were free in all but name, and increasingly prosperous – indeed, they were to become a good deal less so once the British had departed (although no one could have foreseen this). In a famous ballad published in 1765, Benjamin Franklin summed up the contempt which the vigorous young territories had for their 'mother country'.

> We have an old mother that peevish is grown,
> She snubs us like children that scarce walk alone;
> She forgets we're grown up and have sense of our own,
> *Which nobody can deny, deny, which nobody can deny.*
>
> If we don't obey orders, whatever the case;
> She frowns, and she chides, and she loses all patience,
> And sometimes she hits us a slap in the face,
> *Which nobody can deny, &c.*
>
> Her orders so odd are, we often suspect
> That age has impaired her sound intellect:
> But still an old mother should have due respect,
> *Which nobody can deny, &c.*
>
> Let's bear with her humours as well as we can:
> But why should we bear the abuse of her man?
> When servants make mischief; they earn the rattan,
> *Which nobody can deny, &c.*

Know too, ye bad neighbours, who aim to divide
The sons from the mother, that still she's our pride;
And if ye attack her we're all of her side,
*Which nobody can deny, &c.*

We'll join in her lawsuits, to baffle all those,
Who, to get what she has, will be often her foes:
For we know it must all be our own, when she goes,
*Which nobody can deny, deny, which nobody can deny.*

# 2

# *The Lobsters*

If the American Revolution can be said to have begun at the time of the Stamp Act crisis of 1764, of which more later, the Seven Years War – dubbed in America 'the French and Indian War', and labelled by Winston Churchill 'the First World War' – was its catalyst. The mastermind of American independence, the later French Foreign Minister the Comte de Vergennes, who at the time was ambassador to faraway Turkey, commented at the close of the war, 'The colonies will no longer need Britain's protection. She will call on them to contribute toward supporting the burdens they have helped to bring on her, and they will answer by striking off their chains.'

For the real conflict was a deadly struggle for dominance between France and Britain: in this the American colonies were a sideshow, just as two centuries later the war between America and the Soviet Union, was to be played out across the stages of the Third World.

The 'Great War for the Empire' was anticipated in June 1754 by a skirmish in which a twenty-two-year-old major of the Virginia militia, George Washington, was sent to drive out the French who had encroached on Virginian land at Fort Duquesne. Washington surprised and killed a score of Frenchmen, along with their commander, at a site called Great Meadows. The French then surrounded Washington and his men in their crude log stockade, Fort Necessity, and forced them to surrender. With the colonies apparently under imminent threat of French–Indian invasion, the British rushed a large number of troops there to buttress the ill-co-ordinated efforts of the locals. One of these commented:

> The strength of our colonies ... is divided ... Jealous are they of each other – some ill-constituted – others shaken with intestine divisions – and ...

parsimonious even to prodigality. Our assemblies are diffident of their governors – governors despise their assemblies, and both mutually mis-represent each other to the court of Great Britain ... Without a general constitution for warlike operations, we can neither plan nor execute.

On their arrival, the troops were appalled by the greed the colonists displayed: the British were made to pay for access to water from privately owned wells, and were billeted in lodgings 'dearer than would cost in the capital streets of London'. In Pennsylvania a senior British commander lamented upon the 'villainy and rascality of the inhabitants, who to a man seem rather bent upon our ruin ... than give the smallest assistance, which if at last extorted is so infamously charged as shows the disposition of the people in its full glare'. 'I never saw such a set of people, obstinate and perverse in the last degree,' complained one British general.

The British commander sent to conquer the disputed territory of north-western Virginia in 1755 was the sixty-year-old Major-General Edward Braddock. Bluff and self-important, he was furious at the delays hampering the expedition's departure from Fort Cumberland in Virginia. His deputy Quartermaster General railed against the local inhabitants who 'laid themselves out to put what money they could in their pockets, without forwarding our expedition'. Above all, the British could not obtain horses or carts; the local politician who found them some was one Benjamin Franklin, of whom Braddock commented that this was 'about the only instance of ability and honesty I have known in these provinces'.

Franklin's assessment of Braddock was shrewd and less flattering: 'Braddock might probably have made a good figure in some European war. But he had too much self-confidence; too high an opinion of the validity of regular troops; too mean a one of both Americans and Indians.'

Braddock's plan was to take Fort Duquesne and then march on to Niagara and Forenterac, in spite of Washington's preference for a defensive war. Franklin tried to warn him that in such country he would be exposed to ambush. Braddock replied patronizingly, 'These savages may, indeed, be a formidable enemy to your raw American militia, but upon the King's regular and disciplined troops, sir, it is impossible they should make any impression.'

The expedition advanced towards the wild country of north-western Virginia, advancing at a painfully slow pace, until it crossed the Monongahela river, ten miles from Fort Duquesne. On 9 July, Braddock's force marched forward in disciplined ranks across a clearing surrounded on both sides by thickly wooded ravines and was ambushed on both sides by the French and Indians from the cover of the trees. Unable to see the enemy, the ranks broke at last into a headlong retreat, and Braddock, who fought furiously and had four horses shot from under him, was hit in the lungs. Some 750 of his men were killed or wounded, about two thirds of the total, against enemy losses of just 51. Braddock's dying words were 'We shall know better how to deal with them the next time.'

Not for the last time, the British had grossly underestimated the toughness of local American fighters and the difficult terrain, so different from that of Europe. Washington rallied what was left of the force, complaining bitterly that the 'dastardly behaviour of the British soldiers [in panicking] exposed all those who were inclined to do their duty to almost certain death'. The British retreated to Fort Cumberland.

A French thrust from the north pushed aside Colonel James Mercer's courageous forces at Oswego on Lake Ontario. General Montcalm, the French commander, crossed Lake Champlain to Lake George and seized the fort there in 1758. The colonies were now under direct threat.

Elsewhere, the war was proving disastrous for Britain: Admiral Byng surrendered Minorca against impossible odds, and was promptly court-martialled and shot by the British in 1757. From India came news that Calcutta had fallen to the French; Robert Clive's brilliant campaign to retake it, defeat the French, and occupy Bengal had not yet been reported. In Europe, Frederick the Great, Britain's ally, was beaten back by French and Austrian forces and Hanover was taken by France in the summer of 1757.

William Pitt the Elder was summoned in Britain's desperate hour of need. The new Prime Minister rose to the challenge, appointing fresh commanders and deciding on a bold new strategy: while leaving the Indian campaign to Clive, he would delegate the struggle on the Continent to Frederick the Great and use the British navy to cut off France's forces in Canada from resupply. His main effort would be concentrated on Canada.

In 1758 the tide turned: Admiral Boscawen and Generals Amherst and Wolfe stopped the French advance and took Louisbourg, on Cape Breton Island, from behind their lines. Under General John Forbes, and with Washington again in support, a force of 2,500 men made their way across to Fort Duquesne, where Britain had been defeated three years before;

this time scouting parties were sent to check French and Indian positions. Before they reached the fort, the French had left. It was renamed Fort Pitt after the British Prime Minister, and later became Pittsburgh.

In Europe, Frederick the Great won a string of triumphs against the French in 1758. The following year a French fleet was destroyed; further south the British took the French island of Guadeloupe. Fort Niagara fell to the British in July 1759, and Lord Amherst captured Crown Point and Ticonderoga on Lake Champlain.

A month earlier Wolfe had arrived down the St Lawrence with an army of 9,000 men and besieged Quebec. After two months of fruitless bombardment, the British staged the coup of moving 3,200 soldiers up a goat trail to the heights overlooking the city on its apparently impregnable rock rampart above the river. Both Wolfe and Montcalm were mortally wounded in the brief battle that followed. Wolfe's last words on hearing of Britain's victory were 'God be praised, I will die in peace.' Montreal fell to Amherst in September 1760.

But the following year Britain's new King, George III, dismissed Pitt, who wanted to continue the war, and initiated negotiations which led to peace in 1763. The terms were widely criticized in Britain, but at least the French ceded Canada.

From Britain's perspective, the mother country had valiantly defended the colonists. But that was not how the Americans saw it. With the collapse of the French it dawned on them that they no longer needed British defenders to protect them. In addition, the British had, in American eyes, behaved reprehensibly in drawing up the terms of the settlement. For, by the royal proclamation of 1763 under which Britain had occupied French Canada, the large region across the Appalachians which formed the western boundary to the thirteen colonies was to become a huge Indian reserve on which no white settlement could be permitted.

The loathing between the British forces and the colonists had reached near-breaking point. It was most keenly felt between the hardened British professional soldiers and the loosely disciplined, frontier-wise American militia: it is no coincidence that Massachusetts and Virginia, where the British regulars and the American militia had fought most intensely side by side against the French in the Seven Years War, were the two most active colonies in the independence cause later.

The roots of this ill-feeling went back a long way. In 1680 the colonies had raised local militia for defence and internal policing, and all adult males were required to serve on a part-time basis. North America's first local rebellion had taken place as far back as 1675 in Virginia, when Charles II sent an expedition of 1,000 soldiers to put down an uprising against the crabbed and venal royal governor, Sir William Berkeley. The rebellion soon fizzled out, and Berkeley was recalled to England, but 200 soldiers left behind to keep the peace became increasingly ill-fed and unpopular, and were disbanded in 1682.

For the first time the colonists had shown that professional soldiers were not welcome in the colonies: they considered their allegiance was voluntary, not based on coercion. Order was to be enforced by local militia. They liked to enjoy the British Empire's trading benefits and protection, but resented any overt display of political and military supremacy.

The next flare-up had taken place in 1686, when Britain's centralizing King James II decided to strip the then colonies of New Hampshire, Massachusetts, Plymouth and Rhode Island of their separate governments and set them up as the united dominion of New England. Sir Edmund Andros was sent to preside over this supercolony, accompanied by 100 soldiers and a frigate, the *Rose*. Andros, fearing disaffection, placed a few cannon on top of Fort Hill, overlooking the Boston waterfront. His tiny force garrisoned both the fort and Castle Island, a few miles offshore.

The Puritan-dominated local community was appalled by the rough behaviour of the soldiers off duty, and was soon seething: a constable complained that he 'was stabbed as soon as he came out of doors and another constable had his stuff taken out of his house, and had a pass made at him, and was forced to fly for his life, and that by men belonging to the ships that was the King's'.

Andros, as the representative of a Catholic monarch, was hated by Protestant New Englanders. In 1688, as Indians threatened the colony from the north, he conscripted a large body of militiamen to march out and face them just as winter approached. According to the conscripted men, the British officers treated them abominably, executing those who were unable to complete the long and terrible march to desolate outposts in the snow, and torturing others. A soldier was suspended 'by the hand with a cod line clear from the ground only bearing one foot upon a sharp stake a long time, and afterwards tied neck and heels, and after that tied up by the other hand as before, with his other hand and foot tied cross behind him, and after that bound down with his back upon a sharp rail or stake'. The troops returned to Boston without fighting – the expedition a complete failure – to learn that Prince William of Orange had taken James II's throne.

In April 1689 the captain of the *Rose* and others were suddenly seized by local men on the streets of Boston, and Andros fled to Fort Hill. There, after a botched attempt to escape, he and his small garrison surrendered to the townspeople, who also seized the *Rose*. He was sent back to Britain. This act of open mutiny was justified by the colonists as allegiance to the changed regime in England. William and Mary were now in power, and their charter for Massachusetts included the guarantee that no soldiers would return to the colony.

In New York, meanwhile, the deputy governor, Colonel Francis Nicholson, presided over two small garrisons of regular soldiers stationed in Fort James. Nicholson had also unwisely raised some troops of local militia, who were deeply mistrustful of the regulars. Shortly after the fall of Andros, the militia seized control of Fort James and disbanded the regular soldiers, while Nicholson, who had initially threatened to set the town ablaze, fled to England.

The rebel leader – one Jacob Leisler, of German background, who was supported by New York's substantial Dutch community – was regarded by the British as an extremist and, though he professed allegiance to William and Mary, he failed to impress them with his sincerity. Colonel Henry Slaughter was sent to take control, with two companies of redcoats – derided by the Americans as 'lobsters' – dispatched in separate ships from England.

The soldiers arrived first, under the command of Major Richard Ingoldsby. Leisler refused to surrender control, and a series of incidents ensued in which each side tried to intimidate the other until, on 17 March, actual shooting broke out. Two civilian followers of the British were killed and a number were wounded, as well as one soldier. When Slaughter arrived, Leisler still refused to stand down, but Ingoldsby was allowed into the fort. There he called on those within to give up, with the offer of a pardon. They surrendered and were pardoned, but Leisler was tried and hanged.

It was notable that both mini-insurrections had occurred largely in response to what was perceived to be a political change in Britain itself. The Protestant colonists were reacting against the Catholic influence of James II and, so they believed, in favour of William and Mary. They were also demonstrating their repugnance for the uncouth, though highly disciplined, lower-class British regulars. Exactly the same pattern was evident just under a century later, when the colonists perceived – wrongly – that royal authority in England was being usurped by Parliament.

William and Mary promptly took action to end the unwieldy centralized Dominion of New England. Massachusetts Bay and the historic Plymouth Colony were merged almost into a single colony. New Hampshire and New York were restored as royal colonies, and each was given its own independent assembly. Connecticut and Rhode Island remained virtually self-governing, although all the colonies were subject to the largely ineffectual Navigation Acts. A small garrison of redcoats remained in New York, though they were thoroughly despised and unpopular with the locals. New York's British governor, the Earl of Bellomont, had two of them executed for mutiny.

With the outbreak of war between Britain and its two traditional enemies, France and Spain, the northern colonies became alarmed that they would be attacked by the French, and invited the British to take part in a pre-emptive strike. This was to involve a large naval force sailing up the St Lawrence to capture Quebec, while a local force advanced up the wild country across lakes and rivers to seize Montreal from the south. A large and enthusiastic army of militia was raised by the colonists, who eagerly awaited the British forces early in 1709.

To the colonists' fury and dismay, news reached them later in the year that the expedition had been disbanded, possibly because peace with the French was on the cards and there were doubts in London as to the venture's chances of success. The colonists' attempt finally to rid themselves of the French threat to the north had been bitterly disappointed. Instead they had to content themselves with a limited expedition to capture Port Royal, Maryland, which was mounted successfully (the port being renamed Annapolis Royal) but ended in predictable squabbling between royal regular troops and colonial militiamen.

Two years later, in 1711, Britain changed its mind again, and dispatched a major expedition of 4,300 troops and 4,000 sailors under Admiral Sir Hovenden Walker and General John Hill, the brother of Queen Anne's closest confidant. The expedition reached Boston short of supplies, and was grounded on an offshore island to forestall desertion by the harshly disciplined, poorly-paid British soldiers into the rich, beckoning lands of America.

To Admiral Walker's fury, the people of Boston immediately tried to

impose an extortionate rate of exchange upon them, and refused to provision them except on established credit or for cash. He wrote angrily,
'The demands upon exchange, and the prices for provisions, and other
necessaries for the fleet and army in New England were very exorbitant
and excessive; but … we were obliged to comply with them, they being
resolved to make an advantage of our necessities.'

The British command now became increasingly concerned that the
colonists did not want the expedition to succeed. They found that locals
were encouraging the troops to desert and seek employment in New
England – which many did by slipping across to the town in boats. A
British colonel remarked upon 'the ill nature and sourness of these
people whose government, doctrine, and manners, whose hypocrisy and
canting are insupportable … till they are all settled under one government … they will grow every day more stiff and disobedient, more bur-
densome than advantageous to Great Britain.'

Nor could the British easily find pilots to take them up the treacherous St Lawrence. Walker detected 'A very great unwillingness in all the
pilots, for going in that station aboard the men of war, alleging in
general, their incapacity for such a charge, and the long time since many
of them had been up that river. Others complained of the hardship of
compelling them against their wills …; and several of them named
others that would do better in their steads.' But at last, on 20 July, a huge
expedition set off: 12,000 men aboard the fleet, and 2,000 overland to
Montreal. Walker moved his ships as fast as he could: he was terrified of
being trapped in the St Lawrence by autumn ice, which would condemn
his men to die of starvation in the glacial wastes of Canada.

On the fateful night of 23–24 August, however, breaking waves were
suddenly sighted and eight ships went aground, with a loss of 900
British soldiers and sailors – although no Americans. Walker hurriedly
decided to abandon the venture – a remarkably timid decision given the
size of the force of around 11,000 men still in his command. The overland expedition was called off as well. The whole enterprise had proved
a total failure, and the colonists derided the British.

After these hostilities had ended, the people of New Hampshire were
not to experience the threat of war again for a third of a century, until
France joined Spain in its wars against Britain. The main threat to the
northern colonies then came from French privateers based at
Louisbourg, 600 miles to the north of Boston. The New Englanders,

under the governorship of William Shirley, conceived the idea of their own expedition in 1745 to protect their ships with the assistance of British forces. On 24 March, 52 ships carrying 2,800 militiamen under William Pepperell set sail, and the British agreed to send naval support under Commodore Peter Warren. The two men were surprisingly cordial in their relations with one another.

While preparing a massive assault on Louisbourg, they were greeted with news of its surrender. The two commanders then competed to get into the town first, but wrote respectfully of each other's forces to the Prime Minister, the Duke of Newcastle. Warren said that the colonists

> have the highest notions of the rights, and liberties, of Englishmen, and indeed are almost levellers, they must know when, where, how, and what service they are going upon, and be treated in a manner that few military bred gentlemen would condescend to, but if they do the work in which they are engaged, every other ceremony should in my opinion be winked at.

Pepperell wrote that

> Nothing could have contributed more to the success of his Majesty's arms, than the command of the squadron being given to a gentleman of Commodore Warren's distinguished character: he is of such a disposition as makes him greatly beloved by the people in New England, and in the colonies, in general.

But trouble was brewing at a lower level. Under the terms of the surrender, the American militia were denied the opportunity to plunder Louisbourg; meanwhile, on arriving at the port, Warren's army helped itself to £500,000 worth of French prizes. Fistfights broke out between the American soldiers and British sailors. To the Americans' dismay, they were ordered by the British to remain on the island thorugh a long and bitter winter: some 900 perished.

The colonists of the South had more reason to feel dependent on British soldiers than most: the threat to them both from the local Indian populations and from the Spanish in Florida was all too real. In 1732 the southernmost colony of Georgia had been founded under a British officer, James Oglethorpe, with a regiment of regular soliders at his disposal. Seven years later war broke out between Britain and Spain. Oglethorpe eagerly seized the chance to attack the Spanish settlement of San Agustin, 150 miles south of Georgia's capital of Savannah.

In 1740 Oglethorpe assembled a force of his own regulars, a detachment of troops loaned by South Carolina under their own commander, Colonel Alexander Vander Dussen, some Georgian militia and Indians, and a small squadron of the Royal Navy. Approaching San Agustin from the south, the South Carolinians believed they could attack before the Spaniards realized what was happening. The much more cautious British commander refused to do so.

The bold South Carolinians now proposed a night attack using boats from the British naval squadron to capture six armed galleys the Spaniards had positioned across the harbour to protect the fortress and town of San Agustin. The British naval commander balked at the proposal, saying the operation was too risky. The ships then had to move off the coast in a storm, and Spanish supply ships were able to sneak in with food and arms for the beleaguered garrison. The British naval squadron returned and decided it had had enough.

After several weeks' siege the South Carolinians wanted to attack but were as astounded as the Spanish in San Agustin when Oglethorpe gave the order to withdraw. This stirred up a considerable outcry in the southern states, the Americans blaming the British for their lack of boldness, if not outright cowardice, in this expensive fiasco.

In the same year as the shambles at San Agustin, the British had been preparing a massive military expedition against the Spanish in the Caribbean. With promises of generous spoils, the British recruited a volunteer American regiment, all from Virginian militias, under the command of the able and tested lieutenant-governor of Virginia, William Gooch. It was trained by British officers and sergeants, and was divided into 4 battalions and 36 companies, totalling no fewer than 3,500 men.

In the autumn of 1740 they set off from Virginia for Jamaica, where, lacking sufficient accommodation on shore, they remained on board ship on spartan rations, only occasionally visiting the exotic island for women and drink, and picking up tropical diseases. The Americans on the expedition were treated with contempt. General Wentworth, the British commander, commented, 'there are amongst 'em very good men, and some exceeding bad; they are very little acquainted with discipline, but if they prove, what they appear to be, men accustomed to fatigue, I am in hopes that they may do good service'. A navy captain observed that they were 'blacksmiths, tailors, barbers, shoemakers, and all the banditry them colonies affords: insomuch that the other part of the army [the regulars] held them at scorn'. They were used for physical tasks, and to act as substitutes for the hardworking, miserably treated common seamen of the fleet.

The British compounded this idiocy with one much greater: a plan to attack Cartagena, the Spanish Empire's military stronghold in the Caribbean, guarded by one of the most impressive and well-built forts in the world. In March 1741, troops were landed near Cartagena and a night attack was mounted on a Spanish strongpoint guarding the approaches to the city. It failed miserably. Wentworth remarked on 'the wretched behaviour of the Americans, who had the charge of the scaling ladders, working tools, etc., which they threw down on the first approach of danger, and thereby occasioned the loss of the greatest part of 'em'.

In mid-April the British gave up the assault and re-embarked for Jamaica. Not until August 1742 did the expedition reach the island, many of the Americans aboard having done no more than menial work for the navy, which had treated them cruelly, and having no spoils of war to show for their dreadful experience. A significant number had died, while the rest returned with a dangerous mixture of hatred for the British and contempt for the abject military failure. The British officers, in return, considered the Americans undisciplined, greedy, cowardly and almost beneath regard.

Three features stand out most strikingly from this desultory record of British military interventions in America during the century preceding the American War of Independence. First, the rarity of these actions. Second, except for the interventions in Massachusetts and New York at the end of James II's reign, the British army intervened not against the colonists but to protect them from outside threats. It cannot be overemphasized that the colonies were virtually self-governing. With no troops at his disposal, the governor did not govern; he presided. There were no police actions, no large permanent garrisons and no intimidating manoeuvres; most of the time few regular soldiers were stationed in America at all – only the colonies' own militias, which existed to defend the territories in the west, and to keep order when necessary. The American War of Independence was to be less an attack on the British connection and its armed forces – which were scarcely in evidence – than an assault on the established order which used the ties with Britain as underpinning for its social and legal authority.

A third factor common to these few interventions was that they left locals far from impressed by British arms. On the few occasions when

British troops did appear, they inspired nothing but dislike and contempt in a rough-and-ready American militia used to irregular fighting
over woods and mountains, and their commanders appeared timid and
incompetent.

As the first large-scale intervention by the redcoats in the colonies, the
'French and Indian War' furiously exacerbated the distrust between
the wretchedly equipped militiamen and the drill-hardened troops of
the King. But ordinary people, too, bitterly resented the army's wartime
attempts at recruitment; in particular the enlistment of servants infuriated propertied men. One pro-British Massachusetts lawyer observed,
'if any native of the province enlists, the enlistment is critically exam-
ined, every imaginary flaw is made a real one, and the desertion of such
a person encouraged. This is the popular temper, and the magistrates,
always in some shape or other dependent upon the people, are in my
opinion too complaisant to it.' One employer complained that the
British soldiers 'stole into our plantations disguised like thieves in the
dead of night, made our servants drunk, forced them to enlist and
carried them off'.

The problem of quartering was equally contentious. Although British
soldiers during the Seven Years War were supposed to be quartered in
public houses, which were to be compensated, there were far too few
such places to accommodate the men. An officer remarked that the
people make 'no great difference between a soldier and a negro'. In
response, the overbearing Scottish peer Lord Loudon, commander-in-
chief of the British forces in America, treated the citizens of Albany, the
capital of New York State, where most of the troops were to be quartered
in winter, with lofty disdain. Loudon remarked that, 'The practice has
always been … that no house has been exempt from quartering the
troops … and from this rule the people of the first fashion in England
have not been exempted.'

A thousand men descended on the inadequate public accommodation
in Philadelphia, and local people were horrified at the prospect of putting
some of them up in private houses. One specious objection was that

> We cannot conceive it … be thought advisable, to quarter the soldiers by
> force on private houses rather than by law on public-houses; and we
> apprehend that if the bought servants, which have been so lately taken
> from the King's good subjects here, and no satisfaction made their
> owners, notwithstanding the Act of Parliament so expressly requires it, are

now to be thrust into their houses, and made their masters, some com-
motions may arise, dangerous to the King's peace.

In the end, the soldiers sought shelter in a new municipal hospital, and
resorted to constructing rudimentary barracks.

In North Carolina soldiers were housed in a half-built church, farm
buildings or tents, while the legislature made provision for extra firewood and blankets for the wretched, shivering troops. Thus were the
'oppressors' – actually come to protect the colonists – treated by the
'oppressed'. One British commander exclaimed, 'I am heartily tired of
the eternal disputes which makes the service so disagreeable in America.'
At last a rough barracks was constructed.

In Boston, Loudon had to threaten to take quarters by force before
the Massachusetts legislature backed down and provided the army with
accommodation. This was very different from the reception usually
received by armies from the peasantry of Europe.

The visiting army was also bombarded with endless litigation glee-
fully brought by the locals. Moreover, the local assemblies insisted on
their authority to control the army's activities. They argued that, as they
paid for some of its provisions, they had the right to choose provincial
commanders, to select military targets, to pick the location of forts, and
to set limits on which local militias might serve alongside the regulars,
and for how long. The British army found it almost impossible to requisition wagons and horses without coercion.

However, when the militia served alongside British regulars in the
war, they were subject to British military discipline, which was ferocious
and implacable. Men could be shot, hanged or sentenced to 1,000 lashes
for relatively small offences. Unsurprisingly, the Americans bitterly
resented this, and deserted in droves. General Wolfe put it savagely: 'The
Americans are in general the dirtiest most contemptible cowardly dogs
that you can conceive. There is no depending on them in action. They
fall down dead in their own dirt and desert by battalions, officers and
all. Such rascals as those are rather an encumbrance than any real
strength to an army.' Wolfe's description notwithstanding, the militiamen learned from their experience.

Another major long-term effect of the French and Indian War was the
militarization of Americans on an unprecedented scale. It was precisely
these trained militias that were to be so effective to the rebel cause in the
American War of Independence. The very 'rascals' who most disliked

British military discipline and traditions were drilled by the British in tactics and the use of weapons: the British had moulded their own future enemies.

The Royal Navy was a further source of friction, far more acute and longstanding than the rare impositions of the army. The navy used American ports as staging posts to enforce the Navigation Acts, to police smuggling, and to protect local shipping. The Americans complained that the British were much more reluctant to perform the last task, with the risks it entailed, than to stop local shipping for contraband, while running protection rackets for their own ships running illegal trade. Even the British admiralty admitted that 'The captains of his Majesty's ships stationed in America have, of late years, taken a very unwarrantable liberty of lying in port with their ships for the greatest part of the time they have remained a[b]road, to the dishonour of his Majesty's service and the disservice of the colonies for whose protection they were appointed.'

The navy's worst impositions were the press gangs – which, of course, were common to Britain's seaports as well. The arrival of Royal Navy ships was often viewed with such dread that merchantmen, fearing their crews would be pressed into service, would keep away from ports, which affected local commerce. Men would frequently desert from Royal Navy ships, which would then have to resort to the press gang to bring themselves up to strength again.

On one occasion at Boston in June 1741 Captain James Scott was besieged in his house by a mob of several hundred protesting at his impressment of men. According to one newspaper, the ship left 'to the great joy of the inhabitants of this town, as well as the owners of vessels and sailors, having greatly stopped the free course of our navigation and prevented supplies from coming to town, by impressing men out of vessels inward bound, coasters and fishermen not excepted, for several weeks past.'

In 1747 another ship in Boston, the *Achilles*, seized forty-eight young men and the town was plunged into three days of rioting. Naval officers had to flee to the governor's residence, and the British even threatened to bombard the town. Only when Boston's leading citizens called for a return to order did calm return. But the day the *Achilles* went, Samuel Adams, soon to be the colonists' most vociferous spokesman against the British, issued 'an address to the inhabitants of the province of Massachusetts Bay in New England, more especially to the inhabitants of Boston occasioned by the late illegal and unwarrantable attack upon their liberties, and the unhappy confusion and disorders consequent thereon'.

Impressment was no small-scale matter, and levels increased sharply during the wars with the French. One night in New York no fewer than 800 were press-ganged – a quarter of the city's adult male population. HMS *Shirley* pressed nearly 100 men in Boston alone. Boston's riot was followed by others, such as the Newport riot of 1765 after five weeks of impressment. Benjamin Franklin was later to condemn impressment of locals because it 'doth not secure liberty, but destroys it … if impressing seamen is of right by common law in Britain, slavery is then of right by common law there; there being no slavery worse than that sailors are subjected to'.

It may seem surprising that none of the American leaders was to make much political capital out of the undoubted abuse that was impressment. To American revolutionary leaders, as to the American Establishment in general, the press gang was a customary way of manning ships which affected only the lowest levels of society – usually merchant seamen – not men of property. It was hardly viewed as an abuse at all. Yet to the class likely to be impressed it was a furious source of grievance. The seamen and harbour workers were to form a reservoir of dedicated support for the American cause, and hardly any took the British side during the War of Independence.

A final important source of contention during the Seven Years War was the colonists' whole-hearted violation of the British embargo on trade with their common enemy, the French. Amazingly, in a war in which the colonists were supposed to be fighting for their own survival against the French and the Indians, they were engaging in a hugely profitable contraband trade with the enemy. This completely frustrated the British blockade of the French coast and was viewed as downright treachery by the British. William Pitt was determined to stamp it out with his Atlantic fleets.

Trade was carried on through supposedly neutral French entrepôts such as the Dutch island of St Eustatius or Danish St Thomas, or under a flag of truce. The supposedly 'British' governors of American states even connived in it. Governor William Penny of Pennsylvania made a financial killing out of selling his authorizations for flags of truce. One British captain observed twenty-nine American vessels using the free port of Monte Cristi in Spanish Haiti. British commanders sometimes sought to blockade American ports as punishment for this – preventing ships from leaving port, which also helped to depress prices for the British troops ashore – but this practice aroused intense American anger. It was sometimes hard to believe that the Americans were fighting on the same side as the British, much less that they were colonial subjects.

By the end of the long-drawn-out war with France, the groundwork for the American Revolution had been laid: all the ingredients for the con-flagration that began barely more than a decade later were present. Already the thirteen colonies, far from behaving as subordinate to British rule, considered themselves on an equal footing with the mother country. They had their own parliaments and political systems. They elected their own officials. They were English-speaking freemen – much freer, indeed, than many of their peers in Britain, where the upper and middle classes remained dominant, though comparatively small and exclusive. They provided their own defence forces and police.

The British had sent no redcoats to suppress the colonies since the 1690s. When British soldiers had arrived, it had been to protect American borders in wars in the south, north or west. The nominally British state governors were usually in close political alignment with the men who ran the local legislatures. Theoretically, the British could crush rebellions in the colonies – but this was only a distant threat.

Despite their virtual autonomy, the colonies derived several benefits from the British connection: protection from the French in the north and the Indians on their borders; privileged access to the greatest entre-pôt in the world; protected sea routes using a British merchant fleet largely constructed from New England timber; a system of rights and privileges within which they fashioned their own society; above all, the model for a stable social order in which men were ranked by wealth and property, to an even greater degree than in England (where aris-tocracy and family connection counted for more). Why give up these privileges? America was already free in all but name, enjoying a status only slightly below that of a modern member of the British Commonwealth.

But the 'French and Indian War' had eliminated the common enemy that made the Americans most reliant on British protection. For the first time in their history they had no need of a militarily strong ally. The war had armed and trained a large number of ordinary Americans, while simultaneously igniting a hatred against the arrogance and brutality of those who armed and trained them. What became known afterwards as the Seven Years War had completely transformed the American perception of themselves as a people incapable of defending their own territory without British assistance. The war nearly bankrupted both France and Britain, leading the former to retire hurt for several years and stoking up the fires of France's own revolution. The war led Britain to embark on two disastrous attempts to get the colonies to pay part of the cost of defending themselves. Finally, it led to Britain's apparent support for American Indian rights, which incensed the tough-minded settlers eager to expand into the American mid-west. It was not so much a dress rehearsal for the War of Independence as that conflict's first act. In it were rooted the independence of the United States, the French Revolution, the establishment of the British Raj in India, and the collapse of the three-hundred-years-old Spanish Empire.

Finally – and fundamentally – the Seven Years War led poor Americans and those with least stake in society to query the colonies' social structure and the authority by which those who lived there were bound. The struggle for independence was indeed to be a revolution, for it was to start from the bottom, among the lower-middle-classes allied to the waterfront mobs of Boston, and the embittered soldiers and sailors who were to confront the staid social order.

All that was needed was a spark to focus the hatred of those people – still a small minority – who felt suffocated by the tidy restraints of American society, their energies frustrated by a hierarchy they had not created and to which the majority of new migrants felt little loyalty. That focus was found when the British, out of understandable motives, decided to attempt to assert colonial authority over a people they had neither understood nor ever really controlled.

# 3

# *Stamp of Authority*

George Grenville, who became Britain's Prime Minister in 1763, has been blamed as the man responsible for Britain's loss of the American colonies, and has gone down in history as one of Britain's greatest failures. Paradoxically, this intelligent, high-minded man represented a dramatic break with the corruption in which British politics had wallowed since the shrewd but venal Sir Robert Walpole had first invented the office of First Lord of the Treasury (Prime Minister).

Grenville was the younger brother of one of the grandees and major political figures of the mid eighteenth century, Richard, Earl Temple, who treated George II with such contempt that the monarch flung directly at him the Order of the Garter he had been compelled to award. Grenville was a serious, principled man with an administrative bent, as well as being a highly effective orator. The brother-in-law of the greatest statesman of the age, the Great Commoner, William Pitt (who was married to Grenville's sister Hester), he was not afraid to fall out with that towering figure, who, at his height, controlled the loyalty of the chattering classes and the mob alike.

Able and utterly uncorrupt, Grenville was brought in to defuse the major political crisis arising from the new young King George III's attempt to reassert the general prerogatives of the throne, nearly a century after James II had similarly tried without sucess. He followed the shambolic and controversial administration of the Earl of Bute, a didactic, schoolmasterly Scot, who had enjoyed immense power behind the scenes as the King's tutor and who was widely, although probably wrongly, believed to be the lover of his mother.

Bute had succeeded the Duke of Newcastle – a deeply corrupt, inarticulate but astute party manager who had run the country for much of the reign of George II and whom George III had been forced to recall when he dumped the overbearing William Pitt and brought to an end the years of war with France and Britain's expansion of empire. Bute proved an immediate and universal disaster as Prime Minister, incapable of standing up to political fire, and the King was forced to bow to public opinion and compromise with a man who was neither corrupt – a condition of the King – nor a stooge of the court – a condition of Parliament.

That man was Grenville, whose family ties with the Great Commoner might also have been expected to secure Pitt's backing. However, Pitt resented any possible rival, and viewed even Grenville with jealousy – which led to an estrangement over American policy. Pitt had earlier described Grenville as 'one of the very best parliament men in the House', and another appraisal after his term of office sums up the character of the new Prime Minister.

> Calm, deliberate, economical, and attentive; steadfast to business, early and late; attached to no dissipations or trifling amusements; always master of himself, and never seen, either at White's with the gamesters, or at Newmarket with the jockies. Regular and exact in his family, and discharging, in the most exemplary manner, every social and religious duty. What is a labour and a fatigue to other men was his greatest pleasure; and those who knew him best in the management of affairs acknowledge that his discernment, capacity, and application were quick, enlarged, and indefatigable.
>
> No minister was ever more easy of access, or gave a more patient or attentive hearing to such as applied to him, and though he entered upon the management of affairs at the most critical conjuncture, with many and great prejudices on certain accounts against him, yet his steady, upright, and able conduct had conciliated the minds of men to him; and nothing, perhaps, could give the wiser and more rational part of mankind better hopes, and better expectations, than to see a man of these distinguished abilities, of this unwearied attention, and of this unblemished integrity, again serving his country, in one of the highest and most important offices of state.

Edmund Burke was famously to say:

> He thought better of the wisdom and power of human legislation than, in truth, it deserves. He conceived, and many conceived along with him, that the flourishing trade of this country was greatly owing to law and institution, and not quite so much to liberty; for but too many are apt to believe regulation to be commerce, and taxes to be revenue.

\*

The very first crisis that confronted Grenville's ministry arose out of the smouldering embers of the Seven Years War. In 1761 the British Board of Trade, responsible for managing the colonies, had decided that all grants of land must come from its own officials, not from the governors, who were viewed as too much in the hands of local interests. This had little effect in stopping the western seepage of the frontiersmen to seize territory from the Indians, which was often accompanied by extreme brutality on both sides, with the settlers gaining the upper hand.

In May 1763 Chief Pontiac of the Ottawa led a full-scale rebellion against the incursions, attacking British forts between Lake Superior and the lower Mississippi, capturing forts and laying siege to Detroit, as well as ravaging settlements in Virginia, Maryland and Pennsylvania and killing hundreds. Fort Pitt came under bitter siege, and was relieved only with great difficulty by British troops under Colonel Bouquet. To Britain's intense relief, the southern tribes failed to join the rebellion, and the Iroquois in western New York State were persuaded to keep out of it, but it was nevertheless the biggest Indian threat to the colonies since their founding. It marked a fateful turning point for British–American relations.

Grenville concluded that the cause of the rebellion had been the land rush and the greed and brutality of the settlers, and in 1763 he obtained a royal proclamation closing off the land west of the Appalachian mountains and the Mississippi river to white migration. But the hardy, impoverished, self-sufficient pioneers who looked to Britain to defend them were not disposed to obey British orders to stay out of Indian lands. They included participants in the Ohio Company, possessed of a royal charter giving them rights to 200,000 acres of land, and among them was the young George Washington. The shareholders discovered that squatters and fur traders had already moved into the disputed territory and were refusing to move, which undercut the Company.

Despite the attempts of the border garrisons to stop them, the white settlers of the north and the west took full advantage of the French–Indian defeat to move westward over the Potomac and seize territory, as well as the valuable fur trade and other commerce coming across the mountains. In the Kanawha valley, the farmers driven out by the Indians in 1763 passed back over the mountains in 1764 and 1765. The migration continued into western Virginia, Maryland and western Pennsylvania, as though no Proclamation Line had ever been announced. Meanwhile, the proclamation itself had stirred up immense resentment against the mother country among the whites. Grenville's policy was undoubtedly humane and respectful of moral rights and justice for the original inhabitants. Unfortunately, it was also unworkable.

The border problem confronted Grenville with another acute problem. It was clear that a strong army was needed to guard the American West, to protect both native Americans and settlers against each other. The Bute government had already decided in principle to send one, with the support of the King, who was reluctant to disband loyal army units after seven years of war. Grenville accepted the logic – fatefully, in view of the extreme unpopularity of British soldiers among both the American militias and the ordinary people they had encountered. Yet there seemed to be no alternative: the militias were in no shape to police the colonies and the increasingly anarchic and dangerous border separating the races.

Just as the land problem had led to the controversy over a standing army, so this army now posed another question; Who was to pay for it? The British, whose treasury had been bled dry by the war with France? Or the Americans, who stood to benefit and in whose defence it was being set up – or so the British believed? Americans, on the contrary, saw it merely as a police force to protect the Indian tribes against them now that the French threat had been removed – a point the British either failed to appreciate or considered actually gave them a moral obligation to intervene.

Thus the real spark for the American War of Independence was to be the right of settlers to go on pushing westward at the bloody expense of the Indians – which led to the decision to send in a British standing army and to tax the Americans to pay for it. Not surprisingly, American writers were later to prefer to concentrate on the taxation rather than the land grabs across the Appalachians as the catalyst of discontent; but the latter were the first link in the chain of causation.

The British were in fact prepared to pay more than £100,000 of the £200,000 cost of maintaining twenty battalions on the American mainland and in the West Indies. But the logically minded Grenville found it inconceivable that the Americans should not pay part of the cost of their own defence.

After the long war against the French, Britain's national debt stood at nearly £123 million (which by one estimate amounts to some £50 billion in today's terms), and within two years it would stand at £137 million.

Taxes in Britain were at punitive levels: there were levies on houses, windows, offices, carriages, spirits, newspapers, sugar, linen and – affecting particularly the poor – beer and tobacco. Rioting in Exeter against a cider tax in May 1763 was a clear warning that the limits had been reached.

Grenville's reasoning is hard to fault. But he failed to take into account the perceptions of the people he was dealing with across the Atlantic. The Proclamation Line and the stationing of a standing army along it infuriated a large number of Americans – in particular, frontiersmen and former members of the militia. The issue of taxation angered the American middle and upper classes – for historically America had been taxed very little, and then only by the local assemblies. The only taxation previously levied by the British was in the form of customs duties.

To the British government it was unacceptable that Britain's American subjects not only had taxes levied upon them at a lower rate than the British themselves, while enjoying the protection, laws, and commercial advantages of the Empire, but now expected the British taxpayer to pay the full cost of policing the western border. The Stamp Act of 1765 required a number of items, including wills, newspapers, calendars, pamphlets, playing cards, dice and college degrees, to obtain an official stamp in return for a small exaction. But to many wealthy Americans the Stamp Act was simply the establishment of a precedent whereby the British could gradually introduce a regime of taxation into the colonies.

Taxation, of course, is a hallmark of the modern state, and is viewed with most hostility by the propertied class, which stands to lose most by it. The Stamp Act was viewed with special hostility because it imposed an 'internal' duty and because, by taxing so many transactions in America, it hit the middle classes as much as the rich. Whitehall's choice of such a tax had been dictated by the practical difficulty of laying any other on America, where customs duties and tariffs were evaded as a matter of course.

The Stamp Act followed a series of lesser revenue-raising measures by the Grenville ministry, most of which were a tightening of existing legislation, rather than the introduction of new taxes. Chief among these measures was the Sugar Act of 1764, which halved the (almost completely avoided) tax of sixpence a gallon on foreign-produced molasses imported into America, but sought to enforce it rigorously. The trade in molasses was huge and underpinned the lucrative rum industry in the colonies. American anger was understandable, especially when a squadron of British warships was sent to enforce the order.

Americans began to complain of other grievances: Whitehall's decision to insist that the Virginia legislature seek Privy Council approval before passing a particular law; new powers awarded to British customs and excise officials in Massachusetts to break into homes and search for smuggled goods; an order allowing the King to revoke judicial appointments; vigorous proselytization by Thomas Secker, Archbishop of Canterbury, of the Church of England in the colonies; and even enforcement of an act prohibiting the felling of pine trees in the colonies.

The provisions to enforce the Sugar Act infuriated the unbureaucratic colonies. More goods were 'enumerated' for export only to Britain (although, as already pointed out, this was probably beneficial to the Americans). Cargoes had to be listed, and prosecutions for evasion could be brought before vice-admiralty courts, where no sympathetic colonial jury would be sitting in judgement. With his customary administrative zeal, Grenville ordered customs collectors to report to their posts or lose their offices. Many collectors, who lived in England while their deputies in America did the work, promptly resigned, and the new class of collectors from both sides of the Atlantic was far less disposed to be bullied by the colonists than its predecessors, leading to a spate of clashes between the new officials and Americans.

In Newport, Rhode Island, a zealous customs schooner was actually fired upon by the town's cannon in 1764. In the same port a customs collector, John Robinson, was seized by a sheriff and a mob and made to walk eight miles before spending two days in jail. Enforcement of the sugar tax particularly incensed American traders who were used to exchanging molasses for slaves from Africa. The New York Assembly indignantly protested at the Sugar Act as an 'innovation'. It argued:

> An exemption from the burden of ungranted, involuntary taxes, must be the grand principle of every free state. Without such a right vested in themselves, exclusive of all others, there can be no liberty, no happiness, no security; it is inseparable from the very idea of property, for who can call that his own, which may be taken away at the pleasure of another? And so evidently does this appear to be the natural right of mankind, that even conquered tributary states, though subject to the payment of a fixed periodical tribute, never were reduced to so abject and forlorn a condition, as to yield to all the burdens which their conquerors might at any

future time think fit to impose. The tribute paid, the debt was discharged; and the remainder they could call their own.

Boston merchants organized a Society for Emergency Trade and Commerce. When rumours of the imminent Stamp Act reached America, a group of representatives and merchants was dispatched across the Atlantic to meet Grenville in May 1764. The Prime Minister was vague about his plans. The London-based Thomas Whateley, who actually drafted the legislation on Grenville's behalf, did consult senior customs officials in America, as well as Jared Ingersoll from Connecticut, a deeply pro-British American later to be one of the victims of the protests. Ingersoll was unequivocal: he wrote in July 1764 that the minds of Americans

> Are filled with the most dreadful apprehensions from such a step's taking place, from whence I leave you to guess how easily a tax of that kind would be collected; 'tis difficult to say how many ways could be invented to avoid the payment of a tax laid upon a country without the consent of the legislature of that country and in the opinion of most of the people contrary to the foundation principles of their natural and constitutional rights and liberties.

In February 1765, just before the act was passed, Ingersoll joined Benjamin Franklin and two others upon the several weeks' voyage across the Atlantic to press the case once more to the British Prime Minister. They were received cordially, and argued that only the colonies could tax themselves – otherwise the British government would be in dispute with elected local assemblies. Grenville dismissed the objection as exaggerated, and turned the tables by asking how much each assembly would contribute towards the cost of America's defence.

The colonists had no answer to this, because they had never considered it: they had made no plans to raise the necessary taxes by themselves. But, in spite of the fury of the frontiersmen, they made no objection to the stationing of British garrisons in America – the cause of the extra expense. Thus their objection was less to the principle of being taxed by a parliament in which they were not represented than to being additionally taxed at all – otherwise they would have brought proposals for self-taxation to the table.

A few days later, on 23 March, the Stamp Act was brought before the House of Commons. In a famous exchange, Charles Townshend, one of Britain's most brilliant, if erratic, young politicians, asked, 'And now will these Americans, children planted by our care, nourished up by our indulgence till they are grown to a degree of strength and opulence, and protected by our arms, will they grudge to contribute their mite to relieve us from the heavy weight of that burden which we lie under?'

The colonists' foremost champion in the chamber, Colonel Isaac Barré – son of a French refugee, and the man who first coined the term 'sons of liberty' in this speech – replied:

They planted by your care? No! Your oppressions planted 'em in America. They fled from your tyranny to a then uncultivated and inhospitable country – where they exposed themselves to almost all the hardships to which human nature is liable, and among others to the cruelties of a savage foe, the most subtle and I take upon me to say the most formidable of any people upon the face of God's earth. And yet, actuated by principles of true English liberty, they met all these hardships with pleasure, compared with those they suffered in their own country, from the hands of those who should have been their friends.

They nourished up by your indulgence? They grew by your neglect of 'em: as soon as you began to care about 'em, that care was exercised in sending persons to rule over 'em, in one department and another, who were perhaps the deputies of deputies to some member of this house – sent to spy out their liberty, to misrepresent their actions and to prey upon 'em; men whose behaviour on many occasions has caused the blood of those sons of liberty to recoil within them; men promoted to the highest seats of Justice, some, who to my knowledge were glad by going to a foreign country to escape being brought to the bar of a court of justice in their own.

They protected by your arms? They have nobly taken up arms in your defence, have exerted a valour amidst their constant and laborious industry for the defence of a country, whose frontier, while drenched in blood, its interior parts have yielded all its little savings to your emolument. And believe me, remember I this day told you so, that same spirit of freedom which actuated that people at first will accompany them still. But prudence forbids me to explain myself further. God knows I do not at this time speak from motives of party heat, what I deliver are the genuine sentiment of my heart.

Nevertheless, the act became law by 245 to 49 votes.

The Stamp Act fused the growing discontent of the wealthy American merchants and professional elite with the simmering anti-Establishment resentment felt by part of the colonies' underclass. It was a potent alliance: the rich feeding upon the frustration of the poor to vent their anger against the common enemy – remote Britain. It also helped to defuse the class antagonism between the two. Men of property had to be careful in case the attack upon the British undermined the social order and the values of which the monarchy was the pinnacle. But at this stage the threat of such an outcome seemed relatively distant.

For the real revolutionaries among the American lower middle class, however, there was much benefit in securing the self-interested, if temporary, backing of the propertied class in an attack on the distant British government. The three principal arguments against the Stamp Act by the wealthy and articulate classes were, first, that the colonies were unrepresented in Parliament; second, that Parliament therefore had no right to tax them; and, third, that 'internal' taxation could be levied only by representative assemblies – a distinction to be drawn with external taxation, the long-standing, if largely evaded, levying of customs duties.

It was perfectly true that the colonies were unrepresented in Parliament. But so too were all the major industrial areas of England, which had expanded exponentially during the boom years of the eighteenth century, ushering in a new era for British politics and society. This was only partially corrected in Britain – remarkably, without revolution – with the passage of the Great Reform Bill half a century later.

Some British apologists in America argued that, theoretically, the Americans were indeed represented in Parliament.

> Our nation is represented in parliament by an assembly as numerous as can well consist with order and dispatch, chosen by persons so differently qualified in different places, that the mode of choice seems to be, for the most part, formed by chance, and settled by custom. Of individuals far the greater part have no vote, and of the voters few have any personal knowledge of him to whom they entrust their liberty and fortune.
>
> Yet this representation has the whole effect expected or desired; that of spreading so wide the care of general interest, and the participation of public counsels, that the advantage or corruption of particular men can seldom operate with much injury to the public.
>
> For this reason many populous and opulent towns neither enjoy nor desire particular representatives; they are included in the general scheme of public administration, and cannot suffer but with the rest of the empire.
>
> It is urged that the Americans have not the same security, and that a British legislator may be wanton with their property; yet if it be true, that their wealth is our wealth, and that their ruin will be our ruin, the parliament has the same interest in attending to them, as to any other part of the nation.

James Otis Jr, leader of the Boston opposition, momentarily also espoused the status quo, but eventually reversed himself.

> To what purpose is it to ring everlasting changes to the colonists on the cases of Manchester, Birmingham and Sheffield, who return no members? If those now so considerable places are not represented, they ought to be … It may perhaps sound strangely to some, but it is in my most humble opinion as good law and as good sense too, to affirm that all the plebeians of Great Britain are in fact or virtually represented in the assembly of the Tuskaroras, as that all the colonists are in fact or virtually represented in the honourable House of Commons of Great Britain.

The issue of whether a parliament in which the colonists were not represented had a right of taxation was trickier. Even though the Americans had no representation in Westminster, the British parliament's right to impose 'external' tariffs and customs duties had always been accepted, partly because the Americans were initially in no position to refuse, and partly because duties were so easy to evade in the smuggling haven that was America's coastline. Moreover, the Americans were to benefit from added British spending in their own defence. The British assumed some rights on this score – unless Americans objected to the notion that a standing army in their defence was unnecessary, which at this juncture was not what they said. Indeed, the British had just incurred colossal expenditures defending America.

The possibility that America might be represented at Westminster was not discussed at this stage. From the mother country's viewpoint it was not unreasonable that the Americans, who paid very low taxes to their own assemblies, should pay tribute to Britain, which was incurring extra expenditure on their behalf.

A third issue then arose: the principle of taxation without representation had already been conceded by the Americans with the acceptance of 'external' taxation, whatever the populist rhetoric of radical leaders. A distinction had therefore to be drawn with 'internal' taxation, which the Americans deemed unacceptable.

The distinction was essentially specious, semantic and legalistic and masked the true objection: that they were being asked to subsidize British troops blocking their westward expansion. As we shall see, the Americans were soon to object even to 'external' taxation, which was used to raise revenue just as much as to 'regulate' trade – its notional purpose – no matter how much the Americans insisted on this as a key

difference. The age-old English cry of 'no taxation without representation', later taken up by the vigorous Virginia lawyer Patrick Henry as
'Taxation without Representation is Tyranny', was a convenient and
powerful slogan with which to channel American frustrations with
Britain – but little more.

Apart from the Proclamation Line, the nub of the problem was that,
just as America's economy and population were growing dramatically,
and America was becoming more assertive than before, Britain had
chosen to exercise a little more power. And the Americans, who had
barely been aware of any real authority being exerted over them before,
would have none of it. The protest was that of free men suddenly
reminded that they were not formally so; of relaxed, prosperous men
accustomed to getting their own way being fined by a remote power for
some petty infringement of the law.

There was a further source of theoretical dispute: the Americans had
reconciled their actual freedom with their theoretical vassalage to Britain
by insisting that they were subjects of the British Crown, not of
Parliament (where they were unrepresented). They worked this into the
tangled assertion that, although loyal subjects of George III, they were
not bound by the actions of ministers or of Parliament. This was doubly
ironic at a time when a political struggle was under way in England
between a monarch asserting his traditional anti-democratic prerogatives and Parliament fighting for its own rights.

Leaving aside the fact that previously they had accepted Parliament's
right to legislate for them without demur, for Americans to assert that
they owed their loyalty directly to the King placed them on dangerous
ground. For Grenville, while deriving his authority both from King and
Parliament, could to some extent be portrayed as Parliament's man. But
what of Bute before him, and Lord North after him – both King's men
par excellence?

In fact George III exerted the authority of the throne more than his
immediate predecessors or successors, particularly in the matter of the
colonies. He was fully cognisant and persuaded of the case for the Stamp
Act. To try to assume a break between a liberty-loving King and a repres-
sive Parliament was entirely contrived – and ultimately contradictory,
for lovers of liberty looked ridiculous pledging their allegiance to a
'despotic' King against his slightly representative Parliament. This line
of argument was quietly abandoned as the dispute progressed and

indeed, the King was to prove the more ardent persecutor of the colonies.

As long as the colonies still professed their loyal obedience to Britain, it is hard not to conclude that every one of the legal arguments adduced against the Stamp Act and the measures that accompanied it was essentially flawed. There were no real grievances, only excuses for creating crisis, after which the Americans could conclude that they would have no alternative but to declare independence. The colonies' defiant stand against a limited assertion of Britain's rarely used powers was a political confrontation and flexing of muscles for which the British had provided the radicals with a pretext.

Meanwhile the government remained blissfully complacent about the storm heading its way. In March 1765 the King and his Prime Minister were reflecting earnestly on how to defuse a row in America over the proposed provision in the Mutiny Act which would allow for the billeting of troops in private houses as well as public ones, to obviate such absurdities as were suffered during the Seven Years War. An American, David Barclay, styling himself a 'clamorous citizen', had written directly to Grenville:

> As this law will increase the power of the commander-in-chief in America, it may not be improper to remark, what everybody seems to agree in, that if America ever throws off its dependence on this country, it will most probably be attempted by some aspiring genius amongst the military ...
>
> The clause in the Mutiny Act, now framing for that part of the King's dominions, making it lawful to billet soldiers on a march in private families, is, in the opinion of every well-wisher to America, and every friend to liberty, such an innovation upon the privileges of those who justly claim the natural rights of this country, that it alarms many well-wishers to the present administration.

The King's view on this occasion had been remarkably conciliatory:

> Though I shall see you [Grenville] to-morrow, not to lose time I send you the letters that have passed between Lord Halifax and the Secretary at War, concerning the difficulties that have occurred in America with regard to the Mutiny Act; Lord Halifax appears to disregard the noise that may be made here in Parliament by extending the quartering of soldiers in private houses in America. As I think that at a time like this all measures should be duly weighed before they are undertaken, I send them to you before I return them to the office. You will plainly perceive that the

Secretary at War, in his answer, though he feels the necessity of some alterations to adapt the act to the circumstances of America, yet seems to decline approving of the mode proposed for rectifying it.

Grenville, in his reply, appeared to consider dropping the controversial proposal:

> On the short examination which I have hitherto been able to give to the letters which have passed between Lord Halifax and the Secretary of War, it seems to me that the clause which your Majesty mentions for extending the power of quartering soldiers in the private houses in America, is that which is by far the most likely to create difficulties and uneasiness, and therefore ought certainly to be thoroughly weighed and considered before any step is taken in it, especially as the quartering of soldiers upon the people against their wills is declared by the petition of right to be contrary to law.

This gentle reasoning was soon hit by a bombshell: a veritable explosion of anger against the Stamp Act. The bewildered British government first learned of the vehemence of the American reaction in a letter from Grenville's chief adviser on American affairs, Thomas Whately. This was a masterpiece of understatement.

> I enclose to you a copy of a letter which I have received from Boston, and which relates to the behaviour of the populace with respect to the stamp officer there: I am told that after that, they proceeded against Mr Hutchinson, the lieutenant-governor, who, though a very popular man, yet having issued warrants for apprehending some of the rioters, was become the object of their resentment: in Rhode Island the collector of the customs and the distributors of the stamps have been obliged to take refuge on board a ship.
>
> There are some disturbances also in Virginia: and the assembly of deputies from the several provinces, in order to apply jointly for a repeal of the act, is soon to be held at New York. The instructions given by one of the colonies to their deputies on this occasion are come over, and, as I hear from one who has seen them, are directly treasonable. I suppose no representation from such a convention of states will be received by parliament, at least it is worth considering whether it should or not. The rage of the people seems not to be confined to the Stamp Act; the officers of the customs are also the object of it, and if that should be avowed, then the clear point is, whether the parliament has a right to impose any taxes at all there.
>
> The language of the ministry is, I am told resolute, and they have

certainly written to Governor Bernard, directing him to enforce the execution of the law vigorously, but I believe they are undetermined about the measures to be taken, and the mode of proceeding if the tumult continues.

The rescue of the murderers of the Cherokees in Virginia is another very serious affair; these people seem to profess that killing an Indian is not a civil offence, and will, I doubt not, bring on an Indian war.

Nearly a month later, on 8 November, Whately sent further details:

I have now got all the particulars of the riot at Boston from the persons I have seen, and the letters I have received.

The first mob was certainly countenanced by the better sort of people, who most severely repented of the part they had taken, when they saw the outrages of the second, and were so sensible of the danger, that in a few minutes after the council had ordered the alarm drum to be beaten, five hundred of them appeared in arms. Fifty of these who formed a corps of cadets meeting the mob, and preparing to fire, dispersed them instantly. No precautions were taken after the first riot to prevent another, and in the meanwhile, Dr Mayhew, one of their pastors, preached on a text out of the Galatians, 'I would they were cut off which trouble you: for, brethren, ye are called unto liberty', and in his sermon inveighed with the utmost vehemence of expression and gesture against the Stamp Act, which, however ridiculous it may seem to us, so irritated his heated audience, that it was with difficulty they were restrained by the observance of the Sabbath, and the next day burst forth into all the violence you have heard of.

The principal mischief was done to Mr Hollowell and Mr Hutchinson, whose furniture and wainscot they cut into shivers with hatchets, and carried off £600 in cash from the one, and £200 in cash, with a £1,000 province bill, from the other.

Since that time a guard has been kept in the town, and at the custom house: some of the rioters are taken, but, as I hear, they wish to proceed against some one, if they can find any such, of no consequence, instead of choosing the most considerable as the most guilty. I have some reason to believe, what you will hardly expect, that you will be told that the appointment of natives [local people] to be distributors [of the stamps] was improper, and the [anti-]smuggling cutters especially in America are to be decried.

These descriptions hardly did justice to the riots that had followed the introduction of the Stamp Act. This is how the fires were ignited, almost simultaneously, in three places splayed down the 1,500-mile coastal strip of North America.

On 30 May 1765 Patrick Henry, a brilliant, pushy young man of twenty-nine, rose to his feet in the modest building housing Virginia's assembly, the House of Burgesses. Only recently elected to the chamber, eloquent and daring, with a womanizer's vanity, Henry had made his name as a lawyer with a vigorous assault on a pillar of the local Establishment – the Anglican clergy, who had sought the full annual allowance of tobacco (Virginia's main commodity export) due to each as part payment of their salary, even in the drought year of 1758. On that occasion Henry had boldly declared that 'a King, by allowing acts of this salutary nature, far from being the father of his people, degenerates into a tyrant and forfeits all rights to his subjects' obedience'. He was greeted with cries of 'Treason'; but he won his case under the benevolent eye of the presiding judge – Colonel John Henry, his own father.

The majority of the state's legislators had left the chamber and only 39 members of the full quorum of 116 were present when the dashing and bold young lawyer introduced a set of resolutions against the Stamp Act, which had just been passed in England. Only the last were direct and to the point, albeit inflammatory. He was rebuked by the Speaker for treasonable language – 'Caesar had his Brutus, Charles the First his Cromwell, and George the Third may profit by their example' – upon which he offered to demonstrate his loyalty to George III 'at the expense of the last drop' of his blood.

For this ambitious power-seeker, the Stamp Act was no more than a pretext for a general attempt to overthrow the establishment of sleepy Virginia. Of his celebrated resolutions, only the three most innocuous were certainly passed by a rump of the assembly of staid and comfortable burghers and planters; in a brilliant piece of media manipulation, the three militant ones were only said to have been passed in newspapers in other colonies.

In Massachusetts in particular, the resolutions were quickly publicised in the press as if they had all been approved. There the House of Representatives was divided into two factions: one led by the lordly Thomas Hutchinson, who liked to ape the manners of the British aristocracy and ran a sprawling nepotistic empire of placement and jobbery under the benevolent eye of the British-appointed governor, the feeble, indecisive Francis Bernard, and a 'popular' faction led by James Otis Sr and the temperamentally unstable, possibly even crazed, James Otis Jr, who, astonishingly, just before passage of the Stamp Act, had meekly conceded the British parliament the right to tax the colonies in his pamphlet *The Rights of the British Colonies* (1764).

When news of Virginia's defiance reached Boston, a group of shop-keepers and manufacturers and the editor and printer of the *Boston Gazette*, Benjamin Edes and John Gill, met at a distillery in Hanover Square, dubbed themselves the 'Loyal Nine', and planned to stage a riot making use of the town's two waterfront gangs, the North End and South End, which had united under a tough, roguish cobbler, Ebenezer Mackintosh. The cabal probably had the backing of Samuel Adams, in many respects the first and the most incendiary of America's revolution-ary leaders, and only one of its members came from the professional classes – John Avery, a Harvard-educated merchant.

The group authorized Mackintosh to lead his waterfront bands – a collection of apprentices, sailors and unemployed men and boys – on the rampage against Andrew Oliver, Hutchinson's brother-in-law, who had been appointed stamp distributor – tax collector – for the colony. Meanwhile Otis Jr had resigned his lucrative job as Advocate General in Boston, making a speech which John Adams, then a successful lawyer (and later the second President of the United States), described as marking the birth of independence:

> Otis was a flame of fire. With a promptitude of classical allusions, a depth of research, a rapid summary of historical events and dates, a profusion of legal authorities, a prophetic glance of his eye into futurity, and a torrent of impetuous eloquence, he hurried away everything before him. American independence was then and there born; the seeds of patriots and heroes were then and there sown, to defend the vigorous youth. Every man of a crowded audience appeared to me to go away, as I did, ready to take arms against writs of assistance. Then and there was the first scene of the first act of opposition to the arbitrary claims of Great Britain. Then and there the child Independence was born.

On 14 August an effigy of Stamp Distributor Oliver, alongside a large boot to represent the Earl of Bute, George III's unpopular former Prime Minister, was found hanging from a tree in Hanover Square, dubbed Liberty Tree. Indignant respectable citizens tried to pull it down, but were intimidated by threats from bystanders. The sheriff and his officers, ordered by Hutchinson to remove the effigy, were threatened with lynching. That evening a mob of several hundred men carried the effigy past the house where Governor Bernard, Hutchinson and his council were in emergency session and down to the waterfront, where they ripped down a new building belonging to Oliver before going on to smash the windows of his town residence. The effigy was beheaded symbolically, stamped upon, and burnt.

Returning to Oliver's house the same evening, the protestors ransacked it and searched several buildings with a view to finding and killing him – which they failed to do. When Hutchinson and the sheriff called upon the mob to disperse, they were showered with stones. The local commander of the militia, which was supposed to keep order, was too alarmed to take action.

The following night the crowd reassembled and, this time with less violence, beat on the door of Hutchinson's house. On 26 August it gathered again, in its curiously organized way, and destroyed two customs officials' houses before moving on to Hutchinson's home. There Massachusetts's foremost political leader was having dinner with his wife and children. The family narrowly escaped, after persuading Hutchinson that they would not leave without him – undoubtedly this saved his life. The house was then systematically ransacked, its exquisite silver and contents were stolen, and its cupboards and doors were pulled down, leaving only an empty shell and the library of 10,000 books; part of the roof was burnt.

This, at last, was too much for the previously respectable city of Boston, and the following day Governor Bernard raised his militia without difficulty, to restore order. But Oliver had decided to resign his post. He was promptly followed in this decision by the stamp distributor for New York, James McIvens, and by New Jersey's William Coxe. 'A storm is rising and I should soon feel it,' remarked the former. New Hampshire's distributor arrived in Boston harbour from England only to be refused landing by the mob. He promptly resigned, for which he was carried to the Exchange Tower in celebration. One junior collector was stripped naked in the freezing weather, and covered in tar and feathers, causing chunks of flesh to peel off. He survived – although his doctor did not expect him to live long.

In Rhode Island, too, violence rose to the surface. The state had extensive powers of self-government, under a seventeenth-century charter, and was virtually democratic, with three-quarters of its male inhabitants entitled to vote for the general assembly. The state was split between two main towns: Providence, dominated by Stephen Hopkins and his clan, and Newport, dominated by Samuel Ward and his supporters.

The small colonial aristocracy dedicated to England and the Anglican Church was led by Martin Howard. He despised the democratic nature of the state, which he described as 'nothing but a burlesque upon order and government'. Howard and his followers were lampooned as the 'Tory Junto' and were accused of plotting against the liberties of the colony. The junto was accused of being

> a little dirty, drinking, drabbing, contaminated knot of thieves, beggars and transports, or the worthy descendants of such, collected from the four winds of the earth, and made up of Turks, Jews and other infidels, with a few renegade Christians and Catholics, and altogether formed into a club of a scarce a dozen at N–p–t. From hence proceed ... petitions to alter the colony forms of government, libels upon all good colonists and subjects, and every evil work that can enter into the heart of man.

In May 1765 a boat which had landed to press men into the British navy had been burnt by a mob of 500 colonists. With the passage of the Stamp Act, Howard and his main supporter, Dr Thomas Moffat, and the stamp distributor, Augustus Johnstone, became the targets of popular anger. Their effigies were burnt on 27 August in Queen Street, respectively labelled as that 'fawning, insidious, infamous, miscreant and parricide', the 'infamous, miscreant, leering Jacobite', and the 'Stamp Man'. All three fled the town. The houses of Howard and Moffat were burnt down, although Johnstone's survived.

The riots were spreading out of control. Pro-British local merchants were threatened by an aggressive and mutinous British sailor, John Webber, who was arrested and placed on board a British ship. An angry mob then threatened to tear Newport apart. Webber was released, whereupon he returned in triumph and trod on the neck of the prostrated sheriff. Johnstone, however, who had resigned his post as distributor, now had the support of the alarmed merchants against the leaders of the mob, and Webber was arrested again.

In Connecticut the dispute took a religious turn. The 'Old Lights' of the Established Church hierarchy were challenged by 'New Lights', Puritan anti-Establishment supporters of the 'Great Awakening' who had arisen in the 1740s to claim they were possessed by the Spirit. The Old Lights had won the initial struggle, and controlled the legislature. The colony's anti-Establishment land speculators – mostly New Lights – were concentrated in the Susquehannah Company and aimed to settle the upper Wyoming valley, which actually belonged to Pennsylvania.

The leader of the Old Lights was Jared Ingersoll, who, although an opponent of the Stamp Act, agreed to act as stamp distributor. He was immediately labelled 'Judas Iscariot' (a play on his initials). One of his aides in New Providence was seized by a mob, put inside a coffin, whose lid was nailed shut, and lowered into the ground. Only as the first clods of earth struck the coffin was he released, on condition he resign his post. Ingersoll's effigy was hung by Connecticut's own version of the Sons of Liberty secret societies in no fewer than five towns. In West Haven 'a horrible monster, of male sex, a giant, 12 feet high whose head was internally illuminated', was burnt. Mock trials were held of 'stampmen, one sentenced to be tied to the tail of a cart, and drawn through all the principal streets in town, and at every corner and before every house should be publicly whipped; and should be then drawn to a gallows erected at least 50 feet high, and be there hanged till he should be dead'. Ingersoll's house in New Haven was surrounded by a mob until he promised not to fulfil his duties.

This extraordinary mass uprising had turned into a class insurrection of the most elemental kind – albeit, as is usually the case, a minority one. In one colony after another the Stamp Act had been the pretext for the dispossessed, the waterfront malingerers, the urban unemployed to rise up against the established order – usually initially at the behest of a radical faction of have-nots and merchants. In Rhode Island, where rioters came from the ruling clique, they had turned venomously against an attempt by the more prosperous to assert control by taking command of the administration of the Stamp Act. In Connecticut, religious radicals had hijacked the anti-Stamp Act cause to deliver a major blow against the clerical establishment (as had happened to a lesser extent in Virginia). Everywhere the Stamp Act had been used as a pretext for the social underdogs to strike against their overlords. It was a revolution – or at least an attempted revolution.

In all this, the question of British control of the colonies was quite secondary. For what mattered was not the largely academic issue of who supposedly ran the colonies from 2,000 miles away, in a continent where people rarely travelled more than twenty miles, but the very primary issue of the domestic social and economic order within the colonies themselves, for which the British Crown was both the pinnacle and the underpinning.

Like most revolutions, the American one was started by disagreeable thugs working for better-educated malcontents; both categories exist in a country at any time. There was nothing special or attractive about the sans-culottes, Bolsheviks, brownshirts or descamisados of the Boston or Newport waterfronts. It was, however, a unique combination of historical accidents to which they owed their ability to ignite a fire which spread across a continent and changed the world.

To one school of American historians, the causes of the American Revolution are straightforward. It was battle between good and evil, between oppressed and oppressor, the result of the yearning of a democratic, vigorous colonial people to be free of an overseas-based, colony-fattened, oligarchic aristocratic society dominated by a King. The lawyer John Adams, as early as 1766, captured the sentiment:

> The people, even to the lowest ranks, have become more attentive to their liberties, more inquisitive about them, and more determined to defend them, than they were ever before known or had occasion to be; innumerable have been the monuments of wit, humour, sense, learning, spirit, patriotism, and heroism, erected in the several provinces in the course of this year. Their counties, towns, and even private clubs and sodalities have voted and determined; their merchants have agreed to sacrifice even their bread to the cause of liberty; their legislatures have resolved; the united colonies have remonstrated; the presses have everywhere groaned; and the pulpits have thundered.

Adams invoked a heroic past for the American settlers.

> Let us read and recollect and impress upon our souls the views and ends of our own more immediate forefathers, in exchanging their native country for a dreary, inhospitable wilderness. Let us examine into the nature of that power, and the cruelty of that oppression, which drove them from their homes. Recollect their amazing fortitude, their bitter sufferings – the hunger, the nakedness, the cold, which they patiently endured, the severe labours of clearing their grounds, building their houses, raising their provisions, amidst dangers from wild beasts and savage men, before they had time or money or materials for commerce. Recollect the civil and religious principles and hopes and expectations which constantly supported and carried them through all hardships with patience and resignation. Let us recollect it was liberty, the hope of liberty for themselves and us and ours, which conquered all discouragements, dangers, and trials.

These noble settlers were imbued, paradoxically, with a British conception of freedom. As the contemporary commentator John Witherspoon wrote:

> It is proper to observe, that the British settlements have been improved in a proportion far beyond the settlements of other European nations. To what can this be ascribed? Not to the climate, for they are of all climates; not to the people, for they are a mixture of all nations. It must therefore be resolved singly into the degree of British liberty which they brought from home, and which pervaded more or less their several constitutions.

Provost Smith of Philadelphia argued that America should

> with reverence look back to the times of ancient virtue and renown. Look back to the mighty purposes which your fathers had in view, when they traversed a vast ocean, and planted this land. Recall to your minds their labours, their toils, their perseverance, and let their divine spirit animate you in all your actions.
>
> Look forward also to distant posterity. Figure to yourselves millions and millions to spring from your loins, who may be born freemen or slaves, as heaven shall now approve or reject your councils. Think, that on you it may depend, whether this great country, in ages hence, shall be filled and adorned with a virtuous and enlightened people; enjoying liberty and all its concomitant blessings, together with the religion of Jesus, as it flows uncorrupted from his holy oracles; or covered with a race of men more contemptible than the savages that roam the wilderness.

To the eloquent twenty-century American political scientist Clinton Rossiter, the American Revolution was primarily a triumph of ideas:

> Conditions in the continental colonies in the pre-revolutionary decade were conducive to political thinking of a libertarian character ... Progress and freedom were the concerns of the time, and a political theory dedicated to progress and freedom was an inevitable result ...
>
> Far more significant than this material progress was the quickened influence of ... the 'factors of freedom'. The 'forces behind the forces' – the English heritage, the ocean, the frontier, and imperial tension – never worked so positively for political liberty as in this decade of ferment. Until the last days before independence the colonists continued to argue as Englishmen demanding English rights. The more they acted like Americans, the more they talked like Englishmen. Heirs of a tradition that glorified resistance to tyranny, they moved into political combat as English Whigs rather than American democrats, reminding the world that 'it is the peculiar right of Englishmen to complain when injured'.

The other basic forces were no less conducive to liberty. In a situation that called desperately for accurate information, firm decisions, and resolute administration, the very distance between London and Boston frustrated the development of a viable imperial policy. In a situation that called no less desperately for colonial understanding of the financial and imperial difficulties facing crown and parliament, the push to the frontier weakened the bonds of loyalty to an already too-distant land. And the Stamp Act and Townshend Acts forced most articulate colonists to reduce the old conflict of English and American interests to the simplest possible terms. Since some Englishmen proposed to consign other Englishmen to perpetual inferiority, was it not simply a question of liberty or slavery?

A second school viewed the Revolution instead as a product of a primal economic struggle, as in Louis Hacker's classic view of the exploitation of American colonists, quoted earlier.

Established though these two positions are, neither bears serious scrutiny. While ideals, and in particular propaganda, were highly important, as were economic grievances – the one as a rallying cry, the other as fuel – as explanations of the Revolution they lack conviction. At that time the colonists enjoyed more autonomy, freedom and self-government than probably any dependency in history; and, following a brief depression after the Seven Years War, the American colonies were enjoying greater prosperity than ever before – a fact attested to by their magnetic effect on external immigration.

The quasi-independence of the American colonies itself helps to explain their assertiveness and struggle for formal independence. As Rossiter points out, it is not men who are chained and oppressed who fight for freedom; usually their enslaved condition dispirits, inhibits and demoralizes them. It is men who are free in all but name, or men who think themselves free but are suddenly faced by unexpected and unpopular exactions. Both these conditions were found in the thirteen colonies. As the eighteenth-century historian David Ramsay put it in his history of the American Revolution:

England had given the Americans full liberty to govern themselves by such laws as the local legislatures thought necessary, and left their trade open to every individual in her dominions. She also gave them the amplest permission to pursue their respective interests in such manner as they thought proper, and reserved little for herself, but the benefit of their trade, and that of political union under the same head ... without charging herself with the care of their internal police, or seeking a revenue from [the colonies], ... [but] contented herself with a monopoly of their trade. She treated them as a judicious mother does her dutiful children. They shared in every privilege belonging to her native sons, and but slightly felt the inconveniences of subordination.

Small was the catalogue of grievances, with which even democratical jealousy charged the parent state. The good resulting to the colonies, from their connection with Great Britain, infinitely outweighed the evil.

# 4

# *The Conciliators*

In July 1765 Grenville had fallen from power – to the satisfaction of George III, who disliked him intensely. His replacement was the Marquess of Rockingham, who led a weak government of Whig grandees, of which the strongest member was the articulate Edmund Burke. This received news of the disturbances in the colonies with alarm, but was content to drift, though the King lamented, 'I am more and more grieved at the accounts in America. Where this spirit will end is not to be said.'

Furiously castigated by Grenville for its indecisiveness, the government also came under intense pressure from British financiers, who deeply resented the loss of trade brought about by the Americans' actions over the Stamp Act, and the damage caused by the disturbances themselves, which they claimed amounted to several million pounds. Rockingham and the King – the latter in particular a man who tried to compensate for his limited intellect and tendency to vacillate with occasional shows of assertiveness, although his instincts were decent enough – decided to bow to the merchants and take the line of least resistance. If they repealed the Stamp Act, perhaps the colonists would settle down and the whole problem would go away.

Their mistake was to believe that the Stamp Act was the cause of American resentments, which in fact lay far deeper: without the Stamp Act some other excuse would soon have been found. This error was compounded by the belief that appeasement was the best response to what was essentially a series of riots by mobs at first instigated by certain powerful interests. However, if the government conceded the colonists' argument of no taxation without representation, it was permitting the authority of the House of Commons to be directly challenged. For, without American representatives present, what right had Parliament to impose any duties at all on the colonies, or its legislative will?

It was William Pitt, still smouldering with resentment at his own recent dismissal, who inadvertently came to the government's rescue. After Grenville's fall, Pitt's failure to be reinstated on his own terms to what he believed to be his mission to give decisive leadership to Britain left him increasingly buffeted by manic depressive moods, yet his oratory and his presence still towered above those of his peers. In a famous speech, he detached the power of taxation from the other functions of government, ripped into the former government of his brother-in-law Grenville, and then declared:

> It is my opinion that this kingdom has no right to lay a tax upon the colonies. At the same time, I assert the authority of this kingdom over the colonies, to be sovereign and supreme, in every circumstance of government and legislation whatsoever ... taxes are a voluntary gift and grant [prerogative] of the Commons alone. In legislation the three estates of the realm are alike concerned, but the concurrence of the peers and the Crown to a tax is only necessary to close with the form of a law. The gift and grant is of the Commons alone.

Rhetorically brilliant as ever, he was in fact advocating an untenable position: for, by giving way over the issue of taxation, Pitt merely bought time over the issue of whether a parliament in which the colonies were not represented had any authority over them at all. The logical consequence was the acknowledgement of their virtual independence, and there are signs that he understood this. But as long as they believed that they still governed the colonies, it would be necessary for King and Parliament to assert themselves sooner or later. Throwing a bone to a baying pack was no solution unless Britain accepted the reality of a purely notional sovereignty over the colonies, which at that stage it was not prepared to do – although, paradoxically, that had long been the reality of its position. The coolly logical Grenville, in an equally impassioned speech smouldering with indignation at his relative's lofty arrogance, took the only defensible pro-government position of the day:

> Protection and obedience are reciprocal. Great Britain protects America; America is bound to yield obedience. If not, tell me when the Americans were emancipated? When they want the protection of this kingdom, they are always ready to ask for it. That protection has always been afforded them in the most full and ample manner. The nation has run itself into an immense debt to give them their protection; and now they are called upon to contribute a small share towards the public expense, an expense

arising from themselves, they renounce your authority, insult your officers, and break out, I might almost say, into open rebellion.

As though the government did not exist, with Grenville delivering the
speech the minister should have made, Pitt sprang into opposition with
one of his greatest speeches:

> I have been charged with giving birth to sedition in America. [The
> Americans] have spoken their sentiments with freedom against this
> unhappy act, and that freedom has become their crime. Sorry I am to hear
> the liberty of speech in this House imputed as a crime. But the imputa-
> tion shall not discourage me. It is a liberty I mean to exercise. No gentle-
> men ought to be afraid to exercise it. It is a liberty by which the gentleman
> who calumniates it might have profited. He ought to have desisted from
> his project. The gentleman tells us, America is obstinate; America is almost
> in open rebellion. I rejoice that America has resisted. Three millions of
> people so dead to all the feelings of liberty, as voluntarily to submit to be
> slaves, would have been fit instruments to make slaves of the rest ...
>
> No minister since the accession of King William thought or even
> dreamed of robbing the colonies of their constitutional right until the era
> of the late administration. Not that there were wanting some, when I had
> the honour to serve his Majesty, to propose to me to burn my fingers with
> an American Stamp Act. With the enemy at their back, with our bayo-
> nets at their breasts, in the day of their distress, perhaps the Americans
> would have submitted to the imposition; but it would have been taking
> an ungenerous and unjust advantage.
>
> The gentleman boasts of his bounties to America. Are not those boun-
> ties intended finally for the benefit of this kingdom? If they are not, he
> has misapplied the national treasures. I am no courtier of America; I stand
> up for this kingdom. I maintain, that the Parliament has a right to bind,
> to restrain America. Our legislative power over the colonies is sovereign
> and supreme. When it ceases to be sovereign and supreme, I would advise
> every gentleman to sell his lands, if he can, and embark for that country.
>
> When two countries are connected together, like England and her col-
> onies, without being incorporated, the one must necessarily govern; the
> greater must rule the less; but so rule it, as not to contradict the funda-
> mental principles that are common to both. If the gentleman does not
> understand the difference between external and internal taxes, I cannot
> help it; but there is a plain distinction between taxes levied for the purpose
> of raising a revenue, and duties imposed for the regulation of trade, for
> the accommodation of the subject; although, in the consequences, some
> revenue might incidentally arise from the latter.
>
> The gentleman asks, when were the colonies emancipated? But I desire

to know, when they were made slaves. But I dwell not upon words. When I had the honour of serving His Majesty, I availed myself of the means of information which I derived from my office: I speak, therefore, from knowledge. My materials were good; I was at pains to collect, to digest, to consider them; and I will be bold to affirm, that the profit to Great Britain from the trade of the colonies, through all its branches, is two millions a year. This is the fund that carried you triumphantly through the last war. The estates that were rented at two thousand pounds a year, threescore years ago, are at three thousand pounds at present. Those estates sold then from fifteen to eighteen years' purchase; the same may now be sold for thirty. You owe this to America: this is the price America pays for her protection. And shall a miserable financier come with a boast, that he can bring a peppercorn into the exchequer, to the loss of millions to the nation?...

A great deal has been said without doors of the power, of the strength, of America. It is a topic that ought to be cautiously meddled with. In a good cause, on a sound bottom, the force of this country can crush America to atoms. I know the valour of your troops. I know the skill of your officers. There is not a company of foot that has served in America, out of which you may not pick a man of sufficient knowledge and experience to make a governor of a colony there.

But on this ground, on the Stamp Act, when so many here will think it a crying injustice, I am one who will lift up my hands against it. In such a cause, your success would be hazardous. America, if she fell, would fall like the strong man. She would embrace the pillars of the state, and pull down the constitution along with her. Is this your boasted peace? Not to sheath the sword in its scabbard, but to sheath it in the bowels of your countrymen?

The Americans have not acted in all things with prudence and temper. The Americans have been wronged. They have been driven to madness by injustice. Will you punish them for the madness you have occasioned? Rather let prudence and temper come first from this side. I will undertake for America, that she will follow the example. There are two lines in a ballad of Prior's, of a man's behaviour to his wife, so applicable to you and your colonies, that I cannot help repeating them:

> Be to her faults a little blind:
> Be to her virtues very kind.

Upon the whole, I will beg leave to tell the House what is really my opinion. It is, that the Stamp Act should be repealed absolutely, totally, and immediately; that the reason for the repeal should be assigned, because it was founded on an erroneous principle. At the same time, let the sovereign authority of this country over the colonies be asserted in as strong terms as can be devised, and be made to extend to every point of legislation whatsoever that we may bind their trade, confine their manufactures, and exercise every power whatsoever – except that of taking their money out of their pockets without their consent.

Thus, the Great Commoner appeared to espouse the resistance of the waterfront rioters and in effect accept the right of Americans to govern themselves – although he did not say so explicitly. The only honest positions were Grenville's, determined to assert British authority, and to a lesser extent Pitt's, prepared to acknowledge this only formally while favouring self-government for the colonies, except on taxation. Grenville, in his last interview with King George on leaving office, had told him defiantly that

he [Grenville] understood that the plan of his [the King's] new administration was a total subversion of every act of the former; that nothing having been undertaken as a measure without His Majesty's approbation, he knew not how he would let himself be persuaded to see it in so different a light, and most particularly on the regulations concerning the colonies; that he besought His Majesty, as he valued his own safety, not to suffer any one to advise him to separate or draw the line between his British and American dominions; that his colonies were the richest jewel of his crown; that for his own part he must uniformly maintain his former opinions both in parliament and out of it.

Now betrayed by his brother-in-law too, he had a frigidly poignant exchange of letters with Pitt after their historic exchange:

Mr Pitt presents his compliments to Mr Grenville, and understanding that his retiring from the committee last night, when Mr Grenville was beginning to speak, gave him displeasure, he desires to assure him that nothing could be further from his thoughts than to mark the least want of personal regard to Mr Grenville, being, in truth, not in a condition to remain in the committee, and having requested their leave to retire.

Mr Pitt begs to inquire after Mrs Grenville's health, which he sincerely hopes is much better, and to present his compliments to her.

Grenville replied:

Mr Grenville presents his compliments to Mr Pitt, and is sorry that he was not in a condition to remain in the committee last night after he had spoken, as Mr Grenville found himself under the necessity of giving an

answer to many passages contained in Mr Pitt's speech, in which he apprehended himself to be personally called upon, and to which he earnestly
wished Mr Pitt could have heard his answer.

Mr Grenville is obliged to Mr Pitt for his assurances that nothing was
further from his thoughts than to mark the least want of personal regard
towards him; and Mr and Mrs Grenville join in returning their thanks for
his inquiry after Mrs Grenville's health, which they hope is better than it
has been, and shall be glad to receive the like favourable account of Mr
Pitt and Lady Chatham.

The government's position – repeal of the Stamp Act in response to
rioting and business pressures, but a continuing assertion of Britain's
right to rule the colonies – was weak, contradictory and dishonest.
Considering that Pitt had gone too far, the government acceded to the
merchants' petitions against the Stamp Act on economic grounds and
abandoned the act as inexpedient, while petulantly asserting that it
retained the right to tax and legislate for the colonies.

On 7 February 1766 Grenville's last-ditch attempt to retain the Stamp
Act went down to defeat in the House of Commons by 274 to 134.
Benjamin Franklin was given a chance to appear as the colonies' spokesman before the House, where he asserted that everything would return
to normal if the Stamp Act was repealed. When asked why the
Americans should pay any taxes at all to the British if they escaped this
one, Franklin replied with a veiled threat: 'At present they do not reason
so, but in time they may possibly be convinced by these arguments.'

Almost entirely under short-term economic pressures, the British
government had caved in. For the group of self-interested American
businessmen likely to be hurt by the act, it must have seemed certain
that the British government would no longer be able to raise significant
revenues from the colonies – which was very satisfactory. For the mobs
they had raised, this was a first triumph in overthrowing the whole
detested social order.

What if Grenville's policy had prevailed – as indeed it would have had
he not fallen from office (which on his account was caused by a disagree-
ment over the colonies)? Could the Stamp Act have been enforced, or
was the Rockingham government only being realistic in beating a
retreat? Any response must be conjectural. But opposition to British rule
per se had not crystallized or been organized at this stage, as was to
happen a decade later.

The precedent of British weakness towards the colonies had now been set. The great majority of Americans wanted nothing more than a stable society, and most were proud of being British subjects. There was no evidence that, however irritated they might be by the Stamp Act, the Sugar Act and other colonial measures, they were prepared to commit violence against the established order, much less engage in open rebellion.

None of the riots was challenged by armed men or muskets; in the absence of British soldiers or a proper police force, a militant minority had intimidated a peaceful majority and their representatives. That the waterfront thugs of Boston, New York and elsewhere had been backed by the powerful moneyed interests of merchants affected by the Stamp Act did not diminish the threat to order.

Significantly, these mobs of scores, and sometimes hundreds, never succeeded in mustering large crowds, let alone the majority of public opinion behind them, although the extent of popular support for the anti-British cause was to change later.

The British had disappeared at the first signs of trouble. This taught the militant minority of colonists two lessons about the mother country: the British would not resist when pushed; and they were apparently too weak to defend the colonies' interests effectively. It also demoralized upholders of the established order who did not like the Stamp Act but did not dispute Britain's authority to enforce it. It may have been a massive misjudgement of Grenville's to introduce the measure, but, once imposed, for the British to repeal it was folly – confirmation to a newly vigorous America that the British were weak and lacking in the resolve necessary to govern the colonies. Thomas Whately hinted as much in a letter to Grenville in May 1766:

> A rumour universally prevails of some very bad news from America, but I cannot hear anything of it authentically. The story is, that they are in arms. This I do not find any foundation to believe. I have been told that private letters say they will not be content with the repeal, which they say is of as little consequence as the Stamp Act, both being nullities, but I have not met with anybody who has received letters.

Two months earlier Thomas Moffatt, the strongly pro-British doctor from Newport, Rhode Island, had made the position clear in a remarkable letter which was passed directly to Grenville. Moffatt had been forced to flee after his house had been destroyed by a mob after the Stamp Act, and he was writing to a friend back home:

The present ministers of state, full of the tenderest and most benevolent sentiments towards America, set out in this undertaking upon a principle of reclaiming the British colonies by marks of their moderation and grace rather than by instances of their power and resentment, which last was much and eagerly insisted on by many, but prudently averted by those at the helm of government, who never have been, nor are yet insensible how much they have hazarded on this occasion for the sake of north America, and how much they have now depending upon the instant and future behaviour of the British American colonies.

If, therefore, the repeal of the Stamp Act is received in North America with the expected and becoming spirit of gratitude and obedience really manifested by the restoration of public and private tranquillity, order and safety, then may the King's ministers and all the true steadfast friends of America have abundant cause to rejoice, and be well satisfied with what they have now accomplished.

But if, on the contrary, the repealing of the Stamp Act should be received and considered by the colonists as a condescension or submission extorted from Sovereign and supreme authority, or if the occasion shall be celebrated with extravagancy and triumph indicatory of such sentiments or opinion, then may the Americans be said to have conspired in betraying their redeemers, and even of bringing them to open shame, and what the ensuing consequences would be to America and them is but too plain to require any explanation from me to you.

Moreover, the extreme divisions of opinion within Britain itself as to how to treat the colonies had been bitterly exposed in Parliament well before confrontation even began – something duly noted by the pro-independence activists. A policy of seeking to enforce the Stamp Act with American support, as Grenville advocated, was never attempted. In fact the protests were later to fizzle out under the dampening weight of the indignation of the peace-loving colonial majority, concerned at the threat to order, and it is hard to believe that many Americans had the stomach, inclination or preparedness to fight in 1766. Possibly they would have returned to the fight years later; and that is indeed what happened after the repeal of the Stamp Act.

That Parliament continued to assert Britain's rights in the colonies, despite having run away at the first confrontation, merely fuelled opposition until the extremists in America, and their wealthy backers, believed the British would run away at every confrontation – which was tragically not to be the case.

*

News of the repeal set off an explosion of joy across America – the newly constituted Sons of Liberty in Boston cheekily marching to see the governor himself. A British officer remarked acidly that the night 'ended in drunkenness, throwing of squibs, crackers, firing of muskets and pistols, breaking of some windows and forcing the knockers off the doors'.

The extremists had taken on the might of the Crown and won, and the result was an immediate radicalization of colonial politics. In May 1766 elections were held for the House of Representatives and council of Massachusetts: nineteen members belonging to the Establishment faction lost their seats and Thomas Hutchinson, as the colony's chief advocate of the Stamp Act, was ousted, along with many of his relations who held public office. In Connecticut the elected governor, Thomas Fitch, who had backed collection of the Stamp Act, was replaced. In New Jersey, New York, the Carolinas and Pennsylvania the results were less clear-cut.

Meanwhile serious disturbances briefly continued. General Thomas Gage, the British commander, wrote:

> In my letter of the 24th of June, I had the honour to acquaint you that his Majesty's Twenty-Eighth Regiment, under the command of Major Browne, had been ordered into Dutchesse county in this province, to assist the civil officers in putting the laws in execution, and to quell some dangerous riots. A small body of the light infantry company was fired upon by the rioters, and three of them wounded: they returned the fire, wounded some, pursued and dispersed the rest, notwithstanding their numbers.
>
> The disturbances had spread into the county of Albany, where a skirmish happened between the sheriff, with about two hundred followers, and a part of the rioters. Some few were killed and wounded on both sides, but the sheriff and his people were put to flight. A great many prisoners have been taken or delivered themselves up, and among them are several principals. After restoring tranquillity to the country, the regiment came to this place, leaving a captain and fifty men to guard the gaols, and brought with them the principal ringleaders of the whole confederacy. The magistrates commend the regiment greatly, as well for their spirit and readiness in apprehending the rioters, as for their strictness of discipline, not having taken the least thing during their stay in the country, and even refusing to plunder the houses of some of the proclaimed rioters, though desired to do it.

In fact the Americans were already preparing for war, as was plain from a letter written by William Gerard Hamilton, one of the earliest independence activists:

As to America, I wish we may not burn our fingers, and do our enemies' work for them, by quarrelling among ourselves. There are, in the different provinces, about a million of people, of which we may suppose at least 200,000 men able to bear arms; and not only able to bear arms, but having arms in their possession, unrestrained by any iniquitous Game Act. In the Massachusetts government particularly, there is an express law, by which every man is obliged to have a musket, a pound of powder, and a pound of bullets always by him: so there is nothing wanting but knapsacks (or old stockings, which will do as well) to equip an army for marching, and nothing more than a Sartorius or a Spartacus at their head requisite to beat your troops and your custom-house officers out of the country, and set your laws at defiance.

There is no saying what their leaders may put them upon; but if they are active, clever people, and love mischief as well as I do peace and quiet, they will furnish matters of consideration to the wisest among you, and perhaps dictate their own terms at last, as the Roman people formerly in their famous secession upon the sacred mount. For my own part, I think you have no right to tax them, and that every measure built upon this supposed right stands upon a rotten foundation, and must consequently tumble down, perhaps, upon the heads of the workmen.

The British government had learned nothing from its previous experience. Soon after repeal of the Stamp Act, the Rockingham ministry fell under the weight of its internal contradictions and the King had to choose between the two dominant figures of the period, both of whom he detested: the rival brothers-in-law Grenville and Pitt, with their diametrically opposite views on America. Compared with Grenville, even the domineering fifty-seven-year-old Pitt seemed preferable.

The Great Commoner was sent for – only to become, from his own choice, no longer a commoner but Earl of Chatham. This removed him from the House of Commons, which he only sporadically attended, but also from day-to-day party management. Instantly he lost much of his popular support. From the radical American point of view, the change could hardly have been bettered (although Chatham insisted that his friend the Duke of Grafton would actually fulfil the role of Prime Minister). But the ministry quickly fell apart, shedding most of its senior ministers, and Grafton reluctantly relied upon the 'King's friends' – non-party gentry loyal to the throne and probably the most obtuse faction in Parliament. Chatham himself fell into one of his periodic bouts of depression, and withdrew to Bath to nurse himself.

He left behind him as the government's strongest figure a brilliant orator but erratic statesman, Charles Townshend, an epileptic from an unstable family background with a chronic shortage of money. Faced as Chancellor of the Exchequer by Britain's continuing financial crisis after the Seven Years War, Townshend now also had the burden of funding a standing army in America costing £400,000 a year – which Grenville's representatives suggested should be reduced by half and paid for by the Americans.

Townshend proposed instead that new customs duties should be collected on glass, paper, lead, paint and tea – given that the Americans accepted 'external' taxation in principle. These should be administered by an American Board of Customs Commissioners based in the colonies. In addition he asked Parliament to suspend the New York assembly, which had refused to abide by the Quartering Act and provide accommodation for the troops in the colonies.

The £40,000 in revenues that these measures would yield were woefully inadequate to pay for the troops, let alone have the slightest impact on reducing government debt. Townshend's further idea was that this money should be used to pay the salaries of royal officials in the colonies, thus removing them from under the control of the local assemblies.

Each of these measures was received by the colonists as a deliberate provocation. After their victory over the Stamp Act, the Revenue Act seemed an entirely unnecessary assertion of the prerogative of taxation. Worse, it affected in particular the richer merchant class which had supported the Stamp Act riots. Townshend was to be sadly stripped of his illusions that 'external' taxation of this kind was acceptable to the colonists. They now resented all additional forms of taxation, and the closure of New York's legislature and removal of the assemblies' right to pay local civil servants was pure provocation in their eyes. Apparently the British had yielded over the Stamp Act only to reassert their arbitrary rights again within months. Incredibly, the measures had been taken by the government of Chatham – their best friend in Britain – although he could disclaim them because he was not formally Prime Minister, which may have been part of his purpose in withdrawing to Bath.

The truth was that the ageing great man of British politics had lost his grip; he had tried to dismiss the domineering and increasingly assertive Townshend, securing the appointment of the conciliatory Lord

North in his place, but had failed. However, in September 1767 four months after pushing through his disastrous measures, Townshend suddenly died, leaving his successor to cope with the consequences.

North's initial prejudices were clear: 'There has been no proof of any real return of friendship on the part of the Americans; they will give no credit for affection ... I am against repealing the last Act of Parliament, securing to us a revenue out of America. I will never think of repealing it, until I see America prostrate at my feet.'

Britain, contrary to the American perception of a sleepy, stagnant, aristocratic colonialist society, was at its most dynamic in the eighteenth century. Like America itself, it was caught up in a whirlwind of economic and social change which in turn was stirring up huge political pressures.

Society and the economy were developing at a furious pace, partly in consequence of the expansion of empire, partly as a result of the end of dynastic wars of succession with the failure of the 1745 rebellion, and partly thanks to the intellectual flowering brought about by the Enlightenment and domestic inventiveness.

The effervescence of the eighteenth century and its light, airy, exuberant art, architecture, literature and criticism were not yet replaced by the ponderousness of the Victorian sense of responsibility to empire and society. The new supremacy of the middle classes, based on prosperity, a flourishing entrepreneurial spirit and technical and business innovation, had not yet resulted in disfiguring urbanization and industrialization.

It was the age of speed, travel and the first generation of bright young things since the Restoration more than a hundred years before. By 1770 turnpike roads, which had barely linked Birmingham, Chester and Manchester with London twenty years earlier, criss-crossed the whole country in an intricate grid from Truro to Aberystwyth, Holyhead, Glasgow, Edinburgh, Berwick-upon-Tweed, Hull, Norwich and Dover. By 1765 there were an astonishing 20,000 private coaches on the road, excluding stagecoaches and hackneys for public transport. The proliferation of private transport broke down rural isolation and local commercial monopolies, bringing prices tumbling. Speed astonishing by the standards of previous generations was now possible. As late as 1740 it still took around six days for a carriage to travel from Chester to London; by 1780 it took just two days. The travelling time from London to

Gloucester was slashed from two days to one. A journey from Bath to Oxford would take only ten hours, at a miraculous speed of seven miles an hour.

The eighteenth-century novelist Richard Graves has one of the characters in his *Columella* comment in 1779 that the most remarkable phenomenon which he has taken notice of in these late years, in his retirement, is the surprising improvement in the art of locomotion, or conveyance from one place to another. 'Who would have believed thirty years ago', he says, 'that a young man would come thirty miles in a carriage to dinner, and perhaps return at night? Or indeed, who would have said, that coaches would go daily between London and Bath, in about twelve hours, which, twenty years ago, was reckoned three good days journey?'

Accidents and congestion had become major problems, along with the new corruption of morals as landowners neglected their estates for the bright lights of the city and young ladies descended on the towns, making new acquaintances among fellow passengers on stage-coaches.

Another revolutionary communications enterprise was also under way – the canals snaking across Britain. In the late 1750s the waterways were constructed to bring cheap coal to Liverpool and Manchester, and by the 1780s bulk goods could be cheaply transported the length and breadth of England via a hugely improved canal system, transforming local economics and making possible the development of cities well away from the coast or from ready sources of raw materials. It was this colossal public investment, harnessing private capital, that enabled the Industrial Revolution to move ahead in earnest.

A revolution was also under way in Britain's countryside: enclosures, by which individual farmers took over common land, were spreading rapidly. The land not already owned by the big estates was being 'privatized'. Nearly 4,000 enclosure acts were passed between 1750 and 1810, affecting roughly a fifth of all land in England and Wales.

The old village communes were replaced by a class of prosperous middling farmers, while the poorer rustics became seasonal labour dependent on the farmers' whim. 'Engrossing' permitted the amalgamation of small tenant farms into bigger units, driving many peasant smallholders off the land.

The contemporary popular novelist Frances Brooke summed up the impact of the changes in her *History of Lady Julia Mandeville*:

It is with infinite pain I see Lord T— pursuing a plan, which has drawn on him the curse of thousands, and made his estate a scene of desolation; his farms are in the hands of a few men, to whom the sons of the old tenants are either forced to be servants, or to leave the country to get their bread elsewhere. The village, large and once populous, is reduced to about eight families; a dreary silence reigns on their deserted fields; the farm houses, once the seats of cheerful smiling industry, now useless, are failing in ruins around him; his tenants are merchants and engrossers, proud, lazy, luxurious, insolent and spurning the hand which feeds them.

While the old privileged relationship between landowner and farm labourer broke down, with many of the latter becoming fodder for the new industries, revolution in the countryside was paralleled by the self-confident expansion of urban Britain. London, with 500,000 inhabitants in 1700, had nearly doubled its population by 1800. Even more impressive in relative terms was the fourfold growth of Birmingham, Manchester and Leeds between 1700 and 1770. The urban population jumped from around a fifth in 1700 to around a third in 1800, or to about 2 million of England's 6 million people.

The second half of the eighteenth century also at last saw a concerted drive for urban improvement. In 1754 Westminster was paved and lighted. Drainpipes replaced spouts; jutting house signs were replaced by numbers. Piped water was introduced, and in 1779 the poet George Keate celebrated: 'The good order preserved in our streets by day – the matchless utility and beauty of their illumination by night – and what is perhaps the most essential of all, the astonishing supply of water which is poured into every private house, however small, even to profusion! – the superflux of which clears all the drains and sewers, and assists greatly in preserving good air, health and comfort'.

Slums and appalling conditions continued to thrive in the approaches to London and other major cities. But the cramped industrial kennels of the Victorian era had not yet appeared.

As the colonies began to inch towards rebellion, the political scene in Britain had been characterized by one major feature: George III's attempt to re-establish himself as the driving force in national affairs, acting as his own prime minister in the chaotic political conditions of the second half of the century. Apart from rejection of the Catholics, nearly the whole of the previous century and three-quarters in British politics had been devoted to a single major institutional struggle: that between the power of the central state, symbolized by the monarchy, and the power of the (diminishing) aristocracy and (increasing) squirearchy and middle classes, symbolized by Parliament.

For nearly a century, under the subdued but tactful Queen Anne, and then under two rarely resident and non-English-speaking monarchs, the Hanoverians George I and George II, Britain had effectively been a republic under Whig grandees. The defeat of the two Stuart rebellions in 1715 and 1745 was, in effect, the final defeat of the absolutist, centralizing powers of the state – or so the new political class believed.

George III – young, vigorous, attractive, English-resident and English-speaking – succeeded the grandfather he despised to the throne, and was determined to reassert the power of the central state against the squabbling, fractious politicians. Britain, now much more developed economically and socially, was suddenly faced with the possibility of constitutional conflict again.

The contest between the two dominant factions – the central state, represented by George III, and the middle classes, represented by Parliament – allowed unharnessed popular sentiment to a bubble up to a level where it threatened to destroy both. Briefly, the cause of John Wilkes – the first great agitator for freedom of expression – became the occasion for nearly revolutionary anger – on the eve of the American Revolution and a decade and a half before the French.

Wilkes – brilliant rake, journalist and polemicist – would not have found himself out of place in revolutionary America, where his blazing political trajectory was eagerly followed. As a young MP he survived exile for publishing seditious libel against the King, and returned to the House of Commons in vociferous opposition, to become Lord Mayor of London in 1774. The shock of rioting and disturbances in his favour forced King and Parliament to come to terms with him, and order and stability endured for the remainder of George III's reign, in spite of the King's mental deterioration. Prosperity and bourgeois virtues helped to settle a kingdom which many feared was on the brink of revolution in the 1770s.

Developing vigorously with a new thrusting entrepreneurial class, and dominated by arguments between central government and legislature, Britain in many ways mirrored the conflicts taking place inside America. The acerbic 'Letters of Junius' best enshrine the militant spirit stalking the land. In one letter in 1769 to the Prime Minister, the Duke of Grafton, the anonymous author (later believed to be Philip Francis, a protégé of Robert Clive) lacerated the government of Britain.

Lord Chatham, Mr Grenville, and Lord Rockingham have successively had the honour to be dismissed as servants of the public to those compliances which were expected from their station. A submissive administration was at last gradually collected from the deserters of all parties, interests and connections; and nothing remained but to find a leader for these gallant, well-disciplined troops. Stand forth, My Lord, for thou art the man. Lord Bute found no resource of dependence of security in the proud, imposing superiority of Lord Chatham's abilities, the shrewd, inflexible judgment of Mr Grenville, nor in the mild but determined integrity of Lord Rockingham. His views and situation required a creature void of all these properties; and he was forced to go through every division, resolution, composition and refinement of political chemistry before he finally arrived at the caput mortuum of vitriol in your Grace. Flat and insipid in your retired state, but, brought into action, you become vitriol again. Such are the extremes of alternate indolence or fury which have governed your whole administration.

Another letter in the same year was addressed to the King in terms of insolence bordering on treason:

The people of England are loyal to the House of Hanover, not from a vain preference of one family to another, but from a conviction that the establishment of that family was necessary to the support of their civil and religious liberties. This, Sir, is a principle of allegiance equally solid and rational, fit for Englishmen to adopt, and well worthy of your Majesty's encouragement. We cannot long be deluded by nominal distinctions. The name of Stuart, of itself, is only contemptible; armed with the sovereign authority, their principles are formidable. The Prince who imitates their conduct should be warned by their example; and while he plumes himself upon the security of his title to the Crown, should remember that, as it was acquired by one revolution, it may be lost by another.

Junius's views on the American colonies were no less trenchant:

The distance of the colonies would make it impossible for them to take an active concern in your affairs if they were as well affected to your government as they once pretended to be to your person. They were ready enough to distinguish between you and your ministers. They complained of an act of the legislature, but traced the origin of it no higher than the servants of the Crown. They deceived themselves with the hope that their Sovereign, if not favourable to their cause, at least was impartial. The decisive, personal part you took against them, has effectually banished that first distinction from their minds. They consider you as united with your servants against America, and know how to distinguish the

Sovereign and a venal parliament on one side, from the real sentiments of the English people on the other ... They left their native land in search of freedom, and found it in a desert. Divided as they are into a thousand forms of policy and religion, there is one point on which they all agree: they equally detest the pageantry of a King, and the supercilious hypocrisy of a bishop.

The constitutional crisis, and underlying fears of a popular revolution, had three crucial consequences. First, the new young King, insecure and assertive, decided that in the affairs of America, as initially with John Wilkes, he must act with vigour and, sometimes, inflexibility: any too direct challenge to his authority could not be borne. Indeed, softness towards America could unleash the domestic unrest never far below the surface in Britain. In this sense the American revolution was merely part of a wider conflict taking place throughout the English-speaking world between the central state and its forces of order and the rest of society.

Second, the British political class became obsessed with domestic issues which in fact were minor compared with the insurrection in the colonies. Third, thanks to this political turbulence at home, although Britain had no shortage of talented politicians, they were usually too domestically preoccupied to make a stand against the King's belligerent prosecution of his argument with America. In the power struggle between, on the one hand, the King, supported by his courtier Bute, and on the other hand the political classes, no fewer than six prime ministers fell in ten years: the great, overmighty William Pitt, considered too dominant by Bute and the King; the political fixer Newcastle; Bute himself, briefly stepping centre-stage, an instant target of popular hatred; Grenville, independent, unpopular and inflexible; Rockingham, considered over-accommodating towards Parliament; and Grafton, no more than a testy puppet.

The King's and Bute's strategy for reasserting royal authority and the power of the central state was to enlist the support of the backbench Tory squirearchy, now alienated by Whig grandees and the new moneyed classes. Unfortunately for the King, these Tories were no more enamoured of an interfering central state than they had ever been, and were largely agnostic politically. Once he had displaced the dominant figures of British politics, he found himself increasingly the prisoner of his own supporters.

Only with the ascent of Lord North, Grafton's successor, was the contest between King and Parliament resolved and some sort of stability returned. North's devious and emollient abilities were exactly what was needed for political peace in Britain: he accommodated the grandees, the Tory squirearchy and the King all at once. But, unhappily, his very flexibility in accommodating first one side, then the other, was the reverse of what was needed in dealing with an epic challenge like that in America. Firm leadership was required either in squaring up to the King and British public opinion and recognizing that the Americans must have self-government under nominal British rule or in squaring up to the Americans and accepting the sacrifices and commitment required, in terms of money and manpower.

Neither occurred. Britain had acted tough under Grenville, soft under Rockingham, tough again under Grafton, and then soft. North became the Prime Minister who vacillated, then decided to stand up to the Americans under royal prodding without ever committing the necessary resources, only to pull out when the going got rough.

Like the great political fixers Sir Robert Walpole, and the Duke of Newcastle before him, North was a brilliant party manager, and for twelve years he brought peace to the troubled British political scene. He was neither as corrupt as Walpole nor as personally unimpressive as Newcastle. As a peacetime prime minister he was probably without equal, defusing the Wilkes issue simply by ignoring it, and brilliantly mediating between King and Parliament so as to give the illusion that each was dominant when in fact the ringmaster was.

The impecunious son of the Earl of Guilford, he was only thirty-eight when he came to power. He was a supremely capable manager of the nation's finances: honest, able, in command and articulate – and with a face like a genial and bleary pig. A contemporary observer, Nathaniel Wraxall, described his extraordinary eloquence:

> He was powerful, able and fluent in debate, sometimes repelling the charges made against him with solid argument, but still more frequently eluding the weapons of his adversaries by the force of wit and humour . . .
> He seldom or never took notes, trusting to his memory for retaining the principal facts which occurred during the previous discussion ... His natural affability rendered him so accessible, and the communicativeness of his temper inclined him so much to conversation that every member of the House found a facility in becoming known to him. It was impossible to experience dullness in his society.

Even the catty Horace Walpole remarked, 'He is indolent, good humoured, void of affectation, of dignity, void of art; and his parts and the goodness of his character would have raised him much higher if he had cared either for power or applause.'

North was a master of that most British of political weapons, false modesty and diffidence. As the American Revolution flared, Britain thus came under the control of a prime minister supremely skilled at conciliation, yet with no wider vision or ability to take a lead.

The structure of British government, as it applied to the colonies, also lent itself to confusion and indecisiveness. Britain had no Foreign Secretary, but separate Secretaries of State for the Northern (north Britain and north Europe) and Southern Departments (south Britain, southern Europe and the East Indies). Only in 1768 was a third, more junior, secretaryship set up – Colonial Secretary, responsible for the colonies on both sides of the Atlantic. Between August 1772 and November 1775 this post was held by Lord Dartmouth, a moderate and sensible man. His department consisted of just two deputy secretaries, six clerks, a porter and a cleaner.

Even so, all the Secretaries of State were very powerful men. They corresponded directly with ambassadors, generals and even spies. They were responsible for arresting criminals and traitors in the areas under their jurisdictions. They could order British troops into the field in those areas, and issued their orders direct. They were in direct contact with the King, and spoke on his behalf. They had full control of patronage in the colonies.

The War Office, also to be intimately concerned with American issues, had just twenty civil servants, reflecting Britain's traditional distrust of a standing army. These administered no fewer than 45,000 men drawn up in 28 regiments of cavalry, 70 of infantry and 3 of foot guards, which had to garrison Gibraltar, Minorca, the West Indies, Ireland, the coast of Britain and America itself, and be ready for external wars and civil disturbances. There were about 40 artillery batteries and a company of Royal Engineers. The army consisted primarily of a number of independent regiments, run by colonels who were professional soldiers, mostly neither aristocratic nor independently rich. The soldiers came from the lowest economic classes, because of the wretched military pay and conditions.

Dartmouth laboured under a further disadvantage: almost anyone with any experience of the colonies did not favour fighting there. This included Dartmouth himself. The peace party was led by Britain's greatest war minister and foremost orator and statesmen, William Pitt, and included Edmund Burke. The Adjutant-General of the British armed forces remarked in 1775 that 'Taking America as it at present stands, it is impossible to conquer it with our British army. To attempt to conquer it internally with our land forces is as wild an idea as ever contraverted common sense.'

# 5

## *Sowing the Teeth*

The first consequence of the Townshend Acts was an immediate outcry in the American press, led by the *Boston Gazette*, and in particular a demand for a boycott of British goods as a tough way of effectively striking back at the Revenue Act. The *Gazette*'s slogan was 'Save your money, and you save your country.'

John Dickinson, a successful American-born lawyer who had bought a large estate, opened the offensive with his apparently moderate 'Letters from a Farmer in Pennsylvania', in which he urged his fellow colonists to 'behave like dutiful children who have received unmerited blows from a beloved parent'. Dickinson argued that, while Parliament had the right to levy customs duties, it had no right to impose them purely for revenue-raising – a fiercely legalistic distinction to overcome the argument that on the occasion of the Stamp Act the colonies had accepted the principle of external taxation. But, a moderate, he urged the colonies to do no more than petition Parliament.

Boston, as always, took the lead in urging 'non-importation' (boycott), and a few small towns followed suit. The response from the colonies towards this call was initially tepid: in January 1768 the Massachusetts House of Representatives actually rejected a call for all colonies to oppose the new taxes, although the leaders of its radical faction pushed through a 'circular letter' condemning the measures two weeks later.

This sparring did not last: Samuel Adams, the popular leader of the radical faction, and James Otis Jr, the erratic head of a separate faction whose sights were trained on Governor Bernard and the remnants of the previously dominant Hutchinson coterie, jointly published an article denouncing the governor as a relative of the Devil. Bernard sued unsuccessfully for libel. Meanwhile, on the anniversary of the repeal of the Stamp Act, mobs took to the streets, although no actual violence broke out.

When two customs officials sought to board the ship *Lydia*, belonging to John Hancock, one of Boston's most prominent merchants and the heir to the biggest fortune in America, they were forcibly removed for lacking the necessary authorization. The new customs officials sent from Britain were appalled to discover the extent of the trade in contraband – only six ships had been seized in New England in two and a half years, and only one successfully prosecuted, the others being released by mobs or on the order of local juries. The American courts were in this respect a sham – far from America groaning under the weight of an oppressive regime of duties, it would be accurate to say that no effective customs at all were being enforced by the time the Revenue Act was enacted. Hancock was exonerated by the Attorney General of Massachusetts.

Two months later, another of Hancock's ships, the *Liberty*, was seized on probably fraudulent allegations that its papers were not in order, and a fight broke out on the Boston wharfside between the mob and the crew of the British man-of-war *Romney*. Samuel Adams made an incendiary speech: 'If you are men, behave like men! Let us take up arms immediately – and be free – and seize all the King's officers! We will not be alone! Thirty thousand men from the country will join us!'

Commodore Hood, the British naval commander, observed the fight:

> On the appearance of the Romney before the town, the riot and disorder seemed to subside, but on a vessel's being seized for illicit trade, belonging to a Mr Hancock (by far the richest man in the province, and the known abettor of tumultuous proceedings), by the comptroller (who went for England about a fortnight past), a numerous and violent mob assembled, and the collector and comptroller, with other officers, were beaten and wounded, the collector's boat burnt, and other acts of a most outrageous nature committed. The lives of the commissioners were threatened, and they were happy in taking shelter by stratagem on board the Romney, where they tarried some days, and then landed at Castle William. They then wrote to me for more aid, and I immediately sent two more ships, which had secured the castle from all attempts at surprising it.

The town was now entirely out of the control of the legal authorities. Meanwhile, 'committees of correspondence' had been set up to co-ordinate action across the colonies. Governor Bernard, who had no troops, was ordered by the British to dissolve the Massachusetts House of Representatives, which he did at the beginning of July. The response was a volley of attacks in the *Boston Gazette*. Bernard despairingly lamented that 'a trained mob' was in control of the town. Hood vividly described the takeover:

Mr Williams, the inspector-general of the customs, who was from home in the late riots, had his house beset on the evening of his return by a vast mob, who, in a tumultuous manner, insisted on seeing Mr Williams, and his appearing at the window. It was demanded that he should immediately go to Liberty Tree, there resign his office, and take an oath never to resume it, which he refused, assuring them, at the same time, that he had friends in the house ready to defend him if his doors were forced. They then insisted he should go to the castle to the commissioners, where they have been prisoners at large many weeks, which he also refused, when much clamour ensued, and much vengeance was threatened; but on assurance being given by Mr Williams that he would meet them at the Town House [in the centre of Boston] next day at noon, they dispersed without doing much mischief.

At the appointed hour Mr Williams went through a mob of many thousands, who opened a passage for him, and, from a window, he repeatedly told them of their proceedings last evening, that he was come agreeable to his promise, and demanded what they had to say to him: not a word of reply was made by any one; all were silent. His resolute behaviour had quite disconcerted them; but he has often since received anonymous letters threatening his life unless he resigns his office.

Colonel Dalrymple, by General Gage's order, holds two regiments in constant readiness to embark from hence, whenever they are required by the governor, or directed by the general. Had this force been landed in Boston six months ago, I am perfectly persuaded no address or remonstrance would have been sent from the other colonies, and that all would have been tolerably, quiet and orderly at this time throughout America. Every day's delay of the only remedy that can prove effectual, has manifestly tended to an increase of bad humour, by which, what would have been without difficulty effected early in the spring, will become an arduous, and probably a fatal undertaking late in the year.

The giving to the colonies such time and opportunity for uniting in opposition to the British acts of parliament, ought, in my humble opinion, by all possible means, to have been prevented ... almost the whole trade of America is more or less illicit.

On 15 August the insurgents fired a cannon and held a large banquet to celebrate their putsch. Soon afterwards it was learned that troops were being sent from England. A convention of Bostonians and the inhabitants of nearby towns met to co-ordinate a response.

The American colonists, as already observed, had been governed by Britain only in name. In Boston that summer of 1768, for the first time, even that nominal power had been abandoned: the mob had ruled. Legally constituted authority had broken down and the British-appointed governor, Bernard, had been helplesss. During this brief rule by the 'Convention' – in fact a revolutionary seizure of power – the leaders had been two radicals: one, James Otis Jr, moved largely by matters of personal gain – he had asserted Parliament's right of taxation only two years earlier; the other, Samuel Adams, a genuine political extremist.

Every revolution has its Danton, Marx and Lenin. Adams fulfilled all three roles in America. Pudgy, eloquent, an intriguer, a populist manipulator of men and an effective lobbyist, cajoling, threatening and bullying, he was also a born, if wordy, propagandist and writer, and was motivated by hatred both for the British and for the established order in Boston and America.

Adams has been largely neglected as a founding father by American historians, who prefer to concentrate on the historically attractive personalities of Washington, John Adams, Jefferson, Madison and Hamilton. Yet he was not just a founding father but, as his biographer Paul Lewis describes, *the* father of American independence. While Washington was still leading the agreeable life of a rich country gentleman in Virginia, Adam was indefatigably plotting, writing, pamphleteering and editorializing for his cause.

He was the quintessential revolutionary, a man who resembled Karl Marx in his chaotic way of working and relentlessly prolific literary output, Lenin in his implacable determination and ruthlessness, Joseph Conrad's secret agent, Mr Verloc, in his furtiveness and ability to plot, and Danton in his likeability and political skills. Like Marx, he was utterly indifferent to his own physical circumstances and to those of his family – although, unlike Marx, he appeared to be relatively faithful to his two wives. Like Marx again, he lived for his cause, with very little time spared for idle social pursuits.

Of medium height, plump, balding (he rarely wore a wig) and bespectacled, Adams had no vanity: his commitment to the cause was absolute. He liked to spend his time in the waterfront taverns of Boston, among the dock workers, sailors and prostitutes (although, it is said, he did not indulge in the last of these).

Adams had been born on 16 September 1722, the son of a Boston brewer, who lost his savings in the Land and Manufacture Bank of Massachusetts in 1740 when the governor closed it down as an anti-inflationary measure; the experience left Adams embittered early by his family's misfortune. Under the influence of a fanatically puritan mother, he was originally destined for a religious career as a Calvinist minister. He attended Harvard, where his master's thesis discussed 'whether it be lawful to resist the supreme magistrate [the King] if the Commonwealth cannot be preserved' – already showing the direction of his thinking. He then attempted to go into business, but lost the £1,000 his father lent him.

When his father died, creditors attempted to seize the estate, but the burly Adams threatened both the sheriff and the would-be purchasers at the sale on no fewer than four occasions, until they gave up. He squandered the inheritance he had regained. A born vote-getter and leader, in 1756 he was elected tax-collector, and proved wildly incompetent in the job, ending his nine-year tenure with the town £8,000 in debt; he never paid. A member of the Caucus Club, a secret society to advance the political, social and financial interests of its members, he became a founder of the Sons of Liberty opposing the Stamp Act. When Adams's wife died in 1757, his mother took care of the children. He remarried happily.

There are conflicting accounts as to whether he drank. At Harvard he was fined for drinking; his cousin John Adams once had to defend him on that score publicly, which is revealing, and some said he had a prodigious capacity. But others said that he did not drink at all. He probably suffered from Parkinson's disease: he had a tremor in his hand and voice, and his handwriting was virtually illegible. Lewis writes:

> Politics became his whole life, and nothing else mattered to him. He loved his wife and children, but took them for granted, and only a rare woman would have tolerated his neglect. He no longer cared what he ate – even raw oysters failed to tempt his palate – and his attire became so slovenly that Elizabeth Adams [his second wife] had to supervise changes in his suits, shirts and underclothes. He acquired a reputation for forgetting his hat and greatcoat when leaving a meeting, even in midwinter, and he frequently walked out of the house without a penny in his pockets. He abandoned his few avocations, and was known to leave the dinner table in

ill-disguised disgust if the conversation veered away from politics. He forgot the names of nonpolitical friends, yet could recall, verbatim, a letter written to him years earlier on a political subject ...

A study of Sam Adams's position in the fight against the Stamp Act reveals certain fundamentals that only a few scholars, down to the present day, have realized. His arguments, if carried to their logical conclusion, demanded a complete separation of the North American colonies from the mother country. No one realized this more than Adams himself, as his correspondence in 1765 and 1766 clearly indicates.

In a letter to a friend in England, identified only as 'G.W.', he wrote at length about what he called the natural rights of all Englishmen and those rights as they applied particularly to Americans. The first settlers in the New World, he declared, had come to the colonies as free men, with total, unlimited authority to establish an independent state, had they chosen to do so. But they had not exercised that privilege, and instead had 'voluntarily' entered into a 'compact' with the British crown. Consequently they remained British subjects, and their 'natural rights' were reaffirmed in the charters that established each of the colonies.

Now, however, the Stamp Act had violated the charter. In other words, the government of Great Britain had deliberately broken its contract with the American people, and this left Americans free to act accordingly. He stopped short of stating that this automatically made Americans an independent people, but he hinted strongly that he took this position.

From the beginning of his dispute with the Crown, Sam Adams realized that his position would be stronger if cloaked in legality, and it did not matter to him that his argument was historically inaccurate and legally specious. The colonists had not moved from England to territory claimed either by another power or by no power. They had crossed the Atlantic as British subjects, and had voluntarily settled in lands claimed by the Crown. The colonial charters had not been contracts, nor had they been so regarded by either the Crown or the colonists. On the contrary, they had been grants which had given the immigrants to the New World permission to settle on Crown property, to develop it for mutual benefit and to retain their standing as British subjects because they were acting on behalf of the Crown.

Adams's activities in the summer of 1768 were among the least admirable of his life. He acted in the name of liberty, but his conduct was a mockery of the word. He used intimidation freely, resorting to violence through brawny lieutenants when necessary, and literally forced the merchants of Boston to disobey the law, regardless of their own wishes, loyalty to the Crown or desire to earn a living as they saw fit. The continuation of these activities over a period of years eventually compelled a number of respectable merchants to leave Boston and migrate either to Halifax, where a large number of refugees settled, or to London. The imminent arrival of British troops hardened Sam Adams's resolve and stepped up his timetable; he was merciless, giving no quarter to those who opposed his ends, and at the same time expecting none.

Contrary to the general view that the American Revolution was a more or less accidental consequence of Britain's insensitive and arrogant behaviour, Adams and his friends worked ceaselessly to provoke the British, setting up the committees of correspondence in every Massachusetts town, as well as in Virginia, Rhode Island, Connecticut, Delaware, Pennsylvania and South Carolina. Only New York was left out. Adams was the head of a well-organized conspiracy; but British blunders were necessary for it to succeed.

His language in opposing the British connection had become harsh and inflammatory in the House of Representatives, with the mob, and in the *Boston Gazette*. America, he claimed, was to be reduced to the 'miserable state of tributary slaves'. His radicalism came close to espousing anarchy. Writing as Determinatus in the *Gazette*, he attacked without restraint:

> I am no friend to 'riots, tumult, and unlawful assemblies', I take upon me to say, any more than his Excellency is: But when the people are oppressed, when their rights are infringed, when their property is invaded, when taskmasters are set over them, when unconstitutional acts are executed by a naval force before their eyes, and they are daily threatened with military troops, when their legislature is dissolved and what government is left is secret as a divan, when placemen and their underlings swarm about them, and pensioners begin to make an insolent appearance – in such circumstances the people will be discontented, and they are not to be blamed.

He argued remorselessly:

> In short, it is the greatest absurdity to suppose it in the power of one, or any number of men, at the entering into society, to renounce their essential natural rights, or the means of preserving those rights; when the grand end of civil government, from the very nature of its institution, is for the support, protection, and defence of those very rights; the principal of which, as is before observed, are life, liberty and property. If men, through fear, fraud, or mistake, should in terms renounce or give up any natural right, the eternal law of reason and the grand end of society

would absolutely vacate such renunciation. The right to freedom being the gift of Almighty God, it is not in the power of man to alienate this gift and voluntarily become a slave.

In Adams, America had a genuinely radical leader who sought to inflame and channel the simmering discontent of the poor of America against not only the British but the established order. Indeed, the constitutional crisis with Britain seemed to be of much lesser importance than the social threat to the wealthy.

In New York a tenants' revolt had broken out in 1766. In South Carolina, civil war had virtually broken out, with the hardy but impoverished frontiersmen in the west setting up vigilante 'regulators' to defy the establishment's tax collectors in the eastern counties; the revolt continued for three years, until it was put down with considerable violence in 1772. In Charleston the mob briefly seized control. In Virginia there were angry confrontations between the eastern 'tidewater' counties and the western ones. In Pennsylvania fighting nearly broke out between the frontier counties and the eastern counties which, although nearly equal in population, had twice as many representatives in the assembly.

Everywhere, resentment against the rich and powerful was stirring among ordinary people: Townshend's Revenue Act provided the latest handle with which to crank it up. Adams was a demagogue of genius and underlying his agitation was a paranoid theory that British actions were merely the beginnings of a drive to subordinate the virtually free colonies to slavery: it was possible to weld the pressure for greater influence for the Anglican Church, the undoubted abuses of placemen and officials (although they were almost all Americans) and the Stamp and Revenue Acts into one giant engine for attempted British reoccupation of the colonies.

In this, Adams and the American radicals had been influenced by *Cato's Letters* (1721), the manifesto of the radical opposition in Britain, the Commonwealthmen, who argued that power

warms, scorches, or destroys, according as it is watched, provoked, or increased. It is as dangerous as it is useful ... it is apt to break its bounds. Public corruptions and abuses have grown upon us; fees in most, if not all, offices, are immensely increased; places and employments, which ought not to be sold at all, are sold for treble value; the necessities of the public have made greater impositions unavoidable, and yet the public has run very much in debt, and as those debts have been increasing, and the people growing poor, salaries have been augmented, and pensions multiplied.

These views, of course, contrasted starkly with those of the leaders of American society, who defined freedom in terms of the ability to own and retain property. Slaves, argued Jonathan Mayhew, the pastor of West Church in Boston, were those

> who are obliged to labour and toil only for the benefit of others; or what comes to the same thing, the fruit of whose labour and industry may be lawfully taken from them without their consent, and they justly punished if they refuse to surrender it on demand, or apply it to other purposes than those, which their masters, of their mere grace and pleasure, see fit to allow.

As one pamphlet made clear, however, most Americans were loyal to the King: 'Have we not repeatedly and solemnly professed an inviolable loyalty to the person, power, and dignity of our sovereign, and unanimously declared, that it is not with him we contend, but with an envious cloud of false witnesses, that surround his throne, and intercept the sunshine of his favour from our oppressed land?'

In short, during the 1760s, the goals of the various groups within the anti-British coalition differed radically; but the revolutionary element was gaining the offensive towards the end of the decade. Indeed, for the colonial aristocracy, there was a threat not just of social unrest in the east, which could probably be contained, but more seriously of a loss of control of the western territories. The colonies were threatening to divide into three segments: radical New England in the north, the anarchic west, and the settled conservative east and south.

Only the existence of a standing army could prevent this happening – a point understood in London – but, as long as the colonies remained under British control, that army would have to be provided by Britain, and this threatened to exacerbate the tensions. Far-sighted political thinkers in colonial America realized that only the creation of some form of political unity for the colonies, and the raising of their own standing army, would prevent them from disintegrating into competing and even warring states in various stages of social collapse, with Britain floundering to control them, and growing ever more unpopular as it did so. In this scenario, it began to seem not an idle cause but a necessity of self-preservation that the fissiparous furies increasingly dividing America should be reined in by the guiding hands of the enlightened colonial aristocracy and their energy channelled against the British.

*

The boycott of British goods spearheaded by Boston spread to the other colonies in a fairly leisurely manner. Even in Boston, Samuel Adams and his 'junto', as his group now styled themselves, could not persuade the merchants to vote for a total ban. The Philadelphians refused outright in June 1768. But, with intimidation being practised in some places, New York, Connecticut, Virginia, Maryland, the Carolinas and Georgia had one after another joined the boycott by the end of the following year. Rhode Island, maverick as ever, declined to, as did New Hampshire.

The move certainly had a popular following, with widespread attempts by housewives and other ordinary Americans to give up luxuries imported from Britain. Yet there was also widespread evasion of the boycott and a kind of inverse 'smuggling' – this time in Britain's favour. The Boston mob tackled this with customary roughness and brutality. When Hutchinson attempted to defy the ban, within two weeks crowds appeared threatening to tear down his warehouse until he caved in. A merchant, Theophilus Lillie, who openly sought to abide by the boycott, made an eloquent appeal. It was, he said,

> strange that men who are guarding against being subject to laws [to] which they never gave their consent in person or by their representative, should at the same time make laws, and in the most effectual manner execute them upon me and others, to which laws I am sure I never gave my consent either in person or by my representative … I had rather be a slave under one master; for if I know who he is, I may, perhaps, be able to please him, than a slave to a hundred or more, who I don't know where to find, nor what they will expect of me.

His reward was the sign 'informer' nailed over his shop by a mob; in the fracas that followed, an eleven-year-old boy was killed.

Violence increased, and tarring and feathering of those who defied the ban was common. The printer of the *Boston Chronicle*, John Mein, who opposed the ban and published the name of those merchants who hypocritically said they observed it but did not do so, had to flee the town altogether aboard a British warship, such was the intimidation of 'Tories' by 'Whig patriots'.

Bernard himself was a weak leader. As the down-to-earth Hood concluded:

> the commissioners … were, as I am told, never properly supported by the governor, and in no one instance did he ever have recourse to the civil

magistrates for putting a stop to any riot or unlawful meeting; and what is yet more extraordinary, he suffered a declaration to be extorted from him, that he had not applied for troops and would not do it, which I am afraid led the lower class of people to greater lengths than they would otherwise have gone, as well as the demagogues also.

Mr Bernard is without doubt a sensible man, but he has a vast deal of low cunning, which he has played off upon all degrees of people, to his own disgrace. His doubles and turnings have been so many, that he has altogether lost his road, and brought himself into great contempt. I cannot help mentioning one circumstance which has come to my knowledge as an officer. He frequently lamented to Captain Corner (whom I sent to Boston early in May for the support of the King's revenue) the distressed condition of Castle William, and was afraid of its being attacked, [of] which Captain Corner (knowing his man) took no notice.

At last he spoke out, and said if he did not send his marines to the castle the populace would certainly take it. Captain Corner replied that he would not only send his marines, but every man in the Romney in support of the castle, if his Excellency would request it of him in a proper manner in writing; his orders from Commodore Hood enjoined him to it in the most express terms; to which Mr Bernard answered – 'I cannot do that, Captain Corner, but I will tell you what you must do, you must write me a letter that the marines on board his Majesty's ship under your command stand in need of being refreshed, and desire my permission for their being landed on Castle William Island, which I will grant.'

Captain Corner begged to be excused, and withdrew. A few days after [Bernard] wrote Captain Corner a proper letter, and ante-dated it. I think this proves the man very clearly. I had a letter from him, dated the 27th of August, requesting I would grant him a ship to carry him to England, having the King's leave to return. I was very sorry it was not in my power to comply with his request, for most certainly the sooner he is out of America the better.

In September 1768 an unusually large number of British warships appeared opposite the Boston waterfront, sailing in line as though ready to fire in the event of an attack. The redcoats, with their bayonets at ready, were ferried to the quayside, terrifying the men who had taken over the town.

At this determined show of force, the Convention 'broke up and rushed out of town like a herd of scalded hogs', according to the pro-British merchant John Mein.

The soldiers had been summoned at the recommendation of General Thomas Gage, commander of the hitherto tiny British forces in America. Gage was the second son of Viscount Gage, a rakish, recently ennobled barrister. Thomas was a professional soldier to his fingertips, and had served at the bloodbath between the British and the French at Fontenoy in 1745, when 30,000 were killed, and at the Battle of Culloden, which saw the brutal defeat of Bonnie Prince Charlie's Highlanders. Ten years later he had been present at Braddock's defeat in the Ohio valley, and had organized the rearguard that salvaged some of the troops, including those of George Washington, early in the Seven Years War. At Fort Ticonderoga, later in the same war, he was ordered to lead the brave but disastrous assault that cost the British 1,600 men. In 1759 he failed to capture Montreal.

Yet it is unfair to denounce him as a serial failure: he was a career soldier who had bravely and effectively carried out his orders, even in adversity. Decent, fair-minded and highly competent, he lacked the imagination necessary in the politically volatile and militarily unprecedented circumstances in which he was now placed. Gage had little education, and a direct, honest manner; he acted on simple principles. He insisted that his soldiers should 'do nothing' but what was strictly legal. He stated both that:

> The strictest orders have been given, to treat the inhabitants on all occasions, with lenity, moderation and justice; that they shall … be permitted to enjoy unmolested the common rights of mankind and that, lenient measures, and the cautious and legal exertion of the coercive powers of government, have served only to render them more daring and licentious.

Although he had substantial estates in New York and New Brunswick through his marriage to an American, Gage had come to loathe, in particular, Bostonians. 'America is a mere bully, from one end to the other, and the Bostonians by far the greatest bullies.' His able subordinate, Lord Percy, shared this view only a few weeks after arriving in Boston, describing the townspeople as 'a set of sly, artful, hypocritical rascals, cruel, and cowards'.

Gage accurately identified the initial cause of the disorder:

> The plan of the people of property, is to raise the lower class to prevent the execution of the law … The lawyers are the source from which these clamours have flowed … merchants in general, assembly men, magistrates

etc have been united in this plan of riots, and without the influence and instigation of these the inferior people would have been quiet ... The sailors who are the only people who may be properly styled mob, are entirely at the command of the merchants who employ them.

But he gradually came to fear that the revolutionary mobs were taking control. In 1770 he recommended 'that Boston will be called to strict account, and I think it must be plain to every man that no peace will ever be established in that province till the King nominates his council, and appoints the magistrates, and all the town-meetings are absolutely abolished; whilst those meetings exist the people will be kept in a perpetual heat.'

New England he described, with a fair degree of accuracy, as a country 'where every man studies law and interprets the laws to suit his purposes'. The Congregational churches, he observed, 'have a particular mania in perverting and turning everything to their own purposes'. He despised his superiors for their displays of weakness: 'You have yielded by bits, and in such a manner, as it appeared that everything was constrained, and extorted from you: such a conduct could not fail to encourage people here to commit every extravagance to gain their ends, and one demand has risen upon another.'

These observations were straightforward and mostly acute. The tragedy was that this simple-minded soldier would be the chief influence upon British policy in 1774, when subtler evaluations were needed.

Colonel Dalrymple, commander of the newly arrived troops, was refused quarters by the leading citizens of Boston and told to lodge his men on Castle Island or in private houses – now possible under the Quartering Act. Dalrymple, however, had no intention of scattering his troops. After a month of squabbling about where they should be housed, while part of the army camped on the common and part in official buildings, they were moved into warehouses which would protect them against the approaching winter.

All the familiar frictions between redcoats and locals that had been evident in the Seven Years War now resurfaced with a vengeance. Desertions were frequent – forty on the night of arrival. Locals accused soldiers of being drunk, of staging thefts, of violating the Sabbath, and of raping and molesting the women. Many of these complaints were clearly exaggerated and there are no recorded instances of rape – which would have invariably been punished by the British with death.

Bostonians were awed by the punishments inflicted on soldiers for disciplinary reasons – hundreds of lashes for trivial offences, usually administered by black drummers, which offended the Bostonians' racialist sensibilities, and even an execution for desertion.

The *Boston Gazette* published a 'journal' of alleged offences committed by the army. The town's eager courts fined soldiers for getting involved in fistfights and for theft. Some soldiers accused of brawling were met with the declaration of the judge:

> Who brought you here? Who sent for you? By what authority do you guard, or march in the streets with arms? It is contrary to the laws … and you should be taken up so offending. We want none of your guards. We have arms of our own, and can protect ourselves. You are but a handful. Better take care not to provoke us. If you do you must take the consequences.

To what extent were the hated soldiers an army of occupation? They were posted in the Neck and by public buildings, and sentries frequently challenged and sometimes arrested formerly carefree Bostonians for threatening behaviour. But the troops had no real power of policing, except when threatened, and the courts and civil authorities were hostile to them. However, many people who resented the takeover of the town by extremists supported them.

Governor Bernard left in August 1769, bowing before the defiance of his authority. Other British forces had been landed at Charleston, South Carolina, without significant opposition, and at New York, where the local assembly at last complied with the Quartering Act. However, the soldiers there decided to cut down the 'liberty tree' on the common, provoking an angry scuffle with hundreds of demonstrators. In January 1770, after soldiers had cut down yet another liberty tree and left its branches on the doorstep of the Sons of Liberty, two days of rioting ensued, with one person being killed and several injured. This was the first fatality in over a year of British military presence – a remarkable tribute to the soldiers' restraint.

Not until March 1770 did matters turn ugly in Boston. After three days of provocation – during which stones wrapped in snow were thrown at soldiers, a private's arm was broken by a club, and another's face was smashed in – on the night of 5 March a group of toughs gathered on King Street, near the Town House. About twenty men surrounded a British sentry, Private Hugh White, accusing him of hitting someone who had insulted him. In the moonlight they taunted him as a 'scoundrel lobster' (on account of his red coat), 'son of a bitch' and 'sentinel', and pelted him with snowballs.

White pulled back to the shelter of the customs house. As the crowd swelled, Captain Thomas Preston ordered six privates and a corporal across the snow to rescue him. When they reached him, the crowd closed in about them and the soldiers formed a semicircle facing outwards, on Preston's orders. Crispus Attucks, a twenty-seven-year-old mulatto of mixed black and Indian blood, six foot two inches tall, led the demonstrators in shouting insults at the soldiers. Oliver Wendell, a Bostonian, takes up the story:

> The people seemed to be leaving the soldiers, and to turn from them when there came down a number from Jackson's corner, huzzaing and crying, damn them, they dare not fire, we are not afraid of them. One of these people, a stout man with a long cord wood stick, threw himself in, and made a blow at the officer; I saw the officer try to ward off the stroke; whether he struck him or not I do not know; the stout man then turned around, and struck the grenadier's gun at the captain's right hand, and immediately fell in with his club, and knocked his gun away, and struck him over the head; the blow came either on the soldier's cheek or hat. This stout man held the bayonet with his left hand, and twitched it and cried, kill the dogs, knock them over. This was the general cry; the people then crowded in.

The lawyer John Adams (second cousin of Samuel), who was later to defend the soldiers in court, asserted that Attucks:

> appears to have undertaken to be the hero of the night and to lead this army with banners, to form them in the first place in Dock Square, and march them up to King Street with their clubs.
>
> His very look was enough to terrify any person [and he] had hardiness enough to fall in upon them, and with one hand took hold of a bayonet, and with the other knocked the man down. To [his] mad behaviour, in all probability, the dreadful carnage of that night is chiefly to be ascribed.

Private Hugh Montgomery, who had been struck and had fallen, fired. After a short pause, the other soldiers also fired several rounds. As the crowd dispersed, they left behind them three dead, two dying and six wounded.

As news of the killings spread, a mob of 1,000 took to the streets, rioting for a whole day. The new governor, Thomas Hutchinson, received the rebel leader, Samuel Adams, who was afraid the bloodshed would become uncontrollable. By agreement the governor had the soldiers jailed, promised a fair trial, and then ordered the troops out of town. The anger subsided.

Paul Revere, an activist local goldsmith and engraver, immediately immortalized the scene of the killing in an engraving of a drawing by Henry Pelham, called *Fruits of Arbitrary Power, or the Bloody Massacre Perpetuated by the State*. The legend of the 'Boston Massacre' was born. Like such famous atrocities as the Black Hole of Calcutta, the incident was wildly exaggerated from the first.

It is worth noting that this was the first significant bloodshed during eighteen months of British troops being stationed in a hostile near-riot environment. Remarkably, although the propagandist account of the event was invaluable to the American cause, the protests, if not the hatred, began to die down after the massacre.

By the autumn, John Adams was able to defend Preston successfully; after his acquittal, the soldiers were tried separately. All were cleared except two soldiers charged with manslaughter, who were merely branded on the thumbs and released. There was no further rioting; in fact common sense seems to have returned to both sides.

In Britain, early in 1770, Grafton's rudderless government had been succeeded by that of the conciliatory, indecisive Lord North, the man best capable of managing George III's always difficult relations with Parliament. Pragmatist though he was, North's judgement of the American question was also simple and harsh:

> The annual taxes born by the people of Great Britain amounted to ten millions sterling; and the number of inhabitants I supposed to be eight millions, therefore every inhabitant paid at least 25 shillings annually. The total taxes of the continent of (North) America amounted to no more than £75,000; the inhabitants were three millions, therefore an inhabitant of America paid no more than sixpence annually.

North acted quickly to lift all the Townshend duties except a minor one on tea; the decision to retain this was passed by a cabinet majority of only one. He also permitted New York to issue bills of credit again for public debts. A cabinet minute made it clear that no further taxation was needed – refuting American claims at the time that Britain was contemplating a new range of measures to squeeze the colonies.

> It is the unanimous opinion of the lords present to submit to his Majesty as their advice that no measure should be taken which can any way

derogate from the legislative authority of Great Britain over the colonies. But that the Secretary of State in his correspondence and conversation be permitted to state it as the opinion of the King's servants that it is by no means the intention of the administration, nor do they think it expedient, or for the interest of Great Britain or America, to propose or consent to the laying any further taxes upon America for the purpose of raising a revenue, and that it is at present their intention to propose in the next session of parliament to take off the duties upon paper, glass, and colours, imported into America, upon consideration of such duties having been laid contrary to the true principles of commerce.

In October 1770 Boston's merchants gave up the non-importation boycott by a crushing majority, in defiance of Samuel Adams. The British had backed away from another major confrontation, arguably as they were on the verge of winning it, leaving the colonists barely anything to complain about unless they were actively seeking a pretext for confrontation – which, of course, some among them were.

The radicals were now desperately in need of a further source of provocation. For three years – during the 'pause' – the British government gave them none. But that did not stop their relentless drive to organize and prepare for the armed conflict and social revolution that they assumed was inevitable. The radicals in their broadest sense were preparing for independence and war as early as 1769. An astonishing and little-noticed letter written by the most moderate of American leaders, George Washington, in April 1769, came close to admitting as much:

At a time, when our lordly masters in Great Britain will be satisfied with nothing less than the deprivation of American freedom, it seems highly necessary that something should be done to avert the stroke, and maintain the liberty which we have derived from our ancestors. But the manner of doing it, to answer the purpose effectually, is the point in question. That no man should scruple, or hesitate a moment, to use arms in defence of so valuable a blessing, on which all the good and evil of life depends, is clearly my opinion. Yet arms, I would beg leave to add, should be the last resource, the dernier resort. Addresses to the throne and remonstrances to Parliament we have already, it is said, proved the inefficacy of. How far, then, their attention to our rights and privileges is to be awakened or alarmed, by starving their trade and manufactures, remains to be tried.

Samuel Adams now publicly advocated independence, publishing a poster which was printed in the *Providence Gazette* and the *Boston Gazette*, but signed merely 'A Son of Liberty':

When I consider the corruption of Great Britain, their load of debt, their intestine divisions, tumults and riots, their scarcity of provisions, and the contempt in which they are held by the nations about them; and when I consider, on the other hand, the state of the American colonies with regard to the various climates, produce, soils, rapid population, joined to the virtue of the inhabitants – I cannot but think that the conduct of Old England towards us, may be permitted by Divine Wisdom, and ordained by the unsearchable providence of the Almighty, for hastening a period dreadful to Great Britain.

By 1770 the rebels' organization was already structured. The Sons of Liberty had emerged in Boston, New York and Philadelphia, and were in constant communication. They were a self-electing revolutionary clique with adherents in most of the principal legislatures, although their numbers varied greatly: only in Massachusetts, and then in times of crisis, did they command a majority of ordinary citizens and their representatives. On the councils which already ran most of the states under the eyes of largely powerless governors they had only the odd adherent.

Their strength lay in 'town meetings' of unelected members which fluctuated in size and could be swollen by that second pillar of the radicals' strength – the mob. The town councils were by no means wholly unrepresentative – at times of crisis they often reflected the genuine indignation of a majority of the (usually urban-based) citizens. But they were easily manipulated.

The two other pillars of the radical cause were their sympathizers in the press and the American militias. The Protestant anti-Establishment Churches – in particular the Calvinists, the Congregationalists and the Presbyterians – had links with the radical organization, although it seems clear that the radicals manipulated the Protestants and their ethics for their own ends rather than the other way around.

It is worth briefly introducing the men who triggered off the American Revolution in Boston. Except for Paul Revere, later noted for his famous ride, and Samuel Adams, their names are unfamiliar – long-eclipsed by those of the men who became immortalized as the 'founding fathers'. Yet these earlier patriots started the American War of Independence.

The principal Boston radical leaders, headed by Samuel Adams, were his cousin John Adams, Josiah Quincy, Joseph Warren, John Hancock, Benjamin Church (initially), Paul Revere, James Warren and his wife, Mercy Otis Warren, the sister of the younger James Otis. Their fluid group consisted primarily of men of lower-middle-class origin and 'mechanicals' – a euphemism for labourers – and their most celebrated meeting place was the Green Dragon Tavern.

Adams, as already noted, was a brilliant agitator and social revolutionary. John Hancock, by contrast, though heir to the largest fortune in New England, was a devout and hardworking Congregationalist, and also wholly committed, from an early age, to the cause of American independence. Earnest, well-dressed and engaged to a lively activist, Dorothy Quincy, Hancock provided money and weight to the conspirators.

Joseph Warren, a practising doctor from a comfortable background, was an extremist in the Samuel Adams mould; his commitment to the anti-British cause was deep-rooted and longstanding. A mild-mannered if wordy orator, he was a personal friend of Hancock's. Benjamin Church, another doctor, was in fact a spy for the British. Although he is believed to have been paid, his prime motive was certainly sympathy for the loyalist cause. Josiah Quincy, though a fine speaker, was a lightweight.

Paul Revere represented the bulk of the conspirators – the mechanicals. A silversmith, goldsmith and engraver by profession, of relatively humble origins from Boston's North End and father to sixteen children, ten of whom died young (as did seven of his eleven brothers and sisters), Revere considered himself a gentleman because of his modest wealth, and was a pillar of the community, as well as a gregarious and respected figure. He was an active Freemason, and an energetic doer rather than a thinker. Revere effectively set up both the Revolution's intelligence organization, watching the movement of British troops in and around Boston, and, even more significantly, a group of 'riders', of which he was the principal, to carry urgent messages from one revolutionary centre to another. Remembered by all American schoolchildren for his midnight ride to warn of British troop movements, which was in fact one of many, he was deeply committed to the cause of American independence at least by the time of the Boston Massacre and probably much earlier.

The quieter James Warren was the principal organizer of the committees of correspondence. His strong-willed wife, Mercy, was a gifted playwright, propagandist and feminist ('I have even considered human nature as the same in both sexes') and, finally, an authoritative historian of the revolution. She became the icon for the tens of thousands of stalwart American women who supported independence.

Although men like Hancock and Joseph Warren lent respectability to the cause, Samuel Adams and probably Revere and their mechanical followers were motivated as much by their hatred of the 'Tory' Establishment in America as by dislike of the British. But all were united in the latter from an early stage. The most intelligent, devious and Machiavellian of them all, straddling both the radical and conservative positions, was John Adams, a lawyer with a finely honed political mind who deserves to be considered the civilian leader of the Revolution.

# 6

## *Storm in a Teacup*

The Stamp Act crisis and the agitation against the Townshend acts, followed by the Boston Massacre, had fired the Sons of Liberty to set up an extensive network of secret town committees across Massachusetts; these were also linked to the trained and armed militias, whose battle experience went back to the wars with the French and Indians. During the years following the repeal of the Townshend Acts, these militias were organizing and gathering arms and ammunition to prepare for the coming armed struggle. War was inevitable as long as Britain did not cede the colonies peacefully: the only issues were when, on what pretext, and who would win. On the British side, some 8,000–10,000 troops in seventeen regiments were stationed in the colonies, the overwhelming majority policing the western frontier, with a handful in Boston, New York, and other seaports.

Between 1770 and 1774, while the militias' preparation went ahead, the radicals assiduously tried to fan the embers of differences between the two sides into a conflagration, with little success. Trade boomed between Britain and America, increasing in value from around £5 million in 1768–70 to £9 million between 1770 and 1774. Illegal trade flourished as well – and attempts by British customs officials to collect revenues were defied as brazenly as ever. A collector in New Jersey was beaten up, and his son was tarred and feathered. A sheriff in Rhode Island threatened to arrest a captain of the Royal Navy, whose appeal to the governor was met with the remark 'To your advice, not to send the sheriff on board any of your squadron, please to know that I will send the sheriff of this colony at any time, and to any place, within the body of it, as I think fit.' Shortly afterwards the colonists boarded his ship and shot the captain in the groin, then actually arrested him.

It was becoming harder by the month to maintain the fiction that

Britain still ran the colonies. Arthur Lee, one of the American representatives in London, now advised Samuel Adams that

'The prospect of a general war in Europe [between Britain and France,
possibly allied to Spain] strengthens daily; and it is hardly probable that
another year will pass away before that event. You cannot, therefore, be
too speedy in preparing to reap full advantage of this opportunity.'

In Massachusetts, the *Boston Gazette* began a major campaign against
the British decision to pay Governor Thomas Hutchinson and
Lieutenant-Governor Andrew Oliver, as well as Supreme Court judges,
from customs revenues. Adams demanded that the assembly be recalled,
and was rebuffed. So he asked the Boston town council to convoke a
'committee of correspondence', a self-appointed hotbed of the radical
faction, which published a pamphlet attacking the army (which had
been withdrawn from the town). 'Our houses, and even our bed-
chambers,' it claimed, 'are exposed to be ransacked, our boxes, trunks
and chests broke open, ravaged and plundered, by wretches, whom no
prudent man would venture to employ even as menial servants.' This
crude propaganda made its way around the colony.

Letters sent by the governor, Hutchinson, to London were dramatically leaked by Benjamin Franklin, who had secured them by question-
able means. They provided explosive propaganda ammunition,
revealing that American loyalists had been urging Britain to take a
tougher line.

Franklin had sent the letters to Thomas Cushing, Speaker of the
Massachusetts House of Representatives, on the (possibly sincere)
understanding that they should not be published. One view was that he
was attempting to shift the onus of blame for intransigence from Britain
to its supporters in America, particularly Hutchinson. He wrote in the
covering letter:

For my own part, I cannot but acknowledge that my resentment against
this country, for its arbitrary measures in governing us, conducted by the
late minister, has, since my conviction by these papers that those measures were projected, advised, and called for by men of character among
ourselves, and whose advice must therefore be attended with all the
weight that was proper to mislead, and which could therefore scarce fail
of misleading; my own resentment, I say, has by this means been exceedingly abated. I think they must have the same effect with you; but I am
not, as I have said, at liberty to make the letters public. I can only allow

them to be seen by yourself, by the other gentlemen of the committee of correspondence, by Messrs Bowdoin and Pitts of the council, and Drs Chauncy, Cooper, and Winthrop, with a few such other gentlemen as you may think fit to show them to. After being some months in your possession, you are requested to return them to me.

As to writers, I can easily as well as charitably conceive it possible that men educated in prepossessions of the unbounded authority of Parliament, etc., may think unjustifiable every opposition even to its unconstitutional exactions, and imagine it their duty to suppress, as much as in them lies, such opposition. But when I find them bartering away the liberties of their native country for posts, and negotiating for salaries and pensions extorted from the people, and, conscious of the odium these might be attended with, calling for troops to protect and secure the enjoyment of them; when I see them exciting jealousies in the Crown, and provoking it to work against so great a part of its most faithful subjects; creating enmities between the different countries of which the empire consists; occasioning a great expense to the old country for suppressing or preventing imaginary rebellions in the new, and to the new country for the payment of needless gratifications to useless officers and enemies; I cannot but doubt their sincerity even in the political principles they profess, and deem them mere time-servers, seeking their own private emolument, through any quantity of public mischief, betrayers of the interest, not of their native country only, but of the government they pretend to serve, and of the whole English Empire.

But Franklin's deviousness emerges in another letter he sent at the same time. He gave advice to use the letters cunningly, so that, 'as distant objects, seen through a mist, appear larger, the same may happen from the mystery in this case'.

Adams demanded the resignation of Governor Hutchinson and Lieutenant-Governor Oliver, and Franklin was sent at the head of a delegation to London to petition for it. Then, in late summer 1773, the details of an apparently trivial act passed by the House of Commons in May reached America.

The act retained the threepence duty on tea, which remained the sole enduring legacy of the Townshend acts, and which America had continued to pay quietly for two years. But the act also gave the East India Company a monopoly on the trade in tea. The purpose of this provision had nothing to do with North America. The British government had ill-advisedly decided to try to save the failing East India Company from bankruptcy by providing it with a captive market. In practice the tea would be far cheaper than that previously imported by Americans, thus benefiting the consumer, while making no difference to importers. But presented as another diktat from London, the act provided a pretext for indignation that was too good for the radicals to miss: their object was now to goad the sleepy British lion into radical action which would allow them to call Americans to arms. Without waiting for Britain's response to the immediate chorus of protests, the Sons of Liberty in Philadelphia and New York issued their denunciations and threats of violence.

The usual tactic was employed – of mass meetings, bullying and threats to coerce the largely indifferent merchants. At a mass meeting in Philadelphia, anyone importing tea from Britain was deemed an 'enemy to his country'. 'Committees for tarring and feathering' were set up which threatened to decant 'ten gallons of liquid tar on a captain's pate – with the feathers of a dozen wild geese laid over that to enliven your appearance'.

As early as September 1773, Adams was to make his view on the act explicit in the *Boston Gazette*:

> But why should administration expect any further petitions? Our senti-ments and resolutions are sufficiently known to them already. We have spoken without reservation. We scorn to say anything that looks like duplicity or cunning. Our petitions have always been expressed in terms decent and temperate, as well as explicit. If they expect we shall alter our tone with a view of having it thought we have altered our sentiments, when in reality we have not, this is a low artifice which Americans will always despise, and therefore it is highly probable they will find them-selves mistaken.
>
> Solomon tells us there is a time to speak and a time to be silent; and perhaps it requires as much wisdom to determine the time as what to speak. Speak ye every man the truth to his neighbour, however inconsis-tent it may be with the maxims of cunning politics, is a rule which ought to be, and ever will be, regarded by an honest community as well as by every honest individual whenever he speaks at all. It is certainly not a time now for Britain and the colonies to prevaricate with each other.
>
> The matter in controversy is of too serious and important a nature to be trifled with. It will be folly for Britain, and with half an eye she may have discerned it already, to attempt to settle this controversy by mere power and brute force. If, perchance, it should be admitted that at present

she is powerful, would it not for all this be wiser for her to consider how long she is likely to remain so? America is daily increasing in numbers and consequently in strength; and the balance of power may be shifted before the most sagacious are aware of it.

In New York the government held out against pressure from the Sons of Liberty, but the tea-bearing ship the *Nancy* was blown off-course by a storm and never arrived. In South Carolina the teas were actually landed, but never sold. In Boston a mob stormed the importers in a warehouse shortly after the arrival of the tea-bearing ship the *Dartmouth* on 28 November. Over the following two days, mass meetings of around 5,000 people – the biggest ever in the history of anti-British agitation – gathered to listen to Adams's incendiary rhetoric:

> if we are prevailed upon implicitly to acknowledge a right to tax us, by receiving and consuming teas loaded with a tax imposed by the British Parliament, we may be assured that, in very short time, taxes of a like or more grievous nature will be laid on every article exported from Great Britain, which our necessity may require, or our shameful luxury may betray us into the use of; and when once they have found the way to rob us, their avarice will never be satisfied until our own manufacturers, and even our land, purchased and cultivated by our hard labouring ancestors, are taxed to support the vices and extravagance of wretches whose vileness ought to banish them from the society of men.
>
> We think therefore, gentlemen, that we are in duty bound to use our most strenuous endeavours to ward off the impending evil, and we are sure that, upon a fair and cool inquiry into the nature and tendency of this ministerial plan, you will think this tea now coming to us more to be dreaded than plague or pestilence; for these can only destroy our mortal bodies, but we never knew a country enslaved without the destruction of their virtue, the loss of which every good man must esteem infinitely greater than the loss of life ...
>
> Now, brethren, we are reduced to this dilemma, either to sit down quiet under this and every other burden that our enemies shall see fit to lay upon us as good-natured slaves, or rise and resist this and every other plan laid for our destruction, as becomes wise freemen. In this extremity we earnestly request your advice, and that you would give us the earliest intelligence of the sense your several towns have of the present gloomy situation of our affairs.

The Sons of Liberty posted guards aboard the *Dartmouth* and forced it to tie up at Griffin's Wharf. There it stayed for two weeks without the tea being disembarked. On the evening of 16 December Adams addressed an angry public meeting, which then spilled out on to the waterfront, where the *Dartmouth* and two more recently arrived tea-bearing vessels, the *Eleanor* and the *Beaver*, were moored.

This 'spontaneous' demonstration had in fact been carefully prepared by the radicals at a series of secret meetings. Some fifty men reporting in a cellular structure to different section commanders, wearing black and red dye on their faces, dressed like Indians (a symbol of American liberty) and wrapped in blankets, went aboard and systematically hauled the casks of tea on deck, pouring them over the side. Around £10,000 worth of tea was destroyed, some 90,000 lb in all. A ballad was promptly sung on the town's streets: 'The Rallying of the Tea Party': 'Rally Mohawks. Bring in your axes, and tell King George we'll pay no taxes on his foreign tea.'

So was born the legend of the Boston Tea Party – another peaceful display of American high jinks, though calculated and provocative in intent, as well as expensively destructive of property. The savage humour served only to strengthen the American propaganda coup – British pro-tests that the incident represented a major act of premeditated piracy committed at the expense of legitimate British merchants, and a further show of intimidation against their fellow countrymen, could be ridi-culed as pompous and humourless.

Bearing the justification of the Tea Party set out for it by Adams, Revere, who had taken part in it, left the following day on one of his great rides to the Sons of Liberty in New York and Pennsylvania on his famous grey saddle horse. (He was to make five such rides during the next two years, one of them by carriage.)

Adams regarded the Tea Party as a virtual declaration of war. He wrote in the *Boston Gazette* with unashamed militancy:

To all nations under heaven. Know ye, that the people of the American world, are millions strong – countless legions compose their united army of free men … America now stands with the scale of justice in one hand, and the sword of vengeance in the other … Let the Britons fear to do any more so wickedly as they have done, for the Herculean arm of this New World is lifted up – and woe be to them on whom it falls! – at the beat of the drum, she can call five hundred thousand of her sons to arms – before whose blazing shields none can stand. Therefore, ye that are wise, make peace with her, take shelter under her wings, that ye may shine by the reflection of her glory.

May the New Year shine propitious on the New World – and virtue
and liberty reign here without a foe, until rolling years shall measure time
no more.

The Boston Tea Party has gone down as one of the great japes of history,
an act to which the British greatly overreacted. It was certainly non-
violent. But the goal of this huge destruction of property was plainly to
goad the British government, so inept for so long, into action. This time
the Sons of Liberty succeeded.

As it happened, the Tea Party had occurred in the absence of General
Gage, on leave in England. While the cat was away … When news of
the attack reached London in mid-January, 1774 Gage's reaction was
instantaneous and uncharacteristically strong for this usually cautious
and defensive man: the 'mutineers' had gone too far. Even Chatham, the
colonies' staunch defender, called the incident 'criminal'.

The King summoned Gage and listened to his recommendations for
firm action, also telling British ministers to 'hear his ideas as to the mode
of compelling Boston to submit to whatever might be thought necessary'. Lord North stated the position with precision shortly afterwards:
'We are not entering into a dispute between internal and external taxes,
not between taxes laid for the purpose of revenues and taxes laid for the
regulation of trade, not between representation and taxation, or legislation and taxation; but we are now to dispute whether we have, or have
not any authority in that country.'

Franklin was already in London with the delegation petitioning for
the removal of Hutchinson and Oliver from office. He was ordered to
attend the Privy Council for an unprecedented ordeal, a tongue-lashing
from the acerbic Solicitor-General, Alexander Wedderburn, who
accused him of deceit in leaking the letters of Thomas Hutchinson.
Wedderburn completed his tirade with the words:

Amidst these tranquil events, here is a man who, with the utmost insen-
sibility of remorse, stands up and avows himself the author of all. I can
compare him only to Zanga, in Dr Young's 'Revenge':–

– 'Know, then, 'twas I –
I forged the letter – I dispos'd the picture –
I hated – I despis'd – and I destroy.'

I ask, my Lords, whether the revengeful temper attributed to the bloody
African is not surpassed by the coolness and apathy of the wily American?

Franklin, dressed in his customary plain suit, listened stoically. One witness wrote: 'At the sallies of Mr Wedderburn's sarcastic wit, all the members of the council, the president himself (Lord Gower) not excepted, frequently laughed outright; no one of them behaving with decent gravity, except Lord North.' Franklin himself reported back to his colleagues in America:

> But the favourite part of his discourse was levelled at your agent, who stood there the butt of his invective ribaldry for near an hour, not a single lord adverting to the impropriety and indecency of treating a public messenger in so ignominious a manner, who was present only as the person delivering your petition, with the consideration of which no part of his conduct had any concern. If he had done a wrong, in obtaining and transmitting the letters, that was not the tribunal where he was to be accused and tried. The cause was already before the chancellor. Not one of their lordships checked and recalled the orator to the business before them, but, on the contrary, a very few excepted, they seemed to enjoy highly the entertainment, and frequently burst out in loud applause. This part of his speech was thought so good that they have since printed it, in order to defame me everywhere, and particularly to destroy my reputation on your side of the water; but the grosser parts of the abuse are omitted, appearing, I suppose, in their own eyes, too foul to be seen on paper; so that the speech, compared to what it was, is now perfectly decent.

Franklin was now afraid of being arrested:

> My situation here is thought by many to be a little hazardous; for if, by some accident, the troops and people of New England should come to blows, I should probably be taken up; the ministerial people affecting everywhere to represent me as the cause of all the misunderstanding; and I have been frequently cautioned to secure my papers, and by some advised to withdraw. But I venture to stay, in compliance with the wish of others, till the result of the Congress arrives, since they suppose my being here might on that occasion be of use; and I confide in my innocence, that the worst which can happen to me will be an imprisonment upon suspicion.

The episode has gone down in American revolutionary folklore as a kangaroo court humiliation of the dignified elder statesman of America. Yet Franklin was far from being an innocent, and his behaviour with the Hutchinson letters revealed political guile bordering on dishonesty. Wedderburn had some good grounds for his attack, although the wisdom of so humiliating one of America's principal spokesmen, and one not clearly committed to armed struggle even at that stage, is another matter.

However, Wedderburn himself was soon afterwards to counsel that there were no grounds for prosecuting the organizers of the Boston Tea Party. Chatham's advice seemed starkest of all:

> I am extremely anxious about the measures now depending, with regard to America, and I consider the fate of Old England as being at stake, not less than that of the new. The violence committed upon the tea-cargo is certainly criminal; nor would it be real kindness to the Americans to adopt their passions and wild pretensions, where they manifestly violate the most indispensable ties of civil society. Boston, therefore, appears to me to owe reparation for such a destruction of the property of the East India Company.
>
> This is, to my mind, clear and evident; but, I confess, it is equally clear to me, that in pursuing this just object, government may become unjust; if they attempt to blend the enforcement of general declared rights of the British Parliament (which I must for ever treat as rights in theory only) with a due satisfaction for a tumultuous act of a very criminal nature. The methods, too, proposed, by way of coercion, appear to me too severe, as well as highly exceptionable in order of time: for reparation ought first to be demanded in a solemn manner, and refused by the town and magistracy of Boston, before such a bill of pains and penalties can be called just.
>
> The whole of this unhappy business is beset with dangers of the most complicated and lasting nature ... Perhaps a fatal desire to take advantage of this guilty tumult of the Bostonians, in order to crush the spirit of liberty among the Americans in general, has taken possession of the heart of government ... but to consent quietly to have no right over their own purse, I conceive the people of America will never be brought to do.

In spite of all the sound and fury, the measures taken by Lord North's government were surprisingly restrained. The port of Boston was closed for trade, except for essentials, until the cost of the spoilt tea was paid and compensation for lost duties was granted to customs men; the government of Massachusetts was to be moved out of Boston; a measure was enacted to allow any royal official accused of a capital crime to be sent to England for trial (this measure was aimed at protecting British soldiers pursuing their duties; it was quickly misrepresented by the extremists as an edict requiring American political prisoners to be sent for trial to London); a new quartering act provided that troops might be billeted with private families; and General Gage was to replace Hutchinson as governor.

The only one of what the Americans dubbed 'the Intolerable Acts' that really stung was a measure by which the council – the governing body of Massachusetts – and most other officials were now to be appointed by the governor, not by the assembly, although this was permitted to continue in existence. Town councils would no longer be allowed to sit without permission, and sheriffs were to nominate juries.

Gage himself, however, soon found he had little real power to prevent Boston's town council meeting against his express instructions; it had become a revolutionary committee, although it had no legal standing. He took no action.

Arthur Lee, in London, wrote with high intelligence and penetrating insight about Lord North to his brother Richard, in Massachusetts:

> If the colonies in general permit this [British retaliation] to pass unnoticed, a precedent will be established for humbling them by degrees, until all opposition to arbitrary power is subdued. The manner, however, in which you should meet this violent act should be well weighed. The proceedings of the colonies, in consequence of it, will be read and regarded as manifestos. Great care, therefore, should be taken to word them unexceptionally and plausibly. They should be prefaced with the strongest professions of respect and attachment to this country; of reluctance to enter into any dispute with her; of the readiness you have always shown, and still wish to show, of contributing according to your ability, and in a constitutional way, to her support; and of your determination to undergo every extremity rather than submit to be enslaved. These things tell much in your favour with moderate men, and with Europe, to whose interposition America may yet owe her salvation, should the contest be serious and lasting.
>
> In short, as we are the weaker, it becomes us to be *suaviter in modo*, however we may be determined to act *fortiter in re*. There is a persuasion here that America will see, without interposition, the ruin of Boston. It is of the last importance to the general cause, that your conduct should prove this opinion erroneous. If once it is perceived that you may be attacked and destroyed by piecemeal, *actum est*, every part will in its turn feel the vengeance which it would not unite to repel, and a general slavery or ruin must ensue.
>
> The colonies should never forget Lord North's declaration in the House of Commons, that he would not listen to the complaints of America until she was at his feet. The character of Lord North, and the consideration of what surprising things he has effected towards enslaving his own country, make me, I own, tremble for yours. Plausible, deep, and

treacherous, like his master, he has no passions to divert him, no pursuits of pleasure to withdraw him, from the accursed design of deliberately destroying the liberties of his country. A perfect adept in the arts of corruption, and indefatigable in the application of them, he effects great ends by means almost magical, because they are unseen. In four years he has overcome the most formidable opposition in this country, from which the Duke of Grafton fled with horror. At the same time he has effectually enslaved the East India Company, and made the vast revenue and territory of India, in effect, a royal patronage.

Flushed with these successes, he now attacks America; and certainly, if we are not firm and united, he will triumph in the same manner over us. In my opinion, a general resolution of the colonies to break off all commercial intercourse with this country, until they are secured in their liberties, is the only advisable and sure mode of defence. To execute such a resolution would be irksome at first, but you would be amply repaid, not only in saving your money, and becoming independent of these petty tyrants, the merchants, but in securing your general liberties.

Although North's reprisals were fairly moderate in British eyes, they were regarded by the Americans as outrageously punitive. As soon as they heard of these measures, Samuel Adams and his supporters responded by calling for a fresh boycott of British goods. Adams fulminated:

For flagrant injustice and barbarity, one might search in vain among the archives of Constantinople to find a match for it. But what else could have been expected from a parliament too long under the dictates and control of an administration which seems to be totally lost to all sense and feeling of morality, and governed by passion, cruelty and revenge? For us to reason against such an act would be idleness. Our business is to find means to evade its malignant design.

This time most of the merchants were hostile to him and called on him to scrap his self-appointed committee of correspondence. When Gage arrived to take up his post as governor of Massachusetts, they offered to pay for the tea destroyed. The call for a nationwide boycott was bitterly resisted by merchants in the cities, who believed that Boston, in particular, had cheated during the short-lived boycott of six years before. But several other ports closed shops in sympathy and sent essential supplies to Boston's poor.

The Sons of Liberty responded to this unexpected American business backlash against the Tea Party by summoning a 'Continental Congress' to co-ordinate action throughout the colonies as a show of solidarity with Boston. Again this was largely self-appointed – except for South Carolina's delegates, who were fairly elected – and Georgia chose to stay away. Hailed by subsequent revolutionary historians as America's first parliament, although in reality no more than a group of radicals drawn from across the colonies, the congress met on 5 September 1774 in Philadelphia.

The congress was composed of representatives from the various legislatures, chosen somewhat at random, with limited previous experience of politics. General Gage dismissed them as a 'motley crew'. Samuel Adams and his more moderate cousin John, the lawyer, accompanied by two others, made the long journey from Massachusetts. John Adams had never travelled more than thirty miles from Boston before, and Sam had scarcely been out of town. The latter declined the post of chairman, preferring to act behind the scenes. He and the man he recognized as Virginia's leader, George Washington, met frequently in private. The radical and militant Boston leaders found soulmates in the belligerent Virginia delegation, whom one observer commended as 'more sensible fine fellows you should never wish to see'. Adams with his crew, and the haughty sultans of the south, juggled the whole conclave of delegates, according to one Maryland observer.

Unlike the urban middle-class Bostonians, the Virginians came chiefly from the gentry class. Among them was Washington – already rich and a military legend who, although 'hard' in appearance, had 'a very young look and an easy soldier-like cut and gesture'. Patrick Henry and Richard Lee, from the same delegation, spoke eloquently for the radical cause. John Dickinson and John Galloway of Pennsylvania – both much more moderate – and James Duane and John Jay of New York also made a striking impression.

Christopher Gadsden of South Carolina urged an armed attack on the British troops in Boston, but public discussion mostly concentrated on the need for economic action. However, in informal meetings the delegates discussed the very real possibility of war. Galloway, leader of the moderates, argued in favour of setting up a joint committee consisting of American representatives and members of the British parliament to legislate for America, but he was outnumbered by those who saw no hope of reconciliation. A Declaration of Rights was issued which stated that the colonists would not accept acts of parliament which violated their rights, and an 'association' was set up to enforce a ban on British exports and imports.

John Adams frankly admitted the deviousness with which the Bostonians worked towards their goal: 'We have had numberless prejudices to remove here. We have been obliged to act with great delicacy and caution. We have been obliged to keep ourselves out of sight, and to feel pulses and sound the depths; to insinuate our sentiments, designs, and desires, by means of other persons; sometimes of one province, and sometimes of another.'

Samuel Adams and Washington discussed war preparations. As Adams wrote on 17 October:

> I have written to some of our friends to provide themselves without delay with arms and ammunition, to get well instructed in the military art, to embody themselves, and prepare a complete set of rules, that they may be ready in case they are called to defend themselves against the violent attacks of despotism. Surely the law of self-preservation will warrant it in this time of danger and doubtful expectation. One cannot be certain that a distracted minister will yield to the measures taken by Congress, though they should operate to the ruin of the national trade, until he shall have made further efforts to lay America, as he imperiously expressed it, prostrate at his feet.

A dramatic stir was caused at the congress when Paul Revere arrived with the news that the British were fortifying Boston and submitted Joseph Warren's 'Suffolk Resolutions'. These described the 'Intolerable Acts' as 'murderous', and urged an end to all taxes and trade with Britain, as well as preparations to be made for war.

> If we arrest the hand which would ransack our pockets, if we disarm the [hand] which points the dagger to our bosoms ... if we successfully resist that unparalleled usurpation of unconstitutional power, whereby our capital is robbed of the means of life; whereby the streets of Boston are thronged with military executioners ... [only then can Americans be free].

On 26 October the congress dissolved itself, having achieved little except the very fact of meeting – which was significant enough. However, it was far from clear that it represented a majority of Americans, or even a significant minority. John Adams was profoundly irked by the moderation of some delegates at the end: 'In congress grumbling and quibbling as usual. Young Ned Rutledge is a perfect Bob o'Lincoln – a sparrow – a peacock – excessively vain, excessively weak, and excessively variable and unsteady – jejune, inane, and puerile.'

The moderate Galloway was deeply dissatisfied, claiming that he had discerned that 'ill-shapen, diminutive brat, independency'. These self-appointed delegates were, on the whole, far less militant than those from Massachusetts and, to a lesser extent, Virginia. The Massachusetts delegates resolved to enforce the association as vigorously as they could, particularly in the western half of the state, where anti-British sentiment was more lukewarm.

In Virginia, strong-arm bullying was used. One schoolmaster was threatened with the closure of his schoolhouse for writing a letter critical of the patriots, and had to earn redemption through a crawling letter in the *Virginia Gazette*:

> I do, most heartily and willingly, on my knees, implore the forgiveness of this country for so ungrateful a return made for the advantages I have received from it, and the bread I have earned in it, and hope, from this contrition for my offence, I shall be at least admitted to subsist amongst the people I greatly esteem, and desire that this may be printed in the *Virginia Gazette*.

As Governor Dunmore remarked, local committees were soon the effective government of the colony:

> The committees walked into the stores of the merchants and forced them to show their books, and woe to the [man] thus betrayed by his ledger. When merchants took advantage of the scarcity to increase prices, they were taken roughly in hand. When charges were brought against alleged violators of the agreement, they were summoned summarily before the committee to exonerate themselves or stand condemned. If condemned, they were denounced and advertised as enemies of their country.

These unelected bodies were replacing the more representative House of Burgesses where the radicals were in a small minority: Virginia, too, was being taken over by a revolutionary movement. George Washington and George Mason organized the militia and enforced a tax to pay for it, requiring the names of those who did not contribute to be reported to them – a clearly intimidatory move. Maryland's committees were almost as vigorous. Pennsylvania, Connecticut and the Carolinas were less enthusiastic, while Georgia showed no interest at all.

After the Congress, Samuel Adams now urged the preparation of 20,000 militia for an immediate attack on the redcoats. As far as the militants were concerned, war was only a matter of months away, provided they could take a large enough section of the population with them.

Opinion in London was hardening too. The King remarked: 'The die is now cast, the colonies must either submit or triumph; I do not wish to come to severer measures but we must not retreat; by coolness and an unremitted pursuit of the measures that have been adopted I trust they will come to submit.'

The British still suffered from one colossal misconception about Massachusetts: they had believed Gage's assertion that the trouble there was caused by only a tiny minority. Gage may initially have been right about this, but he had discovered the discomfiting truth on his return earlier that year. He was highly inoffensive in a letter to the president of congress:

> People would be led to believe, from your letter to me of the 10th instant, that works were raised against the town of Boston, private property invaded, the soldiers suffered to insult the inhabitants, and the communication between the town and country shut up and molested.

> Nothing can be farther from the true situation of this place than the above state. There is not a single gun pointed against the town, no man's property has been seized or hurt, except the King's by the people destroying straw, bricks, etc, bought for his service. No troops have given less cause for complaint, and greater care was never taken to prevent it, and such care and attention was never more necessary, from the insults and provocations daily given to both officers and soldiers. The communication between the town and country has always been free and unmolested, and is so still.

> Two works of earth have been raised at some distance from the town, wide of the roads and guns put in them. The remains of old works, going out of the town, have been strengthened, and guns placed there likewise. People will think differently, whether the hostile preparations throughout the country, and the menaces of blood and slaughter, made this necessary. But I am to do my duty.

Meanwhile government had practically collapsed. As John Adams wrote:

> The difficulties we suffer, for want of law and government, are innumerable; a total stagnation of law, and of commerce almost ... We have no council, no house, no legislature, no executive. Not a court of justice has sat since the month of September. Not a debt can be recovered, nor a trespass redressed, nor a criminal of any kind be brought to punishment.

# 7

# *Powder Alarms*

Whatever the view of most Bostonians, the countryside round about was seething. In mid-October 1774 thousands of men marched towards the city 'completely armed' because of rumours of a British attack from the 3,000-strong garrison there. Gage came to realize the strength of opposition when he decided to try to seize the principal arsenals and powder houses from the New England militia.

The first 'powder alarm' was aimed at the Massachusetts Provincial Powder House in Somerville, about five miles by boat from Boston up the Mystic river, and about ten miles by land. The British excursion from Boston was accomplished successfully, 250 barrels of gunpowder and two cannon being seized by a small force after a night landing from the river side. It provoked uproar among the heavily armed population outside Boston. A traveller reported that

> He never saw such a scene before. All along [the road] were armed men rushing forward – some on foot, some on horseback. At every house women and children [were] making cartridges, running bullets, making wallets [pouches of food], baking biscuits, crying and bemoaning and at the same time animating their husbands and sons to fight for the liberties, though not knowing whether they should ever see them again ... They left scarcely half a dozen men in a town, unless old and decrepit, and in one town the landlord told him that himself was the only man left.

A large crowd converged on Cambridge, outside Boston, and chased the 'Tory' – pro-British – landowners out of town and into Boston, which, however, they refrained from attacking. The size of the popular outburst surprised even Revere, who rejoiced that

> The spirit of Liberty never was higher than at present, the troops have the horrors amazingly. By reason of some late movements of our friends in

the country, our new fangled councillors are resigning their places every day; our justices of the courts, who now hold their commissions during the pleasure of His Majesty, or the governor, cannot get a jury to act with them, in short the Tories are giving way everywhere in our province.

Governor Gage, seriously alarmed by the uprising, reinforced Roxbury Neck, the strip of land which joined Boston to the mainland, and ordered the inhabitants of Boston to surrender their munitions. His 3,000 soldiers in Boston began to take on a beleaguered air, and he meanwhile wrote frantically to London to alert the government to the new size of the problem confronting him. 'The whole country', he wrote, 'is in arms and in motion'. He added, possibly rhetorically, 'From present appearances there is no prospect of putting the late acts in force, but by first making a conquest of the New England provinces ... If you think ten thousand men sufficient, send twenty; if one million is thought enough, give two; you save both blood and treasure in the end.' He also urged the suspension of the Intolerable Acts.

The King and government regarded these pleas as evidence of pure panic unbecoming in a senior general in the British army. They could not have been more wrong. Gage was merely reflecting the new reality on the ground since his return. George III commented that the general's advice was 'the most absurd that can be suggested', and immediately set about looking for a replacement. Only 500 marines were sent to Boston to assist Gage in what he now understood was a general insurrection.

The government, in truth, did not want to listen. It was disturbed by Gage's reports, but continued to regard the rebellion as essentially a local phenomenon confined to Boston. Prime Minister North was deep in an electoral campaign in which, as Burke remarked, 'any remarkable highways rally on Hounslow Heath made more conversation than all the disturbances in America'. But Burke himself was well acquainted with the position: General Charles Lee, the likely commander of American troops and a man with many friends in England, had apprised him of the situation in a brilliant and remarkable letter in December 1774:

I will now ... venture to predict, that unless the Boston Bills (and I may add the Quebec) are repealed, the empire of Great Britain is no more. I have now run through almost the whole colonies, from the north to the south. I have conversed with every order of men, from the first estated gentleman to the poorest planter, and cannot express my astonishment at the unanimous, ardent spirit reigning through the whole. They are determined to sacrifice everything, their property, their wives, and blood, rather than cede a tittle of what they conceive to be their rights. The tyranny exercised over Boston, indeed, seems to be resented by the other colonies in a greater degree than by the Bostonians themselves.

I cannot help being persuaded that those men who first urged the ministry to this accursed fatal step, have, from a wicked shame of acknowledging their misrepresentations, continued still to keep them in the dark. They first assured them of the practicability of the scheme, that the Bostonians would, on the first appearance of any army, and fleet, be frightened into a submission; that their cause would not be considered as the common cause; and now, when they see their error, they cannot muster up honesty or courage to confess it. This I am confident is the case with Hutchinson and his associates; and there is the strongest appearance that my quondam friend, Gage, holds the same dangerous course.

It is somewhat strange, but it is true, that this gentleman should reside so many years in America, and yet be as ignorant of the dispositions of the people of America as he is of those in the moon; indeed, he took all possible means of shutting up the avenues of truth. At New York he never conversed, as I can find, with any but place and contract-hunters, the staff officers, and his own family …

In fact, every circumstance relating to New England, as it appears to me, has been stated quite the reverse of the truth. Not only the principles and deportment of the people, but their qualifications and capacity for war have been misrepresented. Modesty, temperance, and the most inflexible firmness, are united in them …

But what I think is a sufficient proof of the spirit and principles of these people, is the offer which they made to the congress, to abandon their town, and never set foot within their native walls, but with the re-establishment of their liberties. Such instances of virtue and magnanimity are, I know, scarcely credible in your rotten island. It is too bright a strain for their enervated eyes to gaze at. As to their capacity for war, the want of attention to certain circumstances has led the regular officers who served in America into a very great mistake on this head. Their troops [the American militia] were ill-constituted; economy they had none. They neither knew how to cook their provisions, nor keep themselves clean. They were, consequently, much subject to camp disorders; and in their sickness (the same care not being taken of them as of the regulars), they were apt to be dispirited.

They were only enlisted for six months; were, therefore, always new to the service; whereas the regulars, being kept always on foot, grew more knowing and economical every day. I say, without attending to these circumstances, and without reflecting how much worse themselves would have been in the same circumstances, the regulars attributed to a difference of materials in their men what, in fact, ought to have been attributed solely to ignorance of method, and boldly asserted the people of New England to be unfit for war. They shut their eyes to all the evidences of the reverse; to their promptness to action, their superiority in marching, and address in the use of all military instruments; but, above all, their ardour and zeal for the service.

There is one more circumstance which we gentlemen in red never choose to remember, viz – that in all our defeats and disgraces, particularly in those upon the Ohio, the provincials never led the flight, but were the last to leave the field. But be these things as they will, if I have any judgment, the people of New England are, this day, more calculated to form irresistible conquering armies, than any people on the face of the globe. Even the appearance of their individuals is totally changed since I first knew them. Formerly they had a slouching, slovenly air. Now, every peasant has his hair smartly dressed, is erect and soldier-like in his air and gait. This change struck me very much in passing through the provinces of Massachusetts and Connecticut. It must be attributed to the military spirit which they breathe, and their companies of cadets formed in all the towns of any considerable size.

I have been present at the reviews of several of these companies, and was amazed at the exactness and rapidity of their manoeuvres. I shall say nothing of the formidable numbers of light infantry (undoubtedly the best in the world) which their back provinces can produce. In short, sir, it is my persuasion, that should the people of England be infatuated enough to suffer their misrulers to proceed in their measures, this country may scorch her fingers, but they themselves will perish in the flames. This small province of Maryland has already resolved to train and discipline about six thousand men; inclosed I send you the resolves of their convention. Pennsylvania is going to arm; I am not yet informed of their numbers, but they will be very great. I have still hopes that the people at home will open their eyes before it is too late, and not suffer the resentment of a hellish junta to weigh down eternal justice, the interest and honour of the nation, if not its existence.

But however grave the situation in the American colonies, the government contended that the overwhelming majority of the King's subjects there remained loyal. In any event, trade with these troublesome dominions was of a much smaller order than that with the West Indies. So a proper perspective was required. Lord North had handsomely won re-election in September 1774. That same year the King offered command of the British forces in America to Sir Jeffrey Amherst, one of Britain's most distinguished soldiers, but Amherst was married to an American and so declined it. As a contemporary reported: 'They offered him a peerage and everything else he could ask ... and for a week they thought he had consented, but his wife dissuaded him, and he gave answer that he could not bring himself to command against the Americans, to whom he had been so much obliged.' Lord Effingham and Admiral Keppel also declined the appointment, because they did not support the cause.

Lord Clive, Britain's greatest military hero, had expressed his view of the colonies as long before as 1772: 'That the Americans will sooner or later take all of the Spanish possessions and make Cape Horn the boundary of their empire is beyond a doubt.' According to one source, he too was offered supreme command of the British forces in America, but refused ostensibly on health grounds – although almost certainly because he disagreed with the policy. If Clive, by far Britain's best general, had taken on the job, subsequent history might have been very different. But by November 1774 he was dead, apparently by his own hand.

The rebels were now in the full flood of military preparation – indeed, they had been for some time. According to an unknown correspondent from Philadelphia, writing to a British MP:

> The late proclamation forbidding the exportation of gunpowder and fire-arms to America seemed intended to take away from the colonies the power of defending themselves by force. I think it my duty to inform you that the said proclamation will be rendered ineffectual by a manufactory of gunpowder, which has lately been set on foot in this province, the materials of which may be procured in great perfection, and at an easier rate than they can be imported from Great Britain, among ourselves. There are, moreover, gunsmiths enough in this province to make one hundred thousand stands of arms in one year, at twenty-eight shillings sterling apiece, if they should be wanted. It may not be amiss to make this intelligence as public as possible, that our rulers may see the impossibility of enforcing the late acts of parliament by arms. Such is the wonderful martial spirit which is enkindled among us, that we begin to think the whole force of Great Britain could not subdue us. We trust no less to the natural advantages of our country than to our numbers and military preparations, in the confidence and security of which we boast. The four New England colonies, together with Virginia and Maryland, are completely armed and disciplined, the province of Pennsylvania will follow their example; in a few weeks our militia will amount to no less than sixty thousand men.

The 'Provincial Congress of Massachusetts', comprising most of the members of the dissolved assembly, and meeting at Concord, had approved a committee of safety and of supplies. A third of the militia, under the control of the committee of public safety, was organized into fifty-man 'minute companies' – minutemen – ready to move in rapidly mobile units whenever required. An arsenal of 5,000 bayonets and rifles, as well as 20 cannon, and 4 mortars and 20 tons of ammunition, was to be assembled. A system of 'express riders' was set up alongside a spy system under Revere. The express riders were to be one of the most crucial factors in the war. Benjamin Church reported back to Gage, who took no action against the regulars at the Green Dragon in Boston.

The need to stop the rebels building up their arms and ammunition was now paramount in Gage's mind. Revere, falsely believing that Gage was planning an expedition to secure the arsenal at Fort William and Mary, at the entrance to Portsmouth Harbour some fifty miles north of Boston, rode and alerted the forces camped outside on 13 December.

The following afternoon, 400 militiamen, in a fleet of small boats, attacked the fort in a raging snowstorm. There were only six invalid British soldiers to guard the arsenal. They managed to fire three cannon before being overwhelmed, their captain being wounded and one other injured in the first real skirmish of the War of Independence. The British colours were taken down. The Americans took more than 100 barrels of gunpowder and 16 cannon, and released the soldiers they had captured. A week later a British ship, HMS *Scarborough*, reached the ransacked fort. However small-scale this, not the later ambush at Lexington, was the first aggressive action in the war. The British troops had been justified in taking supplies from Somerville, because these belonged to the British state, and no blood was shed. The attack on Fort William and Mary was an illegal act of rebellion.

A third 'powder alarm' was meticulously planned by Gage in February 1775, to seize the munitions in Salem, the capital of Essex County. Revere's spies were arrested in time, and a force of 240 British soldiers sailed up the coast to the port of Mobilehead, five miles away. The Americans managed to raise the drawbridge leading to the munitions dump, and the British troops were surrounded by the growing force of militia.

As the impasse continued, it seemed certain that hostilities would break out. Eventually, however, a pastor mediated a British withdrawal.

The British came away with nothing to show from the expedition, but the episode had increased their feeling of isolation and powerlessness and enhanced American contempt for them.

As the intense New England winter turned into a dismal spring, Gage's men in Boston grew restless and an increasing number deserted – leading to draconian punishments for those who were caught. The water from the town wells grew brackish, and food ran low. Meanwhile, astonishingly, although Boston was under siege, Britain's sworn enemies were allowed to continue to roam the streets. Lord Percy, Gage's second-in-command, lamented that 'the gentleman's [Gage's] great leniency and moderation serve only to make them more staring and insolent'.

On the anniversary of the Boston Massacre, at a meeting house in the town, a large crowd, including the resistance leaders Samuel Adams, John Hancock and Paul Revere, gathered to listen to Joseph Warren thunder forth in his usual rococo oratorical style. British officers present heckled him, and the meeting ended in chaos. Meanwhile newspapers derided the military governor:

> In truth, it's judged by men of thinking,
> That GAGE will kill himself a'drinking.
> Nay, I'm informed by the inn keepers,
> He'll bung with shoe-boys, chimney sweepers.

Samuel Adams fuelled the fire, remarking that Gage was 'void of a spark of humanity, who can deliberately be the instrument of depriving our country of its liberty, or the people of their lives in its defence'.

In Britain, Chatham made one last, desperate bid to salvage the peace after meeting Franklin. Chatham's speech was majestic, and one of his last, as he advocated that the Congress be recognized in exchange for paying revenue, although Americans should not be taxed without their consent. The coercive acts, he said, should be repealed, along with all other offensive acts. It was an ingenious formula based on the acceptance of nominal British sovereignty for America in exchange for virtual independence. There was something noble in this discourse by the dying man with the hawk-like face and bleary eyes, who had to be carried to the chamber. He concluded his great peroration:

> Resistance to your acts was necessary as it was just; and your vain dec-
> larations of the omnipotence of Parliament, and your imperious doc-
> trines of the necessity of submission, will be found equally impotent to

convince, or to enslave your fellow-subjects in America, who feel that tyranny, whether ambitioned by an individual part of the legislature or the bodies who compose it, is equally intolerable to British subjects. The means of enforcing this thraldom are found to be as ridiculous and weak in practice, as they are unjust in principle.

Indeed, I cannot but feel the most anxious sensibility for the situation of General Gage, and the troops under his command; thinking him, as I do, a man of humanity and understanding; and entertaining, as I ever will, the highest respect, the warmest love, for the British troops. Their situation is truly unworthy; penned up – pining in inglorious inactivity. They are an army of impotence. You may call them an army of safety and of guard – but they are in truth an army of impotence and contempt; and, to make the folly equal to the disgrace, they are an army of irritation and vexation ...

I remember, some years ago, when the repeal of the Stamp Act was in agitation, conversing in a friendly confidence with a person of undoubted respect and authenticity on that subject; and he assured me with a certainty which his judgment and opportunity gave him, that these were the prevalent and steady principles of America – that you might destroy their towns, and cut them off from the superfluities, perhaps the conveniences, of life; but that they were prepared to despise your power, and would not lament their loss, whilst they have – what, my Lords? – their woods and their liberty. The name of my authority [Dr Franklin], if I am called upon, will authenticate the opinion irrefragably.

If illegal violences have been, as it is said, committed in America, prepare the way, open the door of possibility, for acknowledgement and satisfaction: but proceed not to such coercion, such proscription; cease your indiscriminate inflictions; amass not thirty thousand; oppress not three millions, for the fault of forty or fifty individuals. Such severity of injustice must for ever render incurable the wounds you have already given your colonies; you irritate them to unappeasable rancour. What though you march from town to town, and from province to province; though you should be able to enforce a temporary and local submission, which I only suppose, not admit – how shall you be able to secure the obedience of the country you leave behind you in your progress, to grasp the dominion of eighteen hundred miles of continent, populous in numbers, possessing valour, liberty, and resistance ...

I trust it is obvious to your lordships, that all attempts to impose servitude upon such men, to establish despotism over such a mighty continental nation, must be vain, must be fatal. We shall be forced ultimately to retract; let us retract while we can, not when we must ...

Every motive, therefore, of justice and of policy, of dignity and of prudence, urges you to allay the ferment in America – by a removal of your troops from Boston – by a repeal of your Acts of Parliament – and by demonstration of amicable dispositions towards your colonies. On the other hand, every danger and every hazard impend to deter you from perseverance in your present ruinous measures – foreign war hanging over your heads by a slight and brittle thread: France and Spain watching your conduct, and waiting for the maturity of your errors; – with a vigilant eye to America, and the temper of your colonies, more than to their own concerns, be they what they may. To conclude, my lords: If the ministers thus persevere in misadvising and misleading the King, I will not say that they can alienate the affections of his subjects from his crown; but I will affirm, that they will make the crown not worth his wearing – I will not say that the King is betrayed; but I will pronounce, that the kingdom is undone.

Franklin, who was present, described the speech:

Lord Chatham, in a most excellent speech, introduced, explained, and supported his plan. But Lord Sandwich rose, and in a petulant, vehement speech opposed its being received at all, and gave his opinion that it ought to be immediately rejected with the contempt it deserved. That he could never believe it to be the production of any British peer. That it appeared to him rather the work of some American; and turning his face towards me, who was leaning on the bar, said he fancied he had in his eye the person who drew it up, one of the bitterest and most mischievous enemies this country had ever known. This drew the eyes of many lords upon me; but as I had no inducement to take it to myself, I kept my countenance as immovable as if my features had been made of wood.

British business was equally aghast. A petition by the Lord Mayor, aldermen and livery of London on 10 April declared its 'abhorrence of measures' which were 'oppressing our fellow-subjects in America', and pleaded that 'no part of the dominions can be taxed without being represented'. The King replied curtly:

It is with the utmost astonishment that I find any of my subjects capable of encouraging the rebellious disposition which, unhappily, exists in some of my colonies in North America. Having entire confidence in the wisdom of my parliament, the great council of the nation, I will steadily pursue those measures which they have recommended for the support of the constitutional rights of Great Britain, and the protection of the commercial interests of my kingdoms.

It was far, far too late for bluster. Joseph Warren described the situation in a letter of 3 April:

If we ever obtain a redress of grievances from Great Britain, it must be by the influence of those illustrious personages whose virtue now keeps them out of power. The King never will bring them into power until the ignorance and frenzy of the present administration make the throne on which he sits shake under him. If America is a humble instrument of the salvation of Britain, it will give us the sincerest joy; but if Britain must lose her liberty, she must lose it alone. America must and will be free. The contest may be severe – the end will be glorious.

The First Brigade of the army marched about four miles out of town three days ago, under the command of a Brigadier-General (Earl Percy), but as they marched without baggage or artillery, they did not occasion so great an alarm as they otherwise would. Nevertheless great numbers, completely armed, collected in the neighbouring towns; and it is the opinion of many, that had they marched eight or ten miles, and attempted to destroy any magazines, or abuse the people, not a man of them would have returned to Boston. The [Massachusetts] congress immediately took proper measures for restraining any unnecessary effusion of blood; and also passed proper resolves respecting the army, if they should attempt to come out of the town with baggage and artillery.

Both sides were preparing for the showdown. As the American militias assembled in their thousands outside the smouldering trap that Boston was becoming, Gage was instructed by the Colonial Secretary, the Earl of Dartmouth, to take firm action. The action clearly envisaged by the British government was the arrest of the rebel leaders. Most of them had already left town, and Gage feared the arrest of those who remained would trigger off an uprising in Boston.

The supremacy and short-sightedness of the hard-line faction in Britain can be gauged by the remarkable speech observed by Franklin from the Earl of Sandwich, famous not just for his invention (a snack to be taken at the gaming table) but also for John Wilkes's brilliant riposte when the Earl told him he would die either of the pox or on the gallows: 'That depends, my lord, whether I embrace your mistress or your principles.' Sandwich was now First Sea Lord:

The noble Lord [Chatham] mentions the impracticability of conquering America; I cannot think the noble Lord can be serious on this matter. Suppose the colonies do abound in men, what does that signify? They are raw, undisciplined, cowardly men. I wish instead of forty or fifty thousand of these brave fellows, they would produce in the field at least two hundred thousand, the more the better, the easier would be the conquest;

if they did not run away they would starve themselves into compliance with our measures.

I will tell your lordships an anecdote that happened at the siege of Louisburg: Sir Peter Warren told me that in order to try the courage of the Americans, he ordered a great number of them to be placed in the front of the army; the Americans pretended at first to be much elated at this mark of distinction, and boasted what mighty feats they would do upon the scene of action. However, when the moment came to put in execution this boasted courage, behold every one of them ran from the front to the rear of the army with as much expedition as their feet could carry them, and threatened to go off entirely if the commander offered to make them a shield to protect the British soldiers at the expense of their blood; they did not understand such usage.

Sir Peter, finding what egregious cowards they were, and knowing of what importance such numbers must be to intimidate the French by their appearance, told these American heroes that his orders had been misunderstood, that he always intended to keep them in the rear of the army to make the great push; that it was the custom of generals to preserve the best troops to the last; that this was always the Roman custom; and as the Americans resembled the Romans in every particular, especially in courage and love of their country, he should make no scruple of following the Roman custom, and made no doubt but the modern Romans would show acts of bravery equal to any in ancient Rome. 'By such discourses as these,' said Sir Peter Warren, 'I made shift to keep them with us, though I took care they should be pushed forward in no dangerous conflict.' Now, I can tell the noble Lord that this is exactly the situation of all the heroes in North America; they are all Romans. And are these the men to fright us from the post of honour? Believe me, my lords, the very sound of a cannon would carry them off, in Sir Peter's words, as fast as their feet could carry them.

# PART II

*George v. George*

# 8

# *Gauntlet of Fire*

It is hard to detect the fearsome visage of a military oppressor in Gage's actions. Rather than arrest the rebel leaders, the British general again chose the path of caution: an expedition in force to seize the rebel arsenal at the town of Worcester to the south-west. Whether he believed that he could still avert war, or was merely anxious to avoid triggering an attack from the thousands of hostile militiamen outside Boston, he was still going out of his way to avoid provoking hostilities. The limited action was justifiable since the British authorities had the right to control the disposal of munitions, if necessary by force, to deter intimidation of the kind already exercised at Salem.

Two young officers, Captain John Brown and Ensign Henry de Bernière, were sent, to scout out the rebel positions at Worcester, along with their batman – dressed 'like countrymen in brown clothes and reddish handkerchiefs round our necks'. At a tavern, a black serving girl easily saw through the officers' disguise because of their dismissive treatment of their batman, who sat at a separate table. From then on 'we always treated him as our companion, since our adventure with the black woman'.

They travelled on through the snow, staying at loyalist taverns in Weston, Marley and Worcester, where they surveyed the town's defence before returning. Increasingly, however, groups of people watched them as they walked, and horsemen would ride up to inspect them before galloping away. Fearing for their lives, the British scouts were saved by a violent snowstorm and managed to trek thirty-two miles through the snow in a single day to Weston, from which they were guided by the loyalist innkeeper to Boston.

The British troops' prospects for a successful expedition to Worcester were not good: the roads were difficult, and there was a dangerous river crossing. The alternative target was Concord, seat of the Provisional Congress and reputedly a major arsenal. Brown and de Bernière were sent out again along the main road, which they found to be dangerous – 'wooded in most places and commanded by hills'. Arriving in Concord, they were impressed by the military preparations there and were received by a loyalist, who was promptly threatened with death by his neighbours. The three men left hurriedly, taking a long, northern route through more exposed countryside.

Satisfied, rather than awed or rendered more cautious by the evidence that the countryside was in arms, Gage appointed Lieutenant-Colonel Francis Smith to lead a redcoat expedition to Concord. A veteran with twenty-eight years' experience, fat and self-indulgent, Smith was a cautious man in Gage's own mould. The commander-in-chief ordered him to respect the law. 'You will take care that the soldiers do not plunder the inhabitants or hurt private property.' Gage knew the dangers Smith faced. As he wrote to London:

> The most natural and eligible mode of attack on the part of the people is that of detached parties of bushmen who from their adroitness in the habitual use of the firelock suppose themselves sure of their mark ... Should hostilities unhappily commence, the first opposition would be irregular, impetuous, and incessant from the numerous bodies that would swarm to the place of action, and all actuated by an enthusiasm wild and ungovernable.

Gage ordered the naval commander, the irascible and obtuse Admiral Graves, to prepare boats to ferry the troops across Back Bay to Cambridge, which he did in full view of the rebels on the mainland. Revere promptly rode to Concord to warn the militia – prematurely – of the preparations. No attack came, and the rebels began to disperse their munitions out of Concord.

Although a Tory supporter reported to the British that only several large cannon and a large quantity of food remained in Concord, Gage seems to have concluded that he could not abort the mission, even though the horse had bolted. He sent groups of heavily armed British officers into the countryside to intercept and intimidate Revere's riders: the rebels believed that he was out to assassinate or capture Hancock or Samuel Adams, the principal resistance leaders.

The same evening, 18 April 1775, a stable boy ran through Boston's streets to tell Revere that the redcoats were preparing to march. This was confirmed by the preparations of the British seamen. Joseph Warren decided to check the story with a confidential source placed at the very summit of the British hierarchy – almost certainly Margaret Gage, the American wife of the British general, whose loyalties were deeply divided.

Gage's deputy, Percy, was astonished to find that ordinary Bostonians on the common knew that the target of the British expedition was the 'cannon at Concord'. Gage almost certainly believed he had been betrayed by Margaret: after this episode, he had her sent away on board a British ship to England, and they separated.

A second American courier, William Dawes, slipped quietly through the guardpoint at Roxbury Neck shortly before Gage ordered it closed. Revere himself made a prearranged signal from the town to the mainland, of two lanterns in the steeple of Christ Church (Old North Church), to warn that the troops were going by water. At 10.15 p.m. Revere embarked aboard a small boat at the north end of town.

According to the myth, Revere needed a cloth to muffle the oars, and a woman watching at a nearby window took off her knickers and dropped them to him, still warm to the touch. Another tale is that Revere forgot his spurs and sent a message attached to his dog's collar to his wife, who sent them back by the same method. Then he rowed across to the mainland, where he mounted his fast and large New England horse, Brown Beauty, which was waiting for him. So began the most celebrated ride in American history.

Revere galloped through the night along the Lexington road, where he was suddenly intercepted by two of Gage's officers on patrol, waiting to stop exactly such a messenger. He turned his horse about and fled, but the two gave chase – one trying to cut across a field to intercept him, but getting stuck in a bog, the other outrun by the experienced horse and rider. He galloped by a roundabout route through the village of Medford, by good fortune slipping past British patrols, to regain the main road at the village of Menotomy.

Arriving in Lexington at midnight, he rode to the local parsonage, where Samuel Adams and Hancock were hiding. There he was challenged gruffly by the guards round the house and told not to make so much noise. He is said to have replied, 'You'll have noise enough before long. The regulars are coming out.' Inside, Revere, Hancock and Adams urgently discussed the likely objective of the British. They decided the British force was too large merely to be seeking to arrest the two leaders:

the aim must be to seize the stores at Concord. William Dawes also arrived shortly afterwards, and the two riders decided to travel on to warn the people of Concord.

Gage knew from Percy that the expedition's objective was already known to the rebels; he also knew that the munitions had been removed from Concord. Did he believe that his interceptors would have prevented news of the expedition reaching Concord itself, or is it more likely that preparations were already so far advanced that he would be disgraced or dismissed if he pulled back now? Perhaps he wanted merely to pull off the propaganda victory of occupying the rebels' capital, seizing some cannon and supplies, and retiring; then he could assure London that he had taken some action, while in practice having done nothing at all and having barely provoked the Americans – he hoped. Whatever the reason, the expedition was a disastrous miscalculation.

A month earlier Samuel Adams had remarked, 'Put your enemy in the wrong, and keep him so, is a wise maxim in politics, as well as in war.' The American rebels were determined to provoke the British into shooting first in a war they had long regarded as inevitable: for only by maintaining the myth of the British aggressor and oppressor could they hope to win recruits among the indifferent, and sometimes actively pro-British, American population. Gage had seemed equally determined to deny them that opportunity – until Whitehall's insistence that something must be done prompted his futile expedition in force to Concord to capture munitions long since departed.

The expedition was a large one – 800–900 men grouped in 21 companies, comprising grenadiers, picked for their size and ability to intimidate, and light infantry, picked for their initiative and vigour. They were equipped with muskets and rifles. The British musket was long and heavy, with a forty-six-inch barrel, weighing nearly eleven pounds. Its lead ball, with a diameter of three-quarters of an inch, in theory had a range of 300 yards, but was only accurate within 60 yards; it could fire three rounds a minute, and the flint often misfired. The ball could only penetrate earthworks up to about an inch and a half, and chip a tree. Rifles, longer even than muskets, had half-inch balls but were much more accurate, up to 200 yards, although they could be fired at the rate of just one round a minute. All of this favoured defenders over attackers. The American militia were largely equipped with fowling pieces (long-barrelled hunting guns), which fired bullets and buckshot, usually carried carefully wrapped in handkerchieves, the powder being carried in horns. Many militiamen also carried short rapiers.

The British troops were ferried across to Cambridge in two batches, and had to wade the last few yards. The landing was confused, because Gage's passion for secrecy meant that few junior officers knew their orders, and because the two units had been merged. They had to wait for provisions to be brought ashore, then march along the shore again through water, after discovering a swamp immediately beyond the beach. It was four hours before they were properly under way.

Soon they had to ford a freezing stream up to their waists so as not to wake the locals by tramping across the bridge. But the presence of 800 men marching past isolated farmhouses and villages could hardly go unnoticed even at that time of night. Everywhere they were sighted by observers who hurried ahead to give further warning.

Smith marched his men at speed – nearly four miles an hour – to Menotomy, where he decided to send his second-in-command, Major John Pitcairn, forward along with the light infantry to seize the bridges at Concord before they could be taken by the militia. This was about four in the morning.

Meanwhile Revere had long since set out from the parsonage at Lexington with Dawes and another companion to ride to Concord, but the party had been ambushed by a group of Gage's interceptors. Dawes got away, returning to Lexington, while Samuel Prescott, the third rider also escaped. Revere, who was captured and interrogated, unsuccessfully tried to steer his captors away from Lexington Green, where Adams and Hancock were hiding. But the British soldiers, alarmed by nearby gunshots, turned their captive loose so as to hurry back to the coast.

Prescott meanwhile had reached Concord at two in the morning and rang the town bell to wake the sleeping citizens. Other express riders carried the news of the British advance across the Massachusetts countryside. Preparations for a general alert had been made long before, relying on the system of raising militias that had been necessary in several wars. The militias were commanded by veterans who had served in the Seven Years War; they exercised twice a week, and were taught to use their muskets and fight from cover. On parade they looked a shambles. One British observer remarked 'It is a curious masquerade scene to see grave sober citizens, barbers and tailors who never looked fierce before, strutting about in their Sunday wigs with muskets on their shoulders.' Yet they were to prove devastatingly effective.

As the militias began to crowd the highways, terrified local countrymen and their families fled the impending conflict. One said, 'The roads
[were] filled with frightened women and children, some in carts with
their tattered furniture, others on foot fleeing into the woods.' Another,
John Tudor, noted in his diary:

> Terrible news from Lexington ... rumour on rumour and men and horses
> driving past, up and down the roads ... People were in great perplexity;
> women in distress for their husbands and friends who had marched ... All
> confusion, numbers of carts, etc. carrying off goods etc. as the rumour
> was that if the soldiers came out again they would burn, kill and destroy
> all as they marched.

Revere, after his lucky escape, meanwhile made his way back to the parsonage at Lexington. To his astonishment, Adams and Hancock were
still there, although British officers were believed to be hunting them.
The parson's daughter, then a girl of twelve, wrote later of the chaos
surrounding the two revolutionary leaders, who had Hancock's aunt
and fiancée with them – 'Aunt Hancock and Dolly Quincy, with their
cloaks and bonnets on, she crying and wringing her hands and helping
mother dress the children, Dolly going round with Father to hide
money, watches and anything down in the potatoes and up in the
garret.'

Hancock was burning to fight, but Revere angrily persuaded them to
leave for a safer hideout, which they did at dawn in Hancock's coach.
Arriving in the small town of Woburn, the high-living Hancock sent
back for a fine salmon given to him by an admirer, along with his aunt
and fiancée. When they arrived, they proceeded to cook the fish, but
before they could settle down to eat it they were warned that redcoats
were coming and had to flee again, to the house of a farmer. There the
hungry Hancock had to be content with boiled salted pork. At dawn,
hearing gunfire in the distance, Samuel Adams knew the war had begun
and relished the bitter struggle to come, announcing, 'This is a glorious
day for America'.

Revere had returned to the parsonage, where he learned that the
British were barely half an hour away. Meanwhile the Lexington militia
had been summoned but, believing they had been given a false alarm,
had gone back to their houses and to a nearby tavern. Their commander
was John Parker, a forty-six-year-old veteran of colonial campaigns and
a farmer. Tall, with a large head and broad brow, he suffered from tuber-

culosis but still cut an impressive figure. He drew his men up for a second time on Lexington Green.

Down the road, the British column spotted the warning beacons lighting the sky and heard the insistent bells tolling their warnings. As dawn began to break, the patrol which had briefly captured Paul Revere met the British troops on the road and informed them that 500 Americans were assembling to fight them at Lexington. With visibility improving, Lieutenant Sutherland could see 'a vast number of country militia going over the hill with their arms for Lexington'. The soldiers were then ordered to load their rifles.

The British seem to have given no thought to retreating, both because this would be shameful and because the soldiers were confident of dispersing any attack by what they considered an ill-organized rabble. Pitcairn's advance guard numbered about 240 soldiers. As they reached Lexington Green they found themselves face to face with around fifty or so militia. Parker, seeing the superior numbers of the British, ordered his militia, 'Let the troops pass by. Don't molest them, without they being first.' He added, 'Stand your ground! Don't fire unless fired upon! But if they want to have a war let it begin here!'

The young marine lieutenant leading the forward troops – Pitcairn was at the back – decided to march straight at the militia drawn up on the green, rather than bypass them along the main road. Pitcairn was dismayed. He galloped forward and sent the rearguard on the bypass road, then galloped across the common to stop his own men, at the same time yelling, 'Throw down your arms, ye villains, ye rebels', as the British vanguard moved across the common. Parker ordered his men to disperse and not to fire, and they began to retreat.

A shot suddenly punctuated the shouts. The British were convinced that it had been fired not by the militia but by a 'provincial' from behind a stone wall, or possibly from the Buckman tavern across the green. Pitcairn had given the order 'Soldiers, don't fire, keep your rounds and surround them.' But some militia claimed they saw a British officer on horseback fire first, or possibly in response to a shot.

Whoever first pulled the trigger and started the war, the advancing British soldiers now loosed off at the retreating enemy with a ragged volley. Pitcairn later reported angrily that 'without any order or responsibility the light infantry began a scattered fire'. Then they began volleying in a more disciplined way, and after that charged with their bayonets. Altogether eight American men were killed and nine wounded while the soldiers ran riot. It had been the Boston Massacre all over again, on double the scale. Only the arrival of Colonel Smith with the rearguard put an end to the bloodletting. He ordered the drums beaten and the excited soldiers back into line. With neither side ostensibly wishing to shoot, the episode had been one of those terrible accidents that happen when jittery troops come within range of each other.

If Smith had even now bowed to common sense and retreated, catastrophe might have been averted. But he had his orders, and the soldiers moved inexorably along the further ten miles to Concord, giving time for a countryside now understandably baying for their blood in revenge to prepare a trap. Within moments of the British departure, 100 militiamen had assembled near the bodies on Lexington Green.

The minutemen militia of Massachusetts, chiefly the younger soldiers, fanned on to a hill overlooking Concord, vowing to fight. Seeing the strength of the approaching column, they withdrew to the town centre, drumming defiantly all the while at the approaching British columns about a third of a mile away. There the waiting militia commanders decided to withdraw all troops to outside Concord, leaving the town to the British.

Marching unhindered through the streets, the British vigorously searched the houses and cut down the local liberty pole, though behaving with decorum towards the remaining inhabitants. They found almost nothing except three 24-pound cannon buried in a yard. Some wooden gun carriages were burnt, and the blaze spread to the town's council house, which both soldiers and inhabitants attempted to save. The smoke was seen in the distance by the impatient watching militia, one of whom said, 'Would you have them burn the town down?' to the senior commander.

Meanwhile soldiers searching Colonel Barrett's farm outside the town, supposedly an arsenal, had turned up nothing, although many guns there had been ploughed into the ground before the British arrived. The latter withdrew across a bridge leading into Concord, as the now angry militia descended in force. To British astonishment, these irregulars 'advanced with the greatest regularity'. Withdrawing further, the British front line collided with the line behind, causing great confusion in the narrow street.

The nervous troops in front opened fire across the bridge without orders, killing some of the advancing Americans. These fired back, and seven soldiers, including four officers, were killed and nine wounded. Losing so many officers, the British facing the Americans suddenly panicked and ran. As one ensign put it, 'the concentration of their fire was such that we was obliged to give way, then ran with great precipitation' – all the way back to where Smith and the grenadiers were still searching for arms in the centre of Concord.

The Americans sent forward a detachment of 200 minutemen across the bridge, and they took up positions behind a wall on a hill. The British decided not to try to dislodge them. Unquestionably, just as the main aggressive advance had been by the British at Lexington, the Americans had initiated the attack at Concord. But they still hesitated to launch a full-scale assault, holding fire on both sides of the bridge as the British contingent rushed back from Barrett's farm into Concord for fear of being cut off. On the road, the retreating troops came across a dying soldier who had been scalped and had his brain and ears removed with a hatchet. It was the first atrocity of the war, and British recruits were appalled by the sudden realization of the nature of the enemy they were dealing with.

The self-willed American militia made a stark contrast in appearance to the disciplined British redcoats. Most were dressed in ordinary working clothes, and wore large hats with floppy brims. Their hair was generally long, and many sported the earlocks then in fashion. They wore thick linen shirts and knitted stockings. One contemporary said that their 'coats and waistcoats were loose and of huge dimensions, with colours as various as the barks of oak, sumac and other trees of our hills and swamps could make them'. Another observed, 'To a man they wore small clothes, coming down and fastening just below the knee, and long stockings with cowhide shoes ornamented by grey buckles.' A rich man was sent home to change after turning up in a gaudy red coat which might be mistaken for a British uniform. Their officers were little better attired. One wore a brown home-made suit; another, 'an old coat, a flopped hat and a leather apron'.

The perspective of the Massachusetts men massing on the hills to watch the British march to and from Concord was, of course, very different from that of the apprehensive recruits below. They were sturdy independent farmers for the most part, living in scattered settlements and leading simple lives, of poor to middling prosperity. They prided themselves on their self-sufficiency, and had long been barely conscious of any attempt by the authorities to enforce their rule. They would be aware of

British authority only when, on occasional forays to market their produce or to shop, they saw soldiers in Boston.

Now they were experiencing a period of deep economic uncertainty, with credit becoming tighter – something blamed on the British – and Boston itself struggling in a recession. On top of this, the traditional safety valve of migration to the west appeared to have been turned off by the British closure of the frontier, and Adams and his supporters had staged a successful campaign to convince them that the British were intending to introduce a huge burden of taxation.

To these sturdy pioneers, the British forces sallying in strength from Boston were not the legitimate representatives of an established order going about their lawful business. They were an occupying force, sent to assert the authority of a distant king whose power had been purely nominal before. The Massachusetts men regarded the sortie from Boston as an act of naked aggression, almost comparable to a foreign invasion. Only during the French and Indian War, when they were fighting alongside the Americans to repel outsiders, had the British previously asserted their authority throughout the countryside – and they had then made a poor impression as allies.

The Americans did not view their build-up of arms and ammunition at Concord and other powder depots as illegal: did not every American family jealously preserve the right to bear arms? Whatever the formal legal position, in their view the British had declared war on them by marching to seize their arsenals, not the reverse. And to the young and eager volunteers massing upon the heights overlooking the road from Concord to Lexington, they themselves were the men of courage, facing heavily armed and disciplined columns of regular soldiers with only crude fowling pieces and sabres, risking their lives from behind rocks and trees to harass the brute military force of an occupying power.

Patching up his wounded as best he could, Smith decided to leave Concord at noon, suddenly realizing that, although the enemy would not face him in open battle, he was caught in a trap. He marched under the shadow of a ridge to the north of the road, but sent troops to occupy this in order to secure his flanks. The advance column moved forward to Merion's Corner, a junction of several lanes where hundreds of militiamen had been assembling. There were now around 1,000 men there, and the two sides briefly exchanged fire.

The British pressed on, supported by flanking parties on either side, but grimly observed that 'all the hills on each side of us were covered with rebels'. It must have been a terrifying sight for the redcoats.

The ragged hordes of militia were well commanded by veterans of the Seven Years War, who now saw the opportunity of staging their first ambush from a hill to the south, its wooded lower slopes providing ample cover for marksmen. Smith guessed the intention, and sent his advance forces charging up the hill, driving the militia back but losing many in the process. Then he pushed on to another choke point, where the woods sloped down to either side of the road. One of the militiamen observed later, 'We saw a wood at a distance, which appeared to be in or near the road the enemy must pass. Many leaped over the wall and made for that wood. We arrived just in time to meet the enemy. There was then, on the opposite side of the road, a young growth of wood well filled with Americans.'

Caught in a deadly crossfire, the British drove through – only to come under fire from an even larger force of militiamen in woods just around the bend, which became known as 'Bloody Curve'. Thirty soldiers were killed compared with four militiamen, who sheltered behind trees and undergrowth and picked off the British at leisure. The British were ordered to run forward at a trot through the ambushers, some 2,000 of whom now closed in pursuit of the regulars.

After this the country opened into farmland, but respite for the soldiers was only momentary: just ahead were two farms with outbuildings close to the road. As the British soldiers trotted forward, American snipers opened fire on them at point-blank range until a British flanking column came round the back of the farms and killed them.

The soldiers were now halfway back to Lexington. Ahead was a rocky hillside which the road skirted to the right. On the hill were stationed the Lexington militia, under Captain Parker, waiting for revenge. Some snipers fired from behind a rock-strewn meadow, but were routed by the British flanking column. But the men on the hill opened up with a deadly series of volleys: among others, Colonel Smith was shot in the thigh and toppled from his horse. The relentless fire brought the British column to a stop.

Major Pitcairn, Smith's second-in-command, now took charge, sending British soldiers up the hill to rout the American snipers, though not before the Americans had taken many casualties. The hill was to be dubbed 'Parker's Revenge'. Pitcairn had learned his lesson: he

sent marines forward to clear the next hill, called The Bluff. They hero-
ically charged up it, suffering the biggest casualties of any unit on the
expedition.

Around the next curve was yet another hill, skirted by woods reaching the roadside – Fiske Hill. Once again, an American musket company
lay in wait until the British were at point blank range. Then they opened
up, hitting Pitcairn. But the courageous officer had merely been injured
in his arm, although his horse was shot from under him. Five soldiers
lay dead around him.

British discipline now at last fell apart. Some soldiers simply sank to
the ground exhausted, waiting for the end. The light-infantry flanking
parties were also flagging; the wounded could scarcely walk. Many of
those desperate men were panting with thirst and made for pools of
water alongside the road, as did some American militia, with whom they
grappled in hand-to-hand fighting. Other soldiers began to run forward
in a crazed, disorderly attempt at escape. The fleeing soldiers passed
another trap, Command Hill, and were now nearly at Lexington Green.
But this was teeming with their vengeful enemy and offered no respite.
Still fifteen miles from sanctuary in Boston, their only hope of survival
was surrender – but they could expect little mercy.

The few remaining officers drew themselves up across the road in
front of the running column and threatened to shoot them unless the
exhausted men regrouped. This they began to do, under relentless
American fire. But hope was gone. As one officer remarked, 'We must
have laid down our arms or been picked off by the rebels at their pleasure.' They were almost out of ammunition.

Suddenly, the British soldiers at the front of the column gave a ragged
cheer. Along the heights just beyond Lexington a disciplined column of
British infantry waited, equipped with cannon, one of which belched
forth a ball which smashed into Lexington's meeting house. The
exhausted troops summoned the strength to run forward to the relief
force.

Three of Britain's elite regiments – the King's Own, the 47th Foot and
the Royal Welch Fusiliers – as well as a battalion of Royal Marines commanded by Lord Hugh Percy, had been sent out from Boston by Gage
in response to a message for help from Smith just before nine o'clock in
the morning. Gage had wanted them to move much earlier, but the
orders had failed to reach the commanders. They moved across Roxbury

Neck into the countryside, taking two six-round cannon with them. Percy was surprised to find that 'all of the houses were shut up and there was not the appearance of a single inhabitant. I could get no intelligence concerning [the first British force] till I had passed Menotomy.' Reaching Menotomy at one o'clock, they learned of the encounter at Lexington Green. A little further on he heard that the whole of Smith's force had been attacked and was in retreat. Percy was apprehensive: 'The whole country we had to retire through was covered with stone walls, and was besides a very hilly stony country.'

Hurrying forward, he reached the heights east of Lexington and ordered his troops to deploy in battle formation as he heard the sound of shots. When from his vantage point he saw the ragged army of red-coats pursued and surrounded on two sides by swarms of militiamen, he ordered his cannon to be fired, scattering the American troops. The fleeing army reached his positions at last, winded and under fire from long-range snipers. Furiously the Royal Welch Fusiliers broke ranks and charged forward at the Americans. As one officer wrote: 'Revenge had so fully possessed the breasts of the soldiers that the battalions broke, regardless of every order, to pursue the affrighted runaways. They were, however, found again, though with some difficulty.'

Percy sent forward some more orderly soldiers with muskets to deter the American militia from advancing any further, and set fire to some houses behind which snipers were sheltering. He meanwhile ordered a council of war. His men, anticipating only minor trouble, had only thirty-six cartridges each, and Smith's tattered column was virtually out of ammunition. Two ammunition wagons sent out by Gage, after Percy had been captured by irregulars, and the six men accompanying them took refuge with an old woman who handed them over to a local militia captain. Lord North's British critics were later to use the episode cruelly: 'If one old Yankee woman can take six grenadiers, how many soldiers would it require to conquer America?'

An officer was dispatched from Lexington in a desperate bid to get help. He succeeded in getting past militia patrols in a circuitous cross-country ride, but arrived in Boston too late to make any difference. Percy meanwhile drew up his men in three strong columns, instead of a single one along the road accompanied by small flanking parties. He argued that 'Very strong flanking parties [were] absolutely necessary, as there was not a stone wall though before in appearance evacuated, from whence the rebels did not fire upon us.'

His strongest troops were at the sides and rear; the carriages bearing the wounded were in the middle, while the marines were also there in reserve to plug any break in the formation, which was a kind of elongated square. He coolly decided to move much more slowly than the panic-stricken Smith, to keep his formation intact. Altogether he had some 1,800 men.

The Americans also had time to take stock. Around fifty regiments amounting to 5,000 men altogether had mobilized, so effective had been the system of express riders and alerts. Their overall commander was Brigadier William Heath, a prosperous, cheerful, pompous farmer who had made a study of military tactics and had been preparing for war with the British for five years. In a tavern at Menotomy, Heath and other commanders met one of the revolutionary leaders, Joseph Warren, who had left Boston that morning, to plan the next stage of the ambush.

Heath had learned much from studying the tactics employed by guerrillas in European warfare as well as Indians. Recognizing that the terrain to the east offered fewer chances of close ambush, he decided to make use of the scattered cover presented by some stone walls, rocks and buildings, to keep around the British forces a moving ring of 'dispersed though adhering' irregulars, acting as individuals, but under a loose command. When Percy's three columns at last set out at 3.45 p.m., the Americans concentrated their attack on the rear, where the Royal Welch Fusiliers bore the brunt of the fighting, moving backwards to exchange places with those immediately behind when they had discharged their muskets. Their colonel was shot and 36 out of 218 members of the regiment were killed that afternoon; they had eventually to be replaced by the marines.

Heath and Warren led other militia units to the left of the British moving square, to tighten the ring of fire, attacking from rough, boulder-strewn pastureland. At first the British, moving along the hills to the south, managed to keep their flank clear; but past Menotomy, several lines of militia joined the attack from that side. Percy observed:

> The rebels attacked us in a very scattered irregular manner, but with perseverance and resolution, nor did they ever dare to form into any regular body. Indeed they knew too well what was proper, to do so. Whoever looks upon them as an irregular mob will find himself very much mistaken. They have men amongst them who know very well what they are about, having been employed as rangers against the Indians and Canadians, and this country being much covered with wood, and hilly, is very advantageous for their method of fighting.

More militia also attacked from the front, while others on horseback would circle, attack, withdraw, then get ahead of the columns to attack again. However, Percy's flanking columns succeeded in rooting out many irregulars who tried to fight from the cover of houses along the road. In this vicious hand-to-hand fighting, which continued in Menotomy, some Americans were killed by the vengeful and hard-pressed British soldiers after surrendering. As one British lieutenant observed, 'The soldiers were so enraged at suffering from an unseen enemy that they forced open many of the houses from which the fires proceeded and put to death all those found in them.'

Another wrote, 'We were now obliged to force almost every house in the road, for the rebels had taken possession of them as galled us exceedingly, but they suffered for their temerity, for all that were found in the houses were put to death.' Presumably this included any civilians as well. Two Americans found boozing in the Cooper Tavern – they must have been very far gone to have stayed as the armies approached – were 'stabbed through in many places, their heads mauled, skulls broke and their brains out on the floor and the walls of the house.'

In Menotomy alone 25 Americans were killed and 9 wounded, to 40 British dead and 80 wounded. Percy wrote with grudging respect of his opponents: 'Many of them concealed themselves in houses and advanced within ten yards to fire at me and other officers, although they were virtually certain of being put to death themselves in an instant'. Enraged by the American attacks, British soldiers went on a plundering spree – which included the church silver – set fire to buildings, and killed livestock, despite their officers' attempts to stop them.

Reaching the still more thickly populated settlements of Cambridge, the soldiers were faced by a large body of militia, which was dispersed by British cannon. But the British were now low on ammunition: as one lieutenant remarked, they fired back 'with too much eagerness, so that at first much of it was thrown away from want about coolness and steadiness which distinguishes troops who have been inbred to the service'.

Approaching the Charles river, a new danger loomed: the Americans had smashed the bridge, and several hundred militia blocked its approaches. Percy suddenly ordered his men down a small lane to the left, which led on to the road to Charlestown. The Americans, taken by surprise by the move, occupied a hill in front of the British – Prospect Hill. Percy blasted at them with the last rounds of his cannon. Another American force threatened, but stopped at a hill to the north.

At last the British reached Charlestown Neck, the narrow opening of the peninsula, and took refuge on the high ground above the town, from which they would be impossible to dislodge. The guns of HMS *Somerset* were now brought to bear on the militia, who finally gave up their pursuit. As Percy later observed, 'We retired fifteen miles under an incessant fire, which like a moving circle rounded and followed us wherever we went.'

It was seven o'clock. Darkness fell, followed by a thunderstorm that soaked the exhausted men to the skin. The British wounded were ferried across to Boston, followed by their comrades, who were replaced by fresh troops. The gauntlet of fire was at an end. Some 273 British soldiers had been killed or wounded, to 95 Americans. Eighteen British officers were casualties, almost all of them Smith's men in the initial stage of the fighting. Across the water in Boston, the last battle had been witnessed from the quayside by hundreds of Bostonians.

# 9

## *Besieged*

The following morning the British woke to an alarming spectacle: a militia force 10,000 strong camped outside Boston. It was America's first army. One British officer wrote, 'The country is all in arms and we are absolutely invested with many thousand men, some of them so daring as to come very near our outposts on the only entrance into town by land. They have cut off all supplies of provisions from the country.'

The British were under siege. De Bernière observed, 'In the course of two days, from a plentiful town, we were reduced to the disagreeable necessity of living on salt provisions, and were fairly blocked up in Boston.' The soldiers were plunged into bitterness. One wrote, 'These people are very numerous, and as bad as the Indians for scalping and cutting the dead men's ears and noses off, and those they get alive, that are wounded, and cannot get off the ground.'

Another, explaining the incident at Concord, wrote, 'Had we not idled away three hours on Cambridge marsh waiting for the provisions that were not wanted, we should have had no interruption at Lexington.' Colonel Smith told the blindingly obvious truth when he declared, 'I can't think, but it must have been a preconcerted scheme in them, to attack the King's troops at the first favourable opportunity.'

Gage himself – blamed by almost everyone for the fiasco – remained cool-headed, seeking to negotiate through Governor Trumbull of Connecticut to cease hostilities. The Massachusetts leaders refused. Gage ordered the surrender of all private weapons in Boston, and permitted any Americans who wished to leave to do so.

Admiral Samuel Graves, his inept naval commander, had tried to stop women and children leaving, arguing that they could be kept as hostages to deter an attack – while arranging his own personal evacuation. Percy reported coldly:

You may depend upon it, that as the rebels have now had time to prepare, they are determined to go through with it, nor will the insurrection here turn out so despicable as it is perhaps imagined at home. For my part, I never believed, I confess, that they would have attacked the King's troops, or have had the perseverance I found in them yesterday.'

A letter from a Bostonian to a friend in Philadelphia gives a flavour of the controversy that would surround the issue of who started the American War of Independence. The militia at Lexington, he said:

to the number of about forty, were drawn out early in the morning near the Meeting House to exercise; upon which the party of light infantry and grenadiers, to the number of about eight hundred, came up to them and ordered them to disperse. The commander replied that they were inno-cently amusing themselves with exercise, that they had not any ammuni-tion with them, and therefore should not molest or disturb them. This answer not satisfying, the troops fired upon them, and killed three or four; the others took to their heels, and the troops continued to fire. A few took refuge in the Meeting House, when the soldiers shoved up the windows, pointed their guns in, and killed three there. This is the best account I can learn of the beginning of the fatal day, and you must naturally suppose that such a piece of cruelty would rouse the country.

The troops continued their march to Concord, entered the town, and refreshed themselves in the Meeting House and Town House. In the latter place they found some ammunition and stores belonging to the country, which, finding they could not bring away by reason of the country people having occupied all the posts round them, they set fire to the house, but the people extinguished it. They set it on fire a second time, which brought on a general engagement at about eleven o'clock. The troops took two pieces of cannon from the countrymen; but their numbers increas-ing, they soon regained them, and the troops were obliged to retreat towards the town ...

When I reflect, and consider that the fight between those whose parents but a few years ago were brothers, I shudder at the thought, and there is no knowing where our calamities will end.

Gage's official account to Dartmouth had 200 militia gathered on Lexington Green, some of whom when faced by the British troops jumped over a wall then fired four or five shots at the troops. Gage admitted that, in response, 'without any order or regularity, the light infantry began a scattered fire, and killed several of the country people, but were silenced as soon as the authority of their officers could make them'.

As far as British atrocities were concerned, Gage wrote to Governor Trumbull:

The intelligence you seem to have received, relative to the late excursion of a body of troops into the country is altogether injurious, and contrary to the true state of facts. The troops disclaim with indignation the barbarous outrages of which they are accused, so contrary to their known humanity. I have taken the greatest pains to discover if any were committed, and have found examples of their tenderness, both to the young and the old; but no vestige of their cruelty or barbarity. It is very possible that in firing into houses, from whence they were fired upon, that old people, women, or children, may have suffered; but if any such thing has happened, it was in their defence, and undesigned.

I have no command to ravage and desolate the country; and were it my intention, I have had pretence to begin it upon the sea-ports, who are at the mercy of the fleet. For your better information, I enclose you a narrative of that affair, taken from gentlemen of indisputable honour and veracity, who were eye-witnesses of all the transactions of that day. The leaders here have taken pains to prevent any account of this affair getting abroad but such as they have thought proper to publish themselves; and to that end the post has been stopped, the mails broke open, and letters taken out; and by these means the most injurious and inflammatory accounts have been spread throughout the continent, which has served to deceive and inflame the minds of the people.

When the resolves of the provincial congress breathed nothing but war; when those two great and essential prerogatives of the King, the levying of troops and disposing of the public monies, were wrested from him; and when magazines were forming, by an assembly of men unknown to the constitution, for the declared purpose of levying war against the King, you must acknowledge it was my duty, as it was the dictate of humanity, to prevent, if possible, the calamities of a civil war, by destroying such magazines. This, and this alone, I attempted.

You ask, why is the town of Boston now shut up? I can only refer you for an answer to those bodies of armed men who now surround the town, and prevent all access to it. The hostile preparations you mention are such as the conduct of the people of this province has rendered it prudent to make, for the defence of those under my command. You assure me the people of your colony abhor the idea of taking arms against the troops of their Sovereign; I wish the people of this province (for their own sakes) could make the same declaration.

You ask, whether it will not be consistent with my duty to suspend the operations of war on my part? I have commenced no operations of war,

but defensive; such you cannot wish me to suspend while I am surrounded by an armed country, who have already begun, and threaten
further to prosecute an offensive war, and are now violently depriving me,
the King's troops, and many others of the King's subjects under my immediate protection, of all the conveniences and necessaries of life, with
which the country abounds. But it must quiet the minds of all reasonable
people when I assure you that I have no disposition to injure or molest
quiet and peaceable subjects; but on the contrary shall esteem it my greatest happiness to defend and protect them against every species of violence
and oppression.

Benjamin Franklin commented ironically:

You will see by the papers that General Gage called his assembly to
propose Lord North's pacific plan; but before they could meet, drew the
sword and began the war. His troops made a most vigorous retreat –
twenty miles in three hours – scarce to be paralleled in history; the feeble
Americans, who pelted them all the way, could scarce keep up with them.

George Washington wrote:

General Gage acknowledges that the detachment under Lieutenant-
Colonel Smith was sent out to destroy private property; or, in other
words, to destroy a magazine, which self-preservation obliged the inhabitants to establish. And he also confesses, in effect at least, that his men
made a very precipitate retreat from Concord, notwithstanding the reinforcement under Lord Percy; the last of which may serve to convince Lord
Sandwich and others, of the same sentiment, that the Americans will fight
for their liberties and property, however pusillanimous in his lordship's
eye they may appear in other respects.

   From the best accounts I have been able to collect of that affair, indeed
from every one, I believe the fact, stripped of all colouring, to be plainly
this, that, if the retreat had not been as precipitate as it was and God
knows it could not well have been more so, the ministerial troops must
have surrendered, or been totally cut off. For they had not arrived in
Charlestown (under cover of their ships) half an hour before a powerful
body of men from Marblehead and Salem was at their heels, and must, if
they had happened to be up one hour sooner, inevitably have intercepted
their retreat to Charlestown. Unhappy it is, though, to reflect that a
brother's sword has been sheathed in a brother's breast, and that the once
happy and peaceful plains of America are either to be drenched with
blood, or inhabited by slaves. Sad alternative! But can a virtuous man hesitate in his choice?

*

It had been a futile, provocative expedition, and Gage bears the prime responsibility for ordering it. Percy merely showed the wisdom of hindsight in realizing that the British side should have expected the quantity and ferocity of the American resistance they found.

Yet certain other features of this first ugly battle of the American War of Independence stand out. In attempting to capture the arsenal at Concord, the British were asserting their hitherto undisputed rights. Moreover, the accumulation of arms, weapons and trained men in Concord was expressly aimed at the British, so it was specious to argue that the British 'provoked' the 'battle' of Concord by sending out their troops to seize it. Long before Smith and his men set out for Concord, the Americans were in a state of rebellion, of which assembling the arsenal was a major part.

Given the record of the British in Boston, and of Gage's almost pusillanimous moderation and reasonableness, it is hard to argue that this was a legitimate act of self-defence by the people against British oppression. The British had failed to arrest the revolutionary leaders hopping in and out of Boston; they had failed up to then even to disarm Bostonians or prevent their anti-British demonstrations, and had made no forays at all into the countryside except to seize munitions depots that might be used against them.

The large deposits set up at Worcester and Concord were a provocation, as was the elaborate system of militia alerts and express riders built up over months, if not years. Concord and Lexington demonstrated that the whole of Massachusetts was an armed camp waiting for the spark to start a conflagration, watching for the signal to move against the British.

Not even the rebels had ever claimed that the British were not the legitimate authority in the area – to do so would have been open rebellion against the British Crown, and they were intent on portraying themselves in the role of victims of British brutality, not aggressors. Although the rebels immediately went to great lengths to gather testimony as to who had fired the first shot at Lexington (which is disputed) and at Concord (which the British did, in panic), the verdict is beside the point.

Had the British committed the small shooting of militiamen on Lexington Green and then been unmolested in Concord, right would have attached to the rebel cause. But the battles of Lexington and Concord were minor skirmishes; the real battle was of the gauntlet the British were forced to run. To portray this carefully organized ambush as a spontaneous reaction against the British 'massacre' at Lexington is stretching credulity to breaking point. Conceivably, had the shootings at Lexington not occurred, there would have been no subsequent attack on the British forces. It is just as likely, such were the numbers, preparedness and positioning of rebel forces along the road, that the American motive in not attacking in earnest until the retreat from Concord had begun was to lure the British as far as possible into the trap before springing it.

American historiography has preferred to concentrate on the romantic heroism of Paul Revere's ride and other minor episodes. That is because the British ignition of the American War of Independence was nothing of the kind, although it was a good excuse. The Americans' carefully constructed military machine outside Boston had set a well-laid trap, and the British had blundered into it, displaying appallingly faulty intelligence.

Modern American studies – such as Joseph Hackett Fischer's perceptive *Paul Revere's Ride*, and those by John Galvin – show how well organized the American militiamen were in mustering, weaponry and tactics. The Americans had been preparing for such an attack for months. Despite the element of revenge for the deaths at Lexington, no serious student can argue that the orchestrated assaults on the British force by up to 7,000 trained and armed American militiamen was a blind act of revenge by downtrodden farmers. It was a declaration of war by rebels yearning for the excuse the British had taken so long to provide. Yet that (even in those days) most legalistic of peoples had not repudiated British rule, and even the likes of Paul Revere continued to refer to the army as 'the regulars' – not 'the British'. The full tally of British 'atrocities' that had led up to that merciless ambush along the sixteen miles from Concord to Boston was five dead in Boston eleven years before, and the half dozen at Lexington during an exchange of fire.

Now nearly 300 British soldiers had been killed or wounded – three times the number of attackers – in a series of rolling ambushes involving several thousand armed and trained militiamen. The American military leaders could be rightly proud of the impressive military skill with which irregulars had routed a major British force in a surprise attack – rendered all the more so since the two sides were not formally at war – staged on their own terrain and at a time of their choosing.

\*

Within days of the defeat, Joseph Warren was at work turning the events into an indignant response by a peace-loving people to British provocation.

> The barbarous murders committed on our innocent brethren, on Wednesday, the 19th instant, have made it absolutely necessary that we immediately raise an army to defend our wives and children from the butchering hands of the inhuman soldiery, who, incensed at the obstacles they met in their bloody progress, and enraged at being repulsed from the field of slaughter, will, without the least doubt, take the first opportunity in their power to ravage this devoted country with fire and sword. We conjure you, therefore, by all that is dear, by all that is sacred, that you give all assistance possible in forming an army. Our all is at stake. Death and devastation are the instant consequences of delay. Every moment is infinitely precious. An hour lost may deluge your country in blood, and entail perpetual slavery upon the few of your posterity who may survive the carnage. We beg and entreat, as you will answer to your country, to your own consciences, and above all, as you will answer to God himself, that you will hasten and encourage by all possible means the enlistment of men to form the army.

Another propagandist wrote:

> I would only ask, if in all your reading of history, you have found an instance of irregular troops, hurried together at a moment's warning, with half the number at first, attacking ... veterans, picked men for 17 miles, and continually firing the whole way, and not losing one third the number they killed? I view the hand of God in it, a remarkable interposition of Providence in our favour.

On 5 May, Gage was denounced by the Massachusetts assembly and at last rejected as a source of legitimate government by the assembly that itself had no legal right to sit:

> Whereas his Excellency General Gage, since his arrival in this colony, had conducted as an instrument in the hands of an arbitrary ministry to enslave this people ... Resolved, that the said General Gage hath, by these means, and many others utterly disqualified himself to serve this colony as a governor ...

But even this was not a declaration of war. Even in Massachusetts, the legalistic radicals could not be certain of carrying public opinion with them, although they did their best to influence it in lurid fashion. The first newspaper account of the battle was headed, below a masthead of forty coffins, 'Bloody Busting by the British or the Runaway Flight of the Royals'.

It had been a savage beginning for the 'glorious cause' of American freedom. The tactics of sniping with muskets, of ambushes from woods, hills and behind boulders and houses, of constant harassment, of the moving front and 'circle of fire', were examples of guerrilla warfare of a kind American soldiers would one day themselves learn to hate. It was just these tactics that were to prove most successful throughout the American War of Independence, until the final British surrender at Yorktown. Their first appearance gave – or should have given – the British a convincing foretaste of what was in store. Certainly the now doomed Gage understood the threat clearly enough:

> The rebels are not the despicable rabble too many have supposed them to be, and I find it owing to a military spirit encouraged amongst them for a few years past, joined with an uncommon degree of zeal and enthusiasm that they are otherwise ... In all their wars against the French they never showed so much conduct, attention and perseverance as they do now.

Britain's Vietnam had begun – and, as with Vietnam, the opposition to the colonial power understood that the first priority was to influence opinion in the home of that power itself.

The first news of the engagement to arrive in Britain came not from Gage but from documents prepared by Americans aboard a fast schooner. These documents included depositions from those present at the battle – which were instantly published in the press. While the North administration prevaricated, this American version of events gained widespread acceptance in England. One of the government's supporters complained, 'The town is full of private letters from America which contain much more particular accounts of the skirmish than are related by the general. They don't do much credit to the discipline of our troops, but do not impeach their readiness and intrepidity.'

While a free press flourished in England, the same could not always be said for New England: the *Massachusetts Gazette* and *Boston Post-Boy*, both previously loyal to Britain, shut down after the battle while the *Boston News Letter* was terrorized into submission by the rebels. Gage's dry factual account made little impression.

The whole sorry tale was later engulfed in myth – in particular that surrounding the midnight ride of Paul Revere. Ebenezer Stiles was the first to paint this:

> Listen my children, and you shall hear,
> Of the midnight ride of Paul Revere,
> On the eighteenth of April, in Seventy-five;
> Hardly a man is now alive
> Who remembers that famous day and year.
>
> For, borne on the night-wind of the past,
> Through all our history to the last,
> In the hour of darkness and peril and need,
> The people will waken and listen to hear,
> The hurrying hoof-beats of that steed,
> And the midnight message of Paul Revere.

Longfellow was next:

> He raced his steed through field and wood
> Nor turned to ford the river,
> But faced his horse to the foaming flood
> They swam across together.
>
> He madly dashed o'er mountain and moor,
> Never slackened spur nor rein
> Until with shout he stood by the door
> Of the church on Concord green.

A war had begun, however, and two key Americans were instantly convinced of it. Thomas Paine, a recent immigrant, had left a disastrous career in England and arrived in the New World in 1774 to embark on a fresh life at the age of thirty-seven. There he started a new career as a journalist, being appointed editor of the *Pennsylvanian Magazine*. He recalled later that when the news of Lexington and Concord reached him 'The country into which I had just set my foot, was set on fire about my ears. No man was a warmer wisher for a reconciliation than myself, before the fatal nineteenth of April, 1775, but the moment the event of that day was known, I rejected the hardened, sullen-tempered Pharaoh of England forever.' John Adams, the most mischievous, querulous, but often moderate leader of the Boston cabal, set out himself to travel the sixteen miles to Concord, where he witnessed the devastation, the burials, the chaotic flight of refugees and the hurried training of militia – all the signs of imminent war. After his trip he announced, 'The die is cast, the Rubicon crossed.'

Even before news of Concord arrived, the British defences were being cranked up. A month after the disaster, on 25 May, a reinforcement of around 5,000 troops reached Boston from England, swelling the besieged garrison to a now formidable 10,000 men. Then, in November, Dartmouth was replaced by an advocate of a much tougher policy towards America, Lord George Germain (formerly Sackville).

Sackville was something of an oddball. In 1759 his failure to order his cavalry forward at the Battle of Minden, where he was a lieutenant-general in the British army, permitted the French to escape annihilation. Sackville was condemned, without reservation, possibly unfairly, in the ensuing court martial. The court found 'that Lord George Sackville is guilty of having disobeyed the orders of Prince Ferdinand of Brunswick … and it is the further opinion of this court that the said Lord George Sackville is, and he is hereby adjudged, unfit to serve his Majesty in any military capacity whatever'.

He escaped execution, however – much to George II's disgust – and was reinstated through the favour of George III.

Undoubtedly able, Germain felt the need to prove the determination and courage which had been brought into question. A grumpy man, obsessed with protocol and punctuality, he and the five principal generals were to be the most important figures in the British prosecution of the War of Independence.

Germain soon moved to replace Thomas Gage, commenting:

> General Gage, with all his good qualities, finds himself in a situation of too great importance for his talents. The conduct of such a war requires more than common abilities. The distance from the seat of government leaves much to the discretion and resources of the general, and I doubt whether Mr Gage will venture to take a single step beyond the letter of his instructions, and whether the troops will have the opinion of him as to march with confidence of success under his command.

As his juniors and later replacements, in his stead, he sent three generals: William Howe – younger brother of Richard, Viscount Howe, the overall commander in America and admiral of the navy forces there – who had led Wolfe's vanguard up the Heights of Abraham at Quebec, but otherwise was quiet-spoken, intelligent and idle by reputation;

Henry Clinton, who suffered from shyness and an almost paranoid inferiority complex; and Johnny Burgoyne, the most colourful, least judicious and most assertive of the three. Horace Walpole wrote of them:

> Howe was one of those brave and silent brothers, and was reckoned sensible, though so silent that nobody knew whether he was or not. Burgoyne had offered himself for this service; he was a vain and ambitious man, with a half understanding that was worse than none; Clinton had not that fault, for he had no sense at all.

Given the additional troops, the three generals made it plain to their nominal superior, Gage, that remaining besieged and inert in Boston was not an option. However desperate the British predicament outside that city, the war had to be carried to the colonists.

The obvious course was to seize Dorchester Heights, which overlooked the city from the south and was a potential threat should the enemy get there first. From this strongpoint they could attack Roxbury to the west, then move north in a loop, securing their hold on the Charlestown peninsula and attacking the rebel stronghold of Cambridge to break the siege. The Americans were tipped off about the plan, however, and decided to move fast, seizing the peninsula, thus posing a threat to Boston from the north.

The stolid Massachusetts farmer placed in charge of the troops outside Boston, General Artemas Ward, had to be pressed into action by his more aggressive subordinates, Brigadier Israel Putnam, a tough fifty-seven-year-old farmer, and Colonel William Prescott, the forty-nine-year-old head of a distinguished local family. A thousand or so militiamen were sent to seize Bunker Hill, the 110-foot hillock just beyond the small 'neck' of the Charleston peninsula, from which it would be difficult for the British to dislodge the Americans.

The expedition set out on the night of 16 June. Once in control of Bunker Hill, they moved on to occupy the smaller 75-foot-high Breed's Hill, which was closer to Boston. Within a few hours they had raised a six-foot earthwork. When dawn broke they were spotted, and the British warship *Lively* opened up on them, soon joined by two other warships, a fortification in Boston and some floating batteries. Most of the shelling pounded harmlessly into the hillside, because the ships' guns could not be raised to the correct angle to hit the men on top, but at least one man near Prescott was decapitated. The Americans' water supply was also destroyed.

After nearly a day's vigorous work the men had built a 330-foot long rampart; but it could be outflanked at either end.

The British were not prepared to let the enemy seizure of a position overlooking Boston go unopposed; their position in the town would become untenable. The American offensive, the first move since Concord, escalated the war. Howe was appointed to command a landing force of 1,500 men on the left flank of the Americans on the Mystic river. Twenty-eight barges ferried these ramrod-straight troops in their red coats, bearing muskets and bayonets, to the landing place at noon.

There Howe found that some 200 Americans had managed to reinforce the left flank, building an improvised barrier of fencing and stones. Reinforced by a further 700 men, Howe staged a diversionary attack on the American right, while the main thrust would be on the left flank. However, the diversionary attack was greatly slowed by the rough ground at the bottom of the hill.

The Royal Welch Fusiliers, leading the main force in lines – instead of the columns prescribed by British military theory since the days of Wolfe, because they lacked space to manoeuvre – attacked with fixed bayonets, straight into American fire. No fewer than ninety-six fell on the beach, lying 'as thick as sheep in a fold', before the fusiliers were forced to retreat. It was now the turn of the burly grenadiers, who were also blown apart by musket fire.

The Americans bloodily repulsed another attack on both right and left before they virtually ran out of ammunition and a fourth assault finally took the British over the parapet.

Meanwhile the British fleet had opened up on Charlestown, and the whole town was spectacularly ablaze. Burgoyne, watching from Boston, gave a vivid description:

> Now ensued one of the greatest scenes of war that can be conceived. If we look to the height, Howe's corps ascending the hill in the face of the entrenchments and in a very disadvantageous ground was much engaged. To the left the enemy pouring in fresh troops by thousands [actually hundreds] over the land, and in the arm of the sea our ships and floating batteries cannonading them. Straight before us, a large and noble town [Charlestown] in one great blaze. The church steeples being of timber were great pyramids of fire above the rest. Behind us, the church steeples and heights of our own camp [and] ... the hills round the country covered with spectators. The enemy all in anxious suspense.
>
> The roar of cannon, mortars, and musketry, the crash of [shot hitting]

churches, ships upon the stocks, and whole streets falling together in ruins
to fill the ear; the storm of the redoubts with the objects above described
to fill the eye, and the reflection that perhaps a defeat would be a final loss
to the British Empire in America to fill the mind, made the whole a
picture and a complication of horror and importance beyond anything
that ever came to my lot to be witness to.

The British fell upon the Americans across the redoubt; many of their
opponents were killed, while the rest made their escape back to Bunker
Hill, and then to the mainland. Among the American dead was Joseph
Warren, Samuel Adams's closest confidant, who had enlisted as a private.
He was killed in the final assault, dressed in his best frock coat, and his
body was stuffed into a hole with that of another private, although it was
later recovered. He was the first significant martyr to the American
cause.

It had proved a pyrrhic victory for the British, as the Americans were
quick to point out: some 226 soldiers had been killed and a staggering
828 wounded, compared to 140 killed and 271 wounded on the
American side. Yet the royalists had carried the day: from a deeply dis-
advantageous position at the bottom of the hill, they had displaced
several hundred men from a fortified position on a height – a nearly
impossible military feat. As the Americans were later to discover at
Hamburger Hill in Vietnam in an eerie parallel almost two centuries
later, such a feat was no small achievement.

It had been essential for the British to take the hill, to prevent the
shelling of Boston. Yet more imaginative British tactics might have
averted so high a toll on their side. Given its strategic position, why had
they abandoned the peninsula, which they had previously controlled, in
the first place? The rump of the column from Concord had had to be
evacuated, of course, but they could have been replaced with fresh
troops. Why had the British not landed further up the Mystic river, at
the choke point of the 'neck' itself, where, backed by their ships, they
could have cut off the Americans – as indeed Clinton urged? The reason
given by the British – that they should not put themselves between two
fires – had some validity: they could only reinforce their beachheads at
a slow rate. A direct attack on Breed's Hill may have been the lesser of
two evils.

Howe had shown himself to be conventional and unimaginative. In
this, the first real engagement of the war, started by the Americans, the
British had gained their objective, but the Americans had inflicted

higher casualties and had won another propaganda victory. They could now boast two 'successes' against the supposedly invincible redcoats.

More important for the Americans, the British aim of occupying Dorchester Heights and looping round to Cambridge was now out of the question. This was to prove a strategic blunder, as Dorchester Heights would pose a threat to Boston if captured by the Americans. But the British were reluctant to risk a bridgehead on the mainland which could be surrounded by American forces and might have to be slowly and disastrously evacuated by sea. As before, caution triumphed.

For all the fresh ideas of Howe, Clinton and Burgoyne, the British now remained cooped up in a city under siege as tightly as before the arrival of reinforcements. This was a second major strategic blunder: for, having decided that the forces outside Boston were too concentrated to risk a sally out of the city, the British frittered away a full nine months, while those forces grew and Britain's loyalist supporters became progressively more demoralized.

If the British could not hope to prevail against Massachusetts, the best course of action was probably to abandon Boston and carry the war to areas where they enjoyed greater support, thereby seizing the initiative. Ignominious as this would be, the alternative was worse: to remain in Boston until the rebels' ceaseless campaign for support across the colonies made them strong enough to force the British out, with even greater loss of face – which was precisely what happened.

The great bulk of Americans were undecided whom to support, while many were openly loyalist. But for months, as the mother country took no initiative, they had no evidence that the British would indeed prevail. Time was to be a decisive factor in the war: the longer it dragged on, the more Americans were to believe the British could not win, and the more weary British educated opinion was to become with the conflict.

There were, to be sure, some logical arguments for the passive stance taken by the British generals. The least convincing was that with winter approaching, both sides should take to their quarters. But delay favoured the Americans, even in winter. Gage and Howe, the senior commanders, were members of the 'dove' faction in Britain, which argued that the less done to antagonize the Americans the better, believing that peace was still possible as the Americans realised the futility of their cause. The more 'hawkish' Clinton and Burgoyne may not have shared this view.

Howe in particular believed that British forces should be preserved at all costs: in the vastness of America, the expeditionary army was too small to take risks. Instead he argued for reinforcements, which the British government was reluctant to send at a time of financial stringency.

# 10

# *The Commander-in-Chief*

The Americans, meanwhile, were anything but inactive. Less than a month after the battle of Breed's Hill (widely dubbed Bunker Hill), John and Samuel Adams were leading the Massachusetts delegation to the second Continental Congress at Philadelphia, accompanied by the young, wealthy and arrogant John Hancock, who believed the hour had come in which he would be nominated leader of a great American army to rout the British from the colonies. The Massachusetts delegation was greeted everywhere with rapture for the colony's heroic role in resisting Britain.

But the delegation also had reason to be apprehensive. So far, Massachusetts alone had taken on the burden of resisting British military might. Unless they could persuade the other delegates to take up arms, the state risked being picked off and crushed as an example while the rest of the colonies looked on passively. Even if the delegates there supported the men from Massachusetts, they had far less control over public opinion in their own states than did the leaders in New England.

It was necessary to act with great dignity, and even the Adams cousins and Hancock refrained from calling for outright independence. The other colonies had accepted the Massachusetts version of events at Lexington and Concord, and of the American 'triumph' at 'Bunker Hill'. They could not be pushed too fast, however, towards the radicals' objectives. John Adams compared Congress to 'a coach and six – the swiftest horses must be shackled and the slowest quickened, that all may keep at an even pace'. John Dickinson of Pennsylvania, who emerged as leader of the moderate faction at the Congress, called for reconciliation with Britain, but was nevertheless pessimistic: 'What topics of reconciliation are now left for men who think as I do, to address our countrymen? To recommend reverence for the monarch, or affection for the mother country? ... No. While we revere and love our mother country, her sword is opening our veins.' Yet Congress still passed resolutions which spoke wistfully of the 'restoration of the former harmony between Great Britain and these colonies so ardently wished for by the latter [that] shall render it prudent and consistent with the overruling law of self-preservation'.

As yet there was no overt aspiration for independence – only for the assertion of American rights. But the Adamses and Hancock had an immediate practical objective: to ensure the other colonies' commitment to the notion of armed resistance against the British. Accordingly they produced a letter from James Warren, president of the Massachusetts Congress, seeking 'direction and assistance' in the armed struggle and recommending that a 'powerful army' be set up – and in particular that the Massachusetts militia be adopted as the embryo of an American army.

From the start the Massachusetts men had a powerful new ally: Benjamin Franklin had returned from England. Initially from Massachusetts, he was an adopted resident of Pennsylvania. To John Adams's delight, the mischievous old septuagenarian 'does not hesitate at our boldest measures, but rather seems to think us too irresolute and backward ... he thinks that we shall soon assume a character more decisive. He thinks that we have the power of preserving ourselves and that even if ... driven to ... independence and to set up a separate state, we can maintain it.'

The New York delegation had also become more radical, with the ponderous Dutch-descended Philip Schuyler its effective leader. Thomas Jefferson attended representing Virginia, along with Washington. However, the great southern landowning families and conservatives were not keen to grant leadership of the struggle to the radical egalitarians of Massachusetts. So an ingenious compromise was adopted: Congress would espouse the cause of Massachusetts – provided that it also assumed direction of the campaign and the army.

The Massachusetts militia was adopted as 'the American Continental Army' and Congress promised to raise ten companies of riflemen in Pennsylvania and Maryland and two light infantry regiments in Virginia, with £2 million in appropriations to be raised by the usual mixture of voluntary and strong-arm methods. But Hancock wanted the command. John Adams wrote:

Hancock himself had an ambition to be appointed commander-in-chief. Whether he thought an election a compliment due to him, and intended to have the honour of declining it, or whether he would have accepted, I know not. To the compliment he had some pretensions ... But the delicacy of his health, and his entire want of experience in actual service, though an excellent militia officer, were decisive objections to him in my mind.

Instead, Adams rose to nominate another man – 'a gentleman whose skill and experience as an officer, whose independence, great talents and excellent universal character would command the approbation of all America and unite the cordial exertions of all the colonies better than any other person in the union.' He noticed that 'mortification and resentment were expressed as forcibly as [Hancock's] face could exhibit them'.

The man Adams nominated was George Washington – certainly the most distinguished soldier in that motley assembly, and pointedly dressed in military uniform. Like Franklin, he already exhibited the authority of a leader; neither, according to Jefferson, spoke more than '10 minutes at a time ... They laid their shoulders to the great points, knowing that the little ones would follow of themselves.'

The leadership of the American cause was being hijacked from the levellers and homespun lawyers of Massachusetts. It was the key decision of Congress, and perhaps of the whole American Revolution until 1787: the propertied classes of the central and southern states were determined to prevail over the social-revolutionary protagonists of the American cause from the beginning. The tension between the two factions was to endure throughout the Revolution, and afterwards, first one side, then the other, gaining the upper hand. The Adamses, and other radicals from Massachusetts, desperately needing support for their cause, had no choice but to go along with Washington for the time being at least.

John Adams, indeed, had privately brokered the Washington nomination. Hancock was overbearing, and John Adams, unlike his cousin Samuel, was no social revolutionary. One delegate wrote:

[Washington] is a gent, highly esteemed by those acquainted with him though I don't believe ... he knows more than some of our [New England officers] but so it removes all jealousies, more firmly cements the southern to the northern ... He is clever, and if anything too modest. He seems discreet and virtuous, no harum scarum ranting fellow but sober, steady and calm.

John Adams wrote to his wife that Washington had been appointed to 'cement and secure the union of the colonies', and she was greatly impressed when she met him later: 'You had prepared me to entertain a favourable opinion of him, but I thought the half was not told me. Dignity with ease and complacency, the gentleman and the soldier look agreeably blended in him. Modesty marks every line and feature of his face.' Even Hancock swallowed his pride, writing to Warren: 'Washington … is a gentleman you will all like. I submit to you the propriety of providing a suitable place for his residence and the mode of his reception.'

Washington's acceptance speech was a model of restraint:

> Though I am truly sensible of the high honour done me in this appointment, yet I feel great distress, from a consciousness that my abilities and military experience may not be equal to the extensive and important trust. However, as the Congress desire it, I will enter upon the momentous duty, and exert every power I possess in the service, and for the support of the glorious cause. I beg they will accept my most cordial thanks for this distinguished testimony of their approbation.
>
> But, lest some unlucky event should happen, unfavourable to my reputation, I beg it may be remembered by every gentleman in this room, that I, this day, declare with the utmost sincerity, I do not think myself equal to the command I am honoured with. As to the pay, I beg leave to assure the congress that as no pecuniary consideration could have tempted me to accept this arduous employment, at the expense of my domestic ease and happiness, I do not wish to make any profit from it. I will keep an exact account of my expenses. Those, I doubt not, they will discharge; and that is all I desire.

He wrote to his wife:

> I am now set down to write to you on a subject, which fills me with inexpressible concern, and this concern is greatly aggravated and increased when I reflect upon the uneasiness I know it will give you. It has been determined in Congress, that the whole army raised for the defence of the American cause shall be put under my care, and that it is necessary for me to proceed immediately to Boston to take upon me the command of it.
>
> You may believe me … when I assure you, in the most solemn manner, that so far from seeking this appointment I have used every endeavour in my power to avoid it, not only from my unwillingness to part with you and the family, but from a consciousness of its being a trust too great for my capacity, and that I should enjoy more real happiness in one month

with you at home, than I have the most distant prospect of finding abroad, if my stay were to be seven times seven years. But as it has been a kind of destiny that has thrown me upon this service, I shall hope that my undertaking it is designed to answer some good purpose.

You might, and I suppose did perceive from the tenor of my letters, that I was apprehensive I could not avoid this appointment, as I did not pretend to intimate when I should return. That was the case. It was utterly out of my power to refuse this appointment, without exposing my character to such censures as would have reflected dishonour upon myself, and given pain to my friends. This, I am sure, could not, and ought not, to be pleasing to you, and must have lessened me considerably in my own esteem. I shall rely, therefore, confidently on that Providence which has heretofore preserved and been bountiful to me, not doubting but that I shall return safe to you in the fall.

I shall feel no pain from the toil or the danger of the campaign; my unhappiness will flow from the uneasiness I know you will feel from being left alone. I therefore beg that you will summon your whole fortitude, and pass your time as agreeably as possible. Nothing will give me so much sincere satisfaction as to hear this, and to hear it from your own pen. My earnest and ardent desire is, that you would pursue any plan that is most likely to produce content, and a tolerable degree of tranquillity; as it must add greatly to my uneasy feelings to hear that you are dissatisfied or complaining at what I really could not avoid.

A second immediate problem was faced by Congress. Assuming that the British would next land in strength in New York, what was that colony's response to be? Again, Congress was conciliatory: New York should remain on the 'defensive' so long as the British troops behaved peaceably and quietly.

The third challenge to Congress came with the astonishing news that in one area at least American irregulars had gone spectacularly on the offensive. A group of Connecticut businessmen had asked Ethan Allen, the thuggish, boisterous leader of a group of hillbillies who had already clashed with New York settlers, to seize the fort of Ticonderoga, a huge tumbledown French bastion at the bottom of Lake Champlain. Its only strategic value was that it commanded the approaches to Canada. The apparent purpose of this bizarre act of belligerence was to blunt a possible British thrust from Canada down this route. The real reason was a decision by Connecticut settlers to seize a slice of territory disputed with New York.

Ticonderoga – more a commune than an outpost – was seized with remarkable ease. The 'garrison' there – 2 British officers and 48 men with

24 women and children – was surprised in its sleep. Its one asset, a wealth of heavy artillery, had been neglected and was easily captured. Two days later Crown Point, another British stronghold in the north manned by just a dozen men, similarly fell. By this time Allen had been joined by a businessman and adventurer from Rhode Island, Benedict Arnold, who had been authorized by the rebels in Massachusetts to take command of the expedition. Both, however, soon lost control of the 200 men who had made the attacks. Meanwhile, the seizure of two barely manned British outposts, hailed as another triumph for the rebellion, further belied any claim by the Americans to be the victims rather than aggressors.

The general chosen to command the unified American army was, by an extraordinary stroke of fate for the Americans, a man of exceptional ability, who has deservedly gone down as one of the greatest men in human history, as well as of his country. This was anything but apparent at the time. George Washington had been a compromise choice, for a straightforward political motive: to gain the support of the southern states and their aristocracy, of which he was a relatively new if impressive representative, behind the conspirators who had triggered hostilities with Britain in Massachusetts.

At the time of his selection, Washington's greatest virtue appeared to be his dullness. A distinguished soldier who had taken part in Braddock's campaign in one of the great defeats of the Seven Years War, he had spent the next sixteen years as a worthy member of the state House of Burgesses, farming and indulging in the agreeable social life of wealthy Virginia. He was perhaps the most militarily experienced member of the Continental Congress, and the fact that he was a member at all showed that he was less placid and conventional than his exterior suggested.

The impression he gave was of an aloof, reserved man with a slightly superior manner and a remarkably high opinion of himself. This impression is confirmed by studies of his early life. By the age of forty-three, when appointed commander of American forces, he seemed to be an American General Gage – cautious, of impeccable military, if slightly nouveau-riche social, background, a soldier's soldier. Thomas Jefferson was to write that Washington's mind was not 'of the very first order... It was slow in operation, being little aided by invention or imagination but sure in conclusion.' John Adams remarked, 'That Washington was not a scholar is certain. That he was too illiterate, unlearned, unread for his station and reputation is equally past dispute.' A friend agreed with this, and complained of him that 'as usual the company was as grave as at a funeral'. He was a stern disciplinarian. There was no hint of the brilliant, daring, shrewdly political military strategist underlying the grey exterior.

Washington had been born in 1732 of a wealthy family of planters which claimed a minor gentry background in England as well as descent from one of the executed leaders of Wat Tyler's rebellion. He was a fourth-generation American – one of the oldest. His father died when he was eleven, and he then grew up in the shadow of his terrifying mother. One of his playmates remarked, 'Of the mother I was ten times more afraid that I ever was of my own parents ... whoever has seen the awe-inspiring air and manner so characteristic of the father of his country will remember the mother as she appeared as the presiding genius of her well-ordered household, commanding and being obeyed.' Astonishingly in one so young, he taught himself the practical skills of life: at thirteen he was already interested in accountancy and legal work.

His mentor was his half-brother Lawrence, a distinguished soldier, who encouraged the teenage George in many pursuits, including living out in the open in the western wilderness, and who on his death left George his large estate, when the young man was only nineteen. Washington, although on the losing side in Braddock's disastrous campaign, came away from the Seven Years War with a formidable reputation as a soldier. In 1759 he married a wealthy heiress, Martha Dandridge, who already had two children, and settled down to a solid and agreeably uneventful life as a farmer, exchanging visits with his friends, attending balls, and hunting with hounds.

Like all the southern landed gentry, he owned slaves, whom he treated humanely but severely. He was a hard taskmaster, endlessly chastizing his slaves for not working harder – one he called 'a very worthless fellow', another a 'lazy, deceitful and impudent huzzy' – or berating those who owed him money. He was socially cold and correct, privately often mean and moody.

As a young man, he had written a verse of banal charm which encapsulated his homespun character:

> These are the things which once possessed
> Will make a life that's truly blessed;
> A good estate on healthy soil
> Not got by vice, nor yet by toil;

Round a warm fire, a pleasant joke,
With chimney ever free from smoke;
A strength entire, a sparkling bowl,
A quiet wife, a quiet soul.

He was tall – six foot two – well built and physically extremely strong. Stiff and awkward in manner, he was shy, reserved and tongue-tied to an almost paralysing extreme. At the age of fourteen he wrote down a passage from a book, *Youth's Behaviour, or Drawing in Conversation among Men*: 'In the presence of others sing not to yourself with a humming noise, nor drum with your fingers or feet. Shake not the head, feet or legs, roll not the eyes, lift not one eyebrow higher than the other, wet not the mouth, and bedew no mans face with your spittle, by approaching too near him when you speak.'

Washington was less unassuming than he appeared. Immensely ambitious, he felt deeply slighted by his failure to prosper in the British army, in which his main, but frustrated, aim had been to gain a regular commission. He complained always of the way the British officers treated him.

Although frustrated and profoundly anti-British as a result of his military experience, he showed formidable self-control. Abigail Adams wrote, 'He has a dignity which forbids familiarity married with an easy, appealing mind which creates love and reverence.' He was extremely modest, rushing from the room when made commander-in-chief of American forces. John Marshall, one of his closest friends who became the first Chief Justice of the United States, wrote that his innate and unassuming modesty was

> Happily blended with a high ... sense of personal dignity, and with a just consciousness of the respect which is due to station. Endowed by nature with a sound judgment, and an accurate and discriminating mind, he ... was guided by an unvarying sense of moral right, which would tolerate the employment only of those means that would bear the most rigid examination.

His measured letter to his wife after his appointment revealed the iron determination beneath the modest exterior. But (as is so rarely the case) the iron will was married to a brilliant military and political mind – unbound by convention, yet wedded to the need for discipline that his idiosyncratic troops so singularly found unnecessary. In some respects the epitome of a martinet, he told his officers, 'Be easy and condescend-

ing in your deportment to your officers, but not too familiar, lest you
subject yourself to a want of that respect which is necessary to support
a proper command.' He later complained that Congress had limited the
number of lashes that could be given his soldiers, and he insisted on the
death penalty for mutineers in 1781.

He was also to show the ruthlessness, adaptability, resilience in adversity, and ability to rein in his own ambition at crucial moments that
together mark true greatness. He was utterly implacable towards his rival
American generals, and immensely politically skilled in dealing with
Congress.

Under the unassuming exterior this rich man on the margins of the
Virginia aristocracy was to display leadership, strength and dignity of
such an order that ultimately the whole American Revolution came to
revolve around him. His ability alone repeatedly helped to pluck victory
from defeat, and his character was to help shape the nature of the regime
that followed independence. The reputations of many of the 'founding
fathers' have been inflated; Washington's, if anything, was understated
through his own deliberate choice, and his very failings serve to
strengthen the reputation of not just a founding father but, after Samuel
Adams, the founding father.

Washington travelled north with apprehension, though eager to take up
his command, and arrived in Cambridge on 2 July with his two chief
subordinates, Charles Lee and Philip Schuyler from New York. The professional soldier from Virginia was unimpressed by the indiscipline of
the men who had started the American Revolution and now lay outside
Boston besieging the British. He wrote in exasperation, 'The abuses in
this army, I fear, are considerable and the new modelling of it, in the face
of an enemy, from whom we every hour expect an attack, is exceedingly
difficult and dangerous.'

In a curious echo of the views of British officers years earlier, he had
a low opinion of Massachusetts soldiers, who elected their own officers:

> An unaccountable kind of stupidity in the lower class of these people pre-
> vails but too generally among the officers of the Massachusetts part of the
> army who are nearly all the same kidney with the privates. There is no
> such thing as getting of officers of this stamp to exert themselves in car-
> rying orders into execution – to curry favour with the men (by whom they
> were chosen, and on whose smiles possibly they may think they may again
> rely) seems to be one of the principal objects of their attention.

He found that men would wander in and out of camp at will, would abandon their sentry duty when they felt like it, would take potshots at the British, and would even sometimes fraternize with the enemy. Their camps were filthy, with latrines, when they were used, filled to overflowing. He set about issuing the detailed orders needed to begin to place the army on a professional basis – ranging from concern that 'stale and unwholesome' food be thrown away to giving the men clean bedding, digging new latrines, and disposing of rubbish around the camp.

The soldiers were expected to conform to new standards of discipline: officers were cashiered and men were fined and lashed for misdemeanours. He ordered the powder the army was so sorely lacking, and built up new fortifications against the British. He declared:

> The continental congress having now taken all the troops of the seven colonies which have been raised, or which may be hereafter raised for the support and defence of the liberties of America, into their pay and service. They are now the troops of the United Provinces of North America and it is hoped that all distinctions of colonies will be laid aside, so that one and the same spirit may animate the whole, and the only contest be, who shall render, on this great and trying occasion, the most essential service to the great and common cause in which we are all engaged.

To prepare for the war, Washington had women sympathizers up and down the colonies sew no fewer than 14,000 coats for the men. Another major problem was the terms of enlistment, under which most of the men's service expired on 31 December. Washington introduced the concept of year-long enlistment, and tried to regroup the army into twenty-six infantry regiments of eight companies (some 700 men) each, a rifle regiment and an artillery regiment.

Enthusiastic as the Massachusetts men had been during the fervour of high summer, getting them to obey the new discipline through the rigours of a New England winter was another matter. By January 1776 only 12,500 men had joined the new Continental Army, and Washington was forced to depend on 7,000 of the ill-disciplined militia he deplored. It was hardly an auspicious start, or evidence of popular enthusiasm for the rebel cause. Washington lamented: 'After the last of this month, our lines will be so weakened that the minutemen and militia must be called in for their defence, these being under no kind of government themselves will destroy the little subordination I have been labouring to establish and run me into one evil, whilst I am endeavouring to avoid another.'

Two other major setbacks had made the Massachusetts men, in particular, pause for thought. The first was the death of the brave, verbose Joseph Warren at Breed's Hill. Then in August another of the original rebel cabal, Dr Benjamin Church, who had been appointed surgeon-general, sent a letter via a prostitute to be delivered to the British, outlining the dispositions of the 'American army outside Boston'. This was intercepted. He had been Gage's spy all along. John Adams was shocked: 'I stand astonished. A man of genius, of learning, of family, of character, a writer of liberty songs and good ones, too, a speaker of liberty orations ... Good God! What shall we say of human nature? What shall we say of American patriots?'

Church was arrested and eventually exiled to the West Indies, but the boat carrying him sank. Within a few months, of the five main leaders of the Massachusetts rebellion, one had been killed, one exposed as a spy, and one passed over as commander of American forces, leaving only the Adams cousins as major players in the American Revolution. Of the two, Samuel Adams, who had orchestrated resistance with bitter effectiveness, had been eclipsed by John, who was younger, more temperate, more intelligent and much more prepared to compromise with the Virginians who had hijacked the cause.

Ironically, the principal issue that had spurred Massachusetts, and in particular its militias, to rebellion – the existence of a standing professional army in its midst – was now a reality, in the shape of a growing professional army of continentals which equally despised the militias.

Dissatisfied as Washington was with his own side, his adversaries' behaviour remained perplexing. While the Americans drilled, regrouped and tried to build themselves up from a position of institutional weakness, the British, bloodied at Breed's Hill, stayed put and watched. Burgoyne, who was a gifted playwright, staged his own amateur theatricals; one sketch, *The Bloodbath of Boston*, was disrupted by American shelling, the audience initially believing this was part of the play. No attempt was made to arrange an expeditionary sally out of town, nor to abandon it. In England, Lord North opined that: 'I cannot help thinking that many of the principal persons in North America will, with the calmness of the winter, be disposed to bring forward a reconciliation. Now they are too angry, too suspicious and too much under the guidance of factious leaders.'

The British were apparently still being misled into believing that reconciliation was possible – although the King took a more militant line:

The authors and promoters of this desperate conspiracy ... meant only to amuse, by vague expressions of attachment to the parent state and the strongest protestations of loyalty to me, whilst they were preparing for a general revolt ... The rebellious war now levied is ... manifestly carried on for the purpose of establishing an independent empire. I am unalterably determined at every hazard and at every risk of every consequence to compel the colonies to absolute submission. It would be better totally to abandon them than to admit a single shadow of their doctrines.

While there was every argument for being prudent in venturing out of Boston, there was none for merely maintaining the status quo. General Howe, who late in 1775 at last had replaced the ineffectual, muddled, conscientiously peace-loving Gage, seemed barely more decisive as a commander.

Meanwhile the Americans, belying their contention that they still did not seek open war and independence from Britain, decided to strike at the soft overbelly of the British – Canada, controlled by a small British garrison and believed to be ripe for revolt: the huge French population there, while not necessarily pro-American, was believed to be deeply anti-British. With the authorization of Congress, there was now mounted one of the most colourful and heroic exploits of the war, though it was to end in debacle and humiliation for the American forces involved.

The American invasion of Canada was to be two-pronged: General Philip Schuyler, from New York, was to lead an expedition by the obvious route, from Fort Ticonderoga up the waterway of the great Lake Champlain, and drive on to Montreal. The second prong was to aim for Quebec along a fantastic route up the Kennebec river in Maine and down the St Lawrence. Washington was fully behind the expedition: he believed that the British Governor General in Canada, Sir Guy Carleton, could not hold both Montreal and Quebec simultaneously. He exhorted to the expeditionaries, 'Come then, ye generous citizens, range yourselves under the standard of General Liberty, against which all the force and artifice of tyranny will never be able to prevail. Use all possible expedition, as the winter season is now advancing. Upon the success of this enterprise, under God ... the safety and welfare of the whole continent may depend.'

On 28 August, Schuyler's second-in-command, the dashing and energetic General Richard Montgomery, who had fought with Wolfe at

Quebec, decided to set out from New York for Fort Ticonderoga while his superior, who was unwell, lingered at Albany. However, Schuyler soon caught up with him at Lake Champlain. The crossing, with 1,200 men, was easy enough, but when they reached the British garrison of 700 men at Fort St John they found themselves mired in mud outside the walls. Schuyler's illness returned and he went back to Albany, while Montgomery maintained a siege for fifty-five days before he was able to persuade the garrison to surrender on generous terms.

Ethan Allen, the hillbillyish leader of the 'Green Mountain Boys', had meanwhile been captured in a reckless attempt to take Montreal with a few hundred men. When Montgomery at last arrived at Montreal, Carleton had already departed, wisely deciding to avoid a fight there and concentrate his forces in Quebec.

In September 1775 the second expedition, under the command of the rash and larger-than-life Benedict Arnold, left from Newbury Fort to the north of Boston by boat. There were a thousand men altogether – three quarters from Massachusetts, the rest from Virginia and Pennsylvania. The Virginians' commander was Daniel Morgan, who, like Washington, had served with Braddock – he had once been given 500 lashes by the British for striking an officer. Of humble origin, he had been a farm labourer and wagoner, and was a gambler, a heavy drinker, a brilliant marksman, and a fiery and natural leader.

The expedition sailed to the mouth of the Kennebec. Faulty intelligence had led them to believe that Quebec was 180 miles away; in fact it was twice that distance. Arnold embarked his troops in *bateaux*, boats capable of carrying six or seven men with their provisions for the journey to the Great Carrying Place. There they plunged deep into the forested wilderness of Maine, shouldering the boats for twelve miles, which exhausted them, before returning to the David river, a fast-flowing and sometimes log-jammed stream.

The rain was torrential, and the men were so sodden that Arnold called them 'amphibious animals'. Most of the provisions had gone bad, and the men had virtually nothing to eat. Soon snow began to fall, and their clothing was inadequate. They were reduced to eating their mascot, a dog, as well as boiled shoe leather, cartridge boxes and shaving soap, and finally a spartan mixture of water and flour. A third of the men decided to turn back. A soldier recorded that the rest 'were so weak that they could hardly stand on their legs ... I passed by many sitting wholly drowned in sorrow ... Such pity-asking countenances I never before beheld. My heart was ready to burst.'

They had now crossed the Height of Land, the watershed between the Kennebec and Chaudière (Cauldron) rivers, and the starving, exhausted men plunged into the boiling rapids past Lake Megani down to Quebec. On the Chaudière, at last, they found a settlement and ate fresh food. They reached the St Lawrence during the first week of November, some seven weeks after setting out from the mouth of the Kennebec: 675 men were left after an epic of endurance which had left the army in a pitiable state.

Arnold positioned his men around the city, which now had a garrison of some 1,800. Unable to attack with inferior forces and without artillery, he prudently withdrew to some twenty miles away, where they would be safe from British attack. His troops were in no condition to fight. A month later Montgomery's forces reached him after journeying up the St Lawrence, bearing cannon, ammunition, winter clothing and food. With 300 reinforcements, the expeditionary force was now of a more respectable size.

They decided to risk all in an attempt to take the town. Many of the men, whose terms of enlistment would end on 31 December, wanted to return. Moreover, in spring the ice blocking the St Lawrence would melt, and the British could bring reinforcements down the waterway. Promising to let the wretched troops plunder the town, the two American commanders waited for a deep snowstorm to cover their attack at 5 a.m. on New Year's Eve.

The assault on Quebec proved a complete fiasco. Struggling forward in the blizzard beneath the rocky fortifications once successfully stormed by Wolfe, the 1,000 American rebels were up against some 2,000 men armed with 150 cannon. The expected surge of support from French-speaking Canadians had not materialized. Arnold had just unwisely signalled his intention to attack by sending a letter demanding the garrison's surrender. The British commander had the letter taken from the messenger with a pair of tongs and dropped it unread into his fire. When the assault got under way, feints were made against several gates, while Montgomery attacked from the west along the bank of the St Lawrence, and Arnold from the north against Lower Town. The British were prepared: Montgomery was killed by a volley and his men were cut down, while the rest retreated in panic. The town bells warned of the approach of Arnold's forces, and cannon mowed the troops down until they took shelter under the Lower Town's houses, where they were caught in a crossfire and surrendered. Some 426 Americans were taken prisoner and 60 killed, after Morgan had twice ascended a ladder into the citadel and been repulsed.

Benedict Arnold, injured in the leg, withdrew a mile outside Quebec. There his forces remained while Arnold begged for reinforcements from the pompous, incompetent, elderly commander in Montreal, General David Wooster. In despair, Arnold gave up his command in April 1776. Meanwhile the indefatigable Franklin led a delegation on an uncomfortable journey to assess the situation in Canada. He was instantly convinced of its 'utter hopelessness'.

An attempt was made to reinforce the American troops in Canada, but when a British army of 13,000 men under Burgoyne arrived in May, according to an American doctor, 'In the most helter skelter manner we raised the siege leaving everything: all the camp equipage, ammunition, and even our clothing, except what little we happened to have on us … Most of our sick fell into their hands.'

Arnold wrote:

> My whole thoughts are now bent on making a safe retreat out of this country; however, I hope we shall not be obliged to leave it until we have had one more bout for the honour of America. I think we can make a last stand at Île-aux-Noix, and keep the lake this summer from an invasion that way. We have little to fear; but I am heartily chagrined to think that we have lost in one month all the immortal Montgomery was a whole campaign in gaining, together with our credit, and as many men, and an amazing sum of money.

He and his wretched troops joined the other American forces at Île-aux-Noix, south of St John's on the way to Lake Champlain, where their strength was an impressive 8,000; but, by now demoralized, they retreated to Crown Point.

The gallant, sorry expedition had been a quixotic disaster – based on false intelligence, ill planned, with too small a force and an unattainable objective. The American army showed itself to be far from capable of taking on the British in open battle. The British tragedy was in failing to learn from the Americans' folly in crossing the wildernesses on extended supply lines into Canada, when they launched their own expedition the other way soon afterwards.

While the ill-fated Canada expedition was under way, and the two armed camps stared at each other across the waters of Boston harbour, another conflagration was lit in Virginia by its loyalist governor, John Murray, Earl of Dunmore. Like the governors of North and South Carolina, in June 1775 he had fled to safety aboard a British warship.

Dunmore had been considering a truly radical measure for the times: the emancipation of slaves, so as to deprive Virginian planters of their labour force and provide recruits for the British side. Governor Josiah Martin of North Carolina had written, 'The whites are greatly out-numbered by the negroes, at least in [South Carolina]: a circumstance that would facilitate exceedingly the reduction of these colonies which are very sensible of their weakness arising from it.'

Dunmore had expressed his view to London that he could 'collect from among the Indians, negroes and other persons' a force large enough to neutralize Virginia. Slaves had already turned up to the governor's mansion offering their services to him, and the House of Burgesses, aware that something was afoot, wrote that 'a scheme, the most diabolical, has been meditated and generally [approved] by a person of great influence to effect freedom to our slaves and turn them against their masters'.

By October 1775 Dunmore's daredevil scheme was under way. One observer, wrote that: 'A declaration his lordship has made, of proclaim-ing all the negroes free who should join him, has startled the insurgents.'

On 7 November Dunmore declared 'all indentured servants, negroes, or others (appertaining to rebels), free, that are able and willing to bear arms, they joining His Majesty's troops, as soon as may be, for the more speedily reducing the colony to a proper sense of their duty, to His Majesty's crown and dignity'.

This proclamation had an electric effect. As far as the southern colo-nies were concerned, the concept of the rights of man and of freedom emphatically did not extend to slaves: one observer in Pennsylvania commented, 'Hell itself could not have invented anything more black than this design of emancipating our slaves.' Another wrote that 'the proclamation will more effectively work an external separation between Great Britain and the colonies than any other expedient which could possibly have been thought of'. Washington wrote, 'If that man [Dunmore] is not crushed before spring, he will become the most for-midable enemy America has; his strength will increase as a snowball is by rolling; and faster, if some expedition cannot be hit upon to convince the slaves and servants of the impotency of his designs.'

Virginian planters were quick to issue their own warnings to the slaves, who, they said, would be treated much worse by the cruel Dunmore than under their masters 'who pity their conditions, who wish in general to make it as easy and comfortable as possible, and who would willingly, were it in their power, or were they permitted, not only prevent any more negroes from losing their freedom, but restore it to such as have already unhappily lost it'. Slaves were warned that the penalty for insurrection was death without benefit of clergy – but those who chose to return would be pardoned. Some recaptured runaway slaves were indeed executed.

As soon as Dunmore issued his proclamation, some 200 slaves made their way to his ships, followed soon afterwards by a further 300. Before more could join him, he overconfidently landed a force of 600 at Greta Bridge near Norfolk, Virginia, and was badly beaten off with the loss of some sixty men; he hurriedly abandoned the town, his last foothold on land. However, boats taken over by small numbers of slaves continued to join him. One prominent planter described the flight of eleven of his servants:

> Last night after going to bed, Moses, my son's man, Joe, Billy, Postillion, John, Mullatto, Peter, Tom, Panticove, Manuel and Lancaster Sam, ran away, to be sure, to Ld. Dunmore, for they got privately into Beale's room before dark and took out my son's gun and one I had there, took out of his drawer in my passage all his ammunition furniture, Landon's bag of bullets and all the powder, and went off in my pettiauger new trimmed, and it is supposed that Mr Robinson's people are gone with them, for a skow they came down in is, it seems, at my landing. These accursed villains have stolen Landon's silver buckles, George's shirts, Tom Parker's new waistcoat and breeches.

Dunmore dubbed his regiment of ex-slaves 'Lord Dunmore's Ethiopian Regiment'. They were kitted out in military uniforms with the words 'Liberty to Slaves' emblazoned across them.

But by March 1776 tragedy had struck the men cooped up on board ship: fever carried off 'an incredible number of people, especially blacks'. Forced off Gwynn's Island, where he sought shelter, the governor and his 100 or so small craft sailed up the Potomac, where they carried out a number of attacks on land, then abandoned sixty of the disease-ridden boats, the remainder sailing northward with 300 freed slaves still aboard. Yet that short time in which a white governor had proclaimed freedom to slaves had awoken the hopes of thousands. In New York a black child was named Lord Dunmore; in Philadelphia blacks shouted his name to harass whites.

*

However mixed his motives, Dunmore had touched on a raw nerve. Rhode Island, Delaware and Connecticut had come out against the slave trade in principle, with lukewarm support from Pennsylvania. But the majority of the colonists – especially in the south – vehemently supported slavery. Washington and Jefferson were both slave-owners.

Moreover, although blacks were initially permitted to join Massachusetts regiments, by the end of 1775 they were excluded from the American forces, probably to discourage slaves from seeking to escape servitude by joining the army, and also to prevent them acquiring guns and military training for fear 'our slaves when armed might become our masters'. Coinciding with Massachusetts's efforts to bring Virginia and the south into the war, this represented an attempt to pander to the slave-owning colonies.

In South Carolina, North Carolina and Maryland, whites were armed for fear of black insurrection. When the Continental Army was set up under Washington, blacks were weeded out. 'Many northern blacks were excellent soldiers, but several troops would not brook [any equality] with whites,' wrote one American commentator.

Horatio Gates, Adjutant General of the American Continental Army, decided that it should not recruit 'any deserter from the ministerial army, nor any stroller, negro or vagabond'. On 8 October 1775 the patriot army's eight principal generals decided to keep both freed blacks and slaves out of the army. 'Negroes, boys unable to bear arms or old men unfit to endure the fatigues of the campaign' were banished.

Massachusetts itself passed an act prohibiting the enlistment of blacks, Indians and mulattos. South Carolina, Virginia, Pennsylvania, Rhode Island, Delaware, New Jersey, New York and Connecticut all followed suit: lunatics, idiots and blacks (in that order) were barred from joining the patriot cause. As manpower shortages made themselves felt later in the war, this was to change; but even the northern colonies without slaves effectively spurned fully a fifth of the American population as unfit to share in the freedom they proclaimed as their guiding principle.

There were, however, flickerings of a conscience. In Britain, hostility to slavery was already an occasional concern of the chattering classes, and emancipation and reform were to reach the top of the political agenda within three decades. In a landmark decision, Chief Justice Mansfield in 1772 ruled on behalf of James Somerset, a slave brought to England, that he 'be discharged'. Slavery, said the Judge, was 'so odious' that 'I cannot say this case is allowed or approved by the law of England.' Three days after the ruling, Lord Mansfield's health was echoed around a ballroom in which 200 blacks and their ladies had gathered 'to celebrate the triumph of their brother Somerset'. The ruling effectively outlawed slavery in England.

The slave trade was a home-grown feature of American and Caribbean society, not imposed by the British, and any attempt by the latter to abolish it would have been viewed as an outrageous interference. The British government was at worst indifferent and had no wish to take on the vested interests of the southern planters or the far more vociferous slave-owning lobby in the West Indies and their representatives in Parliament.

But, inasmuch as the ruling elite paid any attention, it was fashionable to be appalled by the slave trade, which in a matter of years the government was seeking to ban – although not the institution of slavery itself. There was cynicism in the British decision to call for a slave uprising in the southern states – slaves provided recruits for the British, and unsettled the whites there. But, equally, opinion in Britain was moving against slavery, and a clash would have been inevitable had the colonies remained in the British Empire. The southern colonists, of course, were passionate defenders of the institution on which their livelihood depended, and, with few exceptions, the northern colonists were prepared to support them. Samuel Johnson famously remarked that 'the loudest yelps for liberty' came from 'the drivers of Negroes'.

Men like the Reverend Samuel Hopkins, from Newport, Rhode Island, sought to free slaves and use them as missionaries to carry the Gospel back to Africa. The Quaker schoolmaster Anthony Benezet was another emancipationist. As Benjamin Rush wrote in 1773, 'Anthony Benezet stood alone a few years ago, in opposing negro slavery in Philadelphia; and now three-fourths of the province, as well as of the city, cry out against it. A spirit of humanity and religion begins to awaken, in several of the colonies in favour of the poor negroes.'

Thomas Paine's first published essay on his arrival in America was on the subject of slavery: 'That some desperate wretches should be willing to steal and enslave men by violence and murder for gain, is rather lamentable than strange. But that many civilised, nay, Christianised people should approve, and be concerned in the savage practice, is surprising.'

Only very occasionally, slaves who had the necessary financial backing were allowed to buy their freedom. As one group declared: 'We have no property! We have no rights! We have no children! No liberty! No country!'

Massachusetts was the centre of such anti-slavery feeling as there was in America. As early as 1766, Samuel Adams, John Hancock and James Otis Sr had moved for a law 'to prohibit the importation and purchasing of slaves'. There were few slaves in the north anyway, and New Hampshire, Rhode Island, Connecticut and New Jersey all declared themselves against the trade, as did Pennsylvania. One prominent black artisan and minor businessman, Prince Hall, took the British side in Boston.

Phillis Wheatley, at only twenty in 1774, became a prodigy – a poet admired by Voltaire and a powerful advocate of her cause to the Earl of Dartmouth:

> Should you, my lord, while you peruse my song,
> Wonder from whence my love of freedom sprung,
> I, young in life, by seeming cruel fate
> Was snatched from Africa's fancied seat:
> Such, such my case. And can I then but pray
> Others may never feel tyrannic sway?

She petitioned Washington in late 1775:

> Thee, first in place and honours – we demand
> The grace and glory of thy martial band.
> Famed for thy valour, for thy virtues more
> Here every tongue thy guardian aid implore!

He, for fear of offending his Virginian supporters and perhaps reflecting his own prejudices, refused to publish her anthology but offered to make her welcome if she, now freed, ever visited.

By 1783 slavery was all but outlawed by the courts in Massachusetts. In Pennsylvania in 1778, a measure was passed to give children of slaves their freedom when they reached the age of twenty-eight. But measures to abolish slavery were quashed, in Rhode Island, New Hampshire, New York and New Jersey, while in the southern states they were beyond consideration.

It was not quite the most shameful chapter in America's struggle for freedom: that description belongs to the Americans' treatment of the Indians, the native people of America, there long before the colonists themselves had arrived.

\*

In November 1775 Washington had dispatched a tall, fat, gregarious colonel of artillery, Henry Knox, to Ticonderoga to retrieve the British cannon captured there. In an astonishing piece of military professionalism and endurance, Knox succeeded beyond Washington's wildest expectations. He arranged the removal of 44 guns, 14 mortars and a howitzer from the fort on flat-bottomed boats across Lake George. This colossal armoury was then transported 300 miles across the mountains on sleds, crossing the Hudson river no fewer than four times along the journey. One gun broke loose into the water and sank; by February the others were ready for action outside Boston.

Overjoyed to see them, Washington, whose army was by now organized, although not increased to full strength, urged an attack across the ice from Cambridge to Boston. His fellow commanders rejected this, but accepted a lesser plan to mount the artillery on Dorchester Heights, from where they could pound the town at their leisure. Astonishingly, the British had made no move to occupy the heights. They had no confident, competent, instinctively aggressive equivalent of Washington. Scarred by their experience at Breed's Hill, the British did nothing except mount the odd cannonade against the American forces ranged opposite.

On 2 March 1776 the Americans launched a bombardment of Boston which the British answered heavily but ineffectively. Under cover of darkness, 2,000 Americans quietly ascended Dorchester Heights with the cannon and huge bundles of equipment. The icy ground was so hard that it was impossible for the men to dig in. Their ingenious solution was to erect two barricades of earth on Dorchester Point and two on their flanks, the earth having been dragged up on 300 ox carts during that long night.

Meanwhile Washington prepared forces for an attack across the ice should the British attack the heights. Howe, who by now had at last decided in principle to evacuate Boston as untenable, awoke the following morning to find the American guns in place. His naval commander, Admiral Molyneux Shuldham, who had succeeded Graves, now on leave, told him that the navy must move out of reach of the American heavy guns immediately. Howe had no choice but to attack or to watch as Boston was blown to bits.

He prepared to attack; but that night a violent storm forced him to postpone this and the British fleet had to put out to sea. Belatedly, he decided to speed up evacuation of the garrison. Boston was a city under siege in hostile territory, protected only by water: the men had no chance of breaking out without reinforcements and far more vigorous leadership.

After negotiations under a flag of truce, Washington agreed not to attack provided the British left Boston intact. On 17 March, after nearly a year wasted, they sailed away to Halifax, where they could regroup and pursue a more vigorous strategy with the help of reinforcements from Halifax itself and Nova Scotia.

Without losing a single man, Washington had won the first real American victory of the war. Moreover, the British withdrawal from Boston provided the American radicals with a formidable propaganda coup. Abigail Adams chortled, 'The more I think of it, the more amazed I am that they should leave such a harbour, such fortifications, such entrenchments, and that we should be in peaceable possession of a town which we expected would cost us a river of blood.'

Washington's raw and still enthusiastic men and the patriots' supporters across America could boast of having forced the British out of Boston with their tails between their legs. It proved a powerful boost to a cause set back by the recent humiliation in Canada (although this was not widely known, having been hidden from the troops), and greatly increased support for the rebels.

# II

# *We Hold These Truths*

The radicals were now powerfully enouraged in their efforts to persuade the next Continental Congress to aim for outright independence from Britain. Meanwhile Britain's ban on all trade with America, and rumours that the British planned to send major reinforcements, including German mercenaries, played into the radicals' hands. In January 1776 an incendiary pamphlet was published which for the first time cut through all the colonists' protests that their actions were directed not against Britain or the Crown, but only against Parliament and the army.

*Common Sense* by Thomas Paine, one of the greatest best-sellers in American history relative to population, selling 100,000 copies at the time, was a direct attack on the institutions of government in Britain, and on the link between the mother country and the colonies. Above all, it was a radical statement of the rights of Americans, calling for outright independence.

With this document the revolutionaries had regained the initiative and seemed about to win control of the American cause. The conservatives, now led in Congress by John Dickinson, had no choice but to go along with the tide or be swept under in the wake of a social or popular revolution.

Paine's pamphlet was a masterpiece of plain speaking:

> We have it in our power to begin the world over again. The birthday of a new world is at hand, and a race of men, perhaps as numerous as all Europe contains, are to receive their portion of freedom from the events of a few months. Every spot in the old world is overrun with oppression.

The British constitution, it argued, was founded on 'the base remains of two ancient tyrannies' – monarchy and aristocracy. The monarchy was 'the most pernicious invention the devil ever set in force for the propagation of idolatry'. The principle of hereditary succession was a violation of nature, 'otherwise she would not so frequently turn it to ridicule by giving mankind an ass for an heir'. Paine went on:

> Male and female are the distinctions of nature, good and bad the distinction of heaven; but how a race of men came into the world so exalted above the rest, and distinguished like some new species, is worth enquiring into, and whether they are the means of happiness or of misery to mankind ... In England a king hath little more to do than to make war and give away places; which, in plain terms, is to impoverish the nation and set it together by the ears. A pretty business indeed for a man to be allowed eight hundred thousand sterling a year for, and worshipped into the bargain. Of more worth is one honest man to society, and in the sight of God, than all the crowned ruffians that ever lived.

As for the relationship between America and Britain:

> I have heard it asserted by some, that as America hath flourished under her former connection with Great Britain, that the same connection is necessary towards her future happiness, and will always have the same effect. Nothing can be more fallacious than this kind of argument. We may as well assert that because a child has thriven upon milk, that it is never to have meat ... We have boasted the protection of Great Britain, without considering that her motive was interest not attachment; that she did not protect us from our enemies on our account, but from her enemies on her own account, from those who had no quarrel with us on any other account, and who will always be our enemies on the same account. Let Britain waive her pretensions to the continent, or the continent throw off the dependence, and we should be at peace with France and Spain ...

It was powerful stuff, brilliantly written. More than that, it was authentically incendiary and revolutionary in its assertion of republicanism over monarchy. Throughout Europe – and indeed the world – monarchy, usually absolute, held sway. Only in Britain's own civil war nearly a century and half before had revolutionary republican principles briefly taken hold, before being discarded. The French Revolution was still thirteen years away.

Paine himself was a born revolutionary and an American by recent adoption, having arrived from Britain in 1774 with a letter of introduction from Benjamin Franklin. *Common Sense* partly reflected the depth of his bitterness towards a life of abject failure that he blamed on the British authorities and the class system. With little education, Paine had run away from home at the age of sixteen on board a privateer. He tried his hand as a corsetmaker and then as a customs official, being fined and dismissed after four years for 'stamping' – writing reports without making an inspection – on the evidence of a superior who was doing the same, but re-emerging as a kind of trade unionist for his colleagues. (Later he was fined a second time, possibly on account of these activities.) His two marriages had failed wretchedly.

As a journalist in America, this alcoholic ne'er-do-well was a brilliant success. He quickly became an intimate of Samuel Adams, who might have helped write his pamphlet. This cried to heaven:

> Reconciliation … is a fallacious dream … The blood of the slain, the weeping voice of nature cries, 'Tis time to part.' Even the distance at which the Almighty hath placed England and America is a strong and natural proof that the authority of the one over the other was never the design of heaven … Freedom hath been hunted round the globe. Asia and Africa have long expelled her. Europe regards her like a stranger, and England hath given her warning to depart. O! receive the fugitive and prepare in time an asylum for mankind.

Sam Adams now directly attacked George III:

> His speech breathes the most malevolent spirit and determines my opinion of its author as a man of a wicked heart. I have heard that he is his own minister; why, then, should we cast the odium of distressing mankind upon his minions? Guilt must lie at his door. Divine vengeance will fall on his head.

Paine's levelling instincts were buttressed by another radical pamphlet, the anonymous *The People the Best Governors*, which argued that

> [the people] best know their wants and necessities and therefore are best able to govern themselves … The people are now contending for freedom; and would to God they might not only obtain, but likewise keep it in their own hands. There are many very noisy about liberty but are aiming at nothing more than personal power and grandeur. And are not many, under the delusive character of guardians of their country, collecting influence and honour only for oppression? … Social virtue and knowledge … is the best and only necessary qualification of [a representative]. So sure as we make interest necessary in this case, as sure we root out virtue … The notion of an estate has the directest tendency to set up the avaricious over the heads of the poor … Let it not be said in future generations that money was made by the founders of the American states an essential qualification in the rulers of a free people.

This pamphlet was also wildly popular. Its views were, however, anathema to the colonial aristocracy and bourgeoisie (perhaps 250,000 strong), to whom their popularity came as a profound shock. The established order felt it was peering into an abyss of revolution. Landon Carter, a Virginia planter, promptly attacked *Common Sense* as 'replete with art and contradiction … rascally and nonsensical … a sophisticated attempt to throw all men out of principles … which has drove all who espouse it from the justice of their contest'. Even Samuel Adams publicly received it with kid gloves. In a letter to James Warren he wrote, 'Don't be displeased with me if you find the spirit of it totally repugnant to your ideas of government.'

His cousin John, rapidly becoming the spokesman of the pragmatic moderates in the American Revolution, and dedicated to reconciling Massachusetts radicals with Virginia conservatives, reacted more sharply, writing his classic *Thoughts on Government* – the single most important tract in the American Revolution – in response to Paine. Later he was to claim that he 'dreaded the effect so popular a pamphlet might have among the people, and determined to do all in my power to counteract the effect of it'. He continued:

> Although I could not have written anything in so manly and striking a style, I flatter myself I should have made a more respectable figure as an architect if I had undertaken such a work. This writer seems to have very inadequate ideas of what is proper and necessary to be done in order to form constitutions for single colonies as well as a great model of union for the whole.

Paine's ideas, he said, flowed from simple ignorance and a desire to please the democratic party in Philadelphia. Paine was a 'disastrous meteor'.

Adams's thinking borrowed heavily not from Locke's assertions of natural rights, but from Montesquieu's concept of the separation of powers which he believed – wrongly – to be the cornerstone of the British political system. The theory was that if each part of the political system could check the other, tyranny would not emerge. In Congress, he favoured a bicameral system, with one chamber representing the aristocracy, the other the popular will.

The executive would be independent of this, and would consist of a government responsible to a council. Further safeguards against popular rule would be the possession of a veto by the government upon the assembly, and the requirement of a property qualification to vote for the assembly. However, the lower house 'shall be in miniature an exact portrait of the people at large. It should think, feel, reason and act like them' – with the exception, of course, of women, Indians, blacks and the poor.

These ideas were to have a powerful influence in shaping the constitutions of North Carolina, Virginia, New Jersey, New York and finally, in 1780, Massachusetts, and in turn those constitutions were to be the model on which the American constitution itself was to be based. Their chief purpose was to keep 'popular government' under the control of the propertied classes, who had been profoundly shocked by the success of Paine's teachings.

It was becoming clear that the propertied class, if it was to survive, had to channel the upsurge of revolutionary egalitarian sentiment into a rage against the British. So, with remarkable speed, the mood turned against reconciliation with Britain to support for outright independence – endorsed by the American Establishment. In February 1776 Sam Adams urged the colonists to exchange ambassadors with France and Spain, to mint coins, levy taxes and declare full independence. A committee set up by Congress to consider the matter concluded for one last time that the Americans should remain British subjects, but also free men. But, by May, Adams was able to secure passage of his preamble to the bill to set up American state governments:

> Whereas his Britannic Majesty, in conjunction with the lords and commons of Great Britain, has, by a late act of parliament, excluded the inhabitants of these United Colonies from the protection of his crown; and whereas, no answer, whatever, to the humble petitions of the colonies for redress of grievances and reconciliation with Great Britain, has been or is likely to be given; but, the whole force of that kingdom, aided by foreign mercenaries, is to be exerted for the destruction of the good people of these colonies; and whereas, it appears absolutely irreconcilable to reason and good conscience, for the people of these colonies now to take the oaths and affirmations necessary for the support of any government under the crown of Great Britain ... it is [therefore] necessary that the exercise of every kind of authority under the said crown should be totally suppressed, and all the powers of government exerted under the authority of the people of the colonies, for the preservation of internal peace, virtue, and good order, as well as for the defence of their lives, liberties,

and properties, against the hostile invasions and cruel depredations of their enemies.

A month later Richard Henry Lee, a member of the Virginian cabal, pronounced the motion 'That these United Colonies are, and of right ought to be, free and independent states, that they are absolved from all allegiance to the British crown, and that all political connection between them and the state of Great Britain is, and ought to be, totally dissolved ...', which was seconded by John Adams. The radicals were now determined to push the motion through Congress against awakening moderate opposition in New York, New Jersey, Delaware, Pennsylvania, South Carolina and Maryland. The thirty-three-year old Thomas Jefferson was sent to draft a declaration of independence. According to Adams, his motives for giving the torch to Jefferson were that 'Reason first, you are a Virginian and a Virginian ought to appear the head of this business. Reason second, I am obnoxious, suspect and unpopular. You are very much otherwise. Reason third, you can write ten times better than I can.'

Jefferson came from an aristocratic Virginian family on his mother's side (the Randolphs); a bright and gifted writer, he was a serious student of classics, while also being something of a ladies' man in his youth. He became a tobacco planter, managing the family estates, and a lawyer. By the age of twenty-six he had been elected to the House of Burgesses, three years later he married a young widow, Martha Skelton. In the final text of the declaration his denunciation of England was watered down and an eloquent but bitter passage about the British people was removed:

> At this very time too they are permitting their chief magistrate to send over not only soldiers of our common blood, but Scotch and foreign mercenaries to invade and destroy us. These facts have given the last stab to agonising affection, and manly spirit bids us to renounce for ever these unfeeling brethren. We must endeavour to forget our former love for them, and to hold them as we hold the rest of mankind, enemies in war, in peace friends. We might have been a free and a great people together; but a communication of grandeur and of freedom it seems is below their dignity. Be it so, since they will have it. The road to glory and happiness is open to us too. We will climb it in a separate state, and acquiesce in the necessity which pronounces our everlasting adieu.

The sparser, more powerful, prose that was left remains one of the greatest declarations in human history:

We hold these truths to be self-evident, that all men are created equal, that they are endowed by their Creator with certain unalienable Rights, that among these are Life, Liberty and the pursuit of Happiness. That to secure these rights, governments are instituted among men, deriving their just powers from the consent of the governed. That whenever any form of government becomes destructive of these ends, it is the right of the people to alter or to abolish it, and to institute new government, laying its foundation on such principles, and organizing its powers in such form, as to them shall seem most likely to effect their safety and happiness.

When Adams later fell out with Jefferson, he claimed that all these sentiments had been raided from a pamphlet by James Otis Jr – though there is no record of this.

With New York abstaining, the declaration was approved by Congress on 4 July, the bells were rung, and the new American nation celebrated with fireworks and bonfires on 9 July. An equestrian statue of George III was toppled in New York, later to be melted down into 42,000 cartridges. The declaration was solemnly signed on 22 August. John Hancock, as president of Congress, remarked to Franklin, 'We must be unanimous. There must be no pulling different ways, we must all hang together.' To which Franklin replied, 'Yes, we must indeed all hang together, or most assuredly we shall all hang separately.'

Alongside British ineffectiveness and American determination in the conduct of the war, a crucial factor had yet to be brought into play: French support for the colonies. It is not true, as some have argued, that the rebellion would not have started without the tacit support of the French; nevertheless ultimately it was French intervention on the American side that won it. Since the end of the Seven Years War the Comte de Vergennes, the French Foreign Minister, had been biding his time for another clash with his country's old enemy across the Channel.

In the early 1770s France still felt itself too weak to resume hostilities with Britain; but assisting the American rebels to undermine the British Empire was another matter. Foreign Minister Vergennes employed the offices of an extraordinary man – Pierre-Augustin Caron de Beaumarchais, a watchmaker, musician and businessman of modest origins whose greatest claim to fame, like that of the flamboyant Burgoyne, was playwriting: he was the author of *The Barber of Seville* and *The Marriage of Figaro*, both big hits in late eighteenth-century France, and the begetters of the operas of the same names.

Beaumarchais was sent as a spy to London for a meeting with Arthur Lee, the representative of Virginia and, alongside his rival Benjamin Franklin, the most passionate advocate of the American cause. He was soon advocating military support for the rebels. He was put in charge of a bogus continental trading firm to arrange this, Rodriguez Hortalez & Company.

In July 1776 Silas Deane of Connecticut arrived in France as America's envoy to request 200 cannon, 30 mortars, 200,000 lb of powder, and arms and clothing for 25,000 men. Deane was received by Vergennes, who insisted on France's strict neutrality, and refused Deane's request, but told him that French ports were open to the Americans for trade and that American ships laden with military supplies would not be prevented from leaving France. This was hugely encouraging: the Americans were desperately short of arms and in particular of ammunition. Virtually no gunpowder was produced in the colonies, and its essential ingredient – saltpetre – was imported into Europe, much of it from Bengal.

Soon, however, Beaumarchais contacted Deane and it became clear that the French were secretly prepared to pay for gunpowder and arms shipments to America. It was arranged that clandestine shipments would sail from Le Havre, but British intelligence received word through Edward Bancroft, Deane's private secretary, who was a spy, and the French, learning of this, delayed the sailings. Not until 30 April 1777, did they reach Portsmouth, New Hampshire, where the cargoes were a boon for the American war effort. A second convoy was sunk on the way, taking a personal fortune invested by Beaumarchais with it.

Although these were the best-known shipments to America, there was probably a regular arms traffic from Nantes as early as 1774, arranged through Franklin's great friend Montaudoin. In addition, the French used the old Dutch smuggling entrepôt of Statia Island (present-day St Eustatius) in the Leewards both for provisions and for ammunition. Statia was also a way station for ammunition bought from Holland, although the Dutch government officially denied this. Ships would pretend to leave Amsterdam for Africa and then sail to Statia, despite the efforts of British ships to stop them. French ports nearby would grant American ships neutral papers so that they could dock at Statia.

Eventually no fewer than 3,183 vessels docked at this tiny volcanic atoll in thirteen months between 1778 and 1779, as a Dutch admiral reported. Statia also provided a haven for American volunteers, and was a stopping-off point for European volunteers heading for America.

Franklin himself arrived in December 1776 to join Deane and Lee in Paris and Versailles, where they lobbied hard for France to enter the war against Britain. But the three-man mission was regarded by the French as both comical and quarrelsome. Deane – a shallow, ostentatious, free-spending man – was believed to be cheating the Americans by charging them for munitions given freely by the French. While recruiting European officers for the American cause, he advocated that Washington be replaced as American commander-in-chief by a distinguished European veteran – such as the Comte de Broglie – for which he was not forgiven by the former. Worse, later in the war he lost his zeal for the American cause and advocated reconciliation with England.

Arthur Lee suspected and disliked Deane. But he himself was distrusted by the French and was an irascible and awkward personality. John Adams, who was to replace Deane, wrote of Lee, 'His countenance is disgusting, his air is not pleasing, his manners are not engaging, his temper is harsh, sour, and fierce, and his judgment of men and things is often wrong.'

Franklin who completed this extraordinary triumvirate, appeared a symbol of homespun simplicity that seemed a rebuke to the luxury of the French court – which little imagined that its own country was, just thirteen years later, to follow the republican trail blazed by the Americans. Wearing a simple fur cap, spectacles and a brown suit, he captivated the French public. As John Adams wrote of him:

> His name was familiar to government and people, to kings, courtiers, nobility, clergy, and philosophers as well as plebeians, to such a degree that there was scarcely a peasant or a citizen, a valet de chambre, coachman or footman, a lady's chambermaid or a scullion in a kitchen who was not familiar with it and who did not consider him a friend to humankind ... When they spoke of him they seemed to think he was to restore the golden age.

But Adams revealed another side to this 'indolent voluptuary':

> The life of Dr Franklin was a scene of continual dissipation ... of sexual adventures, gluttony and receiving admirers who came to have the honour to see the great Franklin, and to have the pleasure of telling stories about his simplicity, his bald head and scattering straight hairs.

The young French King, Louis XVI, was unimpressed by the Americans. The decisions to support them covertly, without which they could not have survived the early years of the war, and then to join them in alliance, were made by Vergennes for reasons of French national interest. The colourful American emissaries probably played only a limited part in persuading him. For the French, the colonial rebellion was a surrogate war which drained and distracted the British. Without French arms supplies the American war effort would probably have collapsed in 1776.

At last, with the decision to abandon Boston in March 1776, the British cause seemed to have lost its inertia. The British now appeared resolved to fight the war as a war, not a minor police action in which their hands were tied. Major reinforcements sailed to join the Howe brothers, who had withdrawn to Halifax after the fall of Boston.

The combined British forces anchored off Sandy Hook, south of the entrance to New York harbour. There were no fewer than 170 troop transports under the protection of 10 battleships and 20 frigates. Aboard were some 32,000 troops, including 8,000 Germans from Hesse.

Yet, in spite of Gage's recall, the British continued to show extraordinary caution. Landing unopposed on Staten Island on 3 July, they made no move for several weeks. General Howe, like Gage, seemed unwilling to stage a major confrontation for fear that his men could be too easily dispersed. The Americans could always fall back on the countryside for reserves: the British parliament would be deeply reluctant to commit more troops. As Lord Percy put it, 'Our army is so small that we cannot even afford a victory.'

General Howe also may not have wanted to inflict a devastating defeat on the Americans, in the belief that this would sour all chance of negotiations – although few others believed them likely. As was to be the case with America in Vietnam, British policy was to increase the size of the armies in the colonies only gradually in response to circumstances – which prevented them becoming strong enough to deliver a killer blow.

Several weeks after landing at Staten Island, General Howe's forces arrived at Gravesend on Long Island on 22 August. After Washington's triumph at Boston, he had withdrawn the bulk of his army for the defence of New York, where a British attack was rightly expected. It was the Americans' turn to be overconfident. Believing his own propaganda, Washington concluded that the ambush at Concord and Lexington, the Battle of Breed's Hill and the British evacuation of Boston had brought his adversaries to their knees. But in New York matters were altogether different from in Massachusetts. The state was a hotbed of loyalist, pro-British,

'Tory' sentiment, which the rebels – arguing that all Americans hated the British – were unwilling to acknowledge. Later, American commanders were even to consider burning New York to the ground, to deprive the British of a useful base.

In New York, moreover, the positions at Boston were reversed. Holding the city, Washington and his army would be cut off by a numerically superior enemy in countryside that was largely hostile to the rebels. Washington's best tactic would have been to stay out of the city altogether, to give him freedom of manoeuvre, or even to move his forces south to New Jersey. But for the Americans to have abandoned New York would have been a devastating admission of weakness.

Washington decided to make his stand there. In an effort to avoid the fate of the British in Boston, he stationed most of his forces across the East river in Brooklyn: for if the British gained control of this, New York would be at the mercy of their cannon.

But, in doing so, Washington for the first time displayed serious tactical ineptitude, which was nearly to cost America the war and him his command. Placing his forces across the East River meant that they could be surrounded and cut off by the British army and navy, which controlled the sea; a similar consideration was precisely the reason why the British had not occupied Charlestown and Dorchester Heights – although they had control of the sea even there.

Washington believed his position to be strong. To the east his force was protected by the salt marshes at Gowanus Creek. Just in front of Brooklyn village, he stationed the vanguard under General Putnam. Their position was protected by the heavily wooded Guan Heights, stretching beyond them to the south, which were believed to be impassable except in four places – Gowanus on the sea, the Flatbush Pass a mile to the west, the Bedford Pass a mile further on, and the Jamaica Pass three miles beyond that. General Jack Sullivan was placed in charge of the troops holding the Guan Heights.

To the Americans, who were accustomed to fighting in such terrain, and had already inflicted major casualties from above on British troops storming their positions at Breed's Hill, the position must have seemed almost impregnable. They hoped the British would be forced to string their men out in a long line instead of concentrating their forces at a single point. Unfortunately Sullivan, possibly believing the British could not stretch their forces that far, or ignorant of the topography, sent only five men to defend the Jamaica Pass, to the Americans' far left.

Washington sent a stirring exhortation to his men to do their best, coupled with a warning against desertion:

> Remember officers and soldiers, that you are freemen, fighting for the blessings of liberty – that slavery will be your portion, and that of your posterity, if you do not acquit yourselves like men: Remember how your courage and spirit have been despised, and traduced by your cruel invaders; though they have found by dear experience at Boston, Charlestown and other places, what a few brave men contending for their own land, and in the best of causes can do, against base hirelings and mercenaries ...
>
> Be cool, but determined; do not fire at a distance, but wait for orders from your officers ... No such scoundrel [deserters] will be found in this army; but on the contrary, every one for himself resolving to conquer, or die, and trusting to the smiles of heaven upon so just a cause, will behave with bravery and resolution: Those who are distinguished for their gallantry, and good conduct, may depend upon being honourably noticed, and suitably rewarded: And if this army will but emulate and imitate their brave countrymen, in other parts of America, he has no doubt they will, by a glorious victory, save their country, and acquire to themselves immortal honour.

Washington's words were stirring stuff, but General Howe was now to show his greater experience and skill as a commander. Carefully scouting the rebel lines, he arranged for feint attacks to be made on the three western passes in the early morning of 27 August. He dispatched the bulk of his army, with Clinton in the vanguard, Percy and himself in charge of the main force, and Cornwallis in the rear, to the virtually unguarded Jamaica Pass, arriving there at three in the morning, and seizing the five defenders. The British then moved along the old Jamaica Road as silently as they could at dead of night – behind the American front line in the hills.

These perfectly executed moves caught the American forces on the heights in a trap, and only the right flank succeeded in escaping to the Gowanus marshes. By noon around 1,000 Americans had been killed, wounded or captured in the bogs at the expense of only a handful of casualties among the British. British officers were eager to chase the Americans into their entrenched positions around the village of Brooklyn, and might have succeeded in routing the demoralized Americans altogether. But Howe's caution and concern to keep casualties as low as possible among his own men mistakenly prevailed. There were still some 7,500 Americans facing the 15,000 British.

In desperation Washington had 2,000 troops ferried across from New York, to reinforce the Americans. But he was tightening the noose around his own neck, for the British now began to construct trenches and breastworks, as well as a battery 600 yards away from the American line, in preparation for a siege. All that was needed was Admiral Howe's fleet to sail up the East River and cut off the rebels.

# 12

# *Escape from New York*

Providence intervened on the American side. On 28 August 1776, a violent north-easterly storm soaked both sides, damping their ammunition and making the Americans vulnerable to a bayonet charge, which many British officers urged on their commander. More significantly, the weather prevented the British fleet sailing up the East River. General Howe now misjudged badly. Possibly assuming that he would get his chance once his brother the admiral closed the trap with the navy, or that the Americans would be equally immobilized by the storm, or that they would surrender, or even conceivably that peace negotiations were possible if he showed mercy, he bided his time. As Israel Putnam put it, 'General Howe is either our friend or no general. He had our whole army in his power … and yet offered us to escape without the least interruption … Had he instantly followed up his victory, the consequence to the cause of liberty must have been dreadful.'

Washington's officers had convinced him that his position in Brooklyn was untenable and he must evacuate. Overnight on 30 August the storm subsided; a dank and impenetrable mist settled on both positions, and the choppy river settled to glass-like smoothness. For the first time, Washington displayed his genius as a commander. The entire American force of 9,500 men, with all their provisions and ammunition and most of their guns, was evacuated over the river to New York. The following morning the British discovered that the bird had flown. As a British general remarked, 'It cannot be denied but that the American army lay almost entirely at the will of the English. That they were therefore suffered to retire in safety has by some been attributed to the reluctance of the commander-in-chief [Howe] to shed the blood of a people so nearly allied.'

Howe promptly decided that instead of attacking New York City, which would lead to house-to-house fighting and destruction, he would organize a flanking movement further up the East River to bottle up Washington's forces in New York, where they would again be trapped. This was sensible, as New York was a hotbed of pro-British sentiment, and destroying the city would have needlessly antagonized its inhabitants. But the British would have to act with alacrity.

Despite their miraculous escape, there was no disguising the Americans' demoralization. Hundreds of militiamen deserted outright, while Washington and his officers sought frantically to organize musters, court martials and whippings to stop them. In an army where British-style discipline was unknown, this was next to impossible.

Meanwhile Admiral Howe instructed invited American delegates to Staten Island to discuss how to end the war. The British still fondly believed that the whole issue was an unfortunate misunderstanding, failing to realize that the very people to whom they were appealing for peace were the American minority that had been working for independence for years, and would fight to the bitter end.

The admiral was rebuffed by a mission headed by Benjamin Franklin and John Adams. As Franklin argued, 'Forces have been sent out and towns destroyed, that they could not expect happiness now under the domination of Great Britain; that all former attachment was obliterated; that America could not return again to the domination of Great Britain and therefore imagined that Great Britain meant to rest it upon force.'

To the British, however, the end of the war must have seemed very near. Washington's army had narrowly escaped total annihilation; and it could now be cut off in New York, which the commander was doggedly determined to defend until otherwise ordered by Congress. Both Putnam and General Nathanael Greene urged withdrawal from the city, the latter arguing that the Tory stronghold should be burnt down – an indication of the ruthlessness with which the rebels were prepared to punish their own people. Congress sharply overruled Washington and ordered that he should quit New York, and that 'no damage be done to the said city by his troops, on their leaving it: the congress having no doubt of being able to recover the same'.

But time was running out: on 13 September British ships sailed up the East River and blasted away at American defensive earthworks at Kip's Bay. The militia promptly abandoned their positions, and the British landed hundreds of men unopposed. Washington, hearing of the landing, took to his horse and headed towards the British landing site with two New England brigades, while, with eminent good sense, Putnam furiously led a headlong retreat from the New York trap up the west side of Manhattan Island, his forces carrying as many provisions and as much ammunition as they could, but leaving their guns behind.

Washington, on reaching his fleeing troops, for the first time lost his ice-cool composure and started whipping officers and men with his riding cane, dashing his hat on the ground and raging, 'Are these the men with whom I am to defend America?' The American commander-in-chief feared another debacle to match that on Long Island; after his triumph in Boston, this would be humiliation indeed. He would have been captured by the fast-advancing British, but an aide seized his bridle and his horse and pulled him away.

Astonishingly, in spite of his perfectly executed landing, Howe again held back from springing the trap. He sent his troops north and south up the main road, but failed to cross over to the western Hudson river side of Manhattan Island to cut off Putnam's line of retreat. By evening, the American forces were relatively safe at Harlem Heights, north of the city.

A skirmish the following day gave a bloody nose to the British advance guard below the heights, but one of America's best soldiers, Colonel Thomas Knowlton, was killed. Having almost caught their prey, the British veered off into another attack on a defended uphill position, and the fleeing American army was momentarily safe again. Meanwhile the British had routed another army and taken New York. As a British officer remarked, 'The [Americans] had intended to contest every inch of ground. In every street they had made ditches and barricades, and fortified every little eminence about the town. But when the British landed, they fled, leaving their defences to fill up with stagnant water, damaged sauerkraut, and filth.'

Understandably, by this time the British were becoming contemptuous about their enemy's fighting abilities. All the same, Howe, fearing he had too few troops to risk sacrificing them in a significant engagement, remained remarkably cautious.

Rather than storming the heights, his forces remained entrenched before them for nearly a month while preparing the next movement – a pincer this time, leaving a garrison in New York and sending a force up the Hudson and another up the East River. The strategy was again impeccable, but leisurely executed. Some 400 men were landed at Throgg Point, at the bottom of Long Island Sound, on 14 October.

This prompted Washington to evacuate Harlem Heights altogether and march north to White Plains, four days later. He was proving an adept runner. The ever-cautious Howe waited several days before disembarking more troops further up at Pell's Point and Myer's Point and marching to attack the far left of the American position at Chatterton's Hill, which the British took with difficulty at the cost of 229 men to 140 Americans.

Washington was forced to retreat again to a better position at North Castle Heights, only to see the British suddenly withdraw south west towards an American stronghold he had inexplicably left behind on the Hudson, Fort Washington. The skilful tactical movement left Washington floundering. Leaving 10,000 men behind, he crossed the Hudson with 5,000 to threaten the British should they choose to attack Forts Washington and Lee on either side of the river. These garrisons, containing 3,000 and 2,000 men respectively, were supposed to prevent the British fleet from moving up river, but were otherwise useless, and sitting ducks for the British.

What followed was glorified by Washington as a 'war of posts', or a 'defensive' war. It was in fact nothing less than a British chase and an American retreat as the British forces marched in skilful pursuit of the bedraggled, confused American forces. Having left these useless garrisons behind his lines, Washington could do nothing now to save them.

On 16 November, in a three-sided classic attack, the British surrounded and routed the American lines around Fort Washington, at a loss of 300 British dead to 54 Americans, capturing a garrison of 2,900 men and all their stores. It was the biggest victory so far in the war.

Four days later, the most able British commander, Lord Cornwallis, crossed the Hudson to a position just below the other redundant American garrison, Fort Lee, whose commander, General Nathanael Greene, evacuated his 2,000 men in great haste, joining up with Washington's 5,000 in a desperate attempt to escape yet another British trap. Moving with furious urgency, Washington and Greene reached Newark, New Jersey, on 22 November. There they sought to rally their men. But, with their terms of enlistment at an end, 2,000 soldiers decided to abandon an apparently lost cause.

Washington had now had his fill of bitterness, defeat and retreat. He commented:

I am wearied almost to death with the retrograde motion of things, and I solemnly protest that a pecuniary reward of twenty thousand pounds a year would not induce me to undergo what I do; and after all, perhaps to lose my character, as it is impossible, under such a variety of distressing circumstances, to conduct matters agreeably to public expectation.

His force was reduced to just 3,000 men, who escaped in the nick of time on 28 November as Cornwallis and 4,000 British troops arrived in hot pursuit, and even on occasion in sight. Washington reached New Brunswick the following day, and would have been caught but for an order from General Howe to Cornwallis not to engage, and the destruction of the bridge across the Raritan river. Cornwallis was to be criticized for not overcoming both obstacles and destroying Washington's small army once and for all.

Washington's next refuge was Princeton. The British, marching under Howe and rejoined by Cornwallis, almost surrounded them there, but the depleted American forces escaped and at last reached Trenton and the Delaware river, which they crossed, destroying every boat for seventy miles in the process. Howe lingered on the north bank for a week before deciding to pursue no further and return to winter quarters in New York.

It had been one of the great chases in military history, covering some 170 miles in two months. Washington had narrowly escaped with the rump of the American army. The flame of resistance was still flickering, but barely more. His whole campaign from New York to the Delaware had been a string of disasters, defeats, miscalculations and retreats. He had been wrong to risk his army in the defence of New York; wrong to send the bulk of it across to Long Island, and then reinforce it there; wrong in his half-baked defence of Brooklyn; wrong to seek to hold New York after the disaster there; wrong to flee north to White Plains instead of seeking to concentrate his forces in New Jersey, and wrong to leave a large garrison at Fort Washington to be picked off in his wake.

Military ability was apparent only in his well-organized evacuation from Brooklyn; in Putnam's hastily improvised and speedy retreat from New York; and in the army's flight across New Jersey, as well as the finely executed withdrawal across the Delaware. The Americans had shown themselves supremely skilled in the difficult matter of flight. They had suffered two major defeats – at Brooklyn and at Fort Washington – and a minor one at Chatterton's Hill, with only the skirmish at Harlem Heights as a consoling victory. They had been driven from New York, Fort Washington, Fort Lee, Newark, New Brunswick, Princeton and Trenton and, in a separate attack, from Newport in Rhode Island.

Worse still, to the demoralized American high command, New York and New Jersey showed no inclination to rally to the rebel side. The idea of a united American effort to overthrow the British oppressors was in tatters. These states had wholly failed to follow New England's lead and emerge as centres of armed resistance to the British. All were now virtually under British control. The people's conduct, Washington complained, was 'infamous', and their militia were 'a destructive, expensive and disorderly mob' who 'exulted' at British successes. In fact the majority were probably indifferent and eager only for a quiet life, wanting to be on the winning side for motives of self-preservation. But there seemed to be as many, if not more, loyalists as rebel supporters.

The American army had lost around 5,000 men in casualties and prisoners compared with around 1,000 British soldiers. It had been slashed by war, disease and destruction from around 20,000 men to just 3,000 under Washington's command and a further 5,000 left behind under the control of General Charles Lee at North Castle and Peekskill.

The British had also made serious mistakes – notably their failure to follow up their success at Brooklyn and their landing near Harlem and at Throgg's Point, as well as their strangely slow march to New Brunswick. But they had outmanoeuvred the Americans at Brooklyn, had staged skilful flanking moves and fearless landings up the East River, and had spectacularly routed Washington with their marches on Fort Washington and Fort Lee and their effective pursuit of the enemy.

As they returned to winter quarters, the war seemed as good as won. After the disaster in Massachusetts, they had experienced nothing but success. General Howe returned to the comfort of New York and his mistress for the winter. Clinton, who in his quiet way had begun intensely to dislike his commander's cautious instincts, went to Newport. Cornwallis prepared to return to England. The American Congress's capital of Philadelphia, just thirty miles from the British forward position, was within reach. If it could be occupied, a mopping up operation in the south – where enthusiasm for independence was underwhelming – and then the crushing of isolated New England seemed in prospect.

\*

News of another potentially lethal blow to the American cause soon reached the demoralized Washington, across the Delaware, and Congress, which had fled to Baltimore in expectation of an attack on Philadelphia. Washington's second-in-command, General Charles Lee, possessed of a formidable military reputation, had been left in charge of 5,000 troops in North Castle. A Welshman who had fought as a captain of grenadiers in 1756, he had served with Washington in the ill-fated Braddock expedition. Well-read and a linguist, yet temperamental and coarse in his habits, he was foul-mouthed and ill-mannered with a brutish, ugly appearance. He had married an Indian wife and been adopted into the Mohawk tribe of the Bear. Of her he wrote:

> My wife is daughter to the famous White Thunder who is Belt of Wampun to the Senakas – which is in fact their Lord Treasurer. She is a very great beauty, and is more like your friend Mrs Griffith than anybody I know. I shall say nothing of her accomplishments, for you must be certain that a woman of her fashion cannot be without many … if you will allow good breeding to consist in a constant desire to do everything that will please you, and a strict carefulness not to say or do anything that may offend you.

He served in Portugal and became a mercenary for Poland, then all over Europe, where he showed exemplary toughness and bravery.

Lee had presided over one of the few American victories so far: the successful defence of Charleston, South Carolina, at the end of June. A substantial British force under General Clinton had laid siege to some 3,000 men bottled up in Sullivan's Island, which contained the main fortress defending the city – a wooden bastion with sixteen-foot-thick earth-filled ramparts and some twenty-five guns. Lee, dispatched to take part in the town's defence, initially favoured abandoning the fort as a potential 'slaughter pen', but fortunately gave way to the commander on the spot, Colonel William Moultrie.

The British attack proved ineffectual: the troops were unable to cross deep water to storm the fort, and their cannonballs made little impact on the fortification. Moultrie reported that 'We had a morass that swallowed them up instantly, and those that fell in the sand, in and about the fort, were immediately buried, so that very few of them burst amongst us.' The British ships, badly damaged by shots from the fortress, withdrew after twelve hours. With this real, if limited victory, Lee won admirers both in Congress and among American officers.

When Washington had departed south in his ineffectual attempt to prevent the seizure of Fort Washington and Fort Lee, he had left Lee's 5,000 men with the warning that '[The British] may yet pay the army under your command a visit'. Washington's fear – and his motive for leaving so substantial a force at North Castle Heights – was that the British would revert to their old tactic of staging a loop around New England to join up with a force coming south from Canada. If they did not, Washington stressed that Lee should hurry southward and join forces with him: 'I have no doubt of your following, with all possible dispatch, leaving the militia and invalids to cover the frontiers of Connecticut in case of need.' Lee, however, had no confidence whatever in Washington's leadership.

Lee clearly blamed Washington for much of the failure of the New York campaign, and in particular the disastrous loss of Fort Washington. Some of Washington's own staff agreed with Lee. One, Colonel Joseph Reed, wrote to him:

> I do not mean to flatter or praise you at the expense of any other, but I do think it is entirely owing to you that this army, and the liberties of America, so far as they are dependent on it, are not entirely cut off. You ascribe to this our escape from York [Manhattan] Island, King's Bridge and the Plains. And I have no doubt, had you been here, the garrison of Mount Washington would now have composed a part of this army.
>
> And from all these circumstances, I confess, I do ardently wish to see you removed from a place where there will be so little call for your judgment and experience, to the place where they are likely to be so necessary. Nor am I singular in my opinion. Every gentleman of the family, the officers and soldiers generally, have a confidence in you. The enemy constantly inquire where you are and seem to be less confident when you are present.

Lee reflected, 'There are days when we must commit treason against the laws of the state, for the salvation of the state. The present crisis demands this brave, virtuous kind of treason.' He replied to Reed lamenting 'that fatal indecision of mind [on Washington's part] which is a much greater disqualification than stupidity or even want of personal courage'.

Washington, however, intercepted the letter and became aware of the disaffection. Coolly, he asked to be excused for believing the letter to be an official dispatch and for reading 'the contents of a letter which neither inclination nor intention would have prompted me to'. This may have been one of history's glorious accidents, or an example of the suspicious and highly efficient, even duplicitous, personality of the commander-in-chief. Meanwhile, in the same icy tone he repeatedly urged Lee to reinforce him. On 21 November he had written that the 'public interest' required Lee to march. By 27 November, after discovery of the plotting, he urged furiously, 'My former letters were so full and explicit as to the necessity of your marching, as early as possible, that it is unnecessary to add more on that head.'

Lee's delay in reinforcing Washington is hard to explain except as a kind of suppressed mutiny. He may have believed that a major defeat would assure him of the American command. In his defence, he possibly believed that by holding back he could strike more effectively at the British from behind, as they pursued Washington, rather than merely joining up to make a joint stand. Not until early December did he move at a leisurely pace across the Hudson. Not only were the Americans on the run, their two chief commanders were also in bitter rivalry.

The figure of Lee has been so demonized historically, being cast as a fallen angel to Washington's archangel, that the official version of events recounted by Major James Wilkinson must be viewed with some scepticism. Wilkinson was himself a biased observer, acting for his own ambitious master, Horatio Gates, another of the principal American generals, who would himself later challenge Washington's authority and had good motives for remaining a rival.

According to Wilkinson, the slovenly Lee, having risen late on 13 December and settled down to breakfast at ten at an inn some eight miles away from his army at Morristown, wrote a letter to Gates which began, 'The ingenious manoeuvre of Fort Washington has completely unhinged the goodly fabric we had been building. There never was so damned a stroke. Entre nous, a certain great man is most damnably deficient.' At that moment, Wilkinson, who had been ordered by Gates to visit Lee, exclaimed 'Here, sir, are the British cavalry ... around the house'. The general had been caught napping, and was whisked away by a British patrol under the command of a name soon to inspire terror in the American side – Banastre Tarleton.

Congress, reeling from the capture of one of America's best commanders, despairingly declared a day of fasting 'According to the custom of our pious ancestors in times of imminent dangers and difficulties ... to implore of Almighty God the forgiveness of the many sins prevailing among all ranks, and to beg the countenance and assistance of his Providence in the prosecution of the present just and necessary war'.

What was Lee doing so far from the bulk of the army? How had the British received such precise information as to his whereabouts – for the surrounding of the inn was clearly a carefully staged raid based on excellent intelligence. Might he have been planning secret talks with the British and been double-crossed? Could Lee have been betrayed by one of his own officers, irked by his ambition to supplant Washington? Could the latter have betrayed him? Had Gates or Wilkinson inadvertently led the British to Lee's hideout? Had Lee been lured to the inn by the promise of meeting Gates there?

Lee's capture was a major setback for the American cause, but an extraordinary stroke of luck for Washington, whose chief rival had been whisked away at a moment when few Americans had any confidence in their commander-in-chief. Yet it is hard to believe that Washington himself, now across the Delaware, could have been so duplicitous as to have played an active role.

Lee's abduction was also to prove highly convenient to Horatio Gates, now moving through northern New Jersey with a small reinforcement for Washington's army dispatched by General Schuyler from Fort Ticonderoga. The ambitious Gates wanted to be rid of Lee as much as, later, he wanted to be rid of Washington. Lee's henchman Wilkinson had spread the stories of Lee's idleness and sloppiness.

Washington's greatness is so much part of the American myth that it is difficult to accept that at this stage, and later, his authority was far from established over other candidates jousting to take his place. Except for the successful occupation of Dorchester Heights overlooking Boston, and his retreat from Long Island, his command of American forces had been a string of disasters, defeats, retreats and displays of indecision. His sole remaining card seemed to be his skill as a 'political' general – in particular, and unlike the brusque, impetuous, grumpy Lee, in his careful wooing of Congress to retain its confidence.

Even when Lee's leaderless contingent reached Washington, he still had only some 6,000 men, 'Many being entirely naked and most so thinly clad as to be unfit for service. Ten days more will put an end to the existence of our army … Our only dependence now is upon the speedy enlistment of a new army. If this fails, I think the game will be pretty well up.' He begged for greater powers, expressing 'no lust after power, but I wish with as much fervency as any man upon this wide-extended continent for an opportunity of turning the sword into the ploughshare.'

On 27 December Congress accorded him these and also, ludicrously, the authority to raise 104 infantry battalions for terms of three years or until the end of the war, amounting to 76,000 men. This grandiose declaration to set up a paper army was in stark contrast to the reality of the huddled and barely clothed rump living in shabby wooden huts along the banks of the Delaware. But extending the terms of enlistment was important: for a great stride had been made towards Washington's ambition – apparently justified by the war – of establishing a substantial standing army in place of the shambolic, if occasionally effective, guerrilla militias.

# 13

# *Across the Delaware*

Even at the darkest moment of Washington's command, he was able to turn defeat into long-term advantage, both for America's cause and for his own authority. Like other great politicians and (sometimes) great soldiers, with his back to the wall, this normally most cautious and cool-headed of leaders decided to gamble everything on a single throw of the dice.

Without authorization or any sensible strategic objective, hounded across two states and barely escaping with his life, he had two overriding reasons for boldness: he desperately needed a propaganda success to rally Americans at a time when the cause of independence seemed all but extinguished, in order to continue the war through the winter and find new recruits for his shrunken forces, and a single victory would enable Congress to justify retaining him in his command.

Self-interest as much as idealism continued to guide this intensely ambitious and proud man. He was facing imminent dismissal as a disastrous leader, and he knew it. Beset first by Lee and now by Gates, another 'political' general with friends in Congress, who was much more adept in caucuses than on the battlefield, Washington decided to risk the remnants of the army, which faced annihilation if defeated, in a last-ditch bid to save America's and his own reputation – a colossal gamble indeed.

Good intelligence revealed the other side's complacency, unpreparedness and depleted numbers now that Howe had gone back to winter quarters in New York. To Washington this was too good an opportunity to miss, even with his ragged forces. With his career and reputation on the ropes, it must have seemed he had nothing to lose.

Howe had made two colossal misjudgements after the successful autumn campaign, both born of the British belief that victory was now inevitable: first, the decision to leave the desperate, cornered Americans across the Delaware alone and retire with the bulk of his army to winter quarters; and, second, the decision to leave the front line defended by some 2,000 German hussars from Hesse, strung out in a long line from Trenton to Burlington under the overall command of General Carl von Donop, the Trenton troops being under Colonel Johann Rall.

The hussars were brave and tough; they showed little inclination to pay for their provisions, and succeeded in antagonizing many local people, even though a large number of New Jersey's inhabitants had responded to the offer of a full pardon if they supported the King.

With the main British force withdrawn, the rebels were free to move about the countryside, stirring people up and ambushing and harassing British patrols, which were safe only in the towns. Rall's men could not safely move to Princeton, up the road, in units of less than fifty men. In Trenton, itself, according to Rall, the fortifications were useless – not that he expected Washington's broken army to stage any major action.

Fond of drinking and gambling, Rall could be counted on to be engaged upon both on Christmas night. Washington, well informed by his scouts about the Hessian troop positions, planned his attack with precision. He was to command the central thrust crossing the Delaware with some 2,400 men some nine miles north of Trenton. Further down-stream, directly opposite the town, a diversionary force of 700 would land while a smaller force would attack Donop at Mount Holly to the south – a feint designed to tie up Donop's troops and prevent Trenton being reinforced.

As Washington prepared for the crossing, he received news that his current rival, General Gates, who had refused to join the attack, had gone to Philadelphia to argue that it was bound to fail. Major Wilkinson, Gates's aid, reported:

> As I presented the letter to him, he exclaimed with solemnity, 'What a time is this to hand me letters!' I answered that I had been charged with it by General Gates. 'By General Gates! Where is he?' 'I left him this morning in Philadelphia'. 'What was he doing there?' 'I understood that he was on his way to Congress'. He earnestly repeated, 'On his way to Congress!' then broke the seal.

Washington was incensed, but proceeded with his preparations. If he lost, he would be dismissed.

\*

As night fell, the conditions were grim. Huge blocks of ice flowed down the freezing river, and a blizzard lashed the American troops as they embarked on flat-bottomed craft used to transport iron ore downstream. The biggest problem was embarking the horses and eighteen cannon. The huge and efficient Henry Knox presided over this brilliantly. The half-frozen troops, many marching on feet wrapped in cloths for lack of shoes, left trails of blood in the snow. They completed the river crossing only by three o'clock in the morning.

Washington divided his own central force into two columns, one to attack from the river side to the west, the other from the north east, in an effort to surround the town. One of the two southern contingents had been sent to secure the bridge on Assunpink Creek to the south of Trenton, to complete the loop. Neither of the forces got across, owing to the weather and the lesser determination of their commanders. Advancing in the dark, Washington's troops arrived at around 8 a.m. on 26 December, to find the garrison snug in bed after the night's carousing: it had seemed inconceivable that the ragged and God-fearing Americans would advance on Christmas night – especially such a night as this.

Moving quickly in the muffled silence of the snow, they set up field guns in the streets. As the Hessians, startled from their slumbers, fired from their windows, and tumbled downstairs to take up defensive positions, they were mown down by musket and artillery fire. Colonel Rall bravely tried to make a stand on the east side of town, but was mortally wounded by a bullet.

Within an hour it was over, with just 3 Americans dead and 6 wounded compared with 22 Hessians dead, 98 wounded, and 1,000 taken prisoner. Some 500 Hessians escaped to the south across the Assunpink. In addition the Americans had captured 6 cannon and 1,000 muskets. The Hessians had been caught napping by a beautifully executed, heroic (under the arctic conditions) night ambush. It was a remarkable triumph for careful planning and boldness.

The following afternoon, Washington cautiously withdrew across the Delaware, in case the Hessians counter-marched in larger numbers from the south. In fact the Germans abandoned their positions along the river, feeling exposed against an enemy threat of unknown size. Washington then decided, riskily, to recross, although with his back to the river he faced annihilation if the British came up in force.

Summoning American forces from round about, he increased their strength to 5,000 men and 40 guns.

Cornwallis, who had been preparing to leave for England, hurried south with a force of 5,500 men and 28 guns to counter-attack. Moving down from Princeton, he was slowed by guerrilla attacks along the road to Trenton and reached the town on 2 January, only to find that Washington's men had withdrawn across the Assunpink and assembled on the low hills opposite. Cornwallis considered it impossible to cross the creek safely, and decided to delay his major assault until the following morning. With its boats out of reach to the north and its back to the river, Washington's army seemed trapped at last.

But it was Washington's turn to regain the initiative in another astonishingly bold stroke. Doubling his sentries, digging earthworks along the creek, and lighting blazing campfires opposite the British lines to deceive them, at dead of night his forces stole away not southwards but behind British lines in a daring swoop to the north, towards Princeton, from which the British had just come.

By morning he had reached two British regiments left just outside the town, who put up a desperate fight against far superior American forces and managed to push their way through along the road to Trenton, under hot pursuit and in total disarray. The regiment in Princeton itself fled to New Brunswick, while sixty soldiers were captured in a college dormitory. Within days, Washington decided to forestall any British counter-attack by pulling his exultant soldiers out of Princeton and marching them up the forty miles to winter quarters in Morristown. For his part Cornwallis rapidly returned to New Brunswick, to forestall any attack on the large British arms depot there.

Washington had hardly turned the tables. His army was still small, wretched, poorly supplied, and plagued by desertions and a refusal to re-enlist that, over the previous two months, had reduced it to a pitiable 3,000 men. He had still been ejected from the bulk of New York, New Jersey and Rhode Island.

But his series of brilliant guerrilla attacks had salvaged the American cause from utter demoralization. He had proved that American troops could, after all, win a significant battle – for only the second time in the war, the Concord–Lexington ambush being the first. The British were not invincible, and he had momentarily seized the initiative. His means had been bold, imaginative and beautifully executed. He had brilliantly ambushed the Hessians and as cleanly outmanoeuvred the British. He had staged a massive blow for battered rebel pride, as well as his own rep-utation. The image of the grim-faced, determined Washington crossing the Delaware in the bitter winter night of Christmas Day was a potent icon for rallying the dispirited Americans.

By moving up to Morristown, moreover, he had displayed strategic foresight. Far from leaving the road to Philadelphia undefended, he had positioned his force to attack the rear of the British should they decide to push that way. This in fact had been the strategy of his arch-rival Lee: it was much more sensible to threaten the lowland states from the rela-tive security of the lower Appalachians than to do battle in open country.

Morristown – a village of some fifty houses, a church and a tavern – was well sited. From the east, hill passes would slow any surprise advance by the British and give ample warning of their movement; and the Americans could always withdraw through the westward passes into wilder country. Moreover, it was only twenty-five miles from New York, enabling Washington to react to any troop movements south towards Philadelphia or northwards up the Hudson valley.

The British confirmed Washington's good judgement in choosing his winter quarters by staying comfortably in their own place of hiberna-tion. On top of Howe's failure to pursue Washington across the Delaware, and his weak advance guard of Hessians to defend the river, this represented another crass error by the British commander-in-chief. True, a British expedition in midwinter would have been uncomfort-able, and the Americans would probably have retreated into the hills, entailing a risky British expedition through hills and forest – the Americans' favourite terrain. But the American forces were so vulnerable that they could have been routed and harassed almost to humiliation that winter.

Howe believed that the Americans were on the run anyway, that to carry the fight on to their territory was to risk dispersing his forces and losing precious lives, and that it was better for the British to emerge strengthened after a comfortable winter to do battle later on their own terms in the lowlands. Convinced he was winning and determined to fight only on his own ground, Howe had handed the initiative to Washington.

The latter's view of British strategy was only partly accurate: Howe's 'great end', said Washington, was 'to spread themselves over as much country as they possibly can, and thereby strike a clamp into the spirits of the people, which will effectually put a stop to the new enlistment of

the army, on which all our hopes depend, and which they will most vigorously strive to effect'. That gave Howe more credit for sophistication
than was due: Howe's aim was a decisive engagement in an open battle,
to crush the remnants of the American army. This could work only if
victory was overwhelming: for as long as a rump American army existed,
so too did the low-level resistance and resentment of the rebels' supporters. All Washington's army had to do was survive the winter and seek
some further propaganda success to rekindle recruitment for the
American cause.

Howe needed to eliminate the rebel army, secure large tracts of territory, and enthuse British loyalists in New Jersey. He did none of these
things. Instead, the army stirred up irritation among previously loyal New
Yorkers, who went short of rations, were cold-shouldered by the boisterous British troops, and resented the partying of the commander-in-chief
and his friends – in particular Howe's open flaunting of his mistress.

If the British felt confident of concluding the war successfully in 1777,
they did nothing whatever to advance their cause in the first four months.
While Howe wasted valuable time, American recruitment began to pick
up after a low point in March, when Washington's army had dwindled
still further through desertions. As the hills turned green, congressional
money and soldiers began to swell Washington's ranks. By the end of May
he could boast of an army 9,000 strong and, as ammunition and supplies
poured in from France, the beginnings of a proper arsenal.

The great British dilemma, which preoccupied the military planners
in London as much as in New York, was strategic – how could victory
be achieved in terrain like America? (Essentially the same problem still
faces those who fight guerrilla wars across far-flung and remote countryside to this day.) The man in charge of American policy in London, Lord
George Germain, was what today would be dubbed a 'hawk' – unlike
his predecessor, Lord Dartmouth, an able 'dove' blamed for the failures
at Lexington and Concord.

Aged sixty-one, Germain had long urged a more aggressive policy
towards the colonies. In the winter of 1776–7, he was confronted by a
major problem: three British commanders in America who were all
rivals, cordially detested each other, and had different views of the
correct strategy for winning the war. It was not that the British gave little
thought to how to win that war, or that their strategies were ill thought-
out: rather, they were contradictory.

There were, at this stage, three strategies available to the British, either singly or in combination (later a fourth was to emerge: the southern strategy). The first was what might be dubbed the 'quarantine' strategy: to isolate New England, seen as the infection point for the rest of America, from the other colonies, to restore British rule to the rest, and then go in at leisure to destroy the hard core of resistance in New England.

To achieve this, two simultaneous thrusts were proposed: one southward from Canada, where the British had successfully defeated the Americans, and one up from New York through the Hudson valley to meet the southward pincer at Albany. This strategy had the appeal of simplicity: a surgical amputation of the gangrenous limb of New England looked good on paper, and it would take advantage of the two British strongpoints in the St Lawrence valley and New York.

But it was grotesquely flawed from the beginning. As John Adams later shrewdly observed:

> Discipline and disposition are our resource. It is our policy to draw the enemy into the country, where we can avail ourselves of hills, woods, rivers, defiles, etc., until our soldiers are more inured to war. Howe and Burgoyne will not be able to meet this year [1777] and if they were, it would only be better for us, for we should draw all our forces to a point too. If they were met, they could not cut off the communication between the northern and southern states. But if the communication was cut off for a time, it would be no misfortune, for New England would defend itself, and the southern states would defend themselves.

What on earth would this vast pincer accomplish, beyond the merely symbolic isolation of New England? The British had no chance of fortifying a line 300 miles long to prevent supplies, ammunition and men passing between New England and the other states. Nor, without a far larger force, could they hope to move from that line into the remote woods of New England to eliminate the opposition there any more effectively than they had been able to from Boston.

The only purpose of a pincer would be to produce a British triumph that would demoralize American resistance in the states beyond New England, which was unlikely indeed. Otherwise the scheme, which would over-extend British lines and place British armies at risk to no useful long-term purpose, was overambitious and dangerous.

The second strategy was to seek to control large areas of countryside where the cause of independence had least support, leaving New England alone either to wither on the vine or until an opportunity arose to crush the independence movement there in force. This would reassure the loyalist elements in the central and southern colonies, and encourage them to emerge in large numbers, denying the Americans the possibility of either recruiting or terrorizing them into enlistment, support or passivity. This was the strategy that Washington himself most feared. The disadvantage for the British was that it involved policing a large area with inadequate forces; but it was less obviously pointless and dangerous than the quarantine strategy. It had been briefly tried, and abandoned, with Clinton's ill-fated expedition to Charleston.

The third, more limited and realistic, option was to use maximum British naval power to gain control of the main rivers and urban centres strung along the eastern seaboard of America. If this was done effectively, the cities, urban populations and North American trade would effectively come under British control. Whether the vast American interior was under rebel control or otherwise would then be of little consequence: the urban centres, which the Americans had to use for trade with the outside world, were what mattered. There was a limit, too, to how long the Americans would want to hold the interior if they could not control the ports.

This option, while the least risky for Britain, was seen as somewhat immoral, since it amounted to writing off the large number of loyalist supporters in the interior. It was, however, by far the most likely to succeed from a British point of view, for the eastern seaboard cities could be supplied indefinitely while the British had control of the sea, but the countryside inland might survive but could not hope to prosper if starved of trade.

Provided that the British secured obvious vantage points over the ports, they could hold them indefinitely. It was the kind of strategy that had allowed, for example, the English to subdue Wales in the thirteenth century: secure the fortified outposts along the trading routes, and it doesn't much matter who controls the interior. Its only real disadvantage was that it would involve a long-drawn out struggle, for which the British public might not have the patience.

What was not considered, and could not be at this stage, was whether the British could retain control at all; whether, indeed, the loss of the colonies was inevitable. This issue was bound up (as, with America in Vietnam and countless other insurgency operations before and since) with the depth of the mother country's pocket and commitment to the colonies.

While the 'quarantining' of New England was plainly idiotic to any but its advocates, it represented the tantalizing military prospect of a quick end to the war. The two alternative strategies – policing the middle American countryside as far as the Appalachians or holding the American towns, coast and rivers – both required money, men and staying power, the former strategy much more so than the latter. To hold on to America, Britain would have to make both a judgement and an investment. The judgement would be that outside New England the population was still loyal enough for its allegiance to be retained if people were given the necessary military protection. The investment would be the huge armed forces necessary to provide that protection.

Again, the difficulty was one endemic to guerrilla wars: the largely neutral countryside would support the British only if its people were safe from enemy attack and reprisals; otherwise they would accommodate, voluntarily or involuntarily, the irregulars as a result of persuasion, intimidation, and the guerrillas' spy network and infiltration methods. Given a colossal commitment to policing a huge geographical area, the countryside might be won over at enormous expense. Holding the rivers, coast and ports would be much less expensive, as long as the British retained control of the sea, but would consign the countryside to rule by the rebels even if the latter were forced to their knees economically; the loyalists would be terrorized into submission, and all but the coastal towns would be held by the insurgents.

Of the three options, only the second was both ethical and perhaps tenable in the long term, but it required armies and expenditure of a size the British were unable and unwilling to commit. As in Vietnam two centuries later, the 'freedom fighters' probably did not enjoy majority support, were almost always defeated in pitched battles, and were an irregular and undisciplined force. But they were fighting for their own country and were prepared to intimidate, then retreat in depth, whereas their foreign-based opponents were not prepared to put in the necessary resources.

For, in another eerie parallel, Britain, far from being a country under despotic rule, was governed by public opinion – albeit confined to the considerable and growing middle class, as well as the still influential but no longer dominant aristocracy. The urban middle classes and the country gentry would have to pay for the war, and they were already groaning under the financial exactions arising from the Seven Years War.

While middle-class opinion was strongly in favour of the war, given the colonists' excesses in its early stages, it never favoured an expensive conflict and was unlikely to support a long one. Thus the American War of Independence may have been unwinnable for Britain from the moment the Seven Years War and the Stamp Act crisis had catalysed the formation of an extensive anti-British militia in the colonies.

What slim chance there was of winning depended on abandoning the first crazy scheme for a 'quick kill' in favour of either the second option, which was expensive, or the third one, which was inexpensive but risked leaving the countryside to the rebels. As usual in military policy, it was a matter of choosing the lesser of three evils. What happened was that the British adopted, under separate generals, the first option and a mixture of the second and the third.

British policy was confused and bedevilled by the conflicts of rival policymakers and commanders; but, while the first strategy was to fail in spectacular and expensive fashion, the second and third were to prove sophisticated and very nearly succeeded despite almost hopeless circumstances.

The quarantine approach – dividing New England from the rest of the colonies – seemed the obvious policy in Whitehall, given the extent of British strength in Canada and New York. In the autumn of 1776 General 'Gentleman Johnny' Burgoyne, nominally subordinate to Howe, had returned to England to lobby for this course. It was also favoured by a far more capable commander, Sir Guy Carleton, who as Wolfe's Quartermaster General had been the mastermind behind the successful capture of Quebec from France and an effective and enlightened ruler since, presiding with remarkable skill over the reconciliation of the defeated Catholic colonists and Quebequois to British rule. Carleton had braved furious opposition from both British merchants and the Americans to his policy of reconciliation, but, as he put it, 'the Protestants in Canada are under 400; about 360; but the French inhabitants, who are all Catholics, amount to 150,000!'

Carleton had a strong personality with a furious temper. He lacked scruples under pressure (which served him in good stead when he disguised himself as a Canadian sailor to get past American patrols), and he had a deep contempt for Lord George Germain, his boss. Following the Americans' failure to conquer Canada in the early summer of 1776, the British had hotly pursued them under Carleton's command, with

Burgoyne as his deputy. The British had moved up the Richelieu river to establish a force of some 17,000 at the top end of Lake Champlain, and had put together a fleet of three large ships – which had been systematically dismantled and carried overland past the ten miles of rapids on the Richelieu north of St John's, where the lake navigation begins – with 20 gunboats, 30 launches and 400 small boats. It had been a formidable achievement.

With this force the British proposed to sweep the lake clear of a smaller American naval force of four warships and assorted river craft commanded by the vigorous Benedict Arnold. The British had 94 guns to the rebels' 102, but the British had heavier firepower. Burgoyne was left to command the British troops on shore, while Carleton went aboard to direct the naval operation.

On 11 October 1776 the British sailed right past the American fleet under a strong following wind, and when they realized their mistake they had to move back against it to engage Arnold's fleet lying between Valcour Island and the western shore of the lake. After a furious fight, Arnold's ships slipped away through a line of British ships during the night and would have escaped to safety under the American guns of Fort Ticonderoga had the wind not changed.

But the British caught up and victory was theirs: two thirds of the American vessels were destroyed, 80 men were killed and 120 were taken prisoner. However, enough British vessels were damaged to convince Carleton that it was futile to seek to take Fort Ticonderoga. Overcautiously, he refused even to try to outflank the fort and cut it off from the south, for which he was heavily criticized. It was too late in the year for the British to continue the offensive, and Carleton withdrew his men to winter quarters in Canada, while Burgoyne returned to Britain to argue his case for a full-scale assault down the northern route – this time under his command, not that of the quarrelsome but highly effective Carleton. Germain, disliking Carleton, was deeply impressed by Burgoyne's idea.

# PART III

*The Eagle and the Lion*

# 14

# *The Reason Why*

Johnny Burgoyne came from minor aristocracy (his impoverished father, a gambling addict, was the second son of a baronet). He had been a brave soldier, serving in Portugal, France and Spain, and an enlightened officer, earning the admiration of his troops for the unusual consideration he showed towards them. He formed his own regiment, the 16th Light Dragoons, and issued a code of instructions for it which argued that

> English soldiers are to be treated as thinking beings. Two systems which, generally speaking, divide the disciplinarians; the one is that of training men like spaniels, by the stick; the other, after the French, of substituting the point of honour in place of severity. The followers of the first are for reducing the nature of man as low as it will bear. Sight, hearing and feeling are the only senses necessary, and all qualities of reasoning become not only useless but troublesome The admirers of the latter, who more commonly argue more from speculation than practice, are for exalting rationality, and they are commonly deceived in their expectations. The Germans are the best; the French, by the avowal of their own officers, the worst disciplined troops in Europe. I apprehend a just medium between the two extremes to be the surest means to bring English soldiers to perfection.
>
> [Officers must take every opportunity for] getting insight into the character to each particular man and proportioning accordingly the degree of punishment and encouragement. There are, however, occasions, such as during stable or fatigue duty, when officers may slacken the reins so far as to talk with soldiers; nay, even a joke may be used without harm but to good purpose ...
>
> A short space of time given to reading each day, if the books are well chosen and the subject properly digested, will furnish a great deal of instruction ...

> From the contempt of figures, numberless inconveniences arise. I
> mention, as one of the most trivial, a false return which officers will con-
> tinually sign if they trust the figure part to a sergeant ... One great advan-
> tage which attends an application to this science is that it strongly
> exercises the mind, and common reading becomes a relaxation after it.

These views, though self-evident and patronizing now, were imaginative
in his day, and show Burgoyne to be far from the buffoon he is often
portrayed as. His observations on Continental armies were also shrewd:

> The first principle of the Prussian system is subordination and the maxim
> 'not to reason but to obey'. The effects are attention, alertness, precision
> and every executive quality in the officers which, assisted by the constant
> exercise of the soldiers upon the soundest principles of tactics, enable the
> troops to practice with wonderful ease and exactness, manoeuvres that
> others hardly admit in theory.
>    The ranks are filled up, perhaps more than a third part, with strangers,
> deserters and enemies of various countries ... In an army thus composed
> it is wisdom and sound policy to sink and degrade all intellectual facul-
> ties, and to reduce the man as nearly as possible to mere machinery ...
>    In the Austrian army, the officers have liberality, the soldiers national
> spirit ... In the exercise of arms and the military step the Austrians differ
> but little from the Prussians; they are not yet arrived at the extraordinary
> steadiness of the latter under arms, but cannot fail of soon attaining it,
> with the advantage of seeing their ends compassed with good will and
> little severity ... Zeal, emulation and honour ... will out-do any diligence
> arising from dread of punishment or other slavish punishment.

In private life Burgoyne was a flamboyant and attractive character. In
1751 he had eloped with the daughter of the Earl of Derby, Lady
Charlotte Stanley, eventually winning the old man's grudging assent to
the marriage. A heroic action against the Seville Regiment in Valencia
de Alcántara in 1762 made him a minor public figure.

In 1761 he had been elected to Parliament, where, with a reputation
as a rake and a gambler, he associated with other high spirits such as
Charles James Fox. His most celebrated role there was as parliamentary
inquisitor-in-chief against Robert Clive, the conqueror of Bengal, in
1773. As chairman of the select committee set up to investigate alleged
abuses by the servants of the East India Company, and in particular
Clive, his motives were mixed. First, as a loyal supporter of the King, he
reflected the monarch's own views. Second, the post brought him a high
parliamentary profile. Third, Burgoyne may genuinely have been moved

1. King George III: stubborn re-asserter of the royal prerogative

2. Samuel Adams: Father of the
Revolution and the first Uncle Sam

3. John Adams: the cleverest revolutionary

4. Benjamin Franklin: polymath and
brilliant diplomat

5. Patrick Henry: 'Liberty or death'

6. William Pitt, Earl of Chatham: Empire builder who was America's best friend

7. George Grenville: incorruptible father of the Stamp Act

8. Frederick, Lord North: the King's parliamentary manager

9. The Boston Tea Party: calculated and organized provocation

10. Tarring and feathering: the American way of torture

11. Paul Revere's Ride: the first myth

12. Thomas Paine: popular firebrand of independence

13. The skirmish at Lexington: who fired the first shot?

14. Charles, Lord Cornwallis: tactically skilled, strategically flawed

15. William, Lord Howe: able, laid-back commander who did not believe in his cause

16. Lord George Germain: indecisive, fussy and remote director of the British war effort

17. 'Gentleman Johnny' Burgoyne: magnificent, but a disaster waiting to happen

18. Breed's Hill: Britain's pyrrhic victory

19. New York in flames

20. General Charles Lee: uncouth rival of Washington

21. General Nathanael Greene: the greatest American general

22. General Daniel Morgan: all-American hero

23. John Paul Jones: one-battle admiral and daring raider of British coasts

24. George Washington: a very political general

25. General Horatio Gates: found wanting at the end

26. The Declaration of Independence

27. Crossing the Delaware: birth of the Washington legend

28. Saratoga: surrender and betrayal

29. Winter quarters
at Valley Forge: the
great ordeal

30. The murder
of Jane McCrea:
fact or fiction?

31. Gilbert, Marquis de Lafayette:
Washington's French protégé

32. Jean, Comte de Rochambeau:
able French commander

33. General Benedict Arnold and Major John André: the betrayer and the spymaster

34. Yorktown: the great surrender

35. Alexander Hamilton: Washington's conservative ally

36. Thomas Jefferson: the great romantic

37. Washington is sworn in as President: the revolution turns full circle

by moral indignation, in his somewhat glib and shallow fashion. Finally, Clive, as Britain's greatest living soldier, was a potential commander of British forces in America, and a rival to Burgoyne's ambitions there. Clive's own views on America were moderate, in stark opposition to Burgoyne's belligerent ones. If Clive's reputation was ruined, Burgoyne's military career might prosper.

In the event, Burgoyne's case against Clive was defeated; the Prime Minister, Lord North, who had patronized Burgoyne and was related to him by marriage, voted with him over the Clive affair, but seemed less than impressed, and the two moved apart. As Burgoyne said, 'though I bore respect to Lord North's character, no two persons not in direct enmity could live at a greater distance'.

Burgoyne's views on America were conventionally hawkish. In a parliamentary debate in 1774 he said:

> I look upon America to be our spoilt child, which we have already spoiled by too much indulgence. We are desired to conciliate measures by the Americans; I look upon this measure to have a totally different effect; I think it a misuse of time to go into committee [on this proposal], and that even the enquiry, the news of which will soon reach America, will tend to nothing but to raise hearts, and not appease, but irritate and disturb the more. It is said, if you remove this duty, you will remove all grievances in America; but I am apprehensive it is the right of taxation they contend about; it is the independent state of that country from the legislature of this which is contended for; but I am ready to resist that proposition, and to contend at any future time, against such independence.

However, his more spirited side still broke through outside Parliament. Always attracted to the stage, and a friend of the actor-manager David Garrick, he now wrote professionally for the theatre. His *The Maid of Oaks* achieved a considerable success. Curiously, this sometimes unconventional and attractive character was deeply conventional in other ways – for example in his attitude to America.

In December 1776, shortly after his wife's death, Burgoyne met Lord Germain to whom, it was alleged, he criticized Sir Guy Carleton's decision to withdraw into Canada. He advocated an attack down the north–south Canada lake route, long anticipated by the Americans. He also suggested that a force under Colonel Barry St Leger push across from Lake Ontario to the west along the Mohawk river towards the Hudson valley, to link with the main thrust. He said that once he himself reached Albany the Canadian army should place itself under General

Howe's command – suggesting that he expected the British commander-in-chief to lead a force up the Hudson valley to liaise with the other two, although he did not spell this out.

Germain was by now sufficiently exasperated by Carleton's stubbornness to want him recalled to England, but the King insisted merely that he should be given the job of continuing to rule Canada while another general took charge of military operations to the south. There is little reason to doubt that the flamboyant Burgoyne's main purpose in returning to England was to seek to displace Carleton and lobby for his own scheme of invading America from Canada.

The scheme was not new: Lord Dartmouth had favoured it, and Howe had repeatedly considered it. However, in the autumn Howe had written from New York to Whitehall outlining his plan of campaign for 1777. This would consist of three movements:

> 1st. An offensive army of 10,000 rank and file to act on the side of Rhode Island by taking possession of Providence, penetrating from thence into the country toward Boston and, if possible, to reduce that town. Two thousand men to be left for the defence of Rhode Island, and for making small incursions, under the protection of the shipping, upon the coast of Connecticut. This army to be commanded by Lieut Gen Clinton.
>
> 2nd. An offensive army in the province of New York to move up the North [Hudson] river to Albany, to consist of not less than 10,000 men and 5,000 for New York and adjacent posts.
>
> 3rd. A defensive army of 8,000 men to cover Jersey, and to keep the southern [rebel] army in check by [threatening] Philadelphia, which I would propose to attack, as well as Virginia, provided the success of the other operations will admit of an adequate force to be sent against that province.

Significantly, while Howe proposed the move north to Albany, he made no mention of a liaison with the northern army descending from Canada, and possibly he envisaged the move to Albany as merely preparatory. Even so, he had clearly switched from the idea of a northern pincer to that of direct attacks on Boston and Philadelphia – which he believed would end the war if successful. To achieve all three, however, Howe said he would require an army of 35,000 men – and he believed he had only 20,000 fit for action. Germain replied that Whitehall could spare only another 8,000 or so.

Revising his plan, in a letter which reached Germain in February 1777

Howe decided to abandon the thrust towards Boston and leave 2,000 to defend Rhode Island, 4,000 around New York and 3,000 on the Hudson river while throwing 10,000 into taking Philadelphia. He made no reference to the old north–south pincer strategy, merely remarking that 'we must not look for the northern army to reach Albany before the middle of September'. This particular strategy was clearly to be postponed at least until then, if not abandoned altogether. Philadelphia was to be the target:

> The opinion of people being much changed in Pennsylvania, and their minds in general, from the late progress of the army, disposed to peace, in which sentiment they would be confirmed by our getting possession of Philadelphia. I am from this consideration fully persuaded the principal army should act offensively on that side where the enemy's chief strength will certainly be collected.

Germain wrote back on 3 March, now promising only 3,000 reinforcements, and with no reference to the old plan for a junction of the forces marching up from New York to Albany and down from Canada. This had apparently been dropped from the Colonial Secretary's agenda as well as from Howe's. Germain declared, 'the King entirely approves of your proposed deviation from the plan you formerly suggested, being of the opinion that the reasons which have induced you to recommend this change in your operations are solid and definite'.

However, just a few days earlier, possibly at Germain's request, Burgoyne had submitted to Whitehall a paper called, 'Thoughts for Conducting the War from the Side of Canada'. This outlined in great detail the strategy for an army coming down from Canada, taking Ticonderoga, marching round or crossing Lake George, and thence descending to Albany. He urged:

> Lest all these attempts [frightening the rebels away by Indians and light troops or taking the road by Skenesborough] should unavoidably fail, and it becomes necessary to attack the enemy by water on Lake George, the army at the outset should be provided with carriages, implements and artificers for conveying armed vessels from Ticonderoga to the lake.

Burgoyne concluded:

> These ideas are formed upon the supposition that it is the sole purpose of the Canada army to effect a junction with General Howe, or after co-operating so far as to get the possession of Albany and open the communication to New York, to remain upon the Hudson's river, and thereby enable that general to act with his whole army to the southward.

However, Burgoyne was clearly aware that Howe might not be prepared
to partner him in the pincer movement. In case Howe decided to 'act
with his whole force to the southward' throughout the campaigning
season, Burgoyne suggested that the army descending from Canada
could veer eastward across sixty miles of wild country towards the
Connecticut river, where it might meet up with the garrison on Rhode
Island. This hare-brained idea was quickly dismissed, although Germain
favoured Burgoyne's scheme for advancing down towards Albany.

Sir Henry Clinton, who was expected to be offered the Canadian
command, arrived in London at the end of February and unexpectedly
declined to take it, leaving the field open for Burgoyne. Clinton was
instead offered the job of second-in-command to Howe, who was to lead
the major British offensive against Philadelphia. The probability
remains that Burgoyne was the prime exponent of the expedition from
Canada; that he had used the rift between Germain and Carleton to
deprive the latter of the Canadian command; that he had somehow
engineered the diffident Clinton's refusal to take command himself; and
that he had persuaded the hawkish Germain and the King to adopt his
aggressive tactics. While this must be conjecture, certainly Burgoyne was
the big winner, being offered command of the northern army.

If these assumptions are correct, then the planned expedition from
Canada becomes more clearly a dramatic initiative impressed upon the
British government's hawks by Burgoyne as a speedy resolution to the
war – with himself cast in the role of victorious general. In fact, given
Howe's revised strategy to march south and attack Philadelphia, it
becomes plain that Burgoyne was setting up a contending expedition
with a rival objective – something which Colonial Secretary Germain
and the rest of the British government connived in, perhaps believing
that a double victory would finally crush the Americans.

Although Burgoyne had made a cursory reference to liaising with
Howe's forces, and Germain was to do so more insistently, it seems likely
that the issue was not considered greatly important because Burgoyne
was confidently expected to reach Albany without external support. His
plan never suggested that he would need to be supported by the commander-in-chief in reaching Albany; but it was obvious that Howe
would have to gain control of the Hudson up to Albany in order to
supply his army before the following winter set in.

Thus Burgoyne made his first key mistake. Certain that he could reach Albany unaided, at this stage he neither asked Howe to ensure that help was sent to him from the south nor urged Germain to do so.

If Burgoyne's expedition is seen as essentially a one-army venture, with the British government's collusion, the events of the following weeks fall into place: the astonishing failure of communication by Lord Germain to General Howe; the latter's own contemptuous refusal to acknowledge the northern army's actions; Clinton's failure to advise Howe of the dangers of such a course; and Burgoyne's own failure to seek Howe's support.

Historians have traditionally ascribed these failures to massive incompetence on the part of the British. They can more readily be explained by the professional jealousy of two rival commanders, each seeking to deal the death blow to the American cause and separately encouraged by the British government.

By placing Burgoyne under the purely nominal command of Canada's governor, Sir Guy Carleton, the Colonial Secretary had neatly sidestepped the problem that Burgoyne, as Howe's subordinate, should have taken his orders from the commander-in-chief. Lord Germain and the King possibly saw Burgoyne as the man whose bold initiative would conclude the war, after Howe's caution had singularly failed to do so the previous year. The seeds were thus being sown for one of the greatest disasters in British military history – perhaps the greatest, in view of the momentous consequences.

Events now unfolded so as to doom Burgoyne's expedition even before it had set out. Germain, in giving Burgoyne independence of command from Sir Guy Carleton, whom the British minister disliked, was needlessly offensive, effectively blaming the governor of Canada for the disaster at Trenton. He wrote of his mortification at learning that

> Upon your repassing Lake Champlain [in the previous year], a very considerable number of the insurgents, finding their presence no longer necessary near Ticonderoga, immediately marched from thence and joined the rebel forces in the provinces of New York and Jersey. That unexpected reinforcement was more particularly unfortunate for us as it enabled the rebels to break in with some degree of success upon parts of the winter quarters that were taken up by the army under the command of Sir William Howe.

Germain finished the letter to Carleton with the words:

I shall write to Sir William Howe from hence by the first packet; but you will endeavour to give him the earliest intelligence of this measure and also direct Lieutenant General Burgoyne and Lieutenant Colonel St Leger to neglect no opportunity of doing the same, that they may receive instructions from Sir William Howe. You will at the same time inform them that, until they shall have received orders from Sir William Howe, it is his Majesty's pleasure that they shall act as exigencies require, and in such manner as they shall judge most proper for making an impression on the rebels and bringing them to obedience; but that in doing so they must never lose view of their intended junction with Sir William Howe as their principal object.

Predictably, the furious Carleton promptly resigned his post. Burgoyne had been given command of some 7,000 troops, plus a further 700 or so under the command of Colonel St Leger for a diversionary raid along the Mohawk river, leaving just under 4,000 to garrison Canada.

But despite his promise, Germain never had written to his commander-in-chief – an omission as historic as the misunderstood order that led to the Charge of the Light Brigade at Balaclava. The crotchety, punctilious Colonial Secretary's failure to fulfil his pledge to Carleton has never been convincingly explained. Lamely, he later said that he had issued no specific orders to march to Albany that summer because he had never doubted Howe's intention to do so, but he had intended to send the commander-in-chief a copy of the orders to Carleton, together with a letter setting out Howe's intended part in the operation.

But Howe had made it anything but clear that he still intended to liaise with the northern army under his new plan to attack Philadelphia. The force left at New York would be too small, and only if he had finished the Philadelphia operation by summer would he be in a position to help Burgoyne. Nor did he make any explicit commitment to do so, beyond the throwaway remark that 'We must not look for the northern army to reach Albany before the middle of September' in his letter to Germain, which suggested he saw no role for himself in helping Burgoyne reach Albany.

Even this casual hint was anything but a commitment, given that, owing to the shortage of reinforcements, he had specifically abandoned his earlier plan to move up to Albany with 10,000 men, leaving 5,000 in New York, in favour of the all-or-nothing drive to Philadelphia, leaving a skeleton army of only 4,000 men to hold New York – 1,000 fewer than previously envisaged – and none at all for an expedition up the Hudson.

In view of the new plan's failure to spell out that any of the New York garrison would be destined for the Hudson, or that Howe intended to come to Burgoyne's aid after taking Philadelphia, it seems that Germain was guilty of a fatal dereliction of duty in not explicitly ordering Howe to come to help Burgoyne.

Not only was no specific instruction ever sent to Howe: according to William Knox, Germain's under-secretary, when Carleton's orders had been drafted:

> Lord [Germain] came down to the office on his way to Stoneland, when I observed to him that there was no letter to Howe to acquaint him with the plan or what was expected of him in consequence of it. His lordship started and D'Oyley [the deputy Secretary of War] stared, but said he would in a few moments write a few lines. 'So' said his lordship, 'my poor horses must stand in the street all the time and I shan't be on my time anywhere.' D'Oyley then said he had better go, and he would write himself to Howe and enclose copies of Burgoyne's instructions which he would want to know; and with this his lordship was satisfied, as it enabled him to keep his time, for he could never bear delay or disappointment; and D'Oyley sat down and wrote a letter to Howe, but he neither showed it to me or gave a copy of it for the office, and if Howe had not acknowledged the receipt of it, with a copy of the Instructions to Burgoyne, we could not have proved that he ever saw it.

For the sake of the Colonial Secretary's 'poor horses', the crucial instruction to Britain's commander-in-chief in America was never drafted, for the orders to Carleton and Burgoyne were now forwarded to General Howe (reaching him in early July) with merely a covering note from D'Oyley, containing no explicit instructions for Howe at all, beyond stating that the two men would eventually come under his command and that 'their intended junction with Sir William Howe' was 'their principal object'.

It stretches credulity that so fussy a man as Germain, whose orders to Carleton spelt out the number of men in his expedition down to the last individual ('Second Brigade: Battalion companies of the 20th, 53rd and 62nd regiments deducting 50 from each corps as above – 1,194' etc.) could have made such a colossal blunder through negligence. It is far more likely that his historic omission was deliberate, because he fully expected Howe to be incensed by the decision to detach Burgoyne from his command and virtually give him his own army for a separate expedition intended to bring a quick end to the war.

Howe, denied reinforcements from Britain, might reasonably have expected any available troops in Canada to be ferried down to help him – something Burgoyne had explicitly argued against in his memorandum ('I do not conceive any expedition from the sea can be so formidable to the enemy, or as effectual to close the war as an invasion from Canada'). Howe could only have been furious at Germain's decision to put his subordinate in charge of a competing army undertaking a rival mission.

Germain was in effect too embarrassed to issue a direct order which would indicate his lack of confidence in the cautious Howe – this might have resulted in an angry outburst by the commander-in-chief, like that by Carleton in Canada, or even his resignation. Instead he preferred not to refer the matter directly to him, perhaps bowled along by Burgoyne's optimism.

This interpretation also explains Howe's own response on receiving the copy of the instructions to Carleton and Burgoyne enclosed by d'Oyley in July: his terse acknowledgement no doubt reflected his fury at the government's decision. Howe, who was no fool, would certainly have known of the preparations for Burgoyne's expedition long before. But he would have seen no reason to help a rival subordinate who had withdrawn from his command and commandeered thousands of men badly needed for the success of his own enterprise. If Burgoyne believed he could reach Albany, let him try; Howe was not going to endanger the success of his Philadelphia project by detaching forces to support him. Nor had he been ordered to do so by Germain.

This version also explains why Clinton, who was aware of the dangers of the lack of co-ordination between the two armies, failed to persuade Howe to come to Burgoyne's rescue; the diffident deputy commander shrank from further incensing his furious boss. Finally, it explains why Germain, who wrote to Howe no fewer than eight times from the beginning of March 1777, never once mentioned the planned Canadian offensive, least of all to suggest he co-operate with Burgoyne.

When Burgoyne arrived in Quebec by ship on 6 May, the conditions were in place for the first turning point in the American War of Independence: the two main British armies were virtually under separate commanders, engaged on rival wars. Burgoyne was aware that his situation was 'critical and delicate', and was deeply apprehensive about the reception the slighted Carleton might have in store for him. He need not have worried:

Sir Guy Carleton has received me ... in a manner that, in my opinion, does infinite honour to his private and public character. That he should have wished for the lead in active and important military operations is very natural. That he thinks he has some cause for resentment for the general tenor of treatment he has received from some of the ministers is discernible; but neither his disappointment nor his personal feelings operate against his duty; and I am convinced he means to forward the King's measures, entrusted to my hands, with all the zeal he could have employed had they rested in his own.

William Howe's plan to attack Philadelphia had four objectives: to lure Washington's army into open battle and defeat it; to control as much countryside as possible, encouraging loyalists to come out on the British side; to gain control of the major eastern cities; and to strike a devastating psychological blow by seizing the colonial capital. Striking at Philadelphia would serve all four ends: almost certainly Washington would be forced to defend it; it was the key to military power over a large area; it was a major eastern city; and, as the place where the American Declaration of Independence had been issued, it was a perfect means to strike at enemy morale. Provided Howe could be confident of taking the town, it seemed a much more promising venture than Burgoyne's.

As late as March 1777, Howe's intention was to recross New Jersey by land in order to seize the American capital, thus completing the unfinished business of the year before, ideally with a co-ordinated attack from the sea. But when reinforcements were denied him, and instead were diverted to Burgoyne in Canada, Howe conceived a new plan – to attack Philadelphia only by water, sailing up the Delaware river, which would avoid the risky cross-country journey through New Jersey.

It was a brilliant concept, with only two drawbacks: by embarking his troops, Howe would make it temporarily impossible to reinforce New York or to march to Burgoyne's aid if necessary; and the Delaware river was effectively blocked by the Americans. Further, in choosing not to march back across New Jersey, the British would seem to have abandoned the state's many loyalists. But Howe apparently feared an ambush from the west.

During the next three months of preparation, he staged several sorties and feints both to lure Washington into battle and to deceive the Americans as to his true intentions. He marched his forces beyond the Raritan river, which prompted Washington to move southwards from

Morristown to the heights of Middlebrook. Then Howe withdrew and, when Washington followed, turned on him, nearly crushing the Americans in open battle. He sent forces up the Hudson valley then into Long Island Sound, while the Americans watched bemused as to his objectives.

Washington, knowing that the British were massing for an attack from Canada, was certain that Howe's ultimate destination, by land and by river, was Albany, to link up with Burgoyne. It was with incredulity that the American commander learned on 23 July that Howe had embarked 36 battalions, including a cavalry regiment, on board 260 boats, totalling 18,000 men.

Washington never believed that Howe would sail up the Delaware to capture Philadelphia, but on 31 July he learned that the British fleet had been sighted off the river's mouth. He then learned that, even more remarkably, the ships had sailed on, deterred by the strength of the American defences on the river.

Not until 15 August did the British reappear – this time in Chesapeake Bay, after a stormy and extremely hot forty-seven days at sea which had killed most of Howe's horses. He landed his troops on one side of the Elk river. To the last the British commander had kept the Americans guessing: Washington believed that Howe was headed further south.

At the beginning of August, Washington moved his army of 16,000 men towards Philadelphia, establishing quarters at Wilmington. The British soon afterwards marched forward through the well-provided country-side, ecstatic after their gruelling sea journey, eating well, and often plundering the farms – although Howe imposed severe penalties for those caught. Washington sent detachments to harry the British, while his main force occupied Brandywine Creek, a watercourse bounded by wooded slopes, in an effort to block the British from advancing on the American capital.

So far the British general had shown both audacity and skill, avoiding the potential trap on the Delaware river and catching the Americans by surprise with his move up the Chesapeake. Now his tactical ability was displayed again in by far the most dazzling British campaign of the war. As in the Battle of Long Island, Howe's response to Washington's attempt to block him was to stage a frontal feint attack – in this case on the main American force at Chad's Ford across the Brandywine. At 10 a.m. on 11 September his artillery, under the German Baron Wilhelm von Knyphausen, opened fire across the creek as a prelude to the expected assault.

But six hours earlier Howe had already dispatched his main force on a long march across Jefferson Ford to the north, beyond the furthest American positions. Washington had learned of this move at 9 a.m., but failed to take it seriously enough. So the British succeeded in occupying the strategic heights of Osborne's Hill and advanced on the Americans from the rear: the rebels had been caught napping.

The main American forces along the creek rapidly wheeled around to avoid being taken from behind and to engage the British force. Washington hastily asked General Nathanael Greene, whose men had been standing by in reserve to support the American forces awaiting Knyphausen's attack across the Brandywine, to bring his troops up to plug a gap in the new American front line created by the rapid manoeuvre. This Greene did at a run, his troops covering four miles in forty-five minutes. The British now coolly descended the hill in perfect formation to the strains of 'The British Grenadier', and plunged into a vicious battle. As one British officer described it:

> 'Twas not like those of Covent Garden or Drury Lane. Thou hast seen Le Brun's paintings and the tapestry perhaps at Blenheim. Are these natural resemblances? Pshaw! quoth the captain, en un mot. There was a most infernal fire of cannon and musquetry. Most incessant shouting, 'Incline to the right! Incline to the left! Halt! Charge! Etc.' The balls plowing up the ground. The trees crackling over one's head. The branches riven by the artillery. The leaves failing as in autumn by the grapeshot.

The sound of battle gave Knyphausen his cue to attack at Chad's Ford: the American defenders there had been depleted by the departure of Greene's forces. The German bravely led his men across the river under withering fire, the Brandywine soon being 'much stained with blood'. Knyphausen seized the artillery, and took on the American infantry. Caught between two pincers, the Americans yielded and then panicked, but after some four miles they encountered another American force which slowed them into an orderly retreat.

The American army had survived to fight another day, but it had lost the decisive battle for the defence of the capital. Some 200 Americans had been killed, 500 wounded and 400 captured, compared to around 100 British killed and 450 wounded. Howe had faultlessly outmanoeuvred Washington.

The American commander desperately summoned reinforcements for his army, which had again been weakened by desertions; soon another 1,000 regular soldiers and 2,000 militia arrived from Maryland and New Jersey. He continued to seek to block the British advance. On 16 September a full-scale battle threatened to develop at Warren Tavern, before heavy rain doused the Americans' powder and forced them to retreat.

Washington dispatched some 1,500 men a couple of miles to the south to harass the enemy. But at 1 a.m. on the night of 20 September, after removing the flints from their muskets so they could not be fired accidentally, three British battalions surrounded the American camp at Paoli and massacred the sleeping men with swords and bayonets. As one British officer described it, 'Light infantry bayoneted every man they came up with, the camp was immediately set on fire and this, with the cries of the wounded, formed altogether one of the most dreadful scenes I ever beheld.' Some 300 Americans were killed and 100 were lucky enough to be captured. Only 18 British soldiers died.

Howe was not slow to follow up his advantage: next day he set off towards Reading, travelling up the Schuylkill river, while Washington's forces sought to keep up with him on the other bank. Then, dramatically, he turned back and crossed a ford behind the Americans, dispatching a force of 4,000 redcoats under Cornwallis to seize Philadelphia while his main army of some 9,000 men camped at Germantown five miles to the north. Congress had already fled the capital, and Cornwallis's soldiers entered Philadelphia, which, remarkably, was largely pro-British in sentiment, to the strains of 'God Save the King'. The date was 26 September 1777 – just over fourteen months after the signing of the Declaration of Independence in the same city, and only days after two humiliating defeats for Washington's army.

To many Americans, the war seemed all but over. In propaganda terms, the British victory had been overwhelming. The Americans had been defeated in every pitched battle they had dared to fight, and had now been completely outmanoeuvred by Howe. With Philadelphia lost as well as New York, the cause seemed hopeless.

Against the odds, Washington decided to stage another desperate counter-attack to restore morale, akin to his masterful strike across the Delaware the previous winter. He believed his opportunity arose because Howe kept his army dispersed. The bulk of British forces were at

Germantown, while 3,000 were guarding the supply line from Elktown; more were stationed with Cornwallis in Philadelphia itself, and some 2,000 had been sent east along the Delaware. Once again he was on the ropes, and he exhorted his men to do great deeds: 'Let it never be said that in a day of action you turned your backs on the foe; let the evening no longer triumph.'

On the night of 3 October, with an army barely larger than that of the British at Germantown, he staged a twenty-mile forced march east, from his camp, deploying his forces in four columns down the four roads into the scattered village of Germantown. It was a curious tactic, for it nullified the slight American advantage in numbers. But, starting at five in the morning in a heavy fog, the Americans had the advantage of stealth.

Howe was taken by surprise. After only an hour's sleep, having spent the night gambling – a favourite pastime – he jumped on a horse, shouting 'Form! Form!' at his men, but was forced to fall back. The Americans, recalling the Paoli massacre, were in savage mood, and gave no quarter. A number of British soldiers took refuge in the 'Chew House', a large old stone building, and futile attempts to dislodge them delayed Washington's army for hours.

Nathanael Greene, advancing down Limekiln Road to the east, had also sent one of his units into the fray, and this mistakenly attacked one of the main American columns, under General Wayne. This confusion, and the delay at Chew House, persuaded Howe, with astonishing speed and improvisation, to regroup and launch a counter-attack, forcing the Americans to retreat some twenty miles, their offensive in a shambles.

The British, caught by surprise, had nevertheless won, but they were in no state to pursue. The Americans were later to make much of this, characteristically turning defeat into victory. Wayne wrote:

> Fortune smiled on us for full three hours. The enemy were broke, dispersed and flying in all quarters. We were in possession of their whole encampment, together with their artillery park, etc. etc. A windmill attack was made upon a house ... Our troops ... thinking it something formidable, fell back to assist – the enemy believing it to be a retreat, followed – confusion ensued, and we ran away from the arms of victory open to receive us.

Thomas Paine wrote that the Americans 'appeared to be only sensible of a disappointment, not a defeat'.

Nevertheless, the truth was that Washington's surprise attack, which had come so close to success, had ended in disaster. Washington's tactic of dispersing his army along four roads had been a blunder, his troops had been badly led in firing upon one another, they had wasted time attacking Chew House, and they had been pressed back by a disciplined British counter-attack. Some 650 Americans had been killed or wounded, compared to some 500 British; some 450 Americans were captured. The British had been caught unawares, but had reacted speedily to snatch victory from a seemingly certain defeat.

Determined to open up the Delaware river as a supply line to Philadelphia, on 21 October Howe sent 2,000 men under General Donop to attack the American-held Fort Mercier on the New Jersey side of the waterway. The attack failed, with the loss of 500 men – including the luckless Donop, the man responsible for the failure of the British defences along the Delaware the previous winter, who died with the words 'I perish the victim of my own ambition [presumably in seeking to defend the Delaware line] and the avarice of my prince [in not furnishing him with the means to do so].' This flop by the British made up for the American failure at Germantown.

An attack on Fort Mifflin, a few miles below Philadelphia, was more successful. The British advance was supported by several warships sailing upriver, and by nightfall 'the fort exhibited a picture of desolation. The whole area was ploughed like a field. The buildings [were] hanging in broken fragments, the guns all dismounted.' The Americans evacuated the rest of the garrison along with the defenders of Fort Mercier.

# 15

# *The Trap*

Other things being equal, Howe's capture of the American capital should have signalled the beginning of the end. In every engagement but one the Americans had been mauled – often badly. Only the previous winter's skirmishes had suggested there was life in the American cause. But within weeks Howe's superb achievement in capturing Philadelphia had been overshadowed by news of a disaster slowly engulfing the British army sent under Burgoyne's leadership down from Canada into the wilds of northern New York State.

On 20 June 1777 Burgoyne had assembled his expeditionary force from Canada for the historic march down the Hudson valley that was intended to defeat the American rebels decisively. His army of 7,000 men had gathered at Cumberland Point, some way north of Valcour Island, where the major battle had taken place on Lake Champlain a year before. It consisted of six British battalions, making up two brigades, and two brigades of Germans, all but one of their battalions being Brunswickers, the last Hessians. The army had 35 guns, 6 howitzers and 6 mortars.

There were 300 Indians to act as scouts, some 1,500 Canadians, and another 100 loyalists, their numbers swelling later in the journey briefly to 700, declining to 400 at the campaign's end. Burgoyne was supported by two outstanding officers, his chief of staff, Major-General William Phillips, a veteran of Minden, and General Simon Fraser, in charge of a crack corps of light infantry. The commander of the German troops was Baron Adolf von Riedesel.

Burgoyne launched his campaign with a high-sounding proclamation threatening to punish those who

inflicted arbitrary imprisonment, confiscation of property, persecution and torture unprecedented in the inquisitions of the Romish church

[upon] the most quiet subjects, without the distinction of age or sex, for the sole crime, often only suspicion, of having adhered in principle to the government under which they were born.

He also threatened:

I have but to give stretch to the Indian forces under my direction, and they amount to thousands, to overtake the hardened enemies of Great Britain and America. I consider them the same wherever they may lurk. If not withstanding these endeavours, and sincere inclinations to effect them, the frenzy of hostility should remain, I trust I shall stand acquitted in the eyes of God and men in denouncing and executing the vengeance of the state against the wilful outcasts – the messengers of justice and of wrath await them in the field; and devastation, famine and every concomitant horror that a reluctant but indispensable prosecution of military duty must occasion, will bar the way to their return.

To the Indians, Burgoyne humanely if grandiosely declared:

I positively forbid bloodshed when you are not opposed in arms. Aged men, women, children and prisoners must be held sacred from the knife, even in time of actual conflict. You shall receive compensation for the prisoners you take, but you shall be called to account to scalps.

In conformity and indulgence to your customs … you shall be allowed to take the scalps of the dead, when killed by your fire, and in fair opposition; but on no account, or pretence, or subtlety, or prevarication, are they to be taken from the wounded or even dying.

According to one eyewitness:

The general ordered for them some liquor and they had a war dance in which they throw themselves in various postures, every now and then making most hideous yells; as to their appearance, nothing more horrid can you paint in your imagination, being dressed in such an outré manner, some with the skins of bulls with the horns upon their heads, others with a great quantity of feathers, and many in a state of total nudity: there was one at whose modesty I could not help smiling, and who rather than be divested of any covering, had tied a blackbird before him. Joined to these strange dresses, and to the grotesque appearance, they paint their faces in various colours, with a view to inspire an additional horror.

Burgoyne marched his army down the side of the lake, while his 24 grabs and 400 *bateaux* ferried supplies along the waters. The army advanced at seventeen to twenty miles a day, in perfect order:

In front the Indians went in their birch canoes, containing twenty or thirty in each; then the Advanced Corps in a regular line with the gunboats; then followed the Royal George and Inflexible, towing large booms which are to be thrown across to points of land, with the other brigs and sloops following; after them the first brigade in a regular line; then the generals Burgoyne, Phillips and Riedesel in their pinnaces; next to them the second brigade, followed by the German brigades, and the rear brought up with the sutlers and followers of the army.

The army was accompanied by some 225 women and 500 children, as well as an enormous baggage train laden with officers' belongings, for which Burgoyne was much criticized.

After a few days they reached Crown Point, where they rested. On 30 June they embarked aboard the *bateaux* towards Fort Ticonderoga, at the southern end of the lake, which was manned by some 3,500 Americans. There can be little doubt that the almost surreally self-confident Burgoyne saw the fort and its garrison as the major challenge on the venture. Beyond that, the journey to Albany was only around 100 miles.

Burgoyne had in his papers a letter sent by General Howe to Sir Guy Carleton on 5 April, saying that the British armies to the south could not hope to reinforce him, but only to supply him once he reached Albany:

Having but little expectation that I shall be able from want of sufficient strength in this army, to detach a corps in the beginning of the campaign to act up Hudson's River consistent with the operations already determined upon, the force your Excellency may deem expedient to advance beyond your frontiers after taking Ticonderoga will, I fear, have little assistance from hence to facilitate their approach. As I shall probably be in Pennsylvania when that corps is ready to advance, it will probably not be in my power to communicate with the officer commanding so soon as I could wish; he must therefore pursue such measures as may from circumstances be judged most conducive to the advancement of his Majesty's service, consistent with your orders for his conduct.

The possession of Ticonderoga will naturally be the first object, and without presuming to point out to your Excellency the advantages that must arise by securing Albany and the adjacent country, I conclude they will engage the next attention; but omitting others, give me leave to suggest that this situation will open a free intercourse with the Indians, without which we are to expect little assistance from them on this side.

The further progress of this corps depending so much upon the enemy's movements, cannot be foreseen at this distance of time; still I flatter myself, and have reason to expect, the friends of government in that part of the country will be found so numerous, and so very ready to give every aid and assistance in their power, that it will prove no difficult task to reduce the more rebellious parts of the province. In the meanwhile I shall endeavour to have a corps upon the lower part of the Hudson's river sufficient to open the communication for shipping through the Highlands at present obstructed by several forts erected by the rebels, which corps may afterwards act in favour of the northern army.

I beg your Excellency may be pleased to favour me with the earliest intelligence of your movements and flatter myself some method will be found of conveying it to New York.

Not until much later did Burgoyne believe he required any assistance. A few days after he reached Ticonderoga, the commander-in-chief was preparing to depart in the opposite direction for Chesapeake Bay by ship. At the time, this seemed to matter to neither man: both believed Burgoyne would have little difficulty in reaching Albany and, as already observed, Howe had little inclination to jeopardize his own chance of a spectacular coup in capturing Philadelphia by sending an expedition up the Hudson to make doubly sure of his rival's success.

Neither Howe nor Burgoyne guessed that Fort Ticonderoga would prove so easy to capture. The 'fort' was in fact two fortified positions – one, Fort Carillon, on a peninsula dominating the southern end of Lake Champlain, the other, a hill called Mount Independence across the water on the east side of the lake, commanding the approach to Lake George. The two were joined by a timber bridge defended by a boom covered by artillery on either side.

Burgoyne expected to settle into a long siege of Fort Carillon, with little certainty of success: he was outgunned by 128 American cannon, and his army would be divided on both sides of the mile-wide River George. (It is just conceivable, indeed, that Howe believed Ticonderoga to be so impregnable that Burgoyne would get no further.) In the event the British commander spotted the Achilles heel in the American defence: a sugar-loaf hill called Mount Defiance between the George and South rivers. Lieutenant William Triss, of the Royal Engineers, reported back to Burgoyne that this had

the entire command of the works and buildings both of Ticonderoga and Mount Independence, at a distance of about 1,400 [feet] from the former and 1,500 [feet] from the latter; that the ground might be levelled so as to receive cannon, and that the road to convey them, though difficult, might be made practicable in twenty four hours. This hill also commanded in reverse the bridge of communication; saw the exact situation of their vessels; nor could the enemy during the day make any material movement or preparation without being discovered, even having their numbers counted.

On the first anniversary of the American Declaration of Independence, Triss had reached the summit of Mount Defiance; two days later two 12-pound cannon, had been hauled up it – a remarkable feat. General Arthur St Clair, the American commander, heard of this move and on the same night evacuated his entire garrison towards Skenesborough through the forest to the south, leaving 128 heavy guns and large quantities of ammunition, guarded only by four drunken artillerymen, who were captured in their sleep by the British.

The much-feared siege of Fort Ticonderoga had been a walkover, and lulled the British into an ecstatic sense of false security. It seemed the enemy was melting before them. Simon Fraser, Burgoyne's deputy, now set off with around 800 men in a furious pursuit of the retreating Americans across 'steep and woody hills'. Chasing the Americans towards Hubbardton in this remote area, Fraser's men soon became over-extended, and when they at last caught up, at a strongly defended position called Monument Hill, the Americans seemed likely to trap them. However, the arrival of 200 German reinforcements finally forced the rebels to retreat across the mountains into the Connecticut valley, where their raids against the British gave a taste of the impending ferocity of American resistance. The Americans lost about 300 killed and wounded at Hubbardton, as well as 200 prisoners – a significant defeat. Around 140 British soldiers were killed and wounded.

Meanwhile Burgoyne and the rest of his army had boarded boats and travelled up the South river towards Skenesborough in pursuit of rebel boats. These escaped, but a detachment pursued them all the way to the American stronghold of Fort Anne some fourteen miles to the south. The remnants of the American army dribbled into Fort Edward further south still. Burgoyne, meanwhile, was exultant. He wrote to Germain, 'I have the honour to acquaint your Lordship that the enemy was dislodged from Ticonderoga and Mount Independence on the 6th instant … with the loss of 128 pieces of cannon, all their armed vessels and bateaux, the greatest part of their baggage and ammunition, provision and military stores to a very large amount.' George III, on learning of the fall of Ticonderoga, is said to have jumped for joy, exclaiming 'I have beat them. Beaten all the Americans.'

The rebels had been thrown into near-despondency by the news of yet another crushing defeat, the loss of their northern stronghold. Washington lamented, 'the affair is so mysterious that it baffled even conjecture'. He wrote, 'The evacuation of Ticonderoga and Mount Independence is an event of chagrin and surprise not apprehended, nor within the compass of my reasoning … This stroke is severe indeed and has distressed us much. But … we should never despair. Our situation before has been unpromising and has changed for the better, so I trust it will again.'

Burgoyne, rendered overconfident by this striking success, decided against ordering his force back up the George river and sailing in leisurely fashion down Lake George, at the head of which a tolerable road led to the Hudson river ten miles away. He feared this would look like a retreat, and that he would have to besiege Fort George at the southern end of the lake. Besides, the distance from Skenesborough to Fort Edward – around twenty-eight miles – must have seemed a trifle.

In fact the passage was through appalling country – deep woods intersected by marshes and streams – and the trail had been sabotaged wherever possible by the retreating rebels. Burgoyne wrote later:

> The toil of the march was great, but supported by the utmost alacrity. The country was a wilderness, in almost every part of the passage the enemy took the means of cutting large timber trees on both sides of the road so as to lay across and lengthwise with the branches interwoven. The troops had not only layers of them to remove in places where it was impossible to take any other direction, but also they had above forty bridges to construct and others to repair, one of which was of logwood over a morass, two miles in extent.

Advancing at the snail's pace of a mile a day, Burgoyne's army arrived at Fort Edward, which had been evacuated by the Americans, on 30 July after three weeks. The exhausted soldiers were in no condition to proceed further.

The British commander was becoming increasingly concerned about his over-extended lines of supply across 185 miles. Although well equipped with ammunition, he had only a month's food left, and no supplies were available in the inhospitable surrounding country. He needed to protect his back by keeping a detachment at Fort George, which the Americans had abandoned, and at Fort Anne. He sent an urgent request to Sir Guy Carleton for support to man Fort Ticonderoga; but the northern commander refused, replying that Germain had ordered him not to spread his troops.

Burgoyne was forced to send two battalions – some 900 men in all – to garrison Ticonderoga, reducing his army to just 4,600 men. Growing apprehensive that his position was too exposed, he wrote to Carleton:

> I must do as well as I can but I am sure your Excellency as a soldier will think my situation a little difficult. A breach in my communication must either ruin my army entirely or oblige me to return in force to restore [the communications] which might mean the loss of the campaign. To prevent a breach Ticonderoga and Fort George must be in very respectable strength and I must beside have posts at Fort Edward and other carrying places. These drains, added to the common accidents and losses, will necessarily render me very inferior in point of numbers to the enemy, whom I must expect always to find strongly posted.

Realization was dawning that he would need support from Howe – not knowing that the commander-in-chief had already departed some hundreds of miles to the south several days before. Gentleman Johnny was beginning to lose some of his self-confidence. Although, encouragingly, several hundred loyalists had rallied to his side, he was feeling dangerously isolated in this hostile, densely wooded and watery territory.

A misfortune had also occurred which the rebels inflated to giant proportions for propaganda purposes. Burgoyne's tactic of using Indians had stirred up great controversy in England – even though he had only some 300. Chatham had furiously denounced the tactic: 'We had sullied and tarnished the arms of Britain for ever by employing savages in our service, by drawing them up in a British line, and mixing the scalping-knife and the tomahawk with the sword and the fire-lock.'

Burke had ridiculed Burgoyne's appeal to the Indians to behave with humanity: it was, he said, as if 'at a riot on Tower Hill, the keeper of the wild beasts had turned them loose and declared my gentle lions, my sentimental wolves, my tender-hearted hyenas, go forth, but take care not to hurt men, women, or children.'

Interestingly, the more visceral racism was displayed by the British government's radical critics – although such views were commonplace at the time.

In taking Fort Edward, the Indians reportedly had killed a black man and woman and scalped a family of seven. More sensationally, a beautiful young American loyalist, the twenty-three-year-old Jane McCrea, reputedly with hair reaching to the ground, had allegedly been seized by Indians as she made her way to a rendezvous with her lover, an officer in Burgoyne's army, and had then been murdered and scalped. According to an American surgeon, Dr James Thacher, whose testimony was always strongly partisan, 'The Indians [had] made her their prisoner; and on their return to Burgoyne's camp a quarrel arose to decide who should hold possession of the fair prize. During the controversy one of the monsters struck his tomahawk into her skull and immediately stripped off her scalp.' Worse, Burgoyne was not prepared to execute the alleged murderer for fear that his Indians would desert him.

The story did not ring true. The fact that the alleged killer carried her scalp so openly into the camp was itself remarkable – and it subsequently emerged that Jane McCrea had probably been killed by stray rebel shots before she was scalped by the scout as evidence of her death. When her body was exhumed she was found to have three gunshot wounds, while her skull was unbroken. Burgoyne's humane refusal to execute the suspect was, however, swamped by a surge of American racism and another potent myth – the image of Jane McCrea being tomahawked – was to become an icon of the war, and persuaded hundreds of militiamen to rally to the rebel cause.

Burgoyne himself was well aware of the dangers the Indians posed. He was also more than aware of the dangers his men faced in the American outback: he had written long before:

> Accustomed to felling of timber and to grubbing up trees, [the Americans] are very ready at earthworks and palisading, and they will cover and entrench themselves wherever they are for a short time left unmolested with surprising alacrity … Composed as the American army is, together with the strength of the country, full of woods, swamps, stone walls, and other enclosures and hiding-places, it may be said of it that every private man will in action be his own general, who will turn every tree and bush into a kind of temporary fortress, from whence, when he hath fired his shot with all the deliberation, coolness, and certainty which hidden safety inspires, he will skip as it were to the next, and so on for a long time till dislodged either by cannon or by a resolute attack of light infantry.

As the army whiled away the long, hot month of August in the ruins of Fort Edward, Burgoyne realized he had reached a turning point.

Advance was possible only if supplies were brought up sufficient to ensure striking forward and reaching Albany. As he commented, 'From the hour I pass the Hudson River and proceed towards Albany, all safety of communication [with Canada] ceases.'

Some supplies were reaching the British along the road from Fort George at the southern end of Lake George, although 'The road is some parts steep and in others wanting great repair. Of the horses furnished by contract not more than a third part was yet arrived … Fifty team of oxen which had been collected in the country through which I had marched were added to the transport.'

Washington shrewdly assessed Burgoyne's problem. Writing to the American commander at Stillwater, General Schuyler, he commented:

> You mention their having a great number of horses, but they must nevertheless require a considerable number of wagons, as there are many things which cannot be transported on horses. They can never think of advancing without securing their rear, and the force with which they can act against you will be greatly reduced by detachments necessary for that purpose. And as they have to cut out their passage and to remove the impediments you have thrown in their way before they can proceed, this circumstance, with the encumbrance they must feel in their baggage, stores, etc, will inevitably retard their march and give you leisure and opportunity to prepare a good reception for them.

The solution was straightforward, in Burgoyne's view: he endorsed a recommendation by the commander of the German troops, General Riedesel, that he should raid into the fertile country around Bennington to the south-east, which was the source of the American army's own supplies. According to Burgoyne:

> It was well known that the enemy's source of supplies in live cattle from a large tract of country, passed by the route of Manchester, Arlington and other parts of the Hampshire Grants, to Bennington, in order to be occasionally conveyed from thence to the main army [at Stillwaterl]. A large depot of corn and of wheeled carriages was also formed at the same place, and the usual guard was militia, though it varied in numbers from day to day. A scheme was formed to surprise Bennington. The possession of the cattle and carriages would certainly have enabled the army to leave their distant magazines and to have acted with energy and dispatch …
>
> Major General Riedesel has pressed upon me repeatedly the mounting of his dragoons, the men were animated with the same desire, and I conceived it a most favourable occasion to give into their ideas and

solicitations, because in exerting their zeal to fulfil their favourite purpose, they necessarily would effect the greater purpose of my own.

Some 550 men set off, accompanied by three small cannon. However, the German commander of the force, Lieutenant-Colonel Friedrich Baum, was unaware that, in defiance of Schuyler's orders, a senior American commander, General John Stark, had posted himself at Bennington with some 1,800 men. Baum moved noisily, accompanied by a military band on his 'secret raid', and arrived some three miles from Bennington on 16 August.

There he was lured forward into a classic American trap between two contingents of 200 of Stark's militia, each dressed with white paper in their hats, an agreed sign that they were loyalists. Stark suddenly sallied out of the town with the rest of his men, and the bogus supporters opened fire on the Germans. Baum was mortally wounded, and his men were surrounded. A relief force of 500 men dispatched by Burgoyne, who had realized the Germans were in trouble, took thirty-two hours to march twenty-four miles and arrived too late, themselves being mauled and losing their guns as they retreated.

Around 600 loyalists had been killed or captured, while only 30 Americans had died or been wounded. The 170 loyalist prisoners were dragged behind horses in pairs and humiliated. Many of the relief force perished as they tried to make it back to Fort Edward, being picked off by snipers or getting lost. It was the biggest British defeat in the war so far, although Burgoyne tried to put a brave face on it, insisting that it was 'little more than the miscarriage of a foraging party'.

But he had lost a sixth of his already overstretched army and had failed to obtain any supplies, which were more essential daily. Worse, he now knew that he was in deeply hostile territory: 'The New Hampshire Grants, a country unpeopled and almost unknown in the last war, now abounds in the most active and rebellious race on the continent and hangs like a gathering storm on my left.' Far from being on a jaunt, having routed an American army almost without loss, and chased after it into the outback, he faced formidable unseen foes in the woods.

His Indian allies certainly understood the danger. Led by the Chevalier Saint-Luc, they stated that 'On their first joining his army, the sun arose bright and in its full glory; the sky was clear and serene, foreboding conquest and victory; but then that great luminary was surrounded and almost obscured from the sight by dark clouds, which threatened in their bursting to involve all nature in a general wreck and confusion.' Some 200 quit, leaving only 90 in Burgoyne's depleted company of scouts.

Soon there came news of a second shattering blow: Colonel St Leger had been ordered down Lake Ontario to the head of the Mohawk valley to stage an attack from the west before joining up with Burgoyne's force at Albany. St Leger's expedition was to be partly diversionary, partly an effort to rally the Indians in the southern lakes region to the British side. He had some 600 regulars and 1,100 Indians and loyalists, as well as 4 cannon and 4 howitzers.

On 3 August he reached Fort Stanwix, which was held by 600 men behind formidable fortifications. There the very first Stars and Stripes in American history fluttered proudly – made of a white shirt, strips of red cloth from a petticoat, and a blue cloth. St Leger, his path blocked, prepared for a siege. An American relief force of 800 was ambushed by Indians and Tories at Oriskany about seven miles away, both sides losing around 400 men; the Americans were forced to withdraw. The Americans in the fort staged a sortie which hurt the British, but not to the point of forcing them to raise the siege.

Learning of the American defeat at Oriskany, Schuyler, the American commander at Stillwater, sent out a relief force of 900 men under his most brilliant and dashing young commander, Benedict Arnold. A superb propagandist, Arnold sent word ahead of him through Indian spies that the British had been defeated, and the demoralized Mohawks supporting the British broke into the rum stores in St Leger's camp and deserted. Now heavily outnumbered, St Leger wisely decided to abandon the siege and retreat.

Although St Leger had made the right decision, the news that he had been forced to retreat from Fort Stanwix came as a body blow to Burgoyne's army, which now realized that, far from staging a triumphal march to Albany, it was stranded in hostile territory with no hope of reinforcement – whether from the Mohawk valley (although St Leger hoped to loop up with his defeated force by way of Ticonderoga), from Canada, or from the south.

British tactical ineptitude and failure of co-ordination were not mirrored on the American side. Following the initial shock of the loss of Ticonderoga, Schuyler, much criticized as an aloof New York Dutchman by the more matey American generals (most of the New York Dutch were British supporters), showed great skill in assembling artillery, ammunition and men to defend his headquarters at Stillwater. Prodded by Schuyler, Washington dispatched the militias of Massachusetts and Connecticut – the most effective and dedicated fighters for the American cause – to help him. For them, it was Concord and Lexington all over again – the men from the outback materializing to surround an exposed British army.

Burning crops before the British forces, Schuyler's men meanwhile found ready supplies in the fertile New Hampshire Grants to the east. Washington had also sent two young, able and popular generals – Benedict Arnold and Benjamin Lincoln – to Schuyler's help. It was becoming evident to the Americans that Burgoyne's precipitate advance was drawing him into a trap. Washington observed:

> Though our affairs for some days past have worn a dark and gloomy aspect, I yet look forward to a fortunate and happy change. I trust General Burgoyne's army will meet sooner or later an effectual check and, as I suggested before, that the success he has had will precipitate his ruin. From your accounts, he appears to be pursuing that line of conduct which of all others is most favourable to us. I mean acting in detachment. This conduct will certainly give room for enterprise on our part and expose his parties to great hazard. Could we be so happy as to cut one of them off, supposing it should not exceed four, five or six hundred men, it would inspirit the people and do away with much of their present anxiety.

Burgoyne, far from unaware of the danger, had no possibility of reinforcement down the Mohawk valley, or from Canada; he had failed to secure significant supplies; and he had received no communication whatsoever that the army under General Howe's command was on its way from the south – although he had also heard nothing to the contrary. Even if he did secure Albany, there was little hope of surviving there through the long winter without supplies from the south. His regular forces were depleted to around 4,000 men, supported by some 2,000 loyalists and hangers-on.

Although he had no idea of enemy strength, the American army to the south was growing by the day, and by the end of August would reach 16,000 men – a devastating superiority of three to one in actual fighting men. This reflected the aspect of American warfare perhaps least understood by the British, and the most fatal for them: the huge American class of small, self-sufficient or comfortable independent farmers – what would be called the yeoman class in England – although heavily armed, had no disposition to fight as regulars for the American cause, but was ready to do so when the need arose. Thus the strength of the regular army, which in winter dwindled to sometimes laughable proportions – 3,000 to 5,000 men from the poorest and most desperate elements in society – was no reflection of what the Americans could call upon if necessary. Armies five times the size could spring up as the farmer-militiamen, suddenly convinced that they had the enemy in their sights, joined up to surprise a British army, then immediately disappeared again to tend their crops and look after their families. This was especially true in the north, where such independent men were much more numerous.

There were disadvantages, of course: in protracted campaigns the disciplined British almost invariably had the better of Washington's disparate forces. But, as at Concord–Lexington, a huge well-armed opposition could suddenly materialize against the British almost out of nowhere.

With American forces of such superiority ahead, and others infiltrating around the back, with a line of communications nearly 200 miles long, with only a few weeks left of the campaigning season, with no certain prospect of reinforcement, and in remote and hostile country, it was clearly madness to go on. To anyone but the perennially optimistic and ambitious Burgoyne, it was obvious that, like St Leger, he must call a retreat and suspend the operation, holding on to his first gains by wintering at Ticonderoga, and hoping to resume the expedition with reinforcements the following year. It was pure folly to continue the march to Albany now through the kind of heavily wooded, ambush-prone country that suited the Americans best.

At the end of August a small ray of hope arrived in the form of some 500 horses from Canada. Burgoyne's army was still intact, and his men were far from demoralized. As one German officer commented:

> Probably never did an army have less deserters than ours has had and in this connection you must remember that the rebels try to seduce our men to desertion by their emissaries, some of whom are English and some Germans ... We shall be in a position to move on towards Albany. The soldiers desire it. The unhappy occurrence at [Bennington] has not dispirited us. We regret nothing but the loss of brave friends and men ... Fighting in wild woods and bushes is a serious business, and one detachment may easily have better or worse luck than another.

The army was also cheered by the arrival of a group of Mohawks. The British lieutenant Thomas Amburey described them vividly at the time.

When they arrive, as they imagine, in hearing of the camp, they set up the war whoop, as many times as they have number of prisoners. It is difficult to describe … and the best idea that I can convey is that it consists in the sound of whoo, whoo, whoop! which is continued till the breath is almost exhausted, and then broken off with a sudden elevation of voice; some of them modulate it into notes, by placing the hand before the mouth, but both are heard at a great distance.

Whenever they scalp, they seize the head of the disabled or dead enemy, and placing one of their feet on the neck, twist their left hand in the hair, by which means they extend the skin that covers the top of the head, and with the other hand draw their scalping knife from their breast, which is always kept in good order to this cruel purpose, a few dextrous strokes of which takes off the part that is termed the scalp; they are so exceedingly expeditious in doing this, that it scarcely exceeds a minute. If the hair is short, and they have no purchase with their hand, they stoop, and with their teeth strip it off; when they have performed this part of their martial virtue, as soon as time permits, they tie with bark or deer's sinews their speaking trophies of blood in a small hoop, to preserve it from putrefaction, painting part of the scalp and the hoop all round with red. These they preserve as monuments of their prowess, and at the same time as proofs of the vengeance they have inflicted on their enemies.

At one of the Indian encampments, I saw several scalps hanging upon poles in front of their wigwams; one of them had remarkably fine long hair hanging to it. An officer that was with me wanted to purchase it, at which the Indian seemed highly offended, nor would he part with this barbarous trophy, although he was offered so strong a temptation as a bottle of rum.

The appearance of a dead body … is not a pleasing spectacle; but when scalped it is shocking; two, in this situation, we met in our march from Skenesborough to Fort Edward. After so cruel an operation, you could hardly suppose anyone could survive, but when we took possession of Ticonderoga, we found two poor fellows who lay wounded, that had been scalped in the skirmish the day before the Americans abandoned it, and who are in a fair way of recovery. I have seen a person who had been scalped, and was as hearty as ever, but his hair never grew again.

Should I at any time be unfortunate enough to get wounded, and the Indians come across me with an intention to scalp, it would be my wish to receive at once a coup de grace with their tomahawk, which in most instances they mercifully allow.

One of the British officers captured the prevailing mood:

The British are equal to anything … One proof of the spirit of our army, the Ladies do not mean to quit us. Lady Harriet Acland graces the advanced corps of the Army, and Madame Riedesel the German brigades. We have frequent dinners and constantly music; for my part ... this campaigning is a favourite portion of life: and none but stupid mortals can dislike a lively camp, good weather, good claret, good music and the enemy near. I may venture to say all this, for a little fusillade during dinner does not discompose the nerves of even our ladies ... Therefore we set our faces forward, and mean to bite hard if anything dares to show itself. As to numbers of our foes, I believe them great, mais n'importe, what are we not equal to?

The main problem seemed to be weariness. As one German officer commented:

The heat in this region is uncommonly great and exceeds very noticeably the hottest summer day in our fatherland. Almost every day there are thunder showers which, though violent, are soon over. On the other hand, it does not cool off after them and at night, especially towards morning, such a heavy dew or mist falls that it penetrates the tents and soaks the blankets.

The British commander owed it to his forces to get them back to safety intact while there was still time and he could not be cut off in the rear.

Burgoyne's fateful decision was hardly precipitate; he had had weeks to ponder the critical situation of his command. Uncharacteristically for so flamboyant a British commander, he took refuge in following to the letter the orders given to him months before in London. Showing acute awareness of the dangers facing him, he wrote:

When I wrote more confidently, I little foresaw that I was to be left to pursue my way through such a tract of country and hosts of foes without any co-operation from New York; nor did I think the garrison of Ticonderoga would fall to my share alone ...

Had I a latitude in my orders, I should think it my duty to wait in this position [Battenkill] or perhaps as far back as Fort Edward, where my communication with Lake George would be perfectly secure till something happened to assist my movement forward; but my orders are positive to 'force a junction with Sir William Howe'. I apprehend I am not at liberty to remain inactive longer than shall be necessary to collect twenty five days' provisions, and to receive the reinforcements now (and unfortunately only now) on Lake Champlain.

The waiting the arrival of this reinforcement is an indispensable necessity because, from the hour I pass the Hudson's river. and proceed towards Albany, all safety of communication ceases. I must expect a large body of the enemy from my left will take post behind me. I have put out of the question the waiting longer than the time necessary for the foregoing purposes, because the attempt, then critical, depending on adventure and the fortune that often accompanies it, and hardly justifiable but for my orders from the state, would afterwards be consummately desperate.

I mean that by moving soon, though I should meet with insurmountable difficulties to my progress, I shall at least have the chance of fighting my way back to Ticonderoga, but, the season a little farther advanced, the distance increased, and the march unavoidably tardy because surrounded by enemies, a retreat might be shut by impenetrable bars or the elements, and at the same time no possible means of existence remain in the country.

I do not yet despond. Should I succeed in forcing my way to Albany and find the country in a state to subsist my army, I shall think no more of retreat, but at the worst fortify there and await Sir W Howe's operation.

Whatever may be my fate, I submit my actions to the breast of the King and to the candid judgment of my profession, when all the motives become public; and I rest in confidence that, whatever decision may be passed on my conduct, my good intent will not be questioned.

This flew in the face of common sense. Instead of improvising to meet the needs of the situation – essential in an age when instructions from headquarters could take weeks, if not months, to arrive – he professed to be paralysed by his ancient orders. Burgoyne apparently believed that the way out of the trap was to plunge further into it as speedily as possible across the well-defended American lines to capture a heavily fortified base which could not possibly be defended through the winter.

It is almost impossible not to conclude that, whatever his official view, Burgoyne was determined not to be thwarted in his goal of winning a glorious victory, however improbable his chances of success. Retreat was unthinkable. Hubris had got the better of military judgement. Continually invoking the prospect of relief from Howe had given Burgoyne an alibi for failure; yet he had no real reason to believe that his superior was on his way. He complained, 'The want of communication with Sir William Howe is ... a most embarrassing circumstance; of the messengers I have sent, I know of two being hanged, and am ignorant of whether any of the rest arrived.'

In fact, with astonishing negligence, Clinton had sent a message to Burgoyne by only a single courier on 10 August. This had been intercepted. Only on 20 August did Burgoyne learn from a message from

Clinton hidden in strips of paper that General Howe was on his way to Pennsylvania. It must have been an appalling shock. But he still had time to retreat safely. Clinton's letter, although correct as far as it went on 17 July, made it clear that Howe would come to Burgoyne's aid only if Washington himself moved northward; in fact Howe's guess proved correct, and the American commander moved south on his fruitless attempt to defend Philadelphia. Howe wrote:

> I have received yours of the second instant [from Crown Point] on the 15th, have since heard from the rebel army of your being in possession of Ticonderoga, which is a great event, carried without loss. I have received your two letters, viz from Plymouth and Quebec, your last of 14th May, and shall observe the contents. There is a report of a messenger of yours to me having been taken and the letter discovered in a double wooden canteen [water bottle], you will know if it was of any consequence; nothing of it has transpired to us. I observe the same rules in writing to you, as you propose in your letters to me. Washington is waiting our motions here, and has detached Sullivan with about 2,500 men, as I learn, to Albany. My intention is for Pennsylvania where I expect to meet Washington, but if he goes to the northward contrary to my expectations and you can keep him at bay, be assured I shall soon be after him to relieve you.
>
> After you arrive at Albany, the movements of the enemy will guide yours; but my wishes are that the enemy be drove out of this province [New York] before any operations take place in Connecticut. Sir Henry Clinton remains in the command here and will act as circumstances may direct. Putnam is in the Highlands with about 4,000 men. Success be ever with you.

Howe, in this letter, seemed to expect that Burgoyne would make it through to Albany, but he privately expressed the view that this was unlikely: 'I do not suppose [it] can happen this campaign, as I apprehend General Burgoyne will find full employment for his army against that of the rebels opposed to him.' The taking of Fort Ticonderoga made success only marginally more probable. But it was clear, at least from the tone of Howe's letter, that Burgoyne could not expect reinforcements from the army in the south.

His only hope was of troops from Clinton, defending New York with 7,000 men. Clinton had been a devoted supporter of the northern strategy, and had unsuccessfully urged it on Howe before the latter's departure for Philadelphia. But, even though the main American army had departed for the south, he timorously feared the consequences of leaving New York undefended, until it was too late. This problem was to recur.

Of the five men most culpable for the gathering military disaster – the greatest in British history in terms of its consequences – Burgoyne must stand head and shoulders above the rest. None can be exonerated. The King and Lord Germain had ordered the expedition. Clinton was weak-willed and inanimate and did little to prevent the failure of orders to reach Howe – because he favoured Burgoyne against Howe.

Howe, understandably furious at Burgoyne's expedition being launched outside his own command with the connivance of the War Office and the King, behaved with almost psychopathic indifference towards the fate of Burgoyne's army while he pursued his own more sensible objectives. But Burgoyne, responsible for proposing, planning and lobbying for the whole enterprise, had several weeks' careful consideration to recognize the predicament in which he and his men found themselves. There was no immediate pressure. Yet, far from aborting the expedition, he chose to move forward suicidally into a noose being tightly pulled around his neck.

In late August he had the chance of retreating with dignity and honour, if not martial valour, to try again the following year. Instead, shallowness, vanity and lust for glory drove on this otherwise not dislikeable man. He never seemed to consider calling it all off, even as news of fresh disasters was brought to him, as American troop strength grew, and as it became apparent that he could place no reliance on Howe's assistance.

Instead Burgoyne prepared to cross the Hudson, which would be much more difficult closer to Albany, and launched a floating bridge. On 13 September the small army crossed its Rubicon and camped in the plain of Saratoga,

> at which place there is a handsome and commodious dwelling house, with outhouses, and exceedingly fine saw- and grist mills, and at a small distance a very neat church, with several houses round it, all of which were the property of General Schuyler. This beautiful spot was quite deserted, not a living creature on it. On the grounds were great quantities of fine wheat, as also Indian corn; the former was instantly cut down, threshed, carried to the mill to be ground, and delivered to the men to save our provisions; the latter was cut for forage for the horses.

*

The Americans' front line, some six miles north of their own camp, was just ten miles away from the British front line. The Americans had command problems of their own. Schuyler, who had been blamed unfairly for the loss of Fort Ticonderoga, had been belatedly dismissed on 4 August. His support for New York's claim to the disputed area of the New Hampshire Grants (now Vermont) against the powerful New Englanders had made him important enemies in Congress. Fortunately for the Americans, the news of his dismissal had taken time to travel, and in the meantime he had skilfully assembled the army to defeat the British.

Schuyler was supplanted by General Horatio Gates – one of the most 'political' generals in the American army, who was backed by Sam Adams, the founder of the American Revolution and still the most powerful man in Congress. Gates, a brilliant administrator as Adjutant General and on excellent terms with several leading congressmen, had already tried to undermine Washington's control the previous year. Now he had instigated Schuyler's removal, seeking credit for the American victory he believed imminent.

The son of the housekeeper of the Duke of Bolton's mistress, Gates was intensely resentful of the British aristocracy, though ingratiating in manner. He was a godson of Horace Walpole. A self-made man, and preeminently a staff officer, he had served alongside Washington and Lee in Braddock's ill-fated campaign, when he was wounded in the chest and narrowly escaped with his life; thereafter he tended to avoid active combat. Gates's folksy style went down well enough with New England's politicians – particularly the Adams cousins – but he was loud-mouthed, superficial and a poor field commander. Washington had not supported his nomination to replace Schuyler.

During Burgoyne's three-week pause, the versatile Benedict Arnold arranged for the Americans to entrench themselves in a cleverly chosen forward position to meet the British: Bemis Heights, a plateau some 200 feet above the Hudson, which flowed past it down a gorge. A formidable defensive barrier was built along this commanding position, directed by Tadeusz Kosciuszko, a young Polish émigré who was a military engineer of genius and had urged fortifying the hill at Ticonderoga whose loss had led to the American collapse there. A three-sided breastwork of earth and logs about 2½ miles in length was erected, with artillery dug in at the corners. The British would have needed a force around three times their actual strength to have any hope of dislodging the Americans.

The only weakness was a hill to the west, which the Americans had not occupied, believing the British would be tied to their supply boats along the Hudson to the east. Burgoyne's scouts, however, had told him of the works, and he sent a column under Simon Fraser, his best commander, to attempt to turn the American flank in the west with 2,000 men. Two other columns – in the centre under his overall command and along the banks of the river under General Riedesel – also marched towards the rebel-held heights, occupied by several thousand Americans, who were largely concealed from the British.

Just past midday on 19 September, Burgoyne's middle column of four battalions emerged in a large clearing in wooded country commanded by Freeman's Farm, where it encountered sporadic fire but drove out the American defenders and occupied the buildings. Meanwhile, the Americans had had the same idea as the British, and Arnold had persuaded Gates to let him lead a sortie out of the heights to the west, in an effort to take the British flank. With a shock, Arnold's men ran headlong into Fraser's position, hidden by vegetation, and were forced back by the artillery, recovering enough to attempt to take Freeman's Farm in the centre.

Meanwhile Fraser had stopped his advance in order to protect the British army from American flanking, abandoning his objective of seizing the heights. The British rearguard who had captured the farm came under increasing pressure from Arnold's forces, who outnumbered them two to one. Incessant volleys of rifle fire encircled them from the surrounding woods and, while they withstood every actual attempt to dislodge them, the British could not pursue the Americans further for fear of being scattered and becoming easy prey for the rebels in the forest. Pinned down in the farm, the British were now losing the contest in a deadly war of attrition. By four o'clock the position had become desperate. Arnold begged Gates for reinforcements to break through the beleaguered British centre at the farm, which would have decided the battle, but none came.

Riedesel, commanding the German troops to the east, abandoned his cautious view that he must stand by his guns and supplies along the Hudson at all costs and came to the rescue, enabling the British to attack across the clearing in front of the farm, which forced the Americans back to their entrenchments on Bemis Heights. Remarkably, although heavily outnumbered, the British had maintained their position at Freeman's Farm, but had gained nothing more, and were no closer to punching through to the south. Gates's adjutant, Colonel James Wilkinson, provided a succinct eyewitness description of the battle:

> The theatre of action was such, that although the combatants changed ground a dozen times in the course of the day, the contest terminated on the spot where it began. This may be explained in a few words. The British line was formed on an eminence in a thin pine wood, having before it Freeman's farm, an oblong field stretching from the centre towards its right, the ground in front sloping gently down to the verge of this field, which was bordered on the opposite side by a close wood; the sanguinary scene lay in the cleared ground, between the eminence occupied by the enemy and the wood just described; the fire of our marksmen from this wood was too deadly to be withstood by the enemy in line, and then they gave way and broke, our men rushing from their covert, pursued them to the entrance, where, having their flanks protected, they rallied, and charging in turn drove us back into the wood, from whence a dreadful fire would again force them to fall back; and in this manner did the battle fluctuate, like waves of a stormy sea; with alternate advantages for four hours without one moment's intermission.
>
> The British artillery fell into our possession at every charge, but we could neither turn the pieces upon the enemy, nor bring them off; the wood prevented the last, and the want of a match the first, as the lint stock was invariably carried off, and the rapidity of the transitions did not allow us time to provide one. The slaughter of this brigade of artillerists was remarkable, the captain and thirty-six men being killed or wounded out of forty-eight. It was truly a gallant conflict, in which death by familiarity lost its terrors, and certainly a drawn battle, as night alone terminated it; the British army keeping its ground in rear of the field of action, and our corps, when they could no longer distinguish objects, retiring to their own camp.

Riedesel wrote bitterly:

> Thus had General Riedesel with his German troops, once more saved the English from a great misfortune, having unquestionably decided the engagement in their favour. Notwithstanding, however, the praise which the German troops received for their bravery on this occasion, General Burgoyne, and a few other English commanders, regarded the German general with secret envy. Indeed, they would gladly have passed over his merits, had such a thing been possible. British pride did not desire the acknowledgement of bravery other than their own, as we shall see more plainly in the future.

*

The toll had been high: some 500 British dead or taken prisoner in an army in which every man counted, to 400 American casualties. Burgoyne prepared to renew the attempt to find a way around the enemy lines to the west the following morning, and the troops slept on the battlefield in preparation, amid complaints of being 'almost frozen with cold'. But Fraser persuaded Burgoyne that the troops were in no shape to move the following day. The same night a letter in code at last arrived from Clinton, proposing to come to his relief:

> You know my good will and are not ignorant of my poverty. If you think two thousand men can assist you effectually, I will make a push at Montgomery [the principal fort in the highlands] in about ten days, but ever jealous for my flanks. If they make a move in force on either of them I must return to save this important post. I expect reinforcements every day. Let me know what you would wish.

# 16

## *Someone had Blundered*

Burgoyne now pinned his hopes on this slender lifeline. He decided to call off a second attack on Bemis Heights and order his men back to the position at Freeman's Farm, in the confident expectation that Clinton's army would force the Americans to divert part of their reinforcements southward to meet the challenge, or indeed retreat altogether. With self-deluding optimism, he argued that from the moment Clinton's letter had arrived:

> I was in hourly expectation, I thought a justly founded one, of [Clinton's attack on the highlands] operating to dislodge Mr Gates entirely or to oblige him to detach a large portion of his force. Either of these cases would probably have opened my way to Albany. In these circumstances could the preference upon these alternatives admit of a moment's reflection? To wait for so fair a prospect of effecting at last the great purpose of the campaign, or to put a victorious army under all the disadvantages of a beaten one by a difficult and disgraceful retreat; relinquishing the long-expected co-operation; and leaving Sir Henry Clinton's army, and probably Sir William Howe's, exposed with so much of the season to run, to the whole force of Mr Gates, after he should have seen me on the other side of the Hudson.

It was a huge stake to gamble on a limited thrust by 2,000 men whom Clinton had not even promised would attempt to reach Albany. For two and a half precious weeks, as their supplies ebbed away, Burgoyne's army sat facing the entrenched and vastly stronger American position at Bemis Heights. While the Americans were being steadily reinforced and had ample supplies, the British position deteriorated. According to Lieutenant Amburey:

> Our present situation is far from being an inactive one, the armies being so near that not a night passes but there is firing and continual attacks

upon the advanced piquets, especially those of the Germans. It seems to be the plan of the enemy to harass us with constant attacks, which they are able to do without fatiguing their army, from the great superiority of their numbers ...

We are now become so habituated to fire that the soldiers seem to be indifferent to it, and eat and sleep when it is very near them; the officers rest in their clothes, and the field officers are up frequently in the night. The enemy, in front of our quarter-guard, within hearing, are cutting trees and making works, and when I have had this guard, I have been visited by most of the field-officers, to listen to them ... The enemy had the assurance to bring down a small piece of cannon to fire as their morning gun, so near to our quarter-guard that the wadding rebounded against the works.

We have within these few evenings, exclusive of other alarms, been under arms most of the night, as there has been a great noise, like the howling of dogs, upon the right of our encampment; it was imagined the enemy set it up to deceive us, while they were meditating some attack ... A detachment of Canadians and provincials were sent out to reconnoitre, and it proved to have arisen from large droves of wolves that came after the dead bodies; they were similar to a pack of hounds, for one setting up a cry, they all joined, and when they approached a corpse, their noise was hideous till they had scratched it up.

Beyond the ground where we defeated the enemy on 19th September, all is hostile and dangerous in an alarming degree. The nature of the ground is peculiarly unfavourable in respect to military operations, it being difficult to reconnoitre the enemy and to obtain any intelligence to be relied upon: the roads, the situation of the enemy, the grounds for pro-curing forage, of which the army is in great want and all parties are in quest of, are often attended with the utmost danger, and require great bodies to cover them.

According to a German officer:

We entrenched the camp including all the outposts and piquets, made a line round the camp and fitted it with redoubts and batteries. Even behind the camp we laid out two great redoubts for the defence of the magazine, train and hospital. We felled thousands of trees to clear fields of fire for the guns ... To do this we moved out every morning an hour before dawn and this caused trouble with the enemy. At that time one could enjoy the fresh morning air, with a very heavy hoar frost; that was followed by a mist which you could actually grasp with your hands and which rarely dispersed before nine o'clock. In the middle of the day there was enough heat to melt you ...

Things began to get very scarce. Nothing came through from Ticonderoga; there is nothing in this desert and the Americans would not let anything come to us from Albany. A bottle of poor red wine cost two reichsthaler, eight silver gröschen in our money, and a pound of coffee came to one reichsthaler, twenty two gröschen, sugar about the same. There was no hope of getting any clothes, although we were tearing ours to pieces every day in this wilderness. Never can the Jews have longed more for the coming of the Messiah than we longed for the arrival of General Clinton. From time to time news of his arrival passed round the camp. It was only rumours though they helped to keep up our spirits.

A further blow for morale was the news that behind the British the outer defences of Fort Ticonderoga had been lost to American forces, including the strategic Mount Defiance. This threatened to cut off the vital British lifeline of supplies from the north. Burgoyne was forced to put his men on half rations.

The British commander's behaviour had now passed from foolhardiness and vanity through to something resembling lunacy. Heavily outnumbered, faced by an enemy occupying a much superior strategic position, having only just avoided defeat at Freeman's Farm through the bravery of his soldiers, and now faced by the very real prospect of being cut off from his over-extended supply route, with barely enough food to survive a fortnight, he stayed where he was, refusing to retreat while it was still possible to do so safely – and continued to plan for an attack to break through enemy lines on the faint hope provided by a single heavily qualified letter from Clinton.

Again, the comparison with Lord Cardigan's behaviour at Balaclava nearly a century later is irresistible. But Cardigan at least had the excuse that he did not know what the enemy dispositions were. Burgoyne, similarly faithful to his orders (which in his case were months out of date), had no such defence. Perhaps he believed that retreat was now impossible, although he made no such observation at the time. But he had dawdled for two weeks; almost certainly he could have retreated in good order during the first few days, before American reinforcements were brought up and infiltrated to the north of him.

The subsequent British defeat at Saratoga is usually seen as a triumph for old-style American harassment from the woods against a dispirited British force; yet, while such attacks did take place on a small scale, the Americans in fact largely stayed in place behind their fortifications. The defeat was to be due to Burgoyne's suicidal impulse always to advance and attack.

Whatever tiny hope there was for Burgoyne's tactics soon fizzled out. Clinton had been encouraged by the arrival of 2,000 British reinforcements in New York and, receiving Burgoyne's desperate plea for support, embarked 3,000 men up to the Hudson on 3 October. His expedition was unexpectedly successful. Two days later, he reached Verplanck Point, a few miles south of Fort Montgomery and Fort Clinton, commanding the rocky approach to the highlands, through which the Hudson flowed. He surprised and took the garrisons there using bayonets and without firing a shot. Some 300 Americans were killed, wounded or taken prisoner, to 40 British killed and 150 wounded. The boom and chain across the river were destroyed, and the American flotilla there was burnt. Clinton then embarked on a vigorous thrust into the highlands, gaining control of the whole region by 8 October, possibly because the American forces had been depleted in order to join Gates's army.

Clinton decided to move no further, refusing to embark his men upstream, citing the absence of specific orders. He believed that Burgoyne's fate was sealed:

> Though this intelligence [of the fall of Fort Ticonderoga] destroyed all my hopes of being in the least serviceable to the northern army, whose fate I now feared was inevitable, it yet was very much my wish to be able to retain the footing we were now possessed of in the Highlands. Every view of that sort was, however, dissipated by my next dispatches from the commander-in-chief [Howe], as I was thereby ordered to send him without delay the Seventh, Twenty-sixth and Sixty-third Regiments, two battalions of Anspach and [the] Seventeenth Dragoons, together with all the recruits and recovered men belonging to the southern army and the Jagers and artillerymen which came by the English fleet – even notwithstanding I might be gone up the North [Hudson] River, agreeable to the intimation I had given him of my intentions in my letter of the 29th of September – except I should be on the eve of accomplishing some very material and essential stroke, being left at liberty in that case to proceed upon it provided I judged it might be executed in a few days after the receipt of his letters.
>
> These orders being too explicit to be misunderstood or obedience to them even delayed, and several of the corps with General Vaughan being particularised in them, I wrote to that general officer on the 22nd of October to direct him to return with all speed. And, receiving soon

afterward another order from Sir William Howe to dismantle Fort Clinton, I was under the mortifying necessity of relinquishing the Highlands and all the other passes over the Hudson, to be reoccupied by the rebels whenever they saw proper. For even had General Burgoyne been fortunately in a situation to have availed himself of my success and been tempted to trust to my support at the time I received these orders, I believe there is no military man who will not allow that I should have had no small difficulty in reconciling the delay an effort of that consequence must have necessarily occasioned with the obedience I owed to so explicit and pressing an order from my Commander in Chief.

He sent a cryptic message to Burgoyne, which never arrived because its bearer was intercepted:

Not having received any instructions from the Commander in Chief relative to the northern army, and ignorant of even his intentions concerning its operations (excepting his wishes that it may get to Albany), Sir Henry Clinton cannot presume to send orders to General Burgoyne. But he thinks it impossible that General Burgoyne could really suppose Sir Henry Clinton had any idea of penetrating to Albany with the small force he mentioned in his letter of the 11th September. What Sir Henry Clinton offered in that letter he has now undertaken. He cannot by any means promise himself success, but he hopes the move may be serviceable to General Burgoyne, as his letter of the 21st intimates that even the menace of an attack will be of use.

Although Clinton, as Howe's deputy, was Burgoyne's superior in the former's absence down south, the tongue-tied, diffident officer would never have presumed to give orders to Burgoyne. But his previous letter had advised Burgoyne that he had only a small force and that it would have been risky to take them up to Albany. Burgoyne's hope was thus entirely based on wishful thinking. Clearly Clinton was not up to the job in Howe's absence, and Burgoyne should not have pinned any hopes on him.

At every stage Clinton had been appraised of Burgoyne's intentions and strongly supported the whole operation. But, abandoned by Howe, his main concern seemed to be to place all responsibility for the affair on his fellow commander's shoulders. Where Burgoyne was foolhardy to the point of idiocy, Clinton was cautious to the point of cowardice. In an extremely dangerous situation for his fellow commander, he took no risks at all.

If either Clinton or Burgoyne had cherished any hope that the expedition up the Hudson would divert enemy troops from Bemis Heights, they were soon disappointed. Gates had his enemy in a trap, and knew it. Fraser and Riedesel, conscious of the British army's desperate position, counselled withdrawal; but Burgoyne would have none of it. Phillips, his second-in-command, gave no opinion. Like a man living in a dream, Burgoyne clung to the wild hope that, with an unexpected thrust forward through enemy lines, he might yet reach Albany (although he had not even begun to consider how to survive once he got there).

On the morning of 7 October Burgoyne sent forward some 1,500 men to reconnoitre the supposedly vulnerable American left, which the rebels had had nearly three weeks to fortify. According to Riedesel, who wanted to retreat, the purpose was 'to ascertain definitely [Gates's] position, and whether it would be advisable to attack him. Should the latter be the case, [Burgoyne] intended to advance on the enemy on the 8th with his entire army; but if he should not think an attack advisable then he would, on the 11th, march back to the Battenkill.'

About a mile out of Freeman's Farm this column stopped, having discovered no way through the American lines. The Americans seized the chance they had been waiting for to attack and cut off a large part of the British force: two American columns were promptly assembled, and at about 2.30 p.m. they 'advanced ... blindly in face of a furious fire' while a flanking party under the capable Daniel Morgan sought to veer round to the west of the British in an effort to get behind them and cut them off from the main camp.

Seeing this, the British themselves swivelled round to try to face them, but this manoeuvre demoralized the Germans on their left (eastern) flank, who fled. As their commander commented:

> They retreated – or to speak more plainly – they left their position without informing me, although I was fifty paces in advance of them. I looked backward toward the position still held, as I supposed, by our German infantry but not a man was to be seen. They had all run across the road into the fields and thence into the bushes, and had taken refuge behind the trees.

The British commander, Major Sir John Acland, was shot through both legs and was thereupon nearly killed by a thirteen-year-old boy, but a nearby American soldier came to his rescue. An American surgeon, tending the wounded, exultantly exclaimed, 'I have dipped my hands in British blood.'

Seeing the desperate situation of the troops so far from camp, Burgoyne sent other forces under Fraser to support them, while ordering them to retire; but the commander bearing the order was shot. Meanwhile Arnold, against orders, had ridden up to the American front line to direct operations in a kind of battle frenzy, appearing to have had a great deal to drink. He immediately spotted the opportunity presented by Fraser's departure to help the stricken column: Freeman's Farm was now badly depleted of defenders.

One American soldier commented of Arnold's demonic leadership 'He was a bloody fellow ... He didn't care for nothing; he'd ride right in. It was "Come on, boys!" 'twasn't "Go, boys!" ... there wasn't any waste of timber in him.'

Leading the American forces in a wild charge across to the British camp, Arnold broke his left leg when his horse was shot from under him. Fraser, reacting to the danger, ordered some of his men back. But he himself was now the target of American marksmen. Two bullets grazed his horse. An aide told him to withdraw. 'My duty forbids it,' he replied. Moments later he was shot in the stomach. According to Baroness von Riedesel, who had accompanied her husband on the expedition,

> I heard skirmishing and firing which by degrees grew louder and louder, until there was a frightful noise ... About 3 o'clock in the afternoon instead of the guests who were to have dined with me they brought in poor General Fraser upon a litter. The dining-table, which had been prepared, was taken away and a bed for the general placed there instead. I sat in a corner trembling. The noise got louder and louder and I feared lest they should bring in my husband also. The general said to the surgeon, 'Do not hide anything from me. Am I going to die?' The ball had gone through his bowels.

Meanwhile Arnold had succeeded in turning the whole British line so that the backs of the British were to the river, and Daniel Morgan's formidable flanking party was virtually behind them. After the capture of a redoubt held by Colonel Breymann on the far right, in which the hated disciplinarian German was killed by one of his own men – perhaps not accidentally – the British were threatened with encirclement. Burgoyne attempted a counter-attack, but darkness was falling. The British had lost about 500 men in the futile sortie, including their best general.

At last Burgoyne – too late – seemed to appreciate the desperate plight of his army. The following day he learned of American moves to infiltrate men to the north and surround the British altogether, with their backs to the river. There was nothing for it but to retreat at last before the ring was closed around him – a manoeuvre he might have performed safely a day or two before. Simon Fraser was buried at sunset under fire from the Americans. The chaplain read the service coolly, 'though frequently covered with dust which the shots threw up on all sides of him'. Ordering campfires to be lit so as to deceive the enemy, and abandoning some 300 wounded in a field hospital, the British departed at night.

The army began to move at nine o'clock at night, Major General Riedesel commanding the vanguard and Major General Phillips the rear. This retreat although within musket shot of the enemy and encumbered by all the baggage of the army was made without loss but a very heavy raid and the difficulties of guarding the bateaux which contained all the provisions, occasioned delays which prevented the army reaching Saratoga until the night of the 9th and the artillery could not pass the fords of the Fishkill till the morning of the 10th. [The troops, by the time they reached the new position, were] in such a state of fatigue that they had not the strength or inclination to cut wood or make fires, but rather sought sleep in their wet clothes and on the wet ground under a heavy rain that still continued.

Yet Burgoyne was heavily criticized for stopping at six o'clock in the morning. Riedesel claimed that had the army marched the entire night, it would have reached Saratoga at daybreak without being attacked by the enemy.

On 9 October, as the rain lashed down, the remaining Indians, scenting defeat, disappeared into the woods and the British were peppered with relentless fire. Baroness von Riedesel recorded:

My chambermaid did nothing but curse her situation, and tore out her hair. I entreated her to compose herself, or else she would be taken for a savage. Upon this she became still more frantic and asked 'whether that would trouble me?' And when I answered 'Yes', she tore her bonnet off her head, letting her hair hang down over her face, and said, 'You talk well! You have your husband! But we have nothing to look forward to, except dying miserably on the one hand, or losing all we possess on the other!' . .. Respecting this last complaint, I promised, in order to quiet her, that I would make good all the losses of herself and the other maid. The latter, my good Lena, although also very much frightened, said nothing.

Toward evening, we at last came to Saratoga, which was only half an hour's march from the place where we had spent the whole day. I was wet through and through by the frequent rains, and was obliged to remain in this condition the entire night, as I had no place whatever where I could change my linen. I, therefore, seated myself before a good fire, and undressed my children; after which, we laid ourselves down together upon some straw. I asked General Phillips who came up to where we were, why we did not continue our retreat while there was yet time, as my husband had pledged himself to cover it, and bring the army through? 'Poor woman,' answered he, 'I am amazed at you! – completely wet through; have you still the courage to wish to go further in this weather? Would that you were only our commanding general! He halts because he is tired and intends to spend the night here and give us a supper.' In this latter achievement, especially, General Burgoyne was very fond of indulging. He spent half the nights in singing and drinking, and amusing himself with the wife of a commissary, who was his mistress, and who, as well as he, loved champagne.

Whether the Baroness was being entirely fair is uncertain. Another remarkable woman on the expedition, Lady Harriet Acland, insisted on returning to her wounded husband through enemy lines. According to Wilkinson, on arrival before the astonished Americans:

The lady was immediately conveyed into the apartment of the major, which had been cleared for her reception; her attendants followed with her bedding and necessaries, a fire was made, and her mind was relieved from the horrors which oppressed it, by the assurance of her husband's safety; she took tea, and was accommodated as comfortably as circumstances would permit, and the next morning when I visited the guard before sunrise, her boat had put off, and was floating down the stream to our camp, where General Gates, whose gallantry will not be denied, stood ready to receive her with all the tenderness and respect to which her rank and condition gave her a claim: indeed the feminine figure, the benign aspect, and polished manners of this charming woman, were alone sufficient to attract the sympathy of the most obdurate; but if another motive could have been wanting to inspire respect, it was furnished by the peculiar circumstances of Lady Harriet, then in that most difficult situation [she was pregnant] which cannot fail to interest the solicitudes of every being possessing the form and feelings of a man ... Major Acland had set out for Albany, where he was joined by his lady.

Once at Saratoga the British troops began to dig earthworks and defences. But they were exhausted, demoralized, undernourished and constantly raked with bullets. Several hundred Americans were now across the Fishkill river on the opposite bank, and other smaller detachments were to their right, on the east side of the camp, again moving to surround them.

Desperately Burgoyne ordered men to scout northward to facilitate a fresh advance, but he had to recall them as the American forward patrols moved towards them. Although not attacking directly across the Fishkill, the Americans also raided the British supply boats on the Hudson and were driven off only with difficulty, the stores having to be unloaded ashore for safety.

On 12 October Burgoyne summoned his officers and they discussed the position. They had enough food to last only a week. News of Clinton's progress was welcome, but he was too late. The only way they could escape was to cross the river at Fort Edward or to veer off to the west towards Fort George – a route never before attempted except by Indians, and certainly not by a large army in retreat; it was soon discovered by scouts to be blocked by enemy forces. The Americans had also set up entrenchments opposite Fort Edward. The British were virtually cut off and surrounded.

The same day, Baroness von Riedesel reported, the American guns opened up against the British:

> I laid myself down in a corner not far from the door. My children laid down on the earth with their heads upon my lap, and in this manner we passed the entire night ... On the following morning the cannonade again began, but from a different side ... Eleven cannon balls went through the house, and we could plainly hear them rolling over our heads. One poor soldier, whose leg they were about to amputate, having been laid upon a table for this purpose, had the other leg taken off by another cannon ball in the very middle of the operation.

The decision was taken to stay put on the heights of Saratoga, where the British had some strategic advantage, in Burgoyne's words, 'in the anxious hope of succour from our friends, or the next desirable experience, an attack from the enemy'.

Fired upon from all sides – from the south, from across the river, and from Morgan's men to the west and behind – Burgoyne finally realized the position was hopeless. He had waited far too long to retreat: he could barely survive a few days, let alone cross the river or escape across the desperately rough terrain to Ticonderoga. As he set out in a later account to Germain:

Disabled in the collateral branches of the army by the total defection of the Indians; the desertion or the timidity of the Canadians and provincials ...; disappointed in the last hope of any timely co-operation from other armies; the regular troops reduced by losses from the best parts, to 3,500 fighting men, not 2,000 of which were British; only three days' provisions, upon short allowance, in store; invested by an army of 16,000 men, and no apparent means of retreat remaining; I called into council all the generals, field-officers and captains commanding corps and by their unanimous concurrence and advice I was induced to open a treaty with Major-General Gates.

Everyone, it seems, was to blame except for the intrepid commander himself. He lashed out at the loyalist commander, Colonel Philip Skene. 'You have brought me to this pass. Now tell me how to get out of it.' Skene answered, 'Scatter your baggage, stores and everything that can be spared, at proper distances, and the militiamen will be so busy plundering them that you and the troops will get clean off.'

Burgoyne sent an aide to negotiate terms. Gates bluntly demanded an unconditional surrender. Yet Burgoyne, for the first time in this sorry tale, now saw his natural gambler's bombast vindicated. He rejected Gates's terms and threatened to fight to the death: 'Lieut. General Burgoyne's army, however reduced, will never admit that their retreat is cut off while they have arms in their hands. They will rush on the enemy determined to take no quarter.' Instead he demanded a 'treaty of convention', not a capitulation, under which the British were not to be taken as prisoners of war but were to lay down their arms under their officers' orders and march to Boston, where they were to be re-embarked to Europe on condition that they would not serve again in America. The loyalists were to be respected and treated as British subjects; and the Canadians were to be sent back to Canada. The officers were to be allowed to retain their small arms, and their baggage was not to be searched.

Astonishingly, Gates agreed. He had no stomach for a fight to the death, which the reckless Burgoyne might well have launched, and besides – although the latter was ignorant of this – Clinton had launched a further offensive, having returned to New York and loaded boats with provisions for up to six months, as well as reinforcements. On 13 October, 2,000 men had pushed further up the Hudson, passing Kingston. This British force was now within fifty miles of Gates's camp; it was relatively small, but Gates could not know that it was inadequate to rescue Burgoyne, even if ordered to do so.

Gates knew that a fight to the finish with the British would be extremely costly; and with the small forces he had deployed behind Burgoyne's camp, he could not be sure of preventing a British retreat. He decided to accept the British terms. Burgoyne had by then heard of Clinton's advance from the south and considered breaking off negotiations, but was persuaded not to do so.

On the morning of 17 October, the agreement reached the night before was formally carried out. To the sound of military bands, 2,442 British soldiers and 2,198 Germans rode out of the British camp, bearing with them 37 cannon. Burgoyne himself appeared in full ceremonial uniform, 'having bestowed so much care on his whole toilet that he looked more like a man of fashion than a warrior'. According to Gates's right-hand man:

> Gates, advised of Burgoyne's approach, met him at the head of his camp, Burgoyne in a rich royal uniform, and Gates in a plain blue frock. When they had approached nearly within sword's length, they reined up and halted … General Burgoyne, raising his hat most gracefully, said, 'The fortune of war, General Gates, has made me your prisoner'; to which the conqueror, returning a courtly salute, promptly replied, 'I shall always be ready to bear testimony that it has not been through any fault of your excellency.'

With gentlemanly propriety, the two settled down to a large banquet. Baroness von Riedesel reported that the dismissed General Schuyler, whose careful planning had made the whole American victory possible, offered her and her children a fine lunch of 'small tongue, beefsteaks, potatoes, ground beans and bread'.

One of the most decisive events in human history thus ended on this bizarrely courteous note. Or so it seemed. In fact the Convention of Saratoga – it was not a formal surrender, still less a 'battle' as usually described (the battles having taken place at Bemis Heights), although it was a great victory of points for the Americans, was now to ignite a furious controversy which conferred upon it an importance far beyond what either victor or vanquished could have believed at the time.

Gates himself behaved with propriety towards the British troops now in his care. But as the British were marched through hostile New England, away from Gates's command, they were treated more roughly. General Stark confined them to go no more than fifty yards from their quarters, on pain of '200 lashes without benefit of court martial'. One sergeant reported that:

It was not infrequent for thirty or forty persons, men, women and children, to be indiscriminately crowded together in one small open hut, their provisions and firewood on short allowance; a scanty provision of straw their bed, their blankets their only covering. In the night-time those that could not lie down, and the many who sat up from the cold, were obliged frequently to rise and shake from them the snow which the wind drifted in at the openings. General Burgoyne, ever attentive to the welfare of his army, remonstrated in a letter to General Gates.

Burgoyne himself hovered between a nervous breakdown and the continual need to shift the blame for the debacle. He wrote:

I have been obliged to deliberate upon the most nice negotiations and political arrangements that required the most undisturbed reflection, under perpetual fire, and exhausted with laborious days and sixteen almost sleepless nights, without a change of clothes, or other covering than the sky. I have been with my army in the jaws of famine; shot through my hat and waistcoat; my nearest friends killed round me; and after all these combined misfortunes and escapes, I imagine I am reserved to stand a war with ministers who will always lay the blame upon the employed who miscarries …

I expect ministerial ingratitude will be displayed, as in all countries and at all times is usual, to remove the blame from the orders to the execution. I think it not impossible that the persons who are most bound to vindicate me will be the first to attack my reputation, those for whom I cheerfully undertook a forlorn hope, and who would have crushed me if I remained inactive, I expect to find my accusers for rashness.

Not all the British suffered hardship. Some American girls wanted to 'bundle with' British officers on the way, one of them seeking to do so with her 'first Briton'. In Boston itself the British were mobbed by curious but polite townspeople. Scores of British soldiers deserted, along with a large number of Germans. But Burgoyne complained of his room, which he was forced to share with General Phillips and their staff. Seven or eight officers were bedded in rooms ten feet square – the revenge of the peoples of Charlestown for the destruction of the town at the beginning of the war.

Meanwhile Burgoyne bombarded his superiors in London with a stream of self-justification. He blamed the inconstancy of the Germans for the defeat, but soon Howe was to become his chief scapegoat. He argued, 'Will it be said that in the exhausted situation described, and in the jaws of famine and invested by quadruple numbers, a treaty which saves the army for the start for the next campaign, was not more than could have been expected?'

Carleton wrote to Burgoyne sympathetically, although not blaming Howe:

> This unfortunate event, it is to be hoped, will in future prevent ministers from pretending to direct operations of war in a country at 3,000 miles distance, of which they have so little knowledge as not to be able to distinguish between good, bad, or interested advices, or to give positive orders in matters which from their nature are ever upon the change: so that the expedience or propriety of a measure at one moment may be totally inexpedient or improper in the next.

# 17

# *Betrayal*

Burgoyne had surrendered to an enemy so determined to prevail that it failed to abide by the traditional rules of war. Gates came under immediate attack from his own side for his agreement with Burgoyne, even though he had reached it for reasons of military expediency – to save his men from a savage final battle which they would win only at huge cost, and to prevent a possible mauling afterwards from the force moving up from New York, whose strength he could not know. That this force was not a strong one determined to liaise with Burgoyne was apparent only with hindsight. Clinton had already performed with formidable efficiency in securing the forts below Albany. Gates defended himself with dignity:

> Lieutenant General Burgoyne, at the time he capitulated, was strongly entrenched on a formidable post, with twelve days' provisions; the capture of Fort Montgomery and the enemy's consequent progress up the Hudson's River, endangered our arsenal at Albany: a reflection which left [Gates] no time to contest the capitulation with Lt General Burgoyne, but induced the necessity of immediately closing with his proposals … this delicate situation abridged our conquest and procured Lt General Burgoyne the terms he enjoys … had an attack been carried against Lt General Burgoyne the dismemberment of our army must necessarily have been such as would have incapacitated it for further action this campaign.

But he was a marked man. Seeking the full credit for the victory at Saratoga, he was now seen as a possible replacement for Washington, whose string of failures had been crowned by his loss of Philadelphia, the new nation's capital. Washington sprang at Gates's Achilles heel. On 5 November he wrote:

> As soon as they [the defeated British troops] arrive [in England] they will enable the ministry to send an equal number of other troops from their

different garrisons to join General Howe here, or upon any other service against the American states ... I think, in point of policy, we should not be anxious for their early departure ... I do not think it to our interest to expedite the passage of prisoners to England; for you may depend upon it that they will immediately upon their arrival there throw them into different garrisons and bring out an equal number.

The commander-in-chief's argument impressed congressmen, now cowed and sheltering in nearby Yorktown, Virginia. Using two flimsy pretexts for breaking a solemn agreement, they noted that some 650 British soldiers had retained their cartouche boxes, violating the agreement (which was in fact debatable), and they pounced on the fact that Burgoyne himself, complaining about his uncomfortable accommodation in Boston, had declared 'the public faith is broke' – which, they said, 'signified that he no longer intended to abide by the convention'.

On 8 January 1778, Congress moved that: 'The embarkation of Lieut-Gen Burgoyne, and the troops under his command be suspended till a distinct and explicit ratification of the Convention of Saratoga shall be properly notified by the court of Great Britain to Congress.' Such satification was not possible, because Britain did not recognize Congress. The Americans then abrogated the agreement drawn up by their commander in the field, without which the British would probably not have surrendered. The Americans would not abide by the rules, for they were fighting for their very existence as a nation – to the death.

Although understandable, it was perhaps the most shameful single episode in the birth of independent America. It gained the Americans 4,000 prisoners without a fight, and reflected particularly badly on Washington as its instigator, bent on destroying the reputation of a rival who had secured the first major victory of the war.

Thus the American triumph at Saratoga became a British catastrophe – the loss of a whole army through a failure to keep faith. The war would bristle with excesses and broken promises on both sides; but never had a senior commander's solemn pledge to obtain a negotiated agreement, instead of a fight to the finish, been so shamelessly repudiated by his superiors. Burgoyne, at least, was allowed to return home on parole. The rest of the army was held prisoner, mostly in Massachusetts, with many, maybe most, eventually deserting to the Americans or becoming settlers there.

News of the disaster had, as always, taken time to percolate across the Atlantic to London. When it did, the impact was devastating. At the end of October Germain had learned of the battle of Freeman's Farm, which suggested that Burgoyne's campaign was in serious trouble. Rumours of a major defeat became rife throughout November. Germain set out the government's view of Burgoyne's mission in the debate on the King's Speech later in the month:

> With regard to the Canada expedition, the honourable gentleman was under a mistake when he imagined that General Burgoyne had orders to fight his way to New York, and there join Sir William Howe: his orders were to clear the country of rebels as far as Albany, which town was pre-scribed to him as the boundary of his expedition, unless circumstances might make it necessary to co-operate with General Howe, in which case he was to assist him to the utmost of his powers.

Early in December a prominent government supporter, Edward Gibbon, wrote:

> Dreadful news indeed. You will see them partly in the papers and we have not yet any particulars. An English army of near 10,000 men laid down their arms and surrendered prisoners of war on condition of being sent to England and of never again serving against America. They had fought bravely and were three days without food. General Fraser with 2,000 men killed. A general cry for peace.

When Germain finally heard the news, it was greeted with dismay and incredulity:

> Charles Fox and Burke pressed Lord George [Germain] to know if the capture of Burgoyne's army was true. He was forced to own he believed it, though he did not know it officially. The opposition, instead of receiv-ing such a national indignity with serious lamentations, insulted the min-isters so much that the majority appeared less dejected than on former days of the session.

Burgoyne on his return was refused a court martial or a formal inquiry to vindicate him, and as a sign of severe censure was denied an audience with the King. In view of the debacle he had led, this was light punish-ment indeed. Two decades earlier, Admiral Byng had been shot for sur-rendering at Minorca – a predicament not of his own making.

In 1782 Burgoyne's career was mysteriously resumed and at the age of sixty, he was appointed commander-in-chief in Ireland, where he fell in love with a singer, Susan Caulfield, and had four children. He wrote three more plays: one a flop, one a modest success, the third, *The Heiress*, a sell-out. He died a respected figure in 1792, and was buried in

Westminster Abbey. For a man who had presided over such a disaster it was not a bad end – particularly in view of the fact that, twenty years before, Robert Clive had been nearly censured for his astoundingly successful career in India, with Burgoyne his prime persecutor, and that Warren Hastings, after a brilliant spell as ruler of India, had been impeached. Burgoyne's lenient treatment reflected official embarrassment at the roles that Howe, Clinton, Germain and even the King himself had played in the catastrophe.

Saratoga was certainly a turning point of the war, although not quite the one it has become in American mythology. Immediately hailed as the defeat that broke the back of the British war effort, its significance was fivefold. First, it rescued the American war effort from what looked, in the autumn of 1777, to be an inevitable and humiliating disaster; without Saratoga the Americans might well have sued for peace after the loss of Philadelphia. Second, it marked the first significant American military victory – unless the ambush at Concord and Lexington or the skirmishes at Trenton and Princeton could be described as such. The Americans had at last won a major battle, the second battle of Bemis Heights; the British were not, after all, invincible in open battle. Third, it proved a colossal propaganda boost to the American cause. Fourth, it dented the initial enthusiasm of British public and parliamentary opinion towards the war, which had always been opposed by a significant minority led by the Earl of Chatham. Finally, and perhaps most significantly, it propelled the French into a long-contemplated declaration of global war on Britain in revenge for their defeat in the Seven Years War.

Before Saratoga, the American cause seemed all but dead. Massachusetts, of course, remained a hotbed of rebellion – and not the least of the British northern campaign's idiocies was that it was staged so close to the centre of the whole struggle for American independence: Massachusetts, Connecticut, New Hampshire, Maine and Rhode Island – all challengers to Gage's army in 1775–6. But the British hold on New York was secure, and now the British had seized the American capital itself.

Desperate as had been the winter the Americans endured in 1776–7, the next, at Valley Forge, was to be even worse, giving little hope that they were capable of defeating the British. After Philadelphia, it seemed to many, especially to the fleeing congressmen in the south, that the Americans had in fact lost the war, until the news came of Saratoga. The rebels desperately needed to show their own people and sympathetic outsiders that their cause was not hopeless, to counterbalance the loss of their capital.

The loss of an army of 4,000 redcoats constituted the biggest single event in the war so far – no matter that defeat had been largely the result of staggeringly inept tactics by a single British commander, the hesitations of another (Clinton) and strategic stupidity by their superiors; nor that it had technically been not a defeat but a negotiated surrender whose terms the Americans had reneged upon. Had the British troops been safely repatriated, Saratoga would have been no more than a setback, as they could have taken up other stations in Europe and other troops could have been sent in their place.

This was to be cited as one of the reasons the Americans revoked the agreement. In fact it is specious: it was obvious to the British and American commanders who negotiated the convention that that was what would happen. Otherwise there would have been no incentive for Burgoyne to negotiate the agreement except to avoid a massacre that he may not in any case have believed was inevitable.

But the American leadership showed ruthlessness in abrogating their commander's word, without which there would have been no agreement at Saratoga. This was the action of revolutionaries with their backs to the wall, fighting for a desperate cause in which they believed. These men stood to lose the war and probably their lives unless they reneged upon the agreement. They had acted with the savagery dictated by self-preservation.

The American cause possessed credibility again. Without Saratoga, the rebel effort might have dribbled away into isolated shows of resistance through the terrible winter of 1777–8. As a turning point, it did not mark the beginning of an American victory, but it averted the certainty of an American defeat.

The second impact of Saratoga was no less significant. Except in New England, the American military performance had so far been abysmal. After the initial successes at Concord and Lexington, the 'glorious defeat' at Breed's Hill and the capture of Boston, the American war machine had been routed at the Battle of Brooklyn and proved a fiasco in the defence of New York. The Americans had then displayed skill only in the speed of their running, and had barely recovered with two brilliant guerrilla raids in Maryland in the winter of 1776–7. The defeats outside Philadelphia and the loss of the capital completed the picture of an army on the run except in the north.

To win popular support, the American army had to show that it was capable of achieving a real victory against the British. Saratoga could be portrayed as a spectacular conventional triumph. American military pride, until then propaganda-based, could now become a reality.

The propaganda impact of Saratoga was, of course, tremendous for a side with communications skills that vastly outmatched those of its British enemy. With remarkable and pioneering effect, the rebels had wrung consolation out of defeat, human pathos out of disaster, heroism out of every setback, and had vastly exaggerated their minor achievements. The Ride of Paul Revere had embroidered the ambushes at Lexington and Concord. Defeat at Breed's Hill had been turned into the victory of Bunker Hill. The propagandists had turned the American disasters at Brooklyn and New York into a tragedy of British brutality and repression. The firefights at Newport and Princeton had been turned into victories, and Washington's crossing of the Delaware into a Caesar-like achievement.

Now a real victory had at last taken place, and this was instantly portrayed as the imminent collapse of British rule in America. Although the 4,000 British redcoats had not actually been taken prisoner, Congress quickly made sure they were. Saratoga was to become the most celebrated victory of the whole war. The real American triumph had been the assembling at short notice of a large army, primarily militia-based, to take advantage of British overconfidence and misunderstanding of the terrain – exactly the same technique on a much larger scale, as was practised at Concord and Lexington.

Saratoga's impact on British opinion was just as dramatic as on American. The British had always been divided about the war – many doubting whether it was necessary, and a few like Chatham whether it could be won at all. When news of Philadelphia's capture arrived it seemed that the British were heading towards triumph. Within a few weeks, news of Burgoyne's surrender suggested that disaster beckoned. It was apparent that the British strategy of isolating Massachusetts, which had already failed once, had now led a British army into a trap; and that cancelled out the taking of Philadelphia. While one paw of the British lion had mauled the American eagle, the other had been bitten off.

The First Lord of the Admiralty, the previously belligerent Earl of

Sandwich, now vigorously argued for the limited strategy of a naval blockade, to hold America's ports and bring the rebels to their knees by squeezing their trade in a long war of attrition. North himself had been thrown into one of his characteristic fits of histrionics and despair by the news of Saratoga – although he had never appeared wholeheartedly behind the expedition of his distant relation Burgoyne. Sandwich's ascendancy reflected the advance of the 'peace party' represented by General Amherst, who urged a withdrawal from the American colonies and the strengthening of British positions in Canada, Florida and Nova Scotia in preparation for an attack on French and Spanish possessions in the West Indies in the war that he – rightly – felt was imminent between the major Continental powers. Germain nearly resigned; North attempted to do so, but was blocked by the King. But North argued that Britain was 'totally unequal' to a war on two fronts with America and France, and urged peace with America. Again, the unhappy Prime Minister was blocked by the King.

There was sound common sense in what both Sandwich and Amherst advanced. By holding a few strategic points along the American coastline, such as New York, while blockading American ports, the British could cripple the enemy while ending the unpopular land war which seemed unwinnable and was antagonizing large sections of the American population. This was not a strategy born of desperation: rather, it reflected an understanding that, however many troops they possessed in America, the British could not hope decisively to dominate this vast continent: a victory in one place would be offset by a defeat elsewhere, and always the American army would retreat, reform and fight again. The sheer size of the territory meant that the rebels would remain undefeated. Britain's only prospect of outright victory after Saratoga was to dispatch a huge army; but this would weaken Britain's own defences, and even then might not succeed.

Britain's further mistake was to send no substantial army to the south, whose population was largely loyal. In the absence of British troops, the loyalists there were largely terrorized into submission by Virginian and local irregulars deploying the necessary arms and ruthlessness.

If war broke out with France, Britain's far more immediately lucrative possessions in the West Indies would be threatened, and the prospect of securing France's possessions also beckoned. For Britain to devote a large army and natural resources to the vastness of America, with its more limited commercial value, was madness. A total rethink now took place.

Amherst argued that a land war with the colonists as part of a general war 'must be feeble in all parts and consequently unsuccessful'. The peace party even urged upon the King an agreement almost on American terms – denying them formal independence, but giving them virtual self-government within a loose commercial and political association with the British Empire. These had been the terms originally proposed by Chatham. Almost certainly American hardliners would have blocked this: what might have been acceptable earlier could not be countenanced after so much blood had been spilt, and particularly after Saratoga.

The fear that the British might settle with the colonists was powerfully felt in Paris. Up to then, the French had benefited hugely from America's drain on British resources, at little cost to themselves. With French supplies intermittently reaching the colonies the latter had absorbed the energies of the rival British Empire. If the two sides settled, or if the colonists surrendered, the British would be reanimated and be free to counter the French.

Saratoga had shown the French that the British could be checked in the colonies, and it was in the French interest to prolong the war. That left them with little alternative but to conclude a closer alliance with the Americans, which would inevitably result in a renewed outbreak of war with the British. For the French, as for the British, the colonies' rebellion had until then been essentially a sideshow in their greater rivalry.

The French decision was not taken without soul-searching. It was far less expensive for the French to fight a proxy war using the American rebels as cannon fodder; unless the French treasury could be certain of winning, another war with Britain could be ruinous – as was indeed to be the case, precipitating the Revolution of 1789. Moreover, France's absolutist government was promoting the cause of a polar opposite – English-speaking republicans rebelling against their rightful sovereign, brandishing such subversive slogans as freedom, equal rights and wider male suffrage.

The spectacle was not wasted on the French intellectual classes, who were inspired by the American example, and especially by the cheeky republican simplicity of Benjamin Franklin – a stark contrast to the lavish magnificence of Louis XVI's Versailles. Many at court, even the King himself, were wary of encouraging the American radicals.

From the American perspective the Comte de Vergennes has usually been lauded as a far-seeing statesman; from the viewpoint of his own ruling class he was an unmitigated disaster, steering his country into a war it could ill afford and did not win and, by encouraging the spread of American revolutionary ideas, contributing directly to the bloody overthrow of the French monarchy and nobility a decade later.

On 6 February 1778 a treaty of amity and commerce was signed, providing for most-favoured-nation trading status between the French and the colonists. A treaty of commerce and defensive alliance was also signed, committing both parties to fight against the common enemy should war break out between Britain and France. The French promised not to seek the conquest of American land lost during the French and Indian War. In addition, 'Neither of the two parties shall conclude either a truce or peace with Great Britain, without first obtaining the formal consent of the other, and they mutually engage not to lay down their arms, until the independence of the United States shall have been formally or tacitly assured by the treaty or treaties that shall terminate the war.'

The French had abandoned their earlier insistence that, before any declaration of war, the Spanish should join the anti-British crusade, almost certainly because they feared an American–British settlement might be imminent. Franklin and Deane skilfully played upon French fears by talking to a British emissary, Paul Wentworth. Franklin, Deane and Lee – that odd trio so often snubbed by the French Crown – were received at last by Louis XVI. Congress, not without its own misgivings – after all, the American colonists were signing up with their old enemy against the English-speaking mother country – approved the treaty in May. On 14 June 1778 France and Britain were at war.

Already, in April, Vergennes had sent a convoy of fifteen ships under the command of Vice-Admiral the Comte d'Estaing, a former soldier. These headed for the mouth of the Delaware and successfully evaded British attempts to attack them on 8 July. With the backing of a great power, the American cause had been hugely boosted. The British were by no means wholly dismayed, having fought and beaten the French before. But the alliance meant that, with so many other commitments across the globe, any prospect of significant British reinforcements to crush the rebels after Saratoga was out of the question. Britain's earlier parsimony had lost it the chance to quash the rebellion convincingly before a general war broke out.

*

General Howe, returning to Philadelphia in early October 1777 after Britain's greatest triumph in the War of Independence, might have been forgiven for behaving as a great victor. The British applied themselves to making life as pleasant as possible. Most of Philadelphia's inhabitants were loyalists, and heartily sick of the drab puritanism imposed by Congress. The British occupied the city's public buildings, including Independence Hall, went on the town with willing local girls, and staged no fewer than fourteen plays through the winter. A loyalist beauty, Rebecca Franks, wrote, 'You can have no idea of the life of continued amusement I live in. I can scarce have a moment to myself. There is a ball every Thursday, never a lack of partners, for you must know 'tis a fixed rule never to dance but two dances at a time with the same person … I am engaged to seven different gentlemen.'

Howe continued his relationship with Mrs Joshua Loring, his mistress from New York. But he soon learned the fate of Burgoyne's army. Although himself a well-balanced and effective leader, he had long since become dissatisfied with the conditions of his command. The Burgoyne episode had been a crude attempt to undermine him by the King and Germain, yet he had been expected to rescue a futile and dangerous expedition – though Germain did not have the temerity to order him to do so directly.

Howe had made mistakes – his failure to trap Washington, his slow pursuit of the American army across New Jersey, his inadequate defence of Trenton. But his record contained three striking successes: the victory at Brooklyn, the capture of New York, and now the capture of the rebel heartland at Philadelphia, with two fine battles to his credit. It was time to go, after his greatest success. He believed the war to be unwinnable.

Writing to Germain, Howe declared that only the dispatch of 35,000 more troops would hold America now – much the same conclusion his predecessor General Gage had reached two years before. Furthermore, Howe declared that, as he no longer enjoyed the government's confidence, he wished to resign. However calm and cheerful he appeared, Britain's only successful general in North America to date must have harboured bitterness, though he did not show it.

Following his resignation, his troops, among whom he remained popular, gave him a terrific regatta on the Delaware river, with fireworks, jousting, a banquet and a ball. The proceedings – vigorously denounced by the city's puritan population – were supervised by John André,

Howe's chief aide and spymaster, who occupied Franklin's comfortable house and pilfered some of his belongings. Howe was publicly displaying that he had not taken the inconstancy of his masters in London to heart.

Although Washington and his staff had been overjoyed by the news of Saratoga, the American commander had no grounds for real optimism. One problem was personal. He had just lost two battles, while his main rival for the American supreme command, Horatio Gates, had just won a spectacular victory at Saratoga. Gates, moreover, was a skilled political general, with many supporters in Congress – including the enormously influential Sam Adams, father of the Revolution and chairman of key congressional committees.

Washington's loss of Philadelphia had been a major strategic setback for the American cause. Worse, he had retreated to a valley near White Marsh, some twelve miles south of the capital, only to be ambushed by the British there at the beginning of December. After a stand-off between the two forces, Washington felt compelled to retreat a further twelve miles to a safer refuge at the village of Valley Forge. He had been joined at last by his wife, Martha, who wrote, 'The general is well, but much worn with fatigue and anxiety. I never knew him to be so anxious as now.' She had not been present at the Delaware encampment the year before. The chosen site had natural defences on two sides in the Schuylkill river and Valley Creek, and control of several thickly wooded hills which could be easily defended. It was also well placed to watch British troop movements. To Washington it seemed not unlike his choice of Morristown the previous year.

However, Valley Forge suffered from two severe disadvantages: there were virtually no buildings there, and local people were themselves suffering extreme privation and could provide only scant supplies. Also, the winter of 1777–8 was far fiercer than the previous one. The army this time was also much larger: some 11,000 men, of whom around 8,000 were fit for duty. They had barely a change of clothing, few shoes and no soap. Food was scarce, and water had to be carried up the steep banks of the Schuylkill to the camp.

The absence of food and provisions reflected the middle colonies' lack of enthusiasm for the American cause. The states too preferred to hang on to their supplies, however much Congress might try to cajole them. The army set about building log cabins, fourteen by sixteen feet, to contain twelve men at a time. The soldiers slept on the floors, and subsisted for a while off firecake, an unleavened bread. At the end of December, and then again in early January and mid-February, the troops virtually ran out of food. Some 500 horses died of starvation.

Congress, officially in charge of provisioning from its confined quarters in Yorktown, proved woefully inept. Produce bought in New Jersey went rotten because it could not be transferred. Philadelphian farmers preferred to sell their crops to the British, who could pay in hard cash, while others shipped flour to New England. Washington quarrelled bitterly with his congressional critics, some of whom, he claimed,

> thought the soldiers were made of sticks or stones and equally insensible of frost and snow, and moreover as if they conceived it easily practicable for an inferior army, under the disadvantages I described ours to be – which are by no means exaggerated – to confine a superior one, in all respects well appointed and provided for a winter's campaign, within the city of Philadelphia, and to cover from depredation and waste the states of Pennsylvania and Jersey …
>
> I can assure these gentlemen that it is a much easier and less distressing thing to draw remonstrances in a comfortable room by a good fire side than to occupy a cold bleak hill and sleep under frost and snow without clothes or blankets; however, although they seem to have little feeling for the naked and distressed soldier, I feel abundantly for them, and from my soul pity those miseries, which it is neither in my power to relieve or prevent.

But Congress itself was merely a rump parliament of between nine and twenty-one members meeting in a courthouse. It eventually issued orders to Washington to plunder the countryside, which he acted upon with the greatest reluctance. With Congress in its present, enfeebled state, Washington was in effect a military dictator – which renewed the mutterings about the peremptory but unsuccessful commander-in-chief.

Two unexpected improvements were to ameliorate this desperate plight. First, Nathanael Greene, an immensely energetic and able officer, was appointed Quartermaster General in March 1778, and revolutionized the cumbersome system of provisioning for the army. As Washington expressed it, 'There is not an officer of the army, nor a man in America, more sincerely attached to the interests of his country. Could he best promote their interests in the character of a corporal, he would exchange, as I firmly believe, without a murmur, the epaulet for the knot.' Greene had no inhibitions about giving orders to forage for hay and livestock in New Jersey and Delaware, which he argued were filled with loyalist sympathizers. Purchasing commissioners were appointed under an incentive system which meant they earned more money the more they seized. This proved highly effective.

A second unexpected blessing during that winter of terrible hardship was the arrival of the self-styled Lieutenant-General Frederick William Augustus Henry Ferdinand, Baron von Steuben, a Prussian émigré recommended warmly by Franklin and Deane. In fact he was no general, merely a captain, and was not a baron either. But his military experience was genuine enough: he had been born into a Prussian military family, and had served as an aide to Frederick the Great. He had been sent by the French to try to knock some organization and discipline into Washington's ragtag army, for fear that their financial support was being squandered.

Large, jovial and expansive, von Steuben made an immediate impression. One American soldier wrote that 'Never before or since, have I had such an impression of the ancient fabled God of War, as when I looked on the baron: he seemed to me a perfect personification of Mars. The trappings of his horse, the enormous holsters of his pistols, his large size, and his strikingly martial aspect, all seemed to favour the idea.'

Von Steuben resisted the temptation to instil Prussian discipline into the Americans – who would probably have rejected it anyway – but devoted himself to organization and drill work, which was welcome to the idle, demoralised and unemployed men at Valley Forge. As he put it, 'In the first place, the genius of this nation is not in the least to be compared with that of the Prussians, Austrians, or French. You say to your soldier, "Do this", and he doeth it, but I am obliged to say, "This is the reason why you ought to do that", and he does it.'

He began by introducing records of each soldier and his terms of enlistment, as well as his arms and ammunition. He insisted upon a proper drilling system, with a uniform way of marching and giving commands. He wrote his rules down in French, using two French-speaking aides to translate them into English. He trained a cadre of drill instructors. Von Steuben was given personal command of 100 men to serve as an 'ideal company', and instead of getting sergeants to drill them he did so himself, swearing vigorously at the troops in German and French – which vastly amused them. One of his aides recalled that he ordered

'"My dear [Captain Benjamin] Walker and my dear Duponceau, come and swear for me in English. These fellows won't do what I bid them." A good-natured smile then went through the ranks and at last the manoeuvre of the movement was properly performed.'

Von Steuben shrewdly realized that the Americans should be given freedom of movement, and established light infantry companies with considerable autonomy. His Black Book of military instructions was to become the Regulations for the Order and Discipline of the Troops in the United States, the official manual of the United States army for thirty years.

It is hard to dignify the dress worn by most soldiers belonging to Washington's Continental Army, let alone the militia, with the term 'uniform'. Men wore thick stockings, shirts and waistcoats with long outer coats, and tricorn hats were fashionable. But there was a huge amount of diversity – from floppy-brimmed flat hats to warm woolly ones – and some wore nothing at all on their heads. At Valley Forge Washington considered it useless to supply soap, because most men had only one shirt and one pair of breeches. Their shoes were often in tatters. Similarly, while blue-grey was a favourite and encouraged colour for coats and waistcoats, browns of every hue and even greens and yellows were common. On one occasion Washington furiously reproached the army's clothier for dressing an entire regiment in British red because no other clothing was available.

The Continental Army was equipped with a smooth-bore flintlock musket which, like the rifle wielded by the British, had a range of around seventy-five yards. Although it was easy and quick to load, the width of its muzzle caused the musket ball to bounce up the long barrel, and accuracy was very poor – on average, only one in eighty hit their target, according to one estimate. Some troops were equipped with the American long rifle (also known as the Kentucky or Pennsylvania rifle). Although this was much more accurate, its narrow bore made it much harder and time-consuming to load, and it could not carry a bayonet.

By the end of March a grateful Washington had appointed von Steuben Inspector-General of the army, and soon after he elevated him to the rank of major-general. With von Steuben's help, Washington had made a giant leap towards creating a more professional army, with profound consequences for the future course of American history.

*

At Valley Forge, the austere, reserved and prickly Washington came to appreciate the qualities of a dashing young Frenchman in a manner that seemed totally out of character. Gilbert du Motier, Marquis de Lafayette, was an exuberant nineteen-year-old when he first arrived in America. He had inherited his title at the age of two, when his father was killed at the Battle of Minden in the Seven Years War. Physically unimpressive, he was no athlete and was shunned at court, where his family was considered comparatively nouveau riche. But he was phenomenally wealthy, with an income of around £300,000 a year by the age of twenty-one, and at the age of sixteen he had been married to the daughter of the Duc d'Ayen, head of one of the noblest families in France, who had taken the youth under his wing.

However, the Duc was not Lafayette's mentor: his military tutor was the Comte de Broglie, a former head of the French secret service, who plotted the extraordinary objective of becoming commander-in-chief of the forces in America in place of Washington, whom he and other French military leaders considered ineffectual, and then, fantastically, the elected leader of America. With an aristocratic Frenchman in charge of the colonies, he believed, the French court could be reconciled to supporting a republican revolution.

De Broglie conspired with Silas Deane, the American envoy, to persuade the wealthy but naive Lafayette, who was facing a personal crisis after his rejection by a girl at court whom he wanted to make his mistress, to buy his own ship and travel to America. Lafayette's companion was Brigadier-General Johann de Kalb, a bogus German baron in on the plot, who had been born into a peasant family and had already acted as a secret agent for the French during the Stamp Act crisis.

Arriving just south of Charleston on 13 June 1778, this odd couple – the young aristocrat, now disobeying his father-in-law and even the King, and the fifty-six-year-old 'baron' of German origin – made their way across country from South Carolina to Philadelphia. There Congress had learned of the Broglie plot; and Lafayette, who was not a party to it, was able to save his position only by offering to serve without pay. De Kalb, a veteran of many years experience, was stripped of his commission, while Lafayette was made a major-general on the strength of his French recommendations. De Kalb threatened angrily to return to France, before Congress, realizing his military skills, awarded him the status he sought, and he then joined Washington to assist him at Valley Forge.

Washington was perplexed at what to do with the youthful Major-General Lafayette:

> What the designs of Congress respecting this gentleman were, and what line of conduct I am to pursue to comply with their designs and his expectations, I know no more than a child unborn, and beg to be instructed. If Congress meant that his rank should be unaccompanied by command, I wish it had been sufficiently explained to him. If, on the other hand, it was intended to invest him with all the powers of a major-general, why have I been led into a contrary belief, and left in the dark with respect to my conduct towards him? ...

The two had dinner together at Philadelphia's city tavern after the British evacuation of the city, and the forty-five-year-old got on famously with the twenty-year-old – Washington, who had no sons of his own, asking the youth to treat him as 'a father and friend'. While there was clearly an instant personal bond between the two, it also seems likely that, with France joining the war, Washington saw the advantage in having at his right hand a prominent Frenchman, whom he could hope to dominate because of the age disparity. Lafayette at his side could act as the eyes and ears of France.

Lafayette, eager for glory, requested command of a division, but Washington sensibly attached him to his personal staff. The young man doted with adolescent hero worship on his commander, 'that inestimable man, whose talents and virtues I admire – the better I know him the more I venerate him. I am established in his house, and we live together like two attached brothers, with mutual confidence and cordiality.'

Lafayette behaved with real courage at the Battle of Brandywine, where he came close to enemy lines and was wounded by a musket ball through his leg. 'Treat him as though he were my son,' Washington told those who helped the youth off the field. By the spring of 1778 he was given command of his own division. For his part Lafayette, who had never been party to de Broglie's plotting, was won over completely by the aloof, shy commander, who, uniquely, made this flamboyant if insignificant-looking Frenchman his chosen confidant and ward.

Another of Silas Deane's recruits proved more troublesome. This was Thomas Conway, an Irishman who had been appointed colonel in the French army and then brigadier-general by Congress. Conway was a skilful commander and, supported by influential sections of Congress, sought to supplant Washington with the victor of Saratoga, Horatio Gates. As one of Deane's recruits, he may also have been in on the de Broglie conspiracy, but he probably realized that only an American general could supplant the commander-in-chief.

After Conway had successfully lobbied to be promoted to major-general and secured the promotion of Gates's right-hand man, James Wilkinson, to brigadier, Washington's unease about him came out into the open:

> General Conway's merit as an officer and his importance in this army exist more in his own imagination than in reality. For it is a maxim with him to leave no service of his own untold, nor to want anything which is to be obtained by importunity ... I would ask why the youngest brigadier in the service should be put over the heads of the oldest and thereby take rank and command of gentlemen who but yesterday were his seniors, gentlemen who, as I will be bound to say on behalf of some of them at least, are of sound judgment and unquestionable bravery ... This truth I am well assured of, that they will not serve under him. I leave you to guess therefore at the situation this army would be in at so important a crisis if this event should take place.

Conway was appointed to the influential job of Inspector-General of the artillery, while Gates became head of the new Board of War, rivalling Washington's increasingly autocratically exercised supreme command. Men like James Lovell, chairman of the committee on foreign affairs, openly canvassed for Washington to be replaced. In a letter to Gates he wrote, 'We want you at different places but we want you most near Germantown. Good God! What a situation we are in! How different from what might have been justly expected! You will be astonished when you know accurately what numbers have at one time and another been collected near Philadelphia to wear out stockings, shoes and breeches.'

Lovell wrote in another letter to Gates:

> You have saved our northern hemisphere, and in spite of consummate and repeated blundering you have changed the condition of the southern campaign, on the part of the enemy, from offensive to defensive ...
>
> We have had a noble army [i.e. Washington's] melted down by ill-judged marches, marches that disgrace the authors and directors and which have occasioned the severest and most just sarcasm and contempt of our enemies. How much are you to be envied, my dear general! How different your conduct and your fortune!

Conway, Spotswood, Connor, Ross and Mifflin resigned, and many other brave and good officers are preparing their letters to Congress on the same subject. In short, this army will be totally lost unless you come down and collect the virtuous band who wish to fight under your banner and with their aid save the southern hemisphere. Prepare yourself for a jaunt to this place – Congress must send for you.

Other congressmen, including John Adams, were also increasingly critical of Washington, albeit for different reasons, and even the powerful Sam Adams may have been manoeuvring against him behind the scenes. In particular, Washington's increasingly arbitrary exercise of his authority and the contempt for Congress displayed at Valley Forge – which was well deserved – offended the puritan instincts of John Adams. After news of Saratoga had arrived, he wrote:

I have been distressed to see some members of this house disposed to idolise an image which their own hands have molten. I speak here of the superstitious veneration that is sometimes paid to General Washington. Although I honour him for his good qualities, yet in this house I feel myself his superior. In private life I shall always acknowledge that he is mine. It becomes us to attend early to the restraining of our army. Congress will appoint a thanksgiving, and one cause of it ought to be that the glory of turning the tide of arms is not immediately due to the commander-in-chief nor to the southern troops. If it had been, idolatry and adulation would have been unbounded, so excessive as to endanger our liberties … Now we can allow a certain citizen to be wise, virtuous, and good without thinking him a deity or a saviour.

The trio of Conway, Gates and Wilkinson, now backed by many congressional leaders, tried to secure Lafayette's support for their attempt to dislodge Washington, possibly correctly believing the young Frenchman to be the chief agent of the French in America. Lafayette, who admired Conway, was even offered the post of commander-in-chief in Washington's place, with Conway as his subordinate.

But Washington, although at that stage a commander-in-chief with a distinctly mixed reputation, was an astute defender of his own position. Learning of the plot – possibly from Lafayette, or from a loyal commander who had heard an indiscretion by James Wilkinson – Washington challenged Conway directly about it and treated him with frigid condescension on a visit to Valley Forge in December. The plot was nevertheless still alive in January 1778, when a professed Washington loyalist, Dr Benjamin Rush, sent an anonymous letter to Virginia's leader, Patrick Henry:

> We have now passed the Red Sea. A dreary wilderness is still before us, and unless a Moses or a Joshua are raised up in our behalf we must perish before we reach the promised land … But is our case desperate? By no means. We have wisdom, virtue and strength enough to save us, if they could be called into action. The northern army has shown us what Americans are capable of doing with a general at their head. The spirit of the southern army is no way inferior … A Gates, a Lee, or a Conway would in a few weeks render them an irresistible body of men.

Henry promptly passed these comments on to Washington, who wrote to Gates, meanwhile denouncing Conway as a 'dangerous incendiary'. Lafayette now made it clear that he would take no part in the plot. He wrote to Washington:

> If you were lost for America there is nobody who could keep the army and the revolution for six months. There are often dissensions in Congress, parties who hate one another as much as the common enemy; stupid men, who without knowing a single word about war, undertake to judge you, to make ridiculous comparisons; they are infatuated with Gates, without thinking of the different circumstances, and believe that attacking is the only thing necessary to conquer.

At this stage Gates, seeing his own pre-eminent position in the conspiracy being undermined, appears to have got cold feet and denounced his own protégé, Wilkinson, for implicating him in the plot through his indiscretion. Wilkinson furiously challenged Gates to a duel, but was mollified by Gates's tearful declaration that he would as soon shoot his own son. Nevertheless Gates disowned Wilkinson, whose promotion to brigadier was rescinded and who was forced to resign as secretary to the Board of War.

Conway himself was demoted from Inspector-General of the artillery and shortly afterwards was badly injured in a duel, after which he begged Washington's forgiveness in a letter which was received with customary coldness. Gates retained his eminence, but the glow after his victory at Saratoga was much reduced. Washington had shown that when it came to power struggles he was a formidable enemy. He wrote archly to Gates in conclusion:

> I am as averse to controversy as any man and had I not been forced into it you never would have had occasion to impute to me even the shadow

of a disposition towards it … And it is particularly my wish to avoid any personal feuds or dissensions with those who are embarked on the same great national interest with myself, as every difference of this kind must in its consequences be very injurious.

He had not yet proved himself to be a great general, but he was a masterly political operator.

# 18

# *World War*

Unaware of the tension in the American high command, the new British commander-in-chief, Sir Henry Clinton, was in a highly unenviable position. The government in London's continuing commitment to a major push in the American land war was uncertain, and in June 1778 Clinton had learned of the imminent arrival of D'Estaing's fleet, which might blockade the Delaware and cut him off in Philadelphia. He decided to make for New York, and loaded 3,000 loyalists aboard his boats on the river, along with two regiments of Hessians and the sick, for a journey by sea, arranging for the remaining 10,000 men and 1,500 wagons to travel overland, strung out in a line twelve miles long. Progress overland was extremely slow, only thirty-five miles being covered in six days.

It was a terrible and humiliating admission of the scale of Britain's setback in America with French entry into the war. Clinton, who had so singularly failed to come to Burgoyne's rescue, now presided over Britain's first major retreat after Boston. His decision was inevitable with the threatened loss of British control of the sea to the French. It was one thing to face an attack from Washington on land when given the reassurance of supplies up the Delaware to Philadelphia, and of escape *in extremis* by sea. It was another if neither condition applied. Possibly Howe had realized this, and had decided to quit so as not to preside over the withdrawal of the army he had triumphantly marched into Philadelphia.

All the same, the withdrawal reflected Clinton's caution and defeatism – almost acknowledging French naval superiority, when in fact the British had a much better record at sea, and that Washington would soon be able to bring superior forces to bear against Philadelphia, which was by no means certain. The retreat need never have taken place had the British promptly reinforced Philadelphia and dispatched further naval forces. Yet again, as Howe had guessed, Whitehall was failing to give the American war priority by sending necessary reinforcements. The war was being lost for the British in London, not America.

Under Clinton's doleful and hesitant leadership, the British were now on the defensive. The gains of two years of war were to be wiped out. The army was returning to New York where it had started in 1776. Moreover, for fear of the French fleet, most of it was not going by sea.

For Washington, the chance to strike at the straggling British line was too good to miss. He had already dispatched Lafayette with some 2,200 men to patrol the country north of Philadelphia; but the inexperienced young Frenchman nearly fell into a trap, and escaped only at the last minute by crossing a ford over the Schuylkill river. When news of the British evacuation reached Washington he immediately mobilized virtually all 11,000 men at Valley Forge, staging a march across fifty-seven miles in six days.

His senior subordinate was once again General Charles Lee, his respected former rival, who had been mischievously released by the British in an exchange for four Hessian officers in April.

Washington's congressional critics may have been trying to elevate Lee as a rival once again, after the fiasco of Gates and Conway. Certainly Washington was not in a strong enough position to brush him to one side. Lee, whose military reputation remained considerable, counselled caution, urging harassment of the British rather than an outright attack. Washington's younger commanders, including Greene and Lafayette, pressed for an attack, as did von Steuben.

Clinton's army, although large, was highly vulnerable. It consisted of a forward column of 4,000 men, a huge baggage train, and some 6,000 of the better soldiers making up the rear under Clinton's most able commander, Lord Cornwallis, in case of attack. With the whole strung out over several miles, either front or rear could be attacked before the rest of the column could be alerted in strength. Already well south of Howe's old route through New Jersey, Clinton decided to veer further south still, to avoid crossing the Raritan, where he feared attack both from Washington's forces and from the northern army under Gates coming south.

On 25 June the British troops set off for Allentown towards Monmouth Court House, some nineteen miles away, with the aim of reaching Sandy Hook and then embarking for New York. Reaching their first objective after a long march in intense heat, the army restarted on 27 June. The same day Washington was just twenty-five miles away, having nearly caught up with the British. The chase across New Jersey of two years before was being reversed, with the Americans now in pursuit.

The following day Washington ordered Lee, whom he had put in charge of the American vanguard in preference to Lafayette, to attack the British rear. On a blistering hot day, Lee led his 5,000 men forward towards a position overlooking Cornwallis's rearguard of 2,000 by a ravine.

There he decided they were too exposed and, issuing confused and contradictory orders, stationed part of his force in a position to the right with their backs to the ravine, where they could be cut off. These avoided being trapped only because the British were unaware of how vulnerable Lee's men were; taking to their heels, the latter set off an undignified retreat of all the American forward forces after only a little light skirmishing – although the Americans were overwhelmingly superior in numbers.

Running back to Washington, supported by the main American army, Lee was angrily upbraided by his commander (who had a furious temper at crucial moments, as he had shown at the fall of New York): 'What is the meaning of this, sir? I demand to know the meaning of this disorder and confusion.'

'The American troops would not stand the British bayonets,' Lee explained.

Washington swore at him. 'You never tried them.'

Lee was reduced to gabbling 'Sir, sir', and claiming that his orders had not been obeyed and that he had been acting on false intelligence.

The British were now in pursuit of Lee's men, and exploded cannon-fire round them. After riding forward to survey the scene, Washington deployed his men in a line behind another ravine. This was a strong position on high ground with a hill on his right and woods on the left. It was now the British turn to blunder. Encouraged by the failed American attack and subsequent disorderly retreat, Clinton's men mounted a series of ill-coordinated attempts to dislodge Washington's entrenched line, which they failed to do. By late afternoon a string of assaults by Cornwallis's cavalry had also failed to break the American line.

The British withdrew at 6 p.m. The Americans were too exhausted to pursue, and by morning the British were already on the march towards the coast and their rendezvous with the fleet under Admiral Howe which would ship them to New York. The Americans refrained from trying to attack again, and the British evacuation was successfully completed on 1 July. Despite near disaster at Monmouth Court House, the complex British retreat had otherwise been a model of its kind, and the evacuation as skilful as any mounted by Washington.

The battle had been yet another near-debacle for Washington, who had lost every fight with the British except at Trenton and Princeton. Casualties were high – some 350 on each side. But what should have been an American walkover – an attack by 5,000 men on a retreating enemy rearguard of 2,000, with the forward troops too far ahead to reinforce them – had flopped dismally, with the British nearly routing the Americans before escaping with their army intact. Washington had been the American commander, and the attack his decision, though he had been urged on by his more impulsive subordinates. Lee, who had advised against the assault, was made the scapegoat through Washington's implacable ferocity when his own reputation was at stake or in dealing with internal rivals. Lee attempted to defend himself. In a letter written immediately after the battle, he argued with spirit:

Camp, English-Town, 1st July, 1778

Sir – From the knowledge that I have of your Excellency's character, I must conclude that nothing but the misinformation of some very stupid, or misrepresentation of some very wicked person, could have occasioned your making use of such very singular expressions as you did, on my coming up to the ground where you had taken post: they implied that I was guilty either of disobedience of orders, want of conduct, or want of courage. Your Excellency will, therefore, infinitely oblige me by letting me know on which of these three articles you found your charge, that I may prepare for my justification; which I have the happiness to be confident I can do to the army, to the Congress, to America, and to the world in general.

Your Excellency must give me leave to observe, that neither yourself, nor those about your person, could, from your situation, be in the least judges of the merits or demerits of our manoeuvres; and, to speak with a becoming pride, I can assert that to these manoeuvres the success of the day was entirely owing. I can boldly say, that had we remained on the first ground – or had we advanced – or had the retreat been conducted in a manner different from what it was, this whole army, and the interests of America, could have risked being sacrificed.

I ever had, and I hope ever shall have, the greatest respect and veneration for General Washington; I think him endowed with many great and good qualities; but in this instance I must pronounce, that he has been guilty of an act of cruel injustice towards a man who had certainly some pretensions to the regard of every servant of his country; and I think, sir, I have a right to demand some reparation for the injury committed; and unless I can obtain it, I must, in justice to myself, when the campaign is closed, which I believe will close the war, retire from a service, at the hand of which is placed a man capable of offering such injuries – but at the same time, in justice to you, I must repeat that I, from my soul, believe that it was not a motion of your own breast, but instigated by some of those dirty earwigs, who will for ever insinuate themselves near persons in high office; for I am really assured that, when General Washington acts for himself, no man in his army will have reason to complain of injustice and indecorum.

Washington replied contemptuously:

Headquarters, English-Town, June 28, 1778

Sir – I received your letter, dated through mistake the 1st of July, expressed, as I conceive, in terms highly improper. I am not conscious of having made use of any singular expressions at the time of my meeting you, as you intimate. What I recollect to have said was dictated by duty, and warranted by the occasion. As soon as circumstances will admit, you shall have an opportunity, either of justifying yourself to the army, to Congress, to America, and to the world in general, or of convincing them that you are guilty of a breach of orders, and of misbehaviour before the enemy on the 28th instant, in not attacking them as you had been directed, and in making an unnecessary, disorderly, and shameful retreat.

I am, sir, your most obedient servant, G. Washington.

Washington had his subordinate arrested and charged with 'disobedience of orders at not attacking the enemy', 'misbehaviour before the enemy by making an unnecessary, disorderly and shameful retreat', and 'disrespect to the commander-in-chief'. Lee was found guilty on all counts.

Stories were circulated that Lee, while a prisoner of the British, had told General Howe that he had opposed the Declaration of Independence in the first place, and that, indeed, he had secretly changed sides. Tales of his crudeness and lust abounded in American circles. Washington's first rival became a recluse, living in a windowless hut in Virginia, then in a town in Pennsylvania, where he died of tuber-culosis in 1782, attended only by his faithful dogs. He had been treated with all the ruthlessness accorded to an unsuccessful revolutionary leader in the power struggles in France after 1789 or in Russia after 1917.

It seems probable that Washington did tell Lee to attack the British, although no record exists of his orders. But he also gave his subordinate discretion to avoid battle *in extremis*. By pulling back from an untenable position, and regrouping in a far stronger one under Washington, Lee may indeed have saved the day after an initial blunder which was as much Washington's fault as his own. As he pointed out correctly to Washington, 'neither yourself, nor those about your person, could, from your situation, be in the least judges of the merits or demerits of our manoeuvres'. Washington had indeed been miles away from the scene of the action he had ordered.

Lee's own regimental and brigade commanders denounced him, saying no retreat had been necessary. Yet their own careers were on the line. They attacked him for not issuing specific orders, and for not instructing them when to make a stand. Lee had been ordered forward too fast, did not know the country, and had been forced into a position that was indefensible. His only alternatives had been to blunder on, with at least part of his army being certainly cut off, in unknown territory, while the rest of the British army was mustered against him, or to back off and save his men. He chose the latter course. It was not a matter of cowardice or disobedience of orders, although it certainly betrayed a degree of incompetence.

The choleric and petulant Washington, meanwhile, had brazenly lied, in claiming he had made no 'use of singular expressions at the time of my meeting you, as you intimate'. General Charles Scott of Virginia said the commander-in-chief 'swore on that day till the leaves shook in the trees'. The faithful Lafayette claimed, 'it is the only time I ever heard George Washington swear'. This is the man who told his father he could not tell a lie – a petty point, perhaps, but Washington himself had been guilty of vindictive pettiness in charging Lee for disrespect to the com-mander-in-chief in his post-battle letters of self-justification, one of which, he pointed out pedantically, was incorrectly dated. Washington had exhibited the same furious temper and rashness that had endan-gered his own life after the failure of his troops to stop the British attack from the East River in 1776.

The real truth was probably that Washington, sensing his British prey was escaping, had to order an attack in unfavourable circumstances. When this failed, he needed a scapegoat. America's implacable military leader was determined to have his whipping boy, and he dispatched a once potent rival with a ruthlessness that led the latter to a squalid death and an unmarked grave.

Clinton's troops were lifted off from Sandy Hook to New York on 1 July. The next day, Congress met for the first time after reoccupying Philadelphia. The city was in good condition, apart from the public buildings that had been occupied by the British, Independence Hall having been used as a hospital and Franklin's house ransacked. Within two days d'Estaing's ships had arrived in the Delaware to buttress the American cause. The French were met with as much decorum as the returning Americans could muster in the capital.

At long last, everything was apparently going the freedom fighters' way. With an army captured at Saratoga, the British retreat from Philadelphia, and a huge French fleet in their support, the joyous congressmen returning to Philadelphia knew that Providence was on their side. Also, the Spaniards seemed certain to intervene against the British.

D'Estaing's fleet soon made its way north. By 11 July it had reached Sandy Hook, where, had it arrived ten days earlier, the fleet would have cut off Clinton's retreating army. With a flagship, the 90-gun *Languedoc*, 12 warships and 6 frigates, as well as 4,000 troops aboard, the French fleet was superior to that of the British under Admiral Howe. After replenishment, the French were eager to do battle. By mid-July Washington's army had reached White Plains. A pincer attack on the British in New York seemed possible. Clinton, sensing danger, had sent 2,000 men to fortify Sandy Hook, where d'Estaing could have unloaded his guns and fired with impunity on Howe's ships. But the French commander discovered that his ships' hulls were too deep to cross the shallow bar across the harbour.

Washington and d'Estaing soon realized that an attack on the strongly fortified city was out of the question. They decided to concentrate on the second British stronghold of Newport, Rhode Island, where a garrison of some 3,000 British soldiers under Sir Robert Pigot seemed all too vulnerable. On 20 July the French fleet attacked off Newport, while an American army under General John Sullivan, strengthened to about 10,000 men, including Lafayette and Nathanael Greene, was poised ready to attack from Providence to the north.

Washington was in ebullient mood: at last, with the support of a magnificent French fleet, the British on the run and hounded into confinement in New York, and the British government doubtful of continuing the war as it wrestled with France for control of the world, the endgame seemed near. The capture of the British army at Newport promised to be another Saratoga. The position of this relatively small garrison, stuck out on a limb, seemed hopeless. Both the Americans and the French had moved with great speed to 'pinch' the British. A historic victory was in the offing.

The French and American commanders drafted a plan in which Sullivan was to land on the unguarded north side of the island, while the French were to land in the west. The British attempted to get their four frigates in Narrangansett Bay to shelter in the port, but were forced to scuttle them when they ran aground. A combined Franco-American triumph seemed imminent.

The imperious d'Estaing, however, despised Sullivan, an Irish servant's son who was impertinent enough to give orders to his social superior. The French considered the American militia under Sullivan a laughable spectacle. 'All the tailors and apothecaries in the country must have been called out, I should think. One could recognize them by their round wigs. They were mounted on bad nags and looked like a flock of ducks in cross-belts. The infantry was no better than the cavalry, and appeared to be cut after the same pattern.' To the French, the Americans were a dismal rabble who had failed to win their war without assistance from superior professional troops.

The French general now had his worst fears confirmed when the excitable Sullivan attacked a day before he was supposed to, on 9 August – because he discerned an opportunity. In disgust, d'Estaing considered calling off his assault, but then landed his men, as arranged, on Conanicut Island in preparation for an assault on Newport itself.

Soon afterwards, however, Admiral Howe unexpectedly appeared with his fleet just seven miles out. D'Estaing needed very little prompting to re-embark his men immediately: he was not prepared to risk being trapped by the British fleet for the ragged American cause. In any event he was anxious to give battle on the open seas. It was Sullivan's turn to be furious.

Out in the Atlantic, the French had the advantage: they had manoeuvred themselves to windward and had more guns: 90 on d'Estaing's flagship, 80 on its support; six others could muster 74, three had 64, and one had 50, compared with Howe's 74-gun flagship, seven warships with 64 guns, and five with 50 each. For two days the two fleets shadowed each other, Howe trying to manoeuvre to windward while avoiding d'Estaing's guns, then the wind began to increase to gale force and the two fleets were blown all over the place.

D'Estaing's flagship, the *Languedoc*, already dismasted and rudderless, was attacked by the *Renown* and saved only when seven French ships came to her aid. The British ship *Somerset* was blown to Cape Cod, where she was shipwrecked and nearly 500 seamen and 21 guns were captured. Several other French ships were dismasted and badly damaged, as were a smaller number of British craft. It was a British victory at sea on points.

But the British had also blocked the Franco-American attack on Rhode Island. The Americans' expected triumph, with their new and powerful French allies, had turned to ashes. Howe anchored his battered fleet off Sandy Hook, while d'Estaing rendezvoused with his fleet at Newport but refused to disembark his men or come to the aid of Sullivan, who had launched a frontal assault on Newport on 14 August. Sullivan was convinced that he would capture the garrison with French support, but without it he had to break off the siege, denouncing the French as traitors. A mob of Americans beat up French sailors, and one was killed. Lafayette himself was insulted and threatened to fight a duel with an American officer. He behaved like a wounded peacock: 'Would you believe that I, one who has the honour of belonging to the leading nation of the world, to a nation which ... is respected and admired by all Europe ... have personally been put in the position of hearing the name of France spoken without respect, and perhaps with disdain, by a herd of Yankees from New England.'

Washington was bitterly disappointed by the missed opportunity: 'If the garrison of that place had been captured, as there was in appearance at least, a hundred to one in favour of it, it would have riven the finishing blow to British pretensions of sovereignty over this country and would, I am persuaded, have hastened the departure of the troops in New York as fast as their canvas wings would carry them away.' But he tried desperately to prevent the feud between the French and the Americans from escalating, blaming the storm for the fiasco.

Sullivan insisted that boldness might have turned the day at Newport and trapped another British army, but that d'Estaing had put the safety of his men and ships first. The French commander might have been right in believing he could have been trapped if he had landed his men at Newport, facing the prospect of leaving them stranded if the British fleet had come up behind. But it was hardly a bold strategy, or one likely to endear him to the Americans.

Anyway, D'Estaing's prime concern was not the American cause, but the French one, for which (as with the British) the West Indies were more important than the northern colonies. He departed with his fleet to Boston. Admiral Howe, now believing he had the advantage, pursued him before deciding not to risk the port batteries there. Meanwhile, Sir Robert Pigot, a veteran of Breed's Hill, prepared to counter-attack Sullivan's forces, while Clinton, for once on the offensive, placed 4,000 men aboard troopships in New York in an effort to trap the American army. But unfavourable winds slowed the British down, and Sullivan evacuated his men from the island just a day before they arrived.

While this was disappointing for Clinton, the bitter episode had approached a major defeat for the Americans. They had twice failed to deliver a killer blow to the British, despite holding an overwhelming advantage. Clinton had escaped to the safety of New York, and the might of a large French fleet had not tilted the balance the colonists' way. Far from Saratoga marking the turning point, they had got stuck in the mud almost immediately, even with French support.

Relations between the two allies immediately plunged to a new low. Ordinary Americans, who recalled the French and Indian War and looked upon Frenchmen as foreigners and papists, now also regarded them as foppish and cowardly. The aristocratic French looked upon the Americans as vulgar rabble. It had not been an auspicious start.

After the American failure at Newport, the war became a stalemate. The Americans retreated west to their virtually impregnable mountain stronghold while the British stayed holed up in New York and to a lesser extent Newport, from which they occasionally made a sortie, seeking to draw the Americans out into pitched battles. Neither side could gain the advantage, and the rest of the middle colonies were a no man's land in between.

To the north, New England was staunch American territory. To the south the British believed that the people were overwhelmingly loyalist – which may have been true earlier on, but the rebels had had years to persuade and intimidate these lands. Those two cautious commanders, Washington and Clinton, seemed made for one another. The American victory at Saratoga had been spoiled by the failed battles at Monmouth Court House and Newport, and the great French fleet had arrived and sailed away.

The British and the French had put the war in the northern colonies on hold while renewing the 'first world war' across a global canvas; the British contemplated no major actions for more than a year, provided they could maintain their foothold in North America.

A brief account of the global war is needed to understand why the British acted as they did, and at what point they decided to renew the American campaign. An underlying theme of this book is that the American rebels did not 'win' the War of Independence – the British lost it. With the monumental myopia, and indeed stupidity, that character-ized British policy under Colonial Secretary Germain and the King, the British singularly failed to understand the strategic long-term signifi-cance of the colonies.

Not until early in 1780 did serious fighting resume in America; mean-while, although significant actions did occur, the rebels strikingly failed to dislodge the British, even though the latter were never weaker and their backs were turned. Washington, theoretically in his strongest posi-tion in late 1778–9, should have won the war then and there. Yet he had barely used his advantage, because his old defects as a commander, inde-cision and overcaution, reasserted themselves.

Still more galling to the Americans was the low priority accorded them by their French allies, for whom North America was also just a minor piece in a global game. While the French now provided a grati-fyingly increased flow of arms and munitions, no army was sent except for the 4,000 aboard the French fleet, and d'Estaing dabbled in the war only occasionally, as though its outcome was insignificant provided it tied down a number of British troops.

The four major theatres in the renewed war between Britain and France were the West Indies; Britain itself, threatened with possible invasion across the Channel; the Mediterranean; and India. After being refitted, the French fleet under Admiral d'Estaing sailed from Boston for St Lucia in the Windward Islands. From there the French were deter-mined to seize other rich plantation settlements, with their sugar, cocoa, spices and coffee. In September 1778 they had adroitly occupied the tiny island of Dominica to add to the three they already controlled – Guadeloupe, Martinique and St Lucia.

Underlining the low priority in which North America was held, on exactly the same date as d'Estaing set sail, 4 November, the British government directed the deeply reluctant Clinton to divest himself of 5,000 troops and eight of Howe's ships, including two 64-gunners, to join the British commander in the West Indies, Rear-Admiral Samuel Barrington. Barrington's reinforcements arrived at his base in Barbados, north of St Lucia. Within three days he had sailed north to the French island, seizing the coastal settlements and forcing the French to retreat inland.

Only a day later d'Estaing's fleet arrived from the north. He found just ten British ships – four of them warships and three small 50-gunners, as well as three frigates – guarding the harbour in a line. He passed them twice, firing broadsides ineffectively. Although, with twelve battleships, d'Estaing's force was much superior, he did not attack; instead he landed his troops, now swollen to 7,000, in a suicidal attempt to take on the strongly fortified promontory of St Vigie.

D'Estaing personally led his men in three attacks. (Although an over-cautious naval commander, he was a courageous land officer, in his own element.) These proved disastrous for the French, who suffered 850 casualties. Returning to his ships, he found that the British had strengthened their sea defences and gave up the attempt. D'Estaing took little further action until June, when he suddenly occupied tiny St Vincent and then British Grenada, the southernmost of the Windwards, in both cases without a struggle. It was poor compensation for the loss of St Lucia.

On 6 July, the full British fleet was united under Admiral John Byron, who had taken control of western-hemisphere operations from the highly competent Howe and then, in the West Indies, from Barrington. Byron approached the French fleet, which was harboured off the coast of Grenada, and launched an immediate, somewhat disorganized attack with seventeen warships and a frigate, leaving three vessels to guard the convoy of twenty-eight troop transports they had been accompanying.

Although bold, Byron had underestimated the strength of the French fleet, which was greater than his in firepower, and which formed a line which loosed off broadsides as he performed the complicated manoeuvre of tacking back in parallel, virtually on its tracks, in order to stay windward of it. Four of his ships were crippled in the broadside, leaving the flagship, at the front, highly exposed. Seeing the danger, two of the ships he had left behind to guard the convoy, the *Suffolk* and the

*Monmouth*, came across the top end of the triangle to lend support to Byron.

They arrived just in time to prevent d'Estaing closing in for the kill, and he veered off to the west, towards the crippled ships, which instantly made off. Surprisingly the French, who could have sunk them, did not give chase. Byron gave orders to his fleet to veer away, licking his wounds and making for St Kitts for repairs, while leaving Grenada to the French. For the British it had been a disaster, and nearly a fatal one; but d'Estaing had once again failed to follow up his advantage. The situation in the West Indies thus reached stalemate by mid-1779, with the British having taken strategic St Lucia, and the French having seized three smaller islands – Dominica, St Vincent and Grenada.

In 1778 the British faced the possibility of invasion across the English Channel. This prevented them from reinforcing their North American fleet, instead concentrating the 'Great Fleet', the home fleet, in the Channel to counter the French navy based at Brest. On 10 July the French set sail under Admiral Orvilliers and sighted the British Channel fleet under Admiral Augustus Keppel seventy miles west of Ushant. Although to windward, the French did not attack, and the British took advantage of a change in the wind to attack the French rear.

The two fleets engaged alongside each other, with the thirty British ships aiming for the French bulwarks and decks to sink their enemies, and the French, seeking to escape, aiming for the British masts and rigging. The French tactic paid off, and Orvilliers' ships got away, albeit with about twice as many casualties as the British. Any possibility of a French landing in England now became unlikely – a major relief to the planners in Whitehall.

While the threat from across the Channel loomed large for the English, the threat in the Mediterranean was not a problem until the summer of 1779, when Spain joined the war on France's side. Further afield, in India, the outbreak of war between Britain and France had immediate results. Britain's highly competent and aggressive proconsul in India, Warren Hastings, immediately ordered the seizure of the remaining French enclaves on the subcontinent, dispatching troops from Calcutta to Madras. British forces seized Chandernagore, the French trading centre in Bengal, and occupied Make, on the west coast. In October 1778 the main French settlement of Pondicherry surrendered to the besieging British. By the end of the year it seemed that they had won the contest in India – although they still had to reckon with Hyder Ali, the ruler of Mysore, who considered the seizure of Make, inside his territory, an act of war.

After six months of renewed global conflict the news from London was thus relatively encouraging. The threat of invasion from France had subsided; Britain's position in the Mediterranean was not yet under threat; Britain's hold on India had been consolidated (although the news took several months to filter through); and honours were slightly on the British side in the West Indies.

# PART IV:

## *The South*

# 19

# *Southern Strategy*

A great panic that the British were hopelessly over-extended around the globe had seized the North ministry on the French declaration of war – in sharp contrast to Pitt's self-confidence in far more difficult circumstances during the previous war. But these fears had proved unfounded, and by 1779 it was even time to turn the heat up a little on the war in the colonies.

But the government was determined not to commit substantial new forces in an expensive land engagement when fresh challenges might emerge across the world. Rather, a subtle new tactic was to be practised – the encouragement of local alliances ('Americanizing' the war, as the Vietnam war would be 'Vietnamized' in the 1970s). If, as the British believed, most Americans opposed the War of Independence and favoured retaining ties with Britain, then they should fight for this link themselves. The two areas to which the strategy would principally apply were the south and the west.

Germain speculated, with his usual glazed optimism, from 3,000 miles away, 'Could a small corps be detached at the same time to land at Cape Fear? … it is not doubted that large numbers of the inhabitants would flock to the King's standard, and that His Majesty's government would be restored in that province also.'

The new strategy had political appeal in Britain: it allowed the American war to continue, without further draining British manpower, and it bolstered the government's main moral argument for continuing the war – that it would be a betrayal to abandon the loyalist majority in America. Admittedly, the British based their wishful thinking on reports from the former governors of South Carolina and Georgia:

> From our particular knowledge of those provinces, it appears very clear to us, that if a proper number of troops were in possession of Charleston …

or if they were to possess themselves of the back country thro' Georgia, and to leave a garrison in the town of Savannah, the whole inhabitants in both Provinces would soon come in and submit ... They cannot retire back for the Indians ... would prevent them – and there is no middle country or situation between the sea coast and the Indian country where any number can retire to and sit down with the least safety – from whence there appears to be an absolute certainty of re-establishing the King's Government in those two colonies, and in a great measure cutting off those supplies, which contribute so much to the support and spirit of the rebellion in general.

But the peace party, reinforced now by Howe's deep scepticism about continuing the war, was also on the offensive: General Charles Grey upheld his old commander in the 'Howe enquiry' before the House of Commons, which began in May 1779.

I think that with the present force in America, there can be no expectation of ending the war by force of arms ... I do not think, from the beginning of June, when I landed at New York, in 1777, to the 20th of November, 1778, there was in that time a number of troops in America altogether adequate to the subduing that country by force of arms.

General James Robertson was called upon to reply for the government, again playing the loyalist card:

The object of the war was to enable the loyal subjects of America to get free from the tyranny of the rebels, and to let the country follow its inclination, by returning to the King's government.

Sporadic skirmishing continued in the north and the centre. After the privations of the previous two years, Washington now established his winter quarters in the more civilized surroundings of Middlebrook, New Jersey, on the banks of the Raritan river. In New York, Clinton, stripped of 5,000 men who had embarked for the West Indies, did not dare to order the 10,000 remaining to return to the attack – a sign of both his inherent timorousness and his reluctance to risk his depleted troops. The winter was also as unseasonably warm as the previous one had been cold, and the troops were reasonably housed and fed.

Washington occupied his time in trying to raise money and troops for the American cause. Nathanael Greene, his Quartermaster General, complained of the passivity of the states: 'The local policy of all the states is directly opposed to the great national plan; and if they continue to persevere in it, God knows what the consequences will be. There is a terrible falling off in public virtue ... The loss of morals and the want of public spirit leaves us almost like a rope of sand.'

Washington supported this gloomy view:

> If I was to be called upon to draw a picture of the times and of the men, from what I have seen, heard, and in part know, I should in one word say that idleness, dissipation, and extravagance seem to have laid fast hold of most of them; that speculation, peculation, and an insatiable thirst for riches seems to have got the better of every other consideration and almost of every order of men; that party disputes and personal quarrels are the great business of the day whilst the momentous concerns of an empire, a great and accumulated debt, ruined finances, depreciated money and want of credit (which in their consequences is the want of everything) are but secondary considerations ... I am alarmed and wish to see my countrymen roused.

In particular, Washington quarrelled with Congress, which he regarded as increasingly venal and incompetent, as well as unable to deliver supplies and money because it had so little authority over the states. Washington's crushing of his two chief military rivals, Lee and Gates, had left him undisputed commander of the American war effort, and, with Congress exerting little authority, the cause increasingly revolved around the personality cult of the commander-in chief, as John Adams had predicted. His chief subordinates were no longer men of independent authority who might challenge him, but rather able young lieutenants like Nathanael Greene or Benjamin Lincoln, or talented if sycophantic foreigners like Lafayette. Even someone as strong as von Steuben, being non-American, could not stand up to him.

A French observer, the Marquis de Barbe-Marbois, gives this picture of Washington in his prime:

> He received us with a noble, modest, and gentle urbanity and with that graciousness which seems to be the basis of his character. He is fifty years old, well built, rather thin. He carries himself freely and with a sort of military grace. He is masculine-looking, without his features being less gentle on that account. I have never seen anyone who was more naturally and spontaneously polite. His eyes are blue and rather large, his mouth and nose are regular, and his forehead open. His uniform is exactly like that of his soldiers. Formerly, on solemn occasions, that is to say on days of battle, he wore a large blue sash, but he has given up that unrepublican distinction.
>
> I have been told that he preserves in battle the character of humanity

which makes him so dear to his soldiers in camp. I have seen him for some time in the midst of his staff, and he has always appeared even-tempered, tranquil, and orderly in his occupations, and serious in his conversation. He asks few questions, listens attentively, and answers in a low tone and with few words. He is serious in business. Outside of that, he permits himself a restricted gaiety. His conversation is as simple as his habits and his appearance. He makes no pretensions, and does the honours of his house with dignity, but without pompousness or flattery ... He is reverent without bigotry, and abhors swearing, which he punishes with the greatest severity. As to his public conduct, ask his compatriots, and the universe ...

His appearance and his actions reveal virtue, and he inspires it in all who surround him ... If you like historical parallels, I might compare him to Timoleon who freed the Sicilians from the tyranny of the Carthaginians, and who joined to his military qualities those which make up an excellent citizen, and who after having rendered his country signal services lived as a private citizen, ambitious neither of power nor honours, and was satisfied to enjoy modestly the glory of having given liberty to a powerful nation.

But, however complete Washington's control over his own camp, he proved unable to project his power against the British. Fearing that the enemy were considering an expedition up the Hudson river to attack the American positions there, Washington left camp at Middlebrook early in June 1779 and entrenched most of his troops hurriedly behind a complex set of terraced fortifications up the Hudson river to West Point. The British seized the two lowest of these – Verplanck Point and Stony Point.

Meanwhile William Tryon, the former governor of New York, led a British expedition along the Connecticut coast to harass rebel sympathizers and destroy such towns as New Haven, Fairfield and Norwalk, hoping to draw Washington's troops down from the uplands into open battle. At sea, American privateers were systematically destroyed in an effort to break the supply chain from abroad.

Another British raiding party, based in Maine, attacked French and American shipping in the north. To counter this, Washington dispatched a ramshackle force of 38 boats carrying 1,200 militia and 800 regulars which arrived in July off the coast of Penobscot Bay and attacked the British raiders' headquarters. In spite of poor defences, the assault failed. After several days in which the two sides confronted one another, four British warships arrived with reinforcements and attacked the American fleet, which dispersed in confusion, many boats running aground. One American wrote:

> To give a true description of this terrible day is out of my power. It would be a fit subject for some masterly hand to describe it in its true colours, to see four ships pursuing seventeen sail of our armed vessels, nine of which were stout ships, transports on fire, men of war blowing up every kind of stores on shore, throwing about, and as much confusion as can possibly be conceived.

The Americans suffered several hundred casualties in this further serious setback. However, it was offset by a spectacular American expedition under General Anthony Wayne to retake Stony Point, a stronghold sited on a rock surrounded on three sides by water, with only a single narrow causeway leading to it across a marsh. It seemed impregnable, but the Americans succeeded in wresting it off the British in a surprise night attack, capturing the entire garrison, and showing remarkable mercy to the inhabitants: only 60 men were killed, while 550 were taken prisoner.

Another attack, on a smaller outpost held by the Hessians at Paulus Hook on the Hudson, was similarly successful, with 60 Hessian casualties and around 160 captured. Both were raiding missions, for the Americans soon abandoned their positions, making off with their prisoners and stores. Soon Clinton withdrew from all his outposts outside New York, fearing another French naval attack, and also evacuated Newport.

America's naval effort in the War of Independence was little more than a series of acts of piracy.

Immediately after the ambush at Concord a British schooner, the *Margarita*, which had threatened to fire on the liberty pole at Mathias, Maine, had been captured and its commander killed by armed men; but this was hardly a naval action, although proclaimed by the rebels as the first in the war. The truth was that the colonies possessed no navy, and could not see much point in having one, even if they could afford it.

Washington initially commissioned the roguish Nicholas Broughton to act as captain of the *Hannah*, the first American warship, a 78-ton schooner. Broughton began by attacking American merchant vessels, declaring they were British, then raided Charlottetown, capturing some of its citizens and bringing them to the dismayed Washington as trophies. Broughton was soon dismissed.

Many American smugglers and privateers used the war as an excuse to attack merchant ships, whether American or British. They also damaged some ships supporting the British expeditionary army in America: in November 1775 a munitions ship, the *Nancy*, laden with arms including 2,000 muskets and 3,000 shells, was run down by the *Lee*. Altogether America's 800 privateers – many little more than boats – captured 2,000 craft worth around £10 million in prize money – a far from negligible contribution to the war effort.

Early in the war the states made a desultory attempt to establish a proper navy. A single warship, the 74-gun *America*, was commissioned, as were two 50-gun frigates and several sloops. Congress pompously set up a naval committee and then a Board of Admiralty which by 1780 commanded no more than a few converted merchantmen described as frigates. Until the French brought a large fleet to challenge British control of the sea, the only significant naval engagements in America were undertaken in the waters of Lake Champlain at the Canadian end of the campaign.

Partly to cover this embarrassment, it was necessary to create an American naval legend; and one was soon to hand. Although there is no evidence that the antics of John Paul Jones had the slightest impact upon the course of the war, or on British military planning towards America, this improbable figure, by outrageously carrying the war to the British mainland and flitting like a gadfly around it, pulled off a spectacular propaganda coup.

Jones, true to the best seafaring traditions, had a distinctly dubious past, although he was never actually a pirate or even a privateer. Born John Paul in Galloway in 1747, at the age of thirteen he was apprenticed aboard a merchant ship plying between England and Virginia before enlisting aboard a slaver. After serving on several such ships, the self-possessed, small young man, who alternated great charm with a vile temper, and drove his subordinates ferociously, was at twenty-one given charge of a small merchantman, on which he had the ship's carpenter flogged. When the man died, Paul was charged with manslaughter, but acquitted.

Five years later, in Tobago, he ran a mutineer through with a sword and had to go into hiding, Two years later he resurfaced as John Paul Jones and volunteered his services to the American navy. Neither his ruthlessness nor his seamanship was in doubt. He was given charge of three craft in succession, and was provisionally appointed captain. He performed well, capturing several merchant prizes. In January 1777 he was given command of a sloop, the *Ranger*, with eighteen guns, and was ordered to sail to France, where he confidently expected to be given command of a larger ship.

This failed to materialize, although he made a favourable impression on Benjamin Franklin, and he decided to make his mark with the *Ranger* anyway. John Adam's wife, Abigail, described him at about this time:

> From the intrepid character he justly supported in the American Navy, I expected to have seen a rough, stout, warlike Roman – instead of that I should sooner think of wrapping him up in cotton wool, and putting him in my pocket, than sending him to contend with cannon-balls. He is small of stature, well proportioned, soft in his speech, easy in his address, polite in his manners, vastly civil, understands all the etiquette of a lady's toilette as perfectly as he does the mast, sails and rigging of his ship … he is said to be a man of gallantry and a favourite amongst the French ladies, whom he is frequently commending for the neatness of their persons, their easy manners and their taste in dress. He knows how often the ladies use the baths, what colour best suits a lady's complexion, what cosmetics are most favourable to the skin.

In April 1778 he set off from Brest for his first famous adventure, in the Irish Sea. He quickly captured two small merchantmen, fired upon a coastguard ship, captured and sank an unarmed schooner and then a sloop, and then briefly engaged an armed sloop, the *Drake*, off Belfast. When this engagement came to nothing, he set sail for his native Scotland, to raid the town of Whitehaven. Arriving there after midnight, he led a raiding party of forty men ashore. They spiked the town's unmanned guns before setting fire to a collier and some small craft. Alerted, the townspeople rushed to the harbour and drove him off.

Nothing daunted, Jones set off up the coast to St Mary's Isle, which he knew from his youth, with the idea of capturing the Earl of Selkirk and ransoming him in exchange for American prisoners. At 10 a.m. he landed with a raiding party of fifteen and surprised the Earl's gardener, who told him that his master was away. So the intrepid burglars set off for the house and helped themselves to the family silver, while the Countess of Selkirk behaved with great presence of mind, calmly welcoming them. Afterwards Jones wrote to her as follows:

> Tho' I have drawn my sword in the present generous struggle for the rights of men; yet I am not in arms as an American; nor am I in pursuit of riches. My fortune is liberal enough, having no wife nor family, and

having lived long enough to know that riches cannot ensure happiness. I profess myself a citizen of the world, totally unfettered by the little distinctions of climate or of country, which diminish the benevolence of the heart and set bounds to philanthropy. Before this war began I had, at an early time of life, withdrawn from the sea service in favour of calm contemplation and poetic ease. I have sacrificed not only my favorite scheme of life, but the softer affections of the heart and my prospects of domestic happiness – and I am ready to sacrifice life also with cheerfulness – if that forfeiture could restore peace and goodwill among mankind.

As the feelings of your gentle bosom cannot but be congenial with mine let me entreat you madam to use your soft persuasive arts with your husband (an influential aristocrat) to endeavour to stop this cruel and destructive war, in which Britain can never succeed. Heaven can never countenance the barbarous and unmanly practices of the Britons in America, which savages would blush at; and which if not discontinued will soon be retaliated in Britain by a justly enraged people. – Should you fail in this, (for I am persuaded you will attempt it; and who can resist the power of such an advocate?) your endeavours to effect a general exchange of prisoners, will be an act of humanity, which will afford you golden feelings on a death bed.

He returned the silver, which he had allowed to be taken only to appease his nearly mutinous crew. By the following morning he had steered back towards Belfast Bight, to see his former adversary the *Drake* emerging into the open sea. Jones engaged, and the captain and his second-in-command were killed in close fighting before the ship surrendered. Jones set off with his prize around the north coast of Ireland after a month of sailing.

This little expedition had an impact far beyond its military importance. The British public, prone to jitters about invasion from France, was mildly alarmed at this exposure of the coastline's vulnerability. The presence of an American ship, albeit from France, was more alarming still: suddenly the primitive colonists appeared capable of striking directly at the mother country across the Atlantic. British opposition newspapers were delighted to blame the ministry for allowing the outrage to happen.

In November 1778, after lobbying for a more significant ship to command, Jones was appointed captain of the *Duc de Duras*, a 900-ton French East Indiaman with 40 guns, six of them 18-pounders and the rest 12-pounders. He was also given command of a French frigate, the

*Pallas*, with 32 guns; an American frigate, the *Alliance*, with 36 guns; a brig, the *Vengeance*, and a cutter. He renamed his own ship the *Bonhomme Richard*, after the French version of Franklin's well-known *Poor Richard's Almanack*, full of folksy invocations and proverbs about how to lead life, and in recognition that his flotilla consisted, with one exception, of French ships and was French supplied and based in France.

The squadron set off from Groix Roads in June 1779, capturing merchantmen as it sailed to the west of Ireland. Two months later almost all of Jones's small squadron had left him – including the *Alliance*, whose captain, Landais, bore a particular malice towards Jones – leaving him only the *Vengeance* for company. The flotilla later reassembled near the Orkneys with a rich crop of small merchant prizes. It had by now instilled alarm in most coastal towns in the north.

As the squadron sailed down the east coast of Scotland, Jones decided to enter the Firth of Forth and threaten to sack Leith unless a ransom was paid. On 17 September he arrived opposite the town, but a gale blew up, forcing him to abandon his project or risk running aground. He sailed south, hoping to attack Newcastle, but the others objected to this plan. At the Humber estuary he decided that discretion was the better part of valour, and veered east to attack small merchant ships.

Soon the *Bonhomme Richard* and the *Vengeance*, together with the *Pallas* and the *Alliance*, appeared off the spectacular white cliffs of Flamborough Head in Yorkshire. There the little squadron sighted a 50-gun frigate, the *Serapis*, and a 20-gun sloop, the *Countess of Scarborough*, accompanying some forty merchantmen. All three of Jones's intrepid squadron ignored his orders to engage and veered away, leaving him to face the *Serapis* alone.

He ran up a British flag, and got reasonably close before being found out and exchanging broadsides. Jones tried to bring his ship right up to the *Serapis* to board her, but, failing to do so, rammed the back of his opponent. Captain Pearson of the *Serapis* called, 'Has your ship struck?' to which Jones famously replied, 'I have not yet begun to fight.'

The two ships now began to manoeuvre against each other, and by accident they were driven together by the wind, which was to Jones's advantage, as the *Serapis* was more manoeuvrable and, in concentrated broadsides, had more guns. Like two giant animals grappling, the two ships remained so close that their guns were almost touching, while the British ship raked the *Bonhomme Richard*'s lower deck and French sharpshooters and grenadiers poured fire on to the British upper decks. The

British 18-pounders soon knocked out the Americans' 12-pounders, but the *Serapis*'s decks were raked by musket fire and grenades, which fell through the hatches and caused severe damage.

The *Pallas* meanwhile returned to overcome the *Countess of Scarborough*, while the *Vengeance* and the *Alliance* sailed around in circles, the latter actually firing at Jones's ship three times, not the British. An attempt by Captain Pearson to board the *Bonhomme Richard* failed. The American officers advised Jones to give up, but he refused, although his ship was in imminent danger of sinking and even its officers were having to man the pumps.

The *Bonhomme Richard* continued to pour fire at the *Serapis*'s mainmast, and at last Pearson himself came up on deck to tear down his colours – no member of his crew dared to do so – and offer his surrender. It had been a bloodbath and a Pyrrhic victory for Jones, 150 of whose men – nearly half the crew – had been killed or wounded, only slightly fewer than the number lost on the *Serapis*. Two days later, with his ship continually taking water, Jones had to shift his crew aboard the *Serapis* and watch the *Bonhomme Richard* sink. It was one of the few occasions in naval history where the victor was the captain of the vessel that had been sunk. Jones wrote afterwards, 'A person must have been an eye witness to form a just idea of this tremendous scene of carnage, wreck and ruin that everywhere appeared. Humanity cannot but recoil from the prospect of such finished horror, and lament that which should produce such fatal consequences.'

He and his squadron made speedily for Texel, in Holland, whose embarrassed government was at a loss what to do with him and his 500 prisoners, before he set out again in December aboard the *Alliance* with his prisoners and squadron, minus the *Serapis*, eluding the British to arrive in mid-February at Lorient in France, where he was feted as a hero.

In the cold light of day, this 'first great battle in American naval history' was basically a single ship-to-ship engagement – a ferocious fight of attrition between a slightly more powerful British ship and an inferior American one in which each side nearly pummelled the other into submission and the British gave way first. The engagement had no strategic significance beyond the British loss of one ship, and the alarums that had crackled around the British coast at Jones's raiding parties – although Jones himself had now wisely left the area.

Nor, apart from its leader's nationality, was this even an American raid. All the ships involved were French, with largely French crews. Landais, who had performed so disastrously, was a French naval officer who had enlisted with the American navy. The French had fitted out and backed the expedition as a diversion from their own invasion plans, and to bolster the American cause.

This the 'Battle of Flamborough Head' undoubtedly did: it had been a huge propaganda triumph, immortalizing Jones as a man of extraordinary courage and seamanship – which he certainly was in circumnavigating the British Isles and thumbing his nose at the British – and as one of the world's great naval commanders – which he certainly was not, having never been effectively more than a captain, exerting virtually no authority over his squadron.

Jones's later career was an anticlimax. While Jones was ashore, Landais succeeded in seizing the *Alliance* and set off for America, where he was finally court-martialled and sacked. Jones was given command of a munitions ship with instructions to sail for America, but was driven back to port by a storm; his ship eventually reached America after failing to capture a British privateer on the way. He was designated captain of the *America*, the sole national warship under construction, but to his dismay this ship was then promised to the French in compensation for one of theirs which had run aground in Boston harbour.

No naval commander has been so lionized for such a brief career as Jones, the subject of many biographies. But he was independent America's only naval hero, and he undoubtedly carried out his spectacular raids with great flair, courage and determination. His exploits – appropriately inflated – gave new heart to the American cause.

In 1778 neither side had distinguished itself, although the Americans had had the better of the skirmishes. Neither Washington nor Clinton displayed the courage to make a major move – and their caution may have been justified, as neither had the strength decisively to defeat the other. Washington could console himself that Britain's commitment to America was plainly dwindling and its resolve might fizzle out altogether; Clinton that he had more or less preserved Britain's position until a time when the mother country might have more resources for the American fight.

With the lull, in July 1779 Lafayette decided to return to France, where he was received as a hero, even by the King and his father-in-law, whom he had disobeyed, as well as the beautiful target of his affections, the Countess of Hunolstein. The young general successfully pleaded for more reinforcements to be sent to America. An expeditionary force of 5,000 was assembled – but Lafayette, to his dismay, was passed over as its commander in favour of the veteran Comte de Rochambeau.

Washington spoke with paternal tenderness of the young man: 'I do not know a nobler, finer soul, and I love him as my own son.' When Lafayette playfully wrote to him, 'I have a wife who is in love with you', Washington replied with a cheery warmth usually alien to the dry martinet, 'Tell [your wife] ... that I have a heart susceptible of the tenderest passion, and that it is already so strongly impressed with the most favourable ideas of her that she must be cautious of putting love's torch to it, as you must be in fanning the flame.'

In late 1778 the British adopted an entirely new strategy. Stalemated in the north, where they were unable to occupy the highlands, they decided to strike out for the 'loyalist heartland' of the south. In November 1778 Clinton despatched 3,500 of his carefully hoarded troops to Tybee Island to invade Georgia. This force, under the command of Lieutenant-Colonel Archibald Campbell, reached the mouth of the Savannah river just before Christmas.

The American commander in Georgia, Robert Howe, rushed a force of 700 Continentals – the American army – and 150 militia from Sunbury to the defence of Savannah after the British had pushed the Americans opposing their landing back to the town. Then the British staged a frontal attack as a diversion, while sending another force around the rear along a path that led through the swamps surrounding Savannah. The attack proved brilliantly successful: 83 Americans were killed and 453 captured, only 3 British soldiers were killed and 10 wounded. The British moved on to take Augusta, and then to defeat an American force sent down from South Carolina at Briar Creek on 3 March 1779. They were now in control of Georgia; it was a promising start for the southern strategy.

Over-optimistically, they set out for Charleston, South Carolina, the biggest city in the south, but they were forced back, and General Benjamin Lincoln, with an army of 1,350, marched to retake Savannah. Lincoln begged the unpredictable Admiral d'Estaing to help trap this small but cheeky British army. In September the French arrived with 22 warships and 10 frigates, as well as 4,000 men, who were landed for the siege. The huge French fleet staged a spectacular bombardment to very little effect against the low sand barriers surrounding the town. Military engineers began the slow, laborious business of constructing siege lines – parallel reinforced trenches – towards the town, and the British seemed doomed.

But after a month d'Estaing became impatient, fearing that the British fleet might arrive and catch his ships with most of the men still ashore. On 9 October he decided to stage a frontal assault without waiting for the siege lines to get closer. But for the overwhelming French and American dominance in numbers, this would usually have been considered a suicidal tactic against well-entrenched defences. So it proved.

Some 3,500 French and 1,000 American troops attacked across a swamp, and within an hour, according to a British officer, the scene was 'filled with mangled bodies and the ditch filled with the dead'. Some 600 Frenchmen and 400 Americans were killed. D'Estaing himself was wounded. Only 150 British soldiers were killed. It was a remarkable stand by a small British force against a vastly superior body of French regulars – the first real battle between the two in America since France had joined the war.

D'Estaing decided to pull out with his ships. His poor leadership had contributed to the debacle, and did nothing to improve the uneasy relationship between the French and American allies. After the capture of Savannah by the British, this was a bitterly disappointing and all too depressingly familiar outcome for the Americans. Although masters of the surprise raid against a smaller force, it seemed they could hardly ever win a pitched battle. Lincoln returned dejected to the stronghold of Charleston, in preparation for the seemingly inevitable assault against it. The small British offensive under Campbell in the south was apparently gaining momentum, prompting the crab-cautious Clinton to consider a larger expedition.

However, a new threat to the British loomed to the south-west. In July 1779 news that Spain had joined the war against the British had reached the energetic Spanish governor of Louisiana, Bernardo de Galvez, who had already clandestinely supplied a staggering amount of money and arms to the American cause. Galvez, who like his masters in Madrid cared nothing for the American cause, but relished the possibility of adding to Spain's vast empire to the south, hurriedly secured New Orleans and then assembled a force of 770 regulars and 300 militia at the mouth of the great Mississippi river with the object of securing the British forts at Manchac, Baton Rouge and Natchez.

The first fell without difficulty. At Baton Rouge Galvez opened fire on the fort's 500 defenders with his heavy guns from the front before unexpectedly bursting in around the back, forcing the British to surrender. Natchez now also surrendered, so that the Spaniards had effectively wrested the whole eastern bank of the Mississippi from the British. They now turned to the main British outposts in Florida: Mobile and Pensacola.

On 11 January 1780, Galvez embarked 750 men in twelve boats, including a frigate, a galliot and two brigs, which sailed down the Mississippi into the Gulf of Mexico. There he was joined by a further 570 men sent from Havana, and the little armada set off for Mobile, landing some 2,000 yards away from the British fort, which was garrisoned by about 300 Englishmen. On 10 March, as the Spaniards began digging their first siege trench, the guns on both sides opened up. The end was never in doubt, and two days later the small garrison sued for peace, before Campbell could rush assistance down from Pensacola, to which he had now moved.

This relief force now returned to Pensacola, which was much more strongly defended by some 1,300 British regulars and 900 loyalists, including 300 blacks and 300 sailors. The garrison was reinforced by eleven British ships in April. Galvez, realizing he had met his match, decided to travel to Havana in person to seek reinforcements.

Assembling a large Spanish army of 4,000 men in Veracruz, Mexico, Galvez set sail for the British stronghold in October 1780. The Spaniards would outnumber the British by more than two to one, and were buttressed by 7 warships, 5 frigates, 3 other armed boats and 50 transports. This formidable force was, however, dispersed by a hurricane, and Campbell took advantage of the delay to try to retake Mobile, without success. Not until March 1781 did a new Spanish fleet leave Havana – including, as one of the Spanish commanders, the young Francisco de Miranda, the father of Latin America's own independence struggle against the Spanish some thirty years later.

To the north, Clinton had at last obtained the British government's authorization for a major strike in the south, to occupy the big American base at Charleston. Clinton's own assessments of the opportunity were confused and contradictory. On the one hand he wrote 'that a solid operation in the proper season against Charlestown, and South Carolina will be of infinite consequence'. On the other he told Germain:

> I have as yet received no assurances of any favourable temper in the prov-
> ince of South Carolina to encourage me in an undertaking, where we must
> expect much difficulty ... The force which the present weakness of General
> Washington's army could enable me to detach, might possibly get posses-
> sion of Charlestown ... but I doubt whether they could keep it, and in the
> present stage of the war, I do not think such a desultory advantage, in that
> quarter, would be beneficial to our interests; it might induce a number of
> persons to declare for us, whom we might afterwards be obliged to
> abandon; and thus might destroy a party, on whom we may depend, if
> circumstance will permit a more solid attempt in a properer season.

In the bitter cold of a New York winter the expedition departed on Boxing Day 1779, consisting of some 5,000 men in 90 transports, accompanied by 14 warships, led by Clinton himself. He felt confident enough of New York's defences and Washington's caution in winter to leave only a skeleton force in the city itself. It was the first major offensive of the war since Saratoga and the British departure from Philadelphia eighteen months before.

Although largely inert for a year, Clinton had at least broken with Howe's annual habit of hibernating. He soon learned to regret that: the journey was appalling. As one German officer wrote, it was 'storm, rain, hail, snow, and waves breaking over the cabin'. One of the ships foundered, and the rest were blown in groups far south of their intended destination of Charleston. The expedition was dogged by the buttoned-up Clinton's intense dislike of the pompous, erratic, elderly British naval commander, Vice-Admiral Marriott Arbuthnot.

Charleston, which had repulsed a British attack earlier in the war, was a formidable prize. A city of some 12,000 inhabitants living in 1,000 or so fine wooden houses in a beautiful peninsula between the Ashley and Cooper rivers, it was the Venice of the south, a jewel of civilization and prosperity founded on slavery, dominated by the immensely wealthy Rice Kings. The population of the surrounding 'low country' was 69,000 blacks, and only 19,000 whites. Josiah Quincy had written of it in March 1773:

> The number of shipping far surpasses all I had ever seen in Boston. I was
> told there were then not as many as common at this season, though about
> 350 sail lay off the town ... This town makes a most beautiful appearance

as you come up to it, and in many respects a magnificent one. Although I have not been here twenty hours, I have traversed the most popular parts of it. I can only say in general, that in grandeur, splendour of buildings, decorations, equipages, numbers, commerce, shipping, and indeed in almost every thing, it far surpasses all I ever saw, or ever expected to see in America. Of their manners, literature, understanding, spirit of true liberty, policy and government, I can form no adequate judgement. All seems at present to be trade, riches, magnificence, and great state in everything: much gaiety, and dissipation.

Richard Lathers, another contemporary observer, wrote:

A rice plantation and two hundred negroes worth about $150,000 to $200,000 furnished an income sufficient to support a family of five to ten persons in comparative luxury, since this enabled them to have carriages and houses, a town house, and a villa in some retreat, in addition to the homestead. The natural increase of the negroes in twenty or thirty years was sufficient to educate the children in high-grade seminaries at home or abroad and to provide marriage portions for the daughters.

The city was defended by around 4,500 men, half of them militia, under the command of the competent if not particularly imaginative Benjamin Lincoln – fat, lame, amiable, and prone to fall asleep without warning. He was aided by the dashing young Polish aristocrat Count Casimir Pulaski, renowned for his bravery – although he had lost every battle he had ever fought. The defences consisted, on the seaward side, of Fort Moultrie, which had frustrated Clinton's attack back in 1776, and Fort Johnson across the estuary, both of which had fallen into disrepair; on the landward or 'neck' side, there was a citadel with redoubts and eighteen guns.

Lincoln, believing that any attack would come from the sea, had fortified the nose of the peninsula and the river defences. Sure enough, six British ships successfully negotiated the entrance to the estuary by using small boats to mark the channels through the sand bar. But on 29 March Clinton, in a shrewd move, marched his soldiers around the landward side, crossing the Ashley river unexpectedly and unopposed at a narrow point about twelve miles above the city.

His force now marched down the Charleston peninsula to within 1,000 yards of the Americans' inadequate landward defences. His chief engineer, Major Moncrieff, supervised a parallel trench built to the fortifications about 800 yards away, within range of the heavy guns (which were highly inaccurate at this distance) but beyond the 400-yard range of the numerous smaller guns on both sides, or of muskets or rifles. Trenches were now constructed advancing towards the American lines, protected by redoubts of sand and earth twelve feet high piled up against wooden frames set up at night.

The heat of the day was intense, and the troops generally rested beyond the range of the guns until dusk. The Americans packed their rounds with jagged pieces of metal, old swords, laths and glass – anything that came to hand – while the British used more conventional shot. As the British lines crept ever closer, the relentless shelling continued by day and by night. Towards the end of April, Pulaski bravely led a sortie of 200 men which nearly cut off the British in the newly constructed third parallel trench, but the Americans were eventually driven back.

As the British moved inexorably forward, Clinton tried to persuade Arbuthnot to bring his ships up the Cooper river to block Lincoln's escape. But the elderly incompetent refused, fearing he would be trapped by fireships. Clinton, with good reason, was exasperated: 'I find by [the] Ad[miral's] letter to [Captain George Elphinstone] he still harps upon delays. He should recollect all the delays occasioned by himself . . . I will once more enumerate them here . . . In appearance we were the best of friends, but I am sure he is false as hell.'

However, the ruthless and able commander of the Tory Legion of cavalry, 'Bloody Ban' – Lieutenant-Colonel Banastre Tarleton – was more prepared for action. Born of a wealthy British merchant family, he was young, energetic and coarse-featured, with a large mouth and nose. He succeeded in occupying strategic positions along the east side of the river, cutting off Lincoln's retreat; Sullivan's Island, with its offshore fortress, was captured.

The American commander, knowing defeat was only a matter of time, asked for a conditional surrender which would permit his men to obtain their freedom eventually – a mirror image of the terms granted Burgoyne at Saratoga. Clinton, certain the Americans could not escape the trap, refused. There was now a furious exchange of fire under the British naval commander's orders. William Moultrie, the commander who had repulsed the last British attack, reported:

> Mortars from both sides threw out an immense number of shells. It was a glorious sight to see them like meteors crossing each other and bursting in the air. It appeared as if the stars were tumbling down. The fire was incessant almost the whole night, cannon balls whizzing and shells hissing continually amongst us, ammunition chests and temporary magazines

blowing up, great guns bursting, and wounded men groaning along the lines. It was a dreadful night! It was our last great effort, but it availed us nothing. After this, our military ardour was much abated.

Charleston surrendered three days later, on 12 May 1780. Some 1,800 American militiamen were generously paroled, and 3,600 American regulars taken prisoner. The toll had been 90 Americans killed and 140 wounded, with 76 British dead and 190 wounded. The British seized a staggering 343 cannon, 6,000 muskets, 376 kegs of powder and 30,000 rounds of ammunition, as well as ample stores and food. An ammunition dump accidentally exploded a few days later, and a further 200 were killed on both sides.

It was the biggest British victory in the war so far (Washington's troops having escaped after the otherwise decisive Battle of Long Island), and Clinton deserves credit for his remorseless, competent handling, as well as his consistent bravery in visiting the front line under fire. It seemed that the southern states lay at the feet of the British.

Clinton behaved with gentility towards the inhabitants of Charleston and offered pardons to any rebels who swore allegiance to the King. His object was to rally the loyalists, believed to be in the majority in the south, although in fact he infuriated some with his leniency towards the Americans. But his proclamation also angered many of those who had surrendered, who were prepared to remain quiet but not actively to support the British. Lord Rawdon, Clinton's subordinate, wrote:

> That unfortunate proclamation of the 3rd of June has had very unfavourable consequences. The majority of the inhabitants in the frontier districts, though ill disposed to us, from circumstances were not actually in arms against us: they were therefore freed from the paroles imposed by Lt Colonel Turnbull and myself; and nine out of ten of them are now embodied on the part of the rebels ... Perhaps, I ought not to question the expediency of that proclamation; but I so immediately feel the effects of it that I may fairly be excused.

Early in June, responding to renewed rumours of the imminent arrival of another large French fleet, Clinton departed for New York with 4,000 troops, leaving the capable Lord Cornwallis in command in the south. It had been an excellent start for the southern strategy. Georgia was in British hands as well as the main city in South Carolina. North Carolina and Virginia were the next targets.

The war now took a savage new turn, foreshadowing an ominous trend in the south. The vicious if effective Tarleton caught up with a column of 350 Virginians at Waxhaw, a village near the North Carolina border, and attacked overwhelmingly. According to an American doctor present, the Americans,

> perceiving that further resistance was hopeless, ordered a flag to be hoisted and the arms to be grounded, expecting the usual treatment sanctioned by civilised warfare. This, however, made no part of Tarleton's creed. His ostensible pretext for the relentless barbarity that ensued was that his horse was killed under him, just as the flag was raised. The demand for quarter, seldom refused to a vanquished foe, was at once found to be in vain. Not a man was spared, and it was the concurrent testimony of all the survivors that for fifteen minutes after every man was prostrate, they went over the ground, plunging their bayonets into everyone that exhibited any signs of life.

More than 100 Americans were killed and 150 wounded, compared to British losses of 19 men. 'The virtue of humanity was totally forgot,' one British officer admitted. The massacre at Waxhaw constituted the worst British atrocity in the war, and was to become the pretext for acts of American savagery. No satisfactory explanation has ever been given for it; Tarleton now deservedly became a monster in American folklore.

British strategy in the south depended on the supposition that loyalists would flock to their support. Fewer than expected did so, and those that did presented problems. Setting up a 'provincial service' had already led to friction with the regular regiments. The loyalist regiments were poorly trained, equipped and officered by their own leaders, and sometimes brutal and corrupt. Some 50 provincial corps were set up, comprising 312 companies, and by 1780 some 10,000 loyalists altogether were serving the British in these separate units.

While the British offensive was under way in earnest in the south, Washington's northern army, which had so singularly failed to make an impression the previous year, was once again in dire straits. Leaving a force at West Point to protect the mountain passes there, in late 1779 he had withdrawn to winter quarters in the old protected upland bastion of Morristown, which was sheltered from major British attack.

Unlike the previous warm winter, conditions in 1779–80 reverted to those of Valley Forge two years before. Several three- and four-day snowfalls resulted in drifting, and men were smothered in their tents. No fewer than twenty-eight snowstorms fell throughout the season, and the

Delaware and Hudson rivers froze over completely. For a time, unable to find food in the countryside and unsupplied by Congress or the states, the army was virtually starving. Many deserted amid a mutinous atmosphere in camp. One Private Martin reported, 'We were absolutely, literally, starved. I do solemnly declare that I did not put a single morsel of victuals into my mouth for four days and as many nights except a little black birch bark, which I gnawed off a stick of wood. I saw several men roast their own shoes and eat them.' The soldiers were reduced to stealing – 'Rob and go', as Martin put it.

Soon Washington's force had dwindled from around 15,000 men to just 5,000, while, from the cosy warmth of log fires, Congress grandly proclaimed its intention to recruit 30,000 more. The commander-in-chief was reduced to railing impotently against the businessmen, profiteers and hoarders whom he believed had let the troops down:

> Monopolisers, forestallers, and engrossers of condign punishment ... It is much to be lamented that each state, long ere this, has not hunted them down as the pests of society and the greatest enemies we have to the happiness of America. I would to God that one of the most atrocious in each state was hung in gibbets upon a gallows five times as high as the one prepared by Hamen. No punishment, in my opinion, is too great for the man who can build his greatness upon his country's ruin.

But he himself had had plenty of time to prepare, and the atrocious weather conditions had caught him by surprise. Once again, it seemed, the tide had turned against the Americans after a wasted year. That winter their spirits were lower than ever, as the army was reduced to a wretched rump, the news filtering back from the south was uniformly bad, and the French intervention had so far proved completely ineffectual. The new system of raising provisions, much vaunted in milder weather under Quartermaster General Greene the year before, had failed, and the commander-in-chief himself could not escape his share of the blame, along with the profiteers and the winter.

Congress was, as ever, a target for Washington's wrath, as he grew increasingly autocratic, convinced of the need for a strong central government for independent America.

> Certain I am, unless Congress speak in a more decisive tone, unless they are invested with powers by the several states competent to the great purposes of the war, or assume them as a matter of right, and they and the states respectively act with more energy than they hitherto have done, that

our cause is lost … One state will comply with a requisition of Congress, another neglects to do it; a third executes it by halves; and all differ either in the manner, the matter, or so much in point of time, that we are always working up hill; and, while such a system as the present one or rather want of one prevails, we shall never be able to apply our strength or resources to any advantage.

He lamented the dreadful state of his army:

I assure you, every idea you can form of our distresses will fall short of the reality. There is such a combination of circumstances to exhaust the patience of the soldiery that it begins at length to be worn out, and we see in every line of the army the most serious features of mutiny and sedition.

He feared that the resistance effort was sputtering out and that the French were on the verge of abandoning them.

The present juncture is so interesting that if it does not produce corresponding exertions it will be a proof that motives of honour, public good and even self-preservation have lost their influence on our minds. This is a decisive moment; one of the most, I will go further and say the most important America has seen. The court of France has made a glorious effort for our deliverance, and if we disappoint its intentions by our supineness, we must become contemptible in the eyes of all mankind, nor can we after that venture to confide that our allies will persist.

When news of the catastrophic loss of Charleston reached him, his spirits plunged further. In January the British, under the Hessian general Wilhelm von Knyphausen, actually dared to stage an offensive aimed at the American base of Morristown, but were blocked at Springfield.

# 20

# *The Turntail and the Turncoat*

A fresh hammerblow for the American cause in the south followed. Congress, learning of the fall of Charleston, had decided to nominate as commander-in-chief in the south one of the few American heroes to stand up to the British offensive. Horatio Gates – plain-speaking victor of Saratoga, a good administrator, and America's only really successful general (although Benedict Arnold had done much to win the battle for him) – was the natural choice to raise the spirits of the troops. This required a rehabilitation for Gates, who had been eclipsed by Washington's crushing of the Conway cabal, and was a reflection of the support he still enjoyed in Congress.

Washington, fearing his rival and much too shrewd to take on the possibly disastrous southern command for himself – even if Congress was disposed to give it to him – preferred the loyal and capable Nathanael Greene for the job. The appointment of the younger and more energetic Greene would have been inspired. But the amiable, easy-going and popular victor of Saratoga was understandably preferred.

Travelling south after his appointment, on 16 July Gates caught up with a force of 1,400 Continentals sent forward under Lafayette's old travelling companion, the German veteran Johann de Kalb, who had failed to arrive in time to save Charleston and was now encamped along the Deep river in North Carolina.

To the German's astonishment, Gates ordered de Kalb's regulars to set off the very next day towards Camden in British-held territory. Gates dubbed their small force the 'Great Army'. In fact it was exhausted and bereft of rations after its rapid march south. De Kalb and Otho Williams, Gates's Adjutant General, recommended that they march to Camden by a circuitous route across fertile territory where provisioning would be easy. But Gates's usual caution seems to have been replaced by the hubris of a man corrupted by his own reputation. He ordered a direct march forward through swampy pine barrens, almost a desert, bereft of crops except for inedible green corn and green peaches. There was very little water, and the heat was overpowering.

After a month of this terrible march, the men were parched, malnourished, suffering from acute diarrhoea and near-mutinous. But Gates's overconfidence was swollen when they were joined by some 1,000 North Carolina militia and 1,000 Virginia militia as they approached the British. Reaching Clermont – a good position – Gates was advised to make a stand, but he chose to press on by night, having issued a ration of molasses to his men in place of rum, which the Americans had long run out of, to fortify them for the imminent battle. Instead, renewed outbreaks of diarrhoea and cramps ravaged the exhausted men, as Williams reported, operating 'so cathartically as to disorder very many'.

Gates had a muster taken of the 'Great Army', believing it to be some 7,000 strong. Instead it numbered barely 3,000 after many had drifted away. He seemed almost to have lost the balance of his mind. On the evening of 15 August 1780, he ordered his men forward, hoping to trap the British, who he believed were unaware of his approach. This time he was nothing if not bold, in contrast to his hesitancy at Saratoga. Indeed the British, under Cornwallis, were ignorant of his movements and by coincidence were moving northward along the same road – the only one in the vicinity – with an army of around the same size. Advance patrols met each other in woods in the night, clashing and drawing back in astonishment.

As dawn broke, the two armies found they were on fields about a mile wide between two swamps; just 250 yards divided them. Neither side could safely retreat in this corridor. Gates deployed his troops with the Virginia militia on the left, the North Carolina militia in the centre, and de Kalb's regulars on the right. Again by coincidence, Cornwallis's strong regular regiments were facing the weakest American militia units, while his own loyalist militia was facing de Kalb's regulars. Behind, Tarleton's lethal cavalry could give support wherever needed. Cornwallis shrewdly observed at once that the American militia regiments were weakening, and that the whole army was in poor condition.

It was Gates, however, who ordered the attack, his raw Virginia militiamen advancing to take advantage of the supposed confusion among the British. Through the smoke of artillery fire, the American militiamen suddenly saw the British regiments' 'firing and huzzaing' – and most promptly turned tail and fled without firing a shot. On the right, however, de Kalb's regulars resisted two British attacks, and then counter-attacked against the loyalist militia, who began to give way.

Sensibly, as the battle wheeled round anticlockwise, the commander of the British right, instead of pursuing the militia, wheeled left, attacking de Kalb's men on their flank, which was now exposed. The huge German fought back valiantly, rallying his men, but his horse was shot from under him and his head was cut open with a sabre. Gates, further back, had meanwhile unsuccessfully attempted to stop the militia's headlong flight. Deciding that all was lost, he abandoned de Kalb and galloped towards Charlotte, sixty miles away, which he reached in the evening. Two days later he reached Hillsboro, 120 miles further on. As Washington's young aide Alexander Hamilton remarked, 'was there ever such an instance of a general running away … from his whole army? And was there ever so precipitous a flight?'

Back on the battlefield, the valiant de Kalb had received eleven wounds before his men surrendered or fled. Cornwallis paid tribute to his enemy, and attempted to save de Kalb's life, but he died of his wounds. The wretched Gates tried to save face in a letter to Washington:

> The victory is far from bloodless on the part of the foe … I shall continue with unwearied endeavours … to recommence an offensive war, and recover all our losses in the southern states. But if being unfortunate is solely reason sufficient for removing me from command, I shall most cheerfully submit to the orders of Congress and resign an office few generals would be anxious to possess and where the utmost skill and fortitude are subject to be baffled by the difficulties which must for a time surround the chief in command here.

Cannily, his old rival did not blame him directly, but faulted the militia for the defeat. Gates attempted to rally his forces as they dribbled into Charlotte, but a court of inquiry was appointed to look into the debacle. This acquitted him – probably so as not to stain the reputation of the victor of Saratoga. But after this self-inflicted American fiasco he was replaced by Greene, whom Washington had preferred two months earlier.

The Battle of Camden was to be described as the worst American defeat of the war. In fact the recent taking of Charleston was a far more impressive British victory. But Camden was an utter humiliation and disgrace for an American hero who had entirely lost his touch.

Meanwhile the Americans sought to salvage their pride through exalting the heroism of de Kalb.

Thomas Sumter, a veteran of the Indian frontier and one of the best and most ruthless American guerrilla leaders, narrowly escaped with his life from a pursuing force under the implacable Tarleton, which ambushed his 800 men at Fishing Creek, inflicting 150 casualties and capturing 310. This was partly redeemed with the Battle of Musgrove's Mill, where 150 loyalists were killed or wounded and 70 taken prisoner.

Camden had been another savage blow to the American cause. It seemed that the rebels' only hope was the French, whose performance at Rhode Island and Savannah had proved so disappointing under d'Estaing.

In Europe the French had abandoned their ideas of invading England, and they realized that the American struggle was on the verge of collapse. Lafayette, petitioning desperately for more French aid, found himself knocking at an open door. In spring 1780, 5,000 men in troop transports accompanied by seven warships and five frigates were sent to the colonies under Rochambeau's command. Meanwhile the disastrous d'Estaing was replaced in the West Indies by Admiral the Comte de Guichen, an able veteran of the Seven Years War.

In the meantime Britain's most formidable naval commander, Admiral Sir George Rodney, who had just pulled off a series of successful engagements off the coasts of Spain and Portugal, also arrived in the Caribbean, to assume command of the British war effort there. Soon after de Guichen's arrival in Martinique, Rodney spotted the reinforced French fleet sailing northward on 16 April. There were twenty-three warships and a smaller vessel sailing between Martinique and Dominica.

With characteristic aggressiveness, Rodney ordered his twenty warships (which included two 90-gunners) in pursuit. Bunching up his ships, and abandoning the traditional naval tactic of attacking in line, one ship against another, he sought to overwhelm the rear of the French fleet with overwhelming firepower. De Guichen understood the manoeuvre. As the British began to close from windward, which gave them the advantage, he ordered his ships to reverse direction so that those previously at the front were now at the back, and could come to the aid of the threatened ships.

Rodney replied by ordering his ships to close to attack the new French rear, changing his targets. His flagship, the *Sandwich*, moved to engage. Although Rodney was now aiming for a different set of ships, he still wanted his fleet to attack in concentration. However, this lightning change in orders confused his captains, in particular the one at the rear of the British line, now the front, Captain Carkett, who had engaged the foremost French ship as he had been previously ordered to do. To avoid stranding him, the other ships in the British line immediately followed suit, engaging their opposite numbers down the line in the traditional manner.

Rodney, right at the back and already in action, was unable to prevent this. After four hours of conventional fighting the British had suffered the greater damage, while the French had the larger casualties. Rodney, who had believed he stood to secure the greatest victory in his glorious career, was incensed with his captains. When the French broke off the engagement he chased them up to the port of Guadeloupe, then returned to St Lucia. After repairs, the French sailed down aggressively towards St Lucia and the British came out to meet them. The two sides played cat and mouse for two weeks, engaging in small skirmishes before returning to base.

Meanwhile the Spanish had decided to send out a fleet to de Guichen's assistance. At the end of August, Admiral José Solano set out from Cadiz with twelve warships and 12,000 soldiers. Rodney attempted to intercept this fleet before it could reach Martinique, but the Spaniards slipped past him. But a staggering 5,000 of Solano's troops had died of illness in the cramped conditions on his ships, and he decided to head for the Spanish base of Havana.

Assisted by de Guichen, the Spaniards proceeded north a second time. In Havana, the French fleet was urged to reinforce Rochambeau's French fleet and army in North America to stage a joint assault upon New York. This offered the possibility of decisive action and the defeat of one European power by another, with the American rebels irrelevant on the margins. Washington, in his desperation – defeated on all fronts and facing yet another long winter – clung desperately to this hope.

Yet the chief significance of the stand-off in the Caribbean had been Rodney's failure to inflict a decisive defeat on the French fleet there. This meant the British could bring no great concentration of naval firepower to bear on the northern colonies away from their more prized West Indian possessions. Rodney was instead compelled to remain in the Caribbean to continue to threaten the considerable French fleet still there.

One possible disaster for the British was averted, however, when de Guichen decided to use his nineteen warships to escort a huge convoy of French merchant ships – about 100 vessels – back across the Atlantic from the West Indies, rather than come to the Americans' aid. Like the British, the French were misguidedly concentrating on the lucrative plantations of the West Indies instead of the economically underdeveloped territories of North America.

The Comte de Rochambeau, the French land commander, who had arrived in Newport on 12 July with 5,000 men, was thus deprived of potentially devastating reinforcements. He had sheltered in the excellent anchorage there, and had succeeded in getting along with the local people, who had been deeply disappointed by the failure of the previous French expedition.

Washington, heartened by the arrival of the French commander's force and the possibility of a liaison with de Guichen's fleet from the West Indies, as well as the prospect of possible reinforcements from Brest, hurried down to meet Rochambeau at Hartford, Connecticut, on 21 September. There he was bitterly disappointed to learn that de Guichen's fleet had disappeared across the Atlantic with the huge merchant convoy.

Rodney, who had set out to encounter the French fleet, believing it to be heading for North America, had anchored off New York with ten warships on 14 September. There he joined up with the two choleric and elderly British commanders of the northern fleet, Vice-Admiral Marriott Arbuthnot and Rear-Admiral Thomas Graves, who had just arrived from Britain with reinforcements. It was the very same Graves who had proved so inept at Boston four years earlier, even suggesting taking American women and children as hostages.

Arbuthnot had taken his force – nine warships and one smaller 50-gunner – to a position off Rhode Island to intercept the French in case they decided to return to the West Indies, and was indignant at Rodney's arrival to assume command. The British naval hero promptly urged Arbuthnot and Clinton to stage a joint attack on the French at Newport, which the two crabby old commanders said was impossible.

Frustrated, Rodney departed in mid-November for the Caribbean, while Graves returned to New York. Rodney's ships were buffeted by hurricanes on the way down, but he was reinforced by eight warships in Barbados. Throughout 1780 the naval confrontation between Britain and France off the American coast and in the West Indies had proved utterly indecisive and frustrating throughout for both sides.

As Washington journeyed back north-west from Connecticut on 23 September, after his disappointing meeting with Rochambeau, he had little idea of the shock that awaited him. Two days later he reached the supposedly formidable American garrison at West Point on the Hudson, commanded by one of the few generals with a legendary reputation, Benedict Arnold. To his surprise, after crossing the Hudson, there was no honour guard under Arnold to welcome the commander-in-chief.

He inspected the fortifications on the Hudson – which were in lamentable condition – before riding up to West Point, where his party, including Lafayette and Henry Knox, as well as Alexander Hamilton, his aide, was told that Arnold had departed in a great hurry that very morning, after news had arrived that a British spy had been captured. The commander of West Point had disappeared in a small barge, pausing only to say goodbye to his wife.

Washington and his aides remained baffled by Arnold's disrespect – until papers seized from the British spy arrived later that day. They contained documents in Arnold's writing, setting out the defences of West Point as well as providing estimates of the size of Washington's army; and the 'spy' was none other than Major John André, Adjutant General to the British army.

André had received the documents in a secret meeting with Arnold the previous night, further downriver, before he had ridden back towards a British sloop, the *Vulture*, which had anchored four miles south of Stony Point. Before reaching it he had been intercepted by three American rebels. André's capture had been the reason why Arnold had fled in his boat. The two men had been conspiring to organize a British attack on poorly defended West Point. Washington, on hearing the news, exclaimed, 'Who can we trust now!' He rode off to order reinforcements for the garrison and hasty repairs to its defences against possible attack 'even tonight'. Nathanael Greene, ordered to Washington's side, promptly put out a statement:

> Treason of the blackest dye was yesterday discovered. General Arnold, who commanded at West Point, lost to every sentiment of honour, of private and public obligation, was about to deliver up that important post into the hands of the enemy. Such an event must have given the American cause a dangerous, if not a fatal wound. Happily the treason has been

timely discovered to prevent the fatal misfortune. The providential train of circumstances which led to it affords the most convincing proofs that the liberties of America are the object of divine protection ... Great honour is due to the American army that this is the first instance of treason of the kind, where many were to be expected from the nature of our dispute.

Arnold's treachery has been mercilessly denounced as being the result of his overwhelming greed and frustrated ambition. A general regarded as the hero of the Maine expedition, the Canada campaign and then, at least in part, of Saratoga was now denounced as a long-standing 'schemer', utterly 'unprincipled' and loyal only to money.

Arnold, always popularly viewed as America's best general, had not obtained the recognition he deserved. As far back as February 1777 he had been passed over as a possible major-general – a decision which shocked Washington himself, who wrote to Congress that Arnold must 'have been omitted through some mistake ... I beg you will not take any hasty steps in consequence of it, but allow proper time for recollection, which I flatter myself will remedy any error that may have been made. My endeavours to that end shall not be wanting.'

Despite this slight, Arnold agreed to stay on, and Washington wrote to him:

> Your determination not to quit your present command, while any danger to the public might ensue from your leaving it, deserves my thanks, and justly entitles you to the thanks of your country.
>
> General Greene, who has lately been at Philadelphia, took occasion to enquire upon what principle the congress proceeded in their late promotion of general officers. He was informed, that the members from each state seemed to insist upon having a proportion of general officers, adequate to the number of men which they furnish, and that as Connecticut had already two major generals, it was their full share. I confess this is a strange mode of reasoning, but it may serve to show you, that the promotion which was due to your seniority, was not overlooked for want of merit in you.

One of the best commanders in the American army had in fact, been passed over for purely political reasons – Connecticut already had its quota of major-generals. Probably this induced a measure of bitterness, but he had behaved with restraint. Certainly he was vain, a flamboyant adventurer, deeply ambitious, and he may have been involved in financial irregularities in Canada.

As a reward for his success at Saratoga, Arnold had been appointed governor of Philadelphia where the people remained heavily committed to the British (loyalist) side. According to the (pro-American) French minister there 'Scarcely one quarter of the ordinary inhabitants of Philadelphia now here favour the cause of [independence]. Commercial and family ties, together with an aversion to popular government, seem to account for this. The same feeling exists in New York and Boston, which is not the case in the rural districts.'

These loyalists deeply resented the tough, retribution-minded attitude of the pro-independence activists, one of whom, Congressman Joseph Reed, urged that 500 loyalists be hanged and their property confiscated. Reed was elected president of the supreme executive council of Pennsylvania. Several Quakers, guilty of no more than non-belligerence, were in fact publicly hanged, and others were imprisoned and fined by the courts. It was urged by others that all collaborators be heavily fined. Congressmen returning to the capital, horrified to see the degree of fraternization that had gone on with the British, passed a law 'to suppress stage playing, horse racing, gaming, and such kinds of diversions, as are productive of vice, idleness, dissipation and a general depravity of principles and manners'.

Arnold, occupying the old headquarters of General Howe, sensibly adopted a policy of leniency and reconciliation towards the pro-British majority, though it brought him into conflict with the vindictive radicals in Congress. In this he was obeying Washington's direct orders, issued in characteristically humane and wise fashion: 'You will take every prudent step in your power to preserve tranquillity and order in the city and give security to individuals of every class and description; restraining, as far as possible, till the restoration of civil government, every species of persecution, insult or abuse, either from the soldiery to the inhabitants or among each other.'

After just eight months in his job, in February 1779 Arnold was forced out by his radical critics, led by Reed, and was charged with profiteering. Tried by court martial in December 1779, he was acquitted on all but two minor charges and was mildly reprimanded by Washington. It is impossible to assess the truth in these charges: certainly profiteering was rife at the time – not least among members of Congress – and the law was often barely respected in a city which had changed hands three times. Arnold's real crime seems to have been his moderation in prosecuting the loyalists.

However in April 1779, immediately after being charged, he had married Peggy Shippen, a local society beauty of eighteen and a friend of Major André, Howe's right-hand man in Philadelphia and soon after his spymaster. Shortly thereafter, employing the code-name 'Gustavus', Arnold made contact with André, writing coded information about troop positions to him in invisible ink between the lines of letters sent by Peggy to a friend in New York. Obviously the accusation against him had precipitated long-dormant sympathies for reconciliation with Britain.

Arnold's justification was that he had sought a reconciliation between the Americans and the British which had been frustrated by extremists in Congress. He later said that he had always considered the Declaration of Independence itself too radical a document, and he distrusted the alliance with the French – as did many Americans with bitter memories of the French and Indian War.

As an opportunist, he may also have believed that by 1779 his side could no longer win – astonishing for one of the architects of America's victory at Saratoga, but probably accurate in view of the rebels' succession of disasters since. Damningly, he asked for £20,000 as the price of leading a major American force into a British trap, and was offered more than half that amount.

Arnold's greed was unforgivable; yet he could have anticipated riches and honours if his own side had won, and he was preparing to risk his reputation: at least he could have expected financial security. More reprehensible was the secretive and treacherous nature of the defection itself.

In July 1780 he was appointed commander of West Point, in recognition of the fact that his bad leg made him incapable of commanding in the field. Arnold fed the British with details of the fortifications, and allegedly had the boom across the river below deliberately weakened so that British ships could break through up the Hudson, as well as generally thinning the garrison. The secret British assault was planned for mid-September, when Washington made his visit. The seizure of West Point by the British would have been a devastating blow for the Americans, rendering Albany almost defenceless, eliminating one of the few impregnable American bases, and possibly breaking the American war effort at last.

Having heard about André's capture, Arnold had hastily fled the same morning, leaving his wife behind. He wrote to Washington from the British ship with a mixture of self-justification and concern for his wife:

On board the Vulture, Sept 25th, 1780, Sir, –

The heart which is conscious of its own rectitude, cannot attempt to palliate a step which the world may censure as wrong; I have ever acted upon the principle of love to my country, since the commencement of the present unhappy contest between Great Britain and the Colonies. The same principle of love to my country actuates my present conduct, however it may appear inconsistent to the world, who very seldom judge right of a man's actions.

I have no favour to ask for myself; I have too often experienced the ingratitude of my country to attempt it; but from the known humanity of your Excellency I am induced to ask your protection for Mrs Arnold, from every insult and injury that the mistaken vengeance of my country may expose her to. It ought to fall only on me. She is as good and as innocent as an angel and is incapable of doing wrong. I beg she may be permitted to return to her friends in Philadelphia or to come to me, as she may choose; from your Excellency I have no fears on her account, but she may suffer from the mistaken fury of the country.

In fact she and their infant son were well-treated. But André, found behind enemy lines wearing a British officer's uniform under his coat, was made the scapegoat. The Americans at first sought to exchange him for Arnold, but the British honourably refused. Just six days after discovery of the affair, in an instant court martial presided over by Nathanael Greene, André was sentenced to death.

Greene, at Washington's implacable insistence, callously refused André's request to be shot, not hanged, as befitted a military officer doing his duty, explaining

He is either a spy or an innocent man. If the latter, to execute him in any way will be murder: if the former the mode of his death is prescribed by law ... Nor is this all. At the present alarming crisis of our affairs, the public safety calls for a solemn and impressive example. Nothing can satisfy it short of the execution of the prisoner as a common spy ... Besides, if you shoot the prisoner, instead of hanging him, you will excite suspicion which you will be unable to allay. Notwithstanding all your efforts to the contrary, you will awaken public compassion, and the belief will become general, that, in the case of Major André, there were exculpatory circumstances, entitling him to lenity, beyond what he received – perhaps entitling him to pardon. Hang him, therefore, or set him free.

André went to his death three days later with exemplary bravery; Washington and his staff stayed away from the execution. Arnold was appointed brigadier in the British army and given charge of the American Legion, a regiment made up mostly of deserters. He was to play a further significant part in the war, proving that his military skills had not abandoned him.

One of independent America's real war heroes, Arnold had been the third of Washington's great commanders to fall, preceded by Lee and Gates. Now Greene and the loyal Henry Knox were Washington's chief lieutenants alongside the foreigners – von Steuben and Lafayette.

For Washington that autumn, the only consolation for Arnold's defection was that the loss of West Point to the British had been avoided. But the betrayal was another blow to what now seemed a lost cause. Britain controlled New York City, and the Americans had not felt strong enough to attempt to dislodge Clinton. The British offensive in the south had conquered Georgia and a large part of South Carolina. Now North Carolina beckoned. The French had arrived in strength at Newport, where they amused themselves, rather as the British did, with balls and diversions; but one French relief fleet had not arrived at all, and the other had sailed away.

Washington – ever dogged, ever the long-distance runner – could cherish only three apparently remote hopes. First, that his obduracy would finally weary the British, their hands already full with the global war with France stretching from India to the Mediterranean, the English Channel to the West Indies. Second, that the French would eventually bring their support to bear more effectively. And, third, that the British army in the colonies would remain too small ever to gain complete victory.

A hint of support for this last hope soon emerged in the south. The British had not expected to win so easily against the regular American forces, but they had banked on a large band of loyalists emerging to support them as soon as it appeared that they were winning. However, while there were some loyalists, the great majority of the southern population wanted nothing more than to lie low and keep out of the fighting.

Whatever people's innate sympathies, the adverse consequences of supporting the British side were usually far more alarming than those of backing the Americans, for the British had only isolated military forces and loyalist militia, while the Americans possessed a network of revolutionaries, partisan fighters and informers throughout the countryside, as well as many armed bands and rebel-leaning bandits who thought nothing of raiding and plundering peaceful farming folk.

The Americans also seemed likely to prevail, simply because they would always be there, while the British might give up. Moreover, during four years when the British had neglected the south, the rebels had terrorized their opponents, so that what had once been a loyalist territory was now a land of fear. The consequences of any show of support for the British could be intimidation, theft and plunder, destruction of property and even death. Small wonder that when, belatedly, a British army arrived, it found the loyalists cowed and unwilling to declare themselves until there was firm evidence that the British would prevail.

# 21

# The Frontier War

One of the least-known, most terrible and most important chapters of the War of Independence was the 'frontier war' – the brutal struggle for land and power along the western boundary of the United States between the native Americans – the 'Indians' – the white settlers and the British. It will be recalled that one of the main, if unstated, motives of the rebellious colonists in the war was burning resentment at the British imposition of the Proclamation Line along the watershed of the Appalachians, beyond which land could not be settled by the whites at the expense of the large Indian population.

Once war broke out between the British and the Americans, from north to south along the western border a no-holds-barred systematic holocaust was carried out against the Indian tribes across the Proclamation Line – largely by militia raised from among the land-hungry white border settlers with the full support of Washington and the American high command. This was devastatingly successful, and opened the way to the full-scale occupation of Indian lands during the following century. Thousands of Indians were massacred in the process, hundreds of their villages burnt and levelled, vast acreages of land laid waste, thousands of tons of crops destroyed, and probably tens of thousands of Indians deliberately starved to death as a result.

The American settlers undoubtedly had a pretext for this: many Indian tribes – although probably not the majority, who were rightly fearful of the consequences of having supported the losing side if the Americans should win – favoured a British victory in the war, because they believed this would protect their lands. The British, anxious to open a new front in the war and tie down American troops to the west, did all they could to encourage the Indians to rise up.

But the small-scale British effort along the frontier and the doomed

Indian raids into settler-held territory – most of them retaliatory – were in no way proportionate to the savagery of the whirlwind unleashed upon the Indians from the east. To the frontiersmen, the war against the British was of secondary importance to the occupation of Indian lands. The only real point at issue is to what extent this frontier war was instigated by or was beyond the control of Washington and Congress. Sadly, the evidence suggests the full complicity of both.

The conflict along the frontier had been simmering since the end of the Seven Years War, with settlers driving back west into Indian territory and the British valiantly, if inadequately, trying to stop the seizure of Indian lands in the late 1760s and early 1770s. In autumn 1770, a trader with the Indians reported, 'Boonesborough was founded by Daniel Boone in April 1765 who opened a land office, disposed of over half a million acres in a few weeks, founded three more settlements, and convened a legislature before the year was out.'

Settlers poured into Kentucky from South Carolina, and in turn Pennsylvanians, West Virginians and Scots poured into South Carolina between 1765 and 1775. Dragging Canoe, leader of the Cherokees, told the British in 1776

> that [the Indians] were almost surrounded by the White People, that they had but a small spot of ground left for them to stand upon and that it seemed to be the intention of the White People to destroy them from being a people. He had no hand in making the bargains but blamed some of their old men who he said were too old to hunt and who by their poverty had been induced to sell their land but that for his part he had a great many young fellows that would support him and that were determined to have their land.

As John Stuart, a British observer, commented:

> In this district amazing great settlements have been made upon tracts held under titles obtained from individuals by taking advantage of their wants and poverty, or by forgeries and frauds of different sorts in which the nation never acquiesced; for they are tenants in common and allow no person, however so great, to cede their lands without the consent of the nation obtained in general council.

Many local invaders were primitive in the extreme. One Spanish official described them as 'nomadic like Arabs and ... distinguished from savages only in their colour, language, and the superiority of their depraved cunning and untrustworthiness'.

Ironically, the tribal lands these brigands invaded were usually settled and cultivated. It is a post-independence fabrication to suggest that the Indians across the Appalachians were nomadic: they were settled and highly efficient farmers. By 1771 one of their chiefs was predicting, 'Unless you [the British] can fall upon some method of governing your people who live between the Great Mountains and the Ohio River and who are now very numerous, it will be out of the Indians' power to govern their young men, for we assure you that the black clouds begin to gather fast in this country.'

After the war, in 1774, in a particularly brutal act, American farmers along the Ohio river had invited a group of Indians into their camp and killed and mutilated them. It was in Ohio, unsurprisingly, that hostilities first broke out in 1775.

The Indian nations were far from united in their support of the British. The British commander in Fort Detroit, Henry Hamilton, and the American Indian agent at Fort Pitt to the east, George Morgan, vied for the support of the Delawares of Ohio. The Iroquois to the north, on the boundaries of New York State, were hostile to the Americans. Further south the Wyandots and other tribes tended to favour the British as American raiding parties became more frequent. The Potowatomis to the west were divided, while the Sauk and Fox Indians on the upper Mississippi tended to support the British. To the south the Creeks, Chickasaws and Cherokees tended to favour the British, while the Choctaws were divided.

The main concern of most tribes was simply to protect their lands from the settlers. Their concept of land tenure was different from the white man's: as one Shawnee chief declared, 'Sell land! As well sell air and water. The Great Spirit gave them in common to all.' Most Indian elders were deeply apprehensive about getting involved in the war at all. The Delawares remained neutral, although one of their chiefs, White Eyes, openly supported the Americans. Flying Crow, chief of the Allegheny Senecas, reproached a young warrior from a neighbouring tribe seeking his assistance against the settlers:

> It is true they have encroached on our lands, but of this we shall speak to them. If you are so strong, brother, and they but as a weak boy, why ask our assistance? It is true I am tall and strong but I will reserve my strength to strike those who injure [us] ... You say they are all mad, foolish, wicked and deceitful – I say you are so and they are wise for you want us to destroy ourselves in your war and they advise us to live in peace.

In the summer of 1776 the Cherokees crossed the mountains to attack the cabins of the encroaching settlers. The American response was swift and brutal. The American commander there, General Charles Lee, drew up a plan to assemble a powerful army to overwhelm the Indians. Colonel Andrew Williamson, at the head of 1,100 troops, marched in August 1776 from South Carolina into the 'Lower Towns' at the southern end of the Cherokee nation, 'destroying all the villages and corn (from the Cherokee border with South Carolina) to the Middle Settlement'. The aim was to starve the villagers out of these areas.

Another pincer from North Carolina – a 2,000-strong force under General Griffith Rutherford – joined up with Williamson at the Hiwassie river. In two weeks, dozens of Cherokee villages were levelled. In October a third force under the Virginian commander Colonel William Christian punched into Cherokee territory from the north. He ordered, 'cut up every Indian cornfield and burn every Indian town'. It was an astonishingly swift, effective and brutal campaign that drew admiration from George Washington.

The wars devastated huge swaths of Indian land, which also coincidentally suffered from a smallpox epidemic that killed thousands. Even Christian was moved to comment:

> The miseries of those people from what I see and hear seem to exceed description; here are men, women and children almost naked. I see very little to cover either sex but some old bear skins, and we are told that the bulk of the nation are in the same naked situation. But this is not the greatest of their evils; their crops this year have been worse than ever was known, so that their corn and potatoes, it is supposed, will all be done before April; and many are already out, particularly widows and fatherless children, who have no men nearly connected with them.

The initial Indian raiding in Ohio was small-scale stuff. More than 400 warriors, mostly Wyandots, set out from Detroit in 32 war groups, and another 400 further south. The Detroit raiders took 20 scalps and 30 prisoners in July 1776. Governor Patrick Henry of Virginia, along with General Edward Hand, commander at Fort Pitt, were determined to inflict exemplary punishment. The dynamic twenty-five-year-old Colonel George Rogers Clark was appointed to recruit 350 men from among the militant frontiersmen (who, explained Hand, 'liked chastising Indians') to go on a daring raid deep into Indian territory, as far as Kaskaskias in the Illinois region, to encircle the Ohio tribes.

In July 1778 he seized the outpost from its tiny British garrison. The

British commander in Ohio, Henry Hamilton, moved south to the fort of Vincennes to counter this, and then moved into winter quarters with his force of 100 men and Indian supporters. In a brilliant counter-move, in January 1779 Clark marched his men through rain-sodden, freezing territory, to surprise Hamilton. Showing the ruthlessness that was as characteristic of him as his bravery, Clark surprised a party of Indians returning to the fort and personally led his men in tomahawking them in full view of the little stockade. Soon afterwards Hamilton surrendered. Clark remarked that 'to exceed them in barbarity was, and is, the only way to make war upon Indians and gain a name among them'.

In the summer of 1778, Iroquois Indians along the borders of Pennsylvania and New York began to stage small-scale raids into both states, destroying farms and capturing more than 100 cattle and 30 horses. Washington planned massive retaliation. One of his senior generals, John Sullivan, was placed in charge of an army of 4,000 Continentals and instructed to destroy all Indian towns without exception. Departing from Canojaharie Creek in late June, this huge punitive army – contrasting with the ill-equipped tribesmen it faced, who were in no position to harass it – methodically levelled every Indian settlement all the way to Tioga near the Pennsylvania–New York border. At Great Genesse 100 houses were burnt and 15,000 bushels of corn destroyed, taking eight hours. Any Indians the Americans met were captured or killed, or fled before them. Sullivan and his officers celebrated Independence Day 1779 with the toast 'Civilisation or death to all the American savages.' To the north, Daniel Brodhead set off on a more limited expedition from Fort Pitt, destroying ten Seneca villages.

Altogether Sullivan burnt forty towns and destroyed 160,000 bushels of corn. The Americans were astonished by the prosperity and extent of these vast settlements. As one army doctor remarked, 'The quality of corn in the towns is far beyond what anybody has imagined.' In fact the Indians were superb farmers, cultivating maize, tobacco, potatoes, tomatoes, peanuts, beans, and more than twenty other crops. Some soldiers pillaged Indian graves and skinned bodies 'from the hips down for bootlegs'.

Although the Iroquois had mostly fled, they faced starvation through the terrible winter of 1780–81, and many lived as refugees in wretched camps near the British outposts. One Onondaga chief reported that when the Americans attacked his village 'They put to death all the women and children, excepting some of the young women, whom they carried away for the use of their soldiers and were afterwards put to death in a more shameful manner.'

To the south meanwhile, in 1779, Chicamauga Cherokee country was invaded in another expedition, and eleven villages as well as 20,000 bushels of corn were destroyed and £25,000 worth of goods seized; a few Indians were killed, the rest fleeing.

All this was no more than official policy. Congress had decreed that 'no mercy' was to be shown to 'those that have been at war against the States'. Washington, in respect of the Iroquois expedition into the Mohawk and Susquehanna valleys, had ordered that his men should act 'To carry the war into the heart of the [Indian] Six Nations; to cut off their settlements, destroy their next year's crops, and do them every other mischief of which time and circumstances will permit … it will be essential to ruin their crops now in the ground and prevent them planting more.'

The next flare-up was in Shawnee territory, between the Iroquois and Cherokees lands. The Shawnee deeply resented Virginian incursions into their Kentucky hunting grounds. When their chief, Cornstalk, was murdered while being held a hostage by the Virginians, and Clark, acting on the orders of Governor Thomas Jefferson, laid waste two Shawnee villages, their patience was exhausted. (Clark had turned his cannon on one village assembly house, to which most of the Indians had fled, massacring those inside.) With the support of a small number of British troops and a single field cannon, the Indians secured a rare victory against Kentucky militia at Blue Licks. Two years later Clark had his revenge, burning five Shawnee villages. As one of their chiefs put it on that occasion, the Americans 'have come like thieves in the night, when the Shawnee warriors were out at their hunting grounds, surrounded one of their towns and murdered all the women and children'.

Late in 1780 a further American expedition was mounted in the south against the Cherokees, who were believed to be planning raiding parties. A volunteer force from North Carolina and Virginia was marched under Colonel John Sevier and Colonel Arthur Campbell into Cherokee territory. Campbell reported that 1,000 houses and 50,000 bushels of corn 'were committed to the flames, or otherwise destroyed'. Sevier's son added 'we destroyed their towns, stock, corn and everything they had to support on'. British reports suggested that women and children had been burnt alive by the ill-disciplined frontier irregulars; a Cherokee chieftain claimed that he had lost 600 warriors to the 'madmen of Virginia'. In one attack, Andrew Pickens' South Carolina militia, on horseback, cut down the fleeing inhabitants as they attempted to escape the open land surrounding their towns.

The bloodletting was not yet over. While skirmishing continued in the south, it was the unfortunate Delawares – who had tried to stay out of the war – who were to suffer next. White Eyes, the chief who had befriended the Americans, was repaid by being killed, possibly by an American assassin. A Moravian missionary, David Zeisberger, who had acted as a scout in Indian country for the Americans, was leading a party of around 100 converted Delawares to the village of Gnadenhutten, their tribal home. A group of Pennsylvanian militia came across them there and were welcomed. The militia promptly took the pro-American Delawares prisoner, occupied the old Moravian schoolhouse in the village, and had the prisoners brought in one by one to be bludgeoned to death – supposedly to save the trouble of taking the prisoners back to Fort Pitt. One of the Delawares survived to tell the story.

The rebels' decision to wage a war without mercy against their Indian opponents was in gross contradiction to the professedly humanitarian and idealistic motives of the War of Independence, and in contrast with American behaviour elsewhere. While irregulars committed acts of savagery, and occasional excesses occurred on both sides, for the most part the rules of civilized conduct in war were respected. It was also unlike the behaviour of contemporary British colonists in India, who rarely committed atrocities against the native people there.

The decision to carry the war into Indian territory on a large scale, to pursue scorched earth tactics, to give no quarter to the fighters, to destroy hundreds of settlements, and to starve the women and children in a deliberate effort to expel them from a great swath of their own territory was not the isolated act of a few settlers or extremists, but the stated policy of both Washington and Congress. Even the 'liberal' Jefferson had called for the Shawnees to be driven from their land or exterminated. By far the blackest and most terrible chapter in the American Revolution, it for ever besmirches the reputations of the founding fathers who ordered it. Could it in any way be justified?

Fear of Indian invasion was certainly one motive. The Indians did occasionally attack along the frontier. Indian fighters also killed savagely and without mercy, routinely scalping and mutilating their enemies and taking no prisoners, although on the whole they did not wage general war against the civilian population. Yet to some extent the Indians were reined in by their British allies. Moreover, the American attack could hardly be justified by the extent of the actual Indian uprising, since most Indians tried at first to stay neutral.

There were two prime motives for the colonists' ruthless tactics. First, carrying the war into Indian territory was undoubtedly the best way of neutralizing the tribes in case they should mount a sustained attack along the western frontier of the states. Colin Calloway, in his detailed and pioneering study of the American Revolution in Indian country, sums this up: 'American troops and militia tramped through the Susquehanna, the Allegheny, the Scioto, Miami, and Tennessee valleys, leaving smoking ruins and burned cornfields behind them. As John Shy has pointed out, colonial military forces were used less often for protection of settlements than for exacting retribution and retaliation.'

American soldiers and militia matched and sometimes exceeded their Indian adversaries in the use of terror tactics. William Henry Drayton and Andrew Williamson of South Carolina advocated that captured Indians should become the slaves of the captors, but the legislature refused, fearing Indian retaliation for such a precedent. Since Indian prisoners brought no reward, soldiers killed them for their scalps. Captain William Moore's contingent captured three Cherokees in their campaign against the Middle Towns in 1776. Moore argued that the prisoners should be kept under guard until Congress approved their sale, but he was obliged to give in to the demands of his men, since 'the greater part swore bloodily that if they were not sold for slaves upon the spot, they would kill and scalp them immediately'. South Carolina paid £75 for male scalps; Pennsylvania offered $1,000 for every Indian scalp. Kentucky militiamen who invaded Shawnee villages dug up graves to scalp corpses.

Barely had the Cherokees launched their attacks on the backcountry settlements than the colonists carried fire and sword to the Indians' towns and villages, bringing the nation to its knees. As usual, the war in Cherokee country revolved around corn. 'Make smooth work as you go,' William Henry Drayton advised the troops. 'Cut up every Indian cornfield, and burn every Indian town.'

The destruction of extensive settlements covering so large an area of territory was in fact a methodical cleansing of the land of its inhabitants, as a result of that relentless pressure for colonization of tribal lands which had triggered Indian hostility to the American settlers in the first place. The American armies were extending the state boundaries even as the war with Britain was being fought: land cleared was land ready for colonization by the settlers.

The Indians had sided with the British as a desperate act of self-defence against American depredations. They had not simply been unlucky in choosing the wrong side. Had they joined the Americans, as some attempted to do, they would have fared no better so far as their land was concerned. Yet their loyalty to the British provided an ideal excuse for the levelling of villages and confiscation of lands. As Calloway summarizes it:

> American Indians could not expect to be accepted in a nation that denied the fruits of an egalitarian revolution to so many of its citizens and that lived with the contradiction of slavery in a society built on principles of freedom. Native Americans had been heavily dependent on, and interdependent with, colonial society and economy before the Revolution. But as Indian land became increasingly biracial rather than triracial in character, consigning most non-whites to the status of blacks, many Indian communities became increasingly multiethnic in nature. But by the nineteenth century, Indian country was envisioned as a place beyond the Mississippi.
>
> Indian people had been virtually everywhere in colonial America, building new worlds on the ruins of old worlds. Despite recurrent conflicts, many British officials had envisaged Indians as part of their North American empire. Southern Indian superintendent John Stuart had recommended to the lords of trade in 1764 that the government continue French policies of gift-giving and evenhanded dealings as the means of 'fixing the British empire in the hearts of the Indians'. Stuart's vision was never realised, of course, but British officials did appreciate the imperial importance of Indian trade and presence, and that meant extending a measure of protection to Indian hunting grounds. The United States looked to build an empire on Indian land, not on Indian trade, and that required the Indians' removal.
>
> The United States looked forward to a future without Indians. The Indians' participation in the Revolution guaranteed their exclusion from the new world born out of the Revolution; their determination to survive as Indians guaranteed their ultimate extinction. Artistic depictions of Indian people showed them retreating westward, suffused in the heavy imagery of setting suns, as they faded from history.

Even while engaged in mortal combat with Britain, the American eagle was spreading its wings westward in continental ambition, at the expense of the native American population and its ancient, settled and pastoral mode of existence – not as wild herdsmen on horseback, but as farmers tending great cornfields.

# 22

# *The Enslaved*

The plight of blacks during the War of Independence was to be of an entirely different order, though also a tragedy. For most blacks, as for the Indians, the enemies of their liberty were the American rebels, not the British. There were around 500,000 slaves of African origin in America in 1778 – at least a sixth of the people of colonial America. Of these, 450,000 lived in the south and only 50,000 in the north (above the Mason–Dixon line with which Americans commonly divide the two). Blacks were a majority in Georgia, South Carolina and North Carolina; they constituted around half the population of Virginia, and a third of that of Maryland. Slaves were the machinery of the south's plantation economy.

To the British, American protestations of love of liberty were pure hypocrisy in a country which retained a deep-rooted commitment to the institution of slavery (which had never existed as an institution in Britain, at least since the Roman occupation, although the slave trade was a source of wealth for many Britons and some 40,000 slaves had been brought there, chiefly by American or West Indian masters). One of Lord North's closest friends, Hans Stanley, held that the Prime Minister 'should not think of either the stature or complexion of any whether he was a Pygmy or a Patagonian, or whether he was white, yellow or black'. When told that the Caribs had an excessive love of women and wine, Isaac Barre, the colonists' foremost British champion, responded that this made them no different from Englishmen.

A few of the more perceptive American leaders, particularly from the north, winced at the contradiction between the rebels' protestations and the institution of slavery – particularly John Adams. James Otis Jr, the Massachusetts firebrand, dealt with it frankly:

> Does it follow that 'tis right to enslave a man because he is black? Will short curled hair like wool instead of Christian hair … help the argument?

Can any logical inference in favour of slavery be drawn from a flat nose, a long or short face? Nothing better [than this] can be said in favour of a trade that is the most shocking violation of the law of nature, has a direct tendency to diminish the idea of the inestimable value of liberty, and makes every dealer in it a tyrant.

But it was easy to be anti-slavery in the north, where the vested interests in favour of it were so much fewer. In the south, where slaves were the mainstay of the economy, such freedom fighters as Jefferson and Washington tied themselves up in paroxysms of self-justification and contradiction on the subject. Jefferson, in his first draft of the Declaration of Independence, asserted that 'The King has waged cruel war against human nature itself violating its most sacred rights of life and liberty in the persons of a distant people who never offended him, captivating and carrying them into slavery in another hemisphere, or to incur miserable death in their transportation thither.'

This was largely untrue. Slavery was a system adopted by the local American and West Indian planters, not one proposed by the British government, although it shared the blame for acquiescing in the trade. Congress struck out the Jefferson passage, not for fear of offending British sensibilities, but because it challenged the very institution on which so much of the American economy was based.

Jefferson – 'born to mastery' – treated his slaves well, but did not free them. However, he argued that slavery was harmful to both master and slave, breeding passion in the former and degradation in the latter. He himself was later alleged to have fathered a child by a slave – a claim which recent DNA testing suggests may be true. But he lacked the courage of his convictions in not pressing for the abandonment of slavery, and he had no doubt about the inherent inferiority of blacks. He poured scorn on the poetry of Phillis Wheatley and on the intellectual capacity of blacks in general. He favoured the freeing and deportation of all slaves, to give work to the whites, since he believed blacks and whites could not coexist peacefully.

Washington, ever the pragmatic politician, at no stage during the War of Independence supported the abolition of slavery, and he was lukewarm about Wheatley's poetic eloquence. In 1785, two years after the end of the war, he refused to sign a petition for the abolition of slavery, but a year later he privately expressed the view that 'There is not a man living who wishes more sincerely than I do, to see a plan adopted for the gradual abolition to it ... it being among my first wishes to see some plan adopted by which slavery may be abolished by law.'

While Washington's views were certainly more enlightened than those of his fellow Virginians, his private beliefs provided little hope to this huge mass of chained and wretched humanity enduring the sufferings of a barbarian age in a country founded on the virtues of freedom. While undoubtedly many slave-owners provided security and reasonably comfortable conditions for their slaves, many did not. Nor can this be excused as simply a failing of the times, a contemporary attitude shared by all which can be condemned only with the wisdom of hindsight.

Much more admirable was the attitude of Benjamin Franklin, who had renounced owning slaves shortly before the Revolution. As far back as 1773 he had called on Phillis Wheatley, and in 1785, while Washington was tying himself in knots to avoid public comment on the subject, Franklin was elected president of the Pennsylvania Society for Promoting the Abolition of Slavery and the Relief of Free Negroes Unlawfully Held in Bondage. Four years later he signed a petition to Congress 'to countenance the restoration of liberty to those unhappy men, who alone, in this land of freedom are degraded into perpetual bondage'.

It was Franklin's last public act, and one of his greatest. Congress replied that it had no power to act on the matter. In fact, under America's new constitution, it had every power to override the states, but it was more concerned to preserve the Union than to protect the rights of its black inhabitants.

The reality of the war itself was that most blacks saw their best chance of winning freedom in supporting the British cause against that of the majority of their slave-owners, the rebels. This was more than justified by the American treatment of the blacks during the war, although there were also many failures on the British side.

The position was summed up by the historian Benjamin Quarles in his pioneering study, *The Negro in the American Revolution* (1961):

On the American side the negro saw only limited military service until the war dragged on into its third year. This negative attitude toward enlisting the colored man sprang from a reluctance to deprive a master of his apprenticed servant or chattel slave, and from the fear of putting guns in the hands of a class of persons most of whom were not free. In the main, the negro was thought of as a servile labourer rather than as a potential warrior. But when manpower needs became acute, whether in the volunteer forces, the militia, or the Continental troops, hesitancies and fears were put into the background and the negro was mustered in.

This procedure typified an attitude toward negro enlistment that would prevail in America's future wars. From colonial times until the twentieth century, the negro would be bypassed in the early stages of conflict. But as the struggle grew arduous, civilian authorities and military commanders would turn to the one great remaining manpower pool, and the negro would emerge from his status as a rejected inferior to become a comrade in arms.

After initially admitting a few blacks, Washington's Continental Army then excluded them once the south had entered the war – out of deference to southerners' concerns about arming and training slaves and encouraging them to escape the plantations to fight. Only some 5,000 blacks ever joined up, of whom many were no more than foot supporters of their infantry, described as 'waiting boys', or 'servants' and the women as 'dragons'. Others worked as spies. Most were simply labourers – ordered, for example, to muster with 'all the shovels, spades, pickaxes and hoes they can provide themselves with'.

The defences at Sullivan's Island which beat off the failed first British offensive on Charleston were built by blacks; these at least were volunteers. But, with manpower shortages running high in the American army, blacks were also press-ganged into labour. This caused problems – not ethical ones regarding treatment of the blacks, but with the need to compensate the slave-owners whose labour had been confiscated: this in the army fighting for freedom against tyranny.

Worse, captured slaves were treated as booty, distributed among the officers to keep, or for the men usually to sell. In some southern states slaves were offered as bribes or 'enlistment bounty', to induce white volunteers to join up. As Quarles chillingly puts it in describing such a project by Thomas Sumter,

> The bonus varied according to rank; a private was to receive one grown negro, whereas a colonel was to receive three grown negroes and a small one. The only hitch in Sumter's scheme was that he had no negroes to begin with; he was hoping to get them from the enemy. Essentially Sumter was dealing in slave futures. General Greene supported Sumter, permitting him to use negroes taken at Ancrams Plantation on the Congaree as a down-payment on the contract with his men. Andrew Pickens, too, organized troops on the basis of enemy slaves-to-come, a plan which came to be known as 'Sumter's lie' in deference to its originator ...

Inevitably every regiment organized on the enemy-slave-bounty basis suffered from arrears in pay. By late April 1782 Henry Hampton's regiment had received only 46 out of 120 slaves due; William Hill's regiment was due 73 large and 3½ small negroes, and the payroll of Wade Hampton's regiment revealed a balance due of 93¾ grown negroes and 'three quarters of a small negro'.

Perhaps no state surpassed Georgia in the variety of ways in which enemy slaves were used as wartime money. On one occasion the state donated a slave to every soldier who had taken part in a successful campaign; in another instance the state exchanged slaves for provisions for the troops. Enemy slaves were transmitted to public officials in payment of salaries; in the fall of 1782 the legislature ordered the commissioners of confiscated estates to send ten slaves to Governor Martin for the support of his family.

A month earlier the legislature had voted slave deliveries to the members of the executive council, 'as otherways there is just reason to fear the public business must inevitably be protracted'.

Slaves also served in America's small navy. The great advantage of black sailors was that they were much less likely to desert than whites, because the appalling conditions aboard ship were no worse, or even better, than in their previous existence. As Quarles writes:

> The negro in the Continental navy usually served in the lowliest rank and occupations. Not uncommon was the coloured semi-servant, such as Britain, a 'captain's boy' on the *Alfred*, first vessel to fly the continental flag. Some negroes carried powder to the guns; among such powder boys were Scipio Brown and Caesar Fairweather, who handled the ammunition in the main and fore hatchways of the frigate *Boston* when she pulled out of a Massachusetts port in May 1777 'bound out on a cruise by God's permission'. The *Boston*'s roster shows, however, that the negro sometimes advanced to higher positions; Cuff Freeman was on the larboard watch and Cato Austin operated the number one gun on the starboard watch. A year later the *Boston* was carrying John Fyds as a 'negro seaman' with wages of £48 a month.

Unsurprisingly, most blacks chose to regard the British side as the lesser of two evils. Those American historians who acknowledge the matter at all counter the charge of mistreatment of the blacks during the War of Independence by insisting that the British were equally cynical, arguing that the latter's only motive in promising to free slaves was to undermine the southern economy, which was dependent on slave labour, and to make up their own acute manpower shortages. Certainly these motives were always present.

Yet the proclamation by the British commander-in-chief, Sir Henry Clinton, on 30 June 1779, like others which granted slaves their freedom if they joined the British, was partly sincere, as had been Lord Dunmore's earlier declaration, because revulsion already existed towards the institution of slavery in Britain.

After Clinton's proclamation, as Quarles writes, 'Slaves had been running away a century and a half before the declaration, but what in peacetime was a rivulet became in time a flood.' Slaves swarmed into boats in Chesapeake Bay to join the British. Others made their way to the British lines on foot. 'The negroes ... multiply amazingly,' declared the governor of Florida. Governor Benjamin Harrison of Virginia, who had signed the Declaration of Independence proclaiming that all were created equal, complained bitterly that he had lost thirty of 'my finest slaves'. Tens of thousands went over.

The Americans retaliated by inflicting dire penalties on slaves caught defecting. One well-known black river pilot, 'Jerry', caught assisting slaves to flee to the British in South Carolina in August 1775, was hanged and his body burnt, in an exemplary sentence for helping slaves join the British. The loyalist governor protested, 'the very act harrows my soul', but the local assembly threatened to carry out the sentence outside his mansion. In 1776 the state imposed the death penalty on any slave joining or supporting the British, and executions were frequently carried out. Virginia did the same, but applied the noose more sparingly. Other, more lenient, states would sell offending slaves who were caught to new owners abroad.

Only James Madison, of the founding fathers from the south, kept his honour by refusing to punish his valet, Billy, who tried to go over to the British. He said he was unable to take action against the slave 'merely for coveting that liberty for which we had paid the price of so much blood, and have proclaimed so often to be the right, and worthy pursuit of every human being'. Billy was sent to Pennsylvania as an indentured servant, and was freed after seven years.

The British treated black newcomers to their ranks much like their own men – which is to say they were subject to the same hardship and discipline endured by British soldiers. In Philadelphia, for example, a company of Black Pioneers was formed. This consisted of 72 'privates', 15 women and 8 children under the command of a British officer. They wore a uniform of black trousers, a white shirt, a sailor jacket, a green greatcoat, and a hat. When the British captured Savannah, blacks were put to work building its defences, much as in the American army. At the siege of Charleston, blacks were extensively used to lay ditches and to clean decks on boats, and with the fall of the city large numbers of blacks came to the British looking for help.

Clinton's response was relatively generous. Slaves previously owned by Americans would be expected to work or fight for the British for the duration of the war, with provisions, clothing and pay, and would then be set free after it. Under commissioner John Cruden, some 5,000 ex-slaves were attached to the British army after the fall of Charleston, being paid two shillings a day as common labourers, or a higher rate for skilled workers. Loyalist owners were, however, hypocritically permitted to keep their slaves provided they treated them humanely, though they were encouraged to hire them out to the army.

The British appalled the Americans by fraternizing with the blacks. In January 1782, for example, British officers held an 'Ethiopian Ball', and were attended by black girls 'dressed up in taste, with the richest silks and false rolls in their heads'. As an American wrote furiously, 'This ball was held at a very capital private house in Charlestown and the supper cost not less than £80 sterling, and these tyrants danced with these slaves until four o'clock in the morning.'

Some 500 blacks helped to construct the defences at Yorktown. They were also particularly adept as spies, mainly because of their close knowledge of the countryside. Black guides were largely responsible for taking the British force under Colonel John Maitland along a path that led through a treacherous swamp which had never been crossed before 'but by bears, slaves and runaway negroes' round the back of the French forces besieging Savannah in October 1779. The town had been taken by the British ten months before through the guidance of a black, Quamino Dolly, who had led them round the American rear.

In Savannah some 200 black troops – a tenth of the garrison – were used, despite the protests of the local whites. Similarly, black soldiers made frequent sallies from Charleston in South Carolina, to the disgust of the American General Sumter, who declared their presence 'sufficient to rouse and fix the resentment and detestation of every American who possesses common feelings'. The blacks were invariably under white command.

In short, British attitudes toward the slaves varied from cynical and self-interested to relatively enlightened. Although slavery was tolerated among the loyalists, they were encouraged to lend slaves to the British,

and the British treated these as ordinary soldiers in the lower ranks –
clothing them, provisioning them, paying them, fraternizing with them,
even arming a significant proportion and in 1782 setting up an elite
cavalry contingent of 100 blacks which saw action at Dorchester –
loyalists all the while huffing that the 'savage nature' of 'our black dragoons' caused them to commit excesses.

One British 'atrocity' against the blacks is often cited by American
writers. It is alleged that, in an early example of bacteriological warfare,
several hundred blacks 'were deliberately infected with smallpox' and
sent off towards the American and French camps at Yorktown. The truth
is hardly admirable, but less lurid. Many blacks contracted smallpox in
the insanitary conditions in which the poorest lived at Yorktown – every
thicket holding its 'wretched negro carcass' in the words of one observer.
'An immense number of negroes have died in the most miserable
manner in York,' commented another.

General Alexander Leslie, on the British side, decided to make use of
them: 'about 700 negroes are come down the river in the smallpox. I
shall distribute them about the rebel plantations,' he wrote brutally. But
they were not 'deliberately infected', which would have been a crime
indeed.

The subsequent fate of the runaways has also been held up against the
British, and it is true that many went to a dismal fate after the end of
the war. But this was a matter less of policy than of the inevitable sufferings faced by the losing side, given the rebels' vindictive efforts to get
their slaves back. The British tried, with considerable difficulty and
against fierce American resistance, to honour their obligations to the
freed slaves, who could expect punishment and renewed enslavement if
handed back to the Americans.

On the day the British surrendered Yorktown in October 1781, the
Americans sent boats to try to prevent slaves escaping aboard British
ships, while the defeated commanders were advised not to take them
aboard and Washington himself issued a proclamation on how they were
to be rounded up and treated – although this was probably in part to
prevent American and French officers helping themselves to slaves
without identifiable masters. The reimposition of slavery on the blacks
was a prime post-war concern for the Americans.

On leaving Savannah in August 1782, the British took some 3,500
former slaves with them to Jamaica and to St Augustine in East Florida.

At Charleston, the British commander, General Alexander Leslie, insisted that the blacks who had supported the British be evacuated: 'There are many negroes who have been very useful, such as at the siege of Savannah and here. Some of them have been guides, and for their loyalty have been promised their freedom.' After fruitless negotiations with the Americans, who wanted their slaves back, the British unilaterally took 5,300 black loyalists aboard their ships in December 1782, taking these too mostly to Jamaica and East Florida.

In New York, an irate George Washington was snubbed by the new British commander-in-chief in America, Sir Guy Carleton (appointed in May 1782), who insisted that it would be 'a dishonourable violation of the public faith to leave the blacks'. Washington fumed as the British repeatedly stalled him: 'I have discovered enough, to convince me that the slaves which have absconded from their masters will never be restored.' The British carried away nearly 3,000 black supporters, consisting of 1,300 men, 900 women and 750 children. All of these were listed in a detailed inventory.

Some 5,000 blacks had left Yorktown aboard British ships – mostly for Jamaica – before the end of the siege there, and many thousands of others had also left clandestinely aboard merchant ships. At least 25,000–30,000 altogether left America with the British – more than a twentieth of the entire black population of the United States. It was a formidable migration. The slaves of the loyalists departing with the British had no option; but the great majority left voluntarily, from fear of retaliation and re-enslavement if they fell into American hands.

Actual numbers arriving in the West Indies suggest that the real figure of black migration from the newly 'liberated' United States may have been much higher. Some 60,000 blacks arrived in Jamaica between 1775 and 1787 for example, while around 7,000 black immigrants arrived in the Bahamas between 1783 and 1785. Around 6,500 went to East Florida, which was expected to remain in British hands but was handed over to the Spaniards, prompting most of them to depart again.

It is impossible to establish how many former slaves from America were re-enslaved in the Caribbean, but many remained free, if extremely poor. Many were cheated of the plots of land they were promised. Several thousand travelled north to Canada with their loyalist masters, and, after persistent petitioning and a good deal of altruistic lobbying from enlightened Englishmen such as William Wilberforce, the Quaker

Granville Sharp and John Clarkson, at least one heroic contingent of 1,100 who had reached Nova Scotia under the leadership of Thomas Peters were resettled in Africa, in a new settlement for freed slaves – Freetown in Sierra Leone – in 1792. A few hundred reached Britain and Continental Europe.

Perhaps the most poignant epitaph on the black American experience during the War of Independence was written in 1787 by the ageing poet (a slave throughout his life) Jupiter Hammon:

> That liberty is a great thing we know from our own feelings, and we may likewise judge so from the conduct of the white people in the late war. How much money has been spent and how many lives have been lost to defend their liberty! I must say that I have hoped that God would open their eyes, when they were so much engaged for liberty, to think of the state of the poor blacks, and to pity us.

# 23

# *American Revival: King's Mountain and Cowpens*

The ferocity engendered by the American campaign against the Indians, and by the defection of a large part of the black slave population to the British, was not the limit of the singular viciousness of the war in the south. Although most frontiersmen aligned with the American cause against the Indians, local land feuds often ensured that some of them joined the British. Similarly, many poorer settlers joined the patriots where the local squirearchy in the lands further east from the frontier was Tory. Land quarrels and score-settling became common as established order broke down. Nathanael Greene commented, 'The animosity between the Whigs and the Tories renders their situation truly deplorable. Some thousand have fallen in this way in this quarter [the south], and the evil rages with more violence than ever. If a stop can not be put to these massacres, the country will be depopulated in a few months more, as neither Whig nor Tory can live.'

Atrocities abounded, as did irregular bands of armed men professing allegiance to neither one side nor the other, who were no more than bandits and scavengers. A loyalist officer from South Carolina observed, 'The whole province resembled a piece of patchwork, the inhabitants of every settlement when united in sentiment being in arms for the side they liked best and making continual inroads into one another's settlements.'

A young American fighter wrote that there were three kinds of patriot:

Those who were determined to fight it out to the last let the consequences be what it might … those who would fight a little when the wind was favourable but as soon as it shifted to an unfavourable point would draw back and give up all for lost … those who were favourable for the cause, provided it prospered and they could enjoy the benefit but would not risk one hair of their heads to attain it.

This irregular warfare frequently deterred law-abiding loyalists from coming out in support of the British: the areas the King's army really controlled were few, and its military sweeps were less of a threat to most people than the possibility of retaliation by a band of murderous back-woodsmen in the name of the republican cause. In this climate of fear, the American guerrillas were more pervasive and stronger than the British army.

A few examples will suffice. For the British, the brutal Major James Wemyss (known for his fondness for 'hanging and burning') had Adam Cusack hanged as a parole-breaker on a roadside gibbet in front of his wife and children. The vicious and obese rebel Benjamin Cleveland had one Tory hanged and, as he kicked, told another that he would suffer the same fate unless he cut his own ears off and left the country for ever. The Tory promptly called for a knife 'which he whetted for a moment on a brick, then gritting his teeth, he slashed off his own ears and left with the blood streaming down his cheeks, and was never heard of after-wards'.

Just after Christmas 1780, the ruthless American cavalry commander William Washington (George's distant relation) slaughtered 150 Tories and captured 40 without the loss of a single man. One eyewitness wrote:

> Here I must relate an incident which occurred on this occasion. In Washington's corps there was a boy of fourteen or fifteen, a mere lad, who in crossing the Tiger River was ducked by a blunder of his horse. The men laughed and jeered at him very much at which he got mad and swore that, boy or no boy, he would kill a man that day or die. He accomplished the former. I remember very well being highly amused at the little fellow chasing around a crib after a Tory, cutting and slashing away with his puny arm, until he brought him down.

Against this, the Tory Levi Smith recounts a story to the credit of General Francis Marion, an elusive guerrilla leader operating in the swamps near Charleston:

> I had nearly taken farewell of this world ... when I perceived Gen Marion on horseback with his sword drawn. He asked in a passion what they were doing there. The soldiers answered, 'We are hanging them people, sir.' He then asked them who ordered them to hang any person. They replied, 'Col. Lee.' Whereupon the little Swamp Fox took over. 'I will let you know, damn you, that I command here and not Col. Lee. Do you know if you hang this man Lord Rawdon will hang a good man in his place, that he will hang Sam Cooper who is to be exchanged for him?'

Whatever the wishes of the majority of the population, the expected surge of loyalist support to the British was confined to the few areas they already controlled, and even there most loyalists refused to fight for the cause.

The new British commander in the south, Lord Cornwallis, was an able aristocrat, imbued with a readiness to seize the offensive and a vigour wanting in both Clinton and Howe. Born the son of the fifth Baron Cornwallis and the niece of Sir Robert Walpole, Britain's first prime minister, he went to Eton and a military academy in Turin before taking part in the Seven Years War. Although an opponent of Britain's policy in America, he became an aide to the King. Following the death of his young wife, he was heartbroken, as well as embittered at being passed over as commander-in-chief in America when Clinton attempted to resign. He never forgave his superior when he resumed command.

In spite of the recent victory at Camden, at which Gates had been soundly defeated, in the autumn of 1780 Cornwallis was left with only one possible strategy for success: to attempt what General Howe had failed to do in the north and pursue an outright victory over the enemy. The alternative was to remain bottled up in the major towns and ports the British controlled – in particular Charleston and Savannah – and wait for the Americans to come to them. But now that the French had entered the war, there was a real danger even to this minimalist strategy – of concentrated French naval strength accompanied by an American land attack. As long as the British pursued the southern strategy, the only sensible course for Cornwallis must have seemed to be to run down the enemy.

Besides, Cornwallis was a much less defensive strategist than either Howe or Clinton, although not nearly so flash or aggressive as Burgoyne. Also, after the Battle of Camden, it seemed that the British were routing American opposition in the south. So the curtain was lifted on the last great act in the American War of Independence: the chase between the armies across the great expanse of the southern states.

The Americans, meanwhile, had also acquired a new leader in the south, who was to prove the best commander in the war after Washington, and possibly exceeded him. He was thirty-eight-year-old Nathanael Greene, who had spent two years as Quartermaster General and, through energy and intelligence, had revolutionized the clothing and feeding of Washington's army. Greene's latest assignment had been to take over as commander at West Point after Arnold's defection, but in October 1780, as he complained to his wife, 'I am ordered away to another quarter. How unfriendly is war to domestic happiness.'

A Quaker, born the son of a former forgemaster and merchant from Rhode Island, Greene married a beautiful girl from a prominent local family, Caty Littlefield. Promoted to run the local militia, he immediately impressed Washington – but his advice to make a stand at Fort Washington in 1776, after the fall of New York, had proved disastrous, and Washington, who shared the responsibility, had made him the scapegoat.

A blunt, self-educated, no-nonsense man with a hard puritan streak, Greene was also highly intelligent, and his experience as Quartermaster General had taught him the importance of good provisioning to motivate his men. He liked to be meticulously well-prepared, scouting out territory before entering it, and methodically noting the location of fords across rivers – usually above waterfalls – and whether southern rivers like the Pee Dee could suddenly rise twenty or thirty feet after rains, thus blocking an army or permitting it to escape. He was to die in debt, prematurely, at the age of forty-four – a tragic end for the greatest of Washington's generals.

After a long string of incompetent or disastrous American generals – Charles Lee, Benjamin Lincoln, Horatio Gates – Greene was an inspired choice, the right man in the right place. As Colonel Moultrie, the great American defender of Charleston, wrote, 'His military abilities, his active spirit, his great resources when reduced to difficulties in the field, his having been quarter-master-general to the army under the commander-in-chief; all these qualities combined together rendered him a proper officer to collect and to organize an army that was broken up and dispersed.'

Cornwallis was wary of his new opponent: 'Greene is as dangerous as Washington. He is vigilant, enterprising, and full of resources – there is but little hope of gaining any advantage over him. I never feel secure when encamped in his neighbourhood.'

Greene had few illusions about the quality of the army he had been called upon to command: it was a shambles, and the only tactic he could conceive for it was hit-and-run attacks against the British. To be caught in an open engagement with the enemy would, he believed, be fatal. To run, he needed to be sure of his line of escape. He called this the 'fugitive war'.

\*

When Greene reached the American army at Hillsboro, North Carolina, on 27 November 1780, he found some 1,400 'naked and dispirited' troops. They were almost all militia of the most undisciplined kind, whose appetite for plunder he compared to 'the locusts of Egypt' which have 'eaten up every green thing'. Greene's first act was to order his second-in-command, the able General von Steuben, to supply the army properly. To cope with the innumerable watercourses of the south, he constructed his own shallow rafts, which he had mounted on wheels to provide a crucial element of mobility.

The fastidious Greene was appalled by the 'savage' civil war raging between Whigs and Tories in North and South Carolina, and found the Whigs themselves divided into three competing factions. He was determined to bring the partisan leaders from the south under control. He told Thomas Sumter:

> The salvation of this country don't depend upon little strokes; nor should this great business of establishing a permanent army be neglected to pursue them. Partisan strokes in war are like the garnish of a table, they give splendour to the army and reputation to the officers, but they afford no substantial national security. They are matters which should not be neglected, and yet they should not be pursued to the prejudice of more important concerns. You may strike a hundred strokes, and reap little benefit from them unless you have a good army to take advantage of your success. The enemy will never relinquish their plan, nor the people be firm in our favour until they behold a better barrier in the field than a volunteer militia who are one day out and the next at home.

It was about as unpromising a command as seemed possible, particularly after the disaster at Camden. But even in that dismal autumn a rare event had occurred to lift rebel spirits during this long war – a victory by America. It had happened almost by accident, had been achieved by the kind of irregular forces Greene most despised, and had largely been brought about through overconfident blundering by a British commander. Yet Thomas Jefferson, now governor of Virginia, was to hail it as 'that glorious victory which was the joyful annunciation of that turn in the tide of success which terminated the revolutionary war'.

In fact, at the time it was an isolated and freak success. But it perfectly illustrated two enduring lessons of the war: that, even if the British won every battle, they could not necessarily win the war while enemy forces remained at large on that huge continent; and that one American victory after a string of British triumphs was enough to threaten the mother country with overall defeat. The British could not afford to lose a single battle, for fear of demoralizing the government and public opinion back home. So far, in the south, they had not done so. Now they were to endure a stinging little defeat in what has become known as the Battle of King's Mountain.

For once a loyalist force had been placed under a Scottish commander, of dash, daring and not a little foolhardiness. His name was Patrick Ferguson, and he was the inventor of the first breech-loading rifle (which, characteristically, the British were not to adopt for 100 years more). As commander of the loyalist militia, he had been given free rein to engage in mopping-up operations against the patriot guerrillas of north-western South Carolina, up against the mountains.

Ferguson's courage and sensitivity quickly won the respect of the cussed loyalists, and through the summer of 1780 he had worked with gusto and success with a few hundred men, cleansing the area of patriot forces who, by a quirk of local politics, were commanded by the local gentry families – men like John Sevier, later first governor of Tennessee, William Campbell, a Virginia aristocrat, and Isaac Shelby, later governor of Kentucky. These men had been forced by Ferguson's offensive to retreat across the Blue Ridge Mountains, where they formed a motley but colourful army of some 850 men, their horses decked out in red and yellow, the men wearing blue hunting shirts. Reaching Gilberton in the foothills, Ferguson cockily issued a challenge that 'if they did not desist from their opposition to British arms, he would march his army over the mountains, hang their leaders, and lay their country waste with fire and sword'.

On 26 September the 'over-mountain men', advancing from the Watauga river to Gilberton, moved to challenge Ferguson's force of around 150 British regular troops and 900 or so loyalists directly. Ferguson prudently began to withdraw towards Cornwallis's army in Charleston, then thought better of it and decided to make a stand. His men climbed a spur, grandly called King's Mountain, some sixty feet above the surrounding ground extending from the mountain range that separates North and South Carolina. Its craggy summit afforded them a good defensive position, but it was not steep and its slopes were covered with deep pine forests, which provided perfect cover for any attack. Here Ferguson wrote to Cornwallis, 'I have taken a post where I do not think I can be forced.' It was an appalling misjudgement.

Ferguson did not know that the over-mountain men had picked up recruits as they approached, swelling their army to 1,400. The rebels reached King's Mountain on the afternoon of 7 October, surrounding it, and forcing the British to gather at one end of the ridge in order to prevent their force being cut in two. That enabled the Americans to climb up on to the abandoned end of the ridge.

Meanwhile the rest of the encircling forces climbed through the dense woods in irregular formations, using their long rifles to pick off the British, for whom the rocks at the top in practice afforded little shelter. Instead the dense trees gave the Americans virtually complete cover. The forest, as a loyalist officer put it, 'sheltered the [patriots] and enabled them to fight in their favourite manner. In fact, after driving in our pickets, they were able to advance ... to the crest ... in perfect safety, until they took post and opened an irregular but destructive fire.'

The disciplined ranks of Ferguson's trained loyalists, staging bayonet charges and firing off volleys that went over the Americans' heads because of the elevation, proved no match for their largely unseen enemy, although for a time they kept away those closing in along the ridge. One young British loyalist described the terrifying scene afterwards, as reported by another:

> As the mountaineers passed over him he would play possum; but he could plainly observe their faces and eyes; and to him those bold, brave riflemen appeared like so many devils from the infernal regions, so full of excitement were they as they darted like enraged lions up the mountain. He said they were the most powerful looking men he ever beheld; not over-burdened with fat, but tall, raw-boned, and sinewy, with long matted hair – such men as were never before seen in the Carolinas.

The Americans staged two assaults, then broke through on the third, as Ferguson himself, in magnificent style, mounted a white charger and, whistling his men into action, staged one last sortie. He was shot from his saddle by a murderous crossfire.

With that the British surrendered, but many continued to be killed, and prisoners were knifed in retaliation for Tarleton's massacre at Waxhaw. Besides, the Americans considered loyalists little more than traitors. Altogether 225 British were killed and 185 wounded, while 700 prisoners were taken. The Americans suffered 90 casualties. As James Collins, a young American soldier, described it:

> The dead lay in heaps on all sides, while the groans of the wounded were heard in every direction. I could not help turning away from the scene

before me with horror, and, though exulting in victory, could not refrain from shedding tears … On examining the dead body of their great chief [Ferguson], it appeared that almost fifty rifles must have been levelled at him at the same time. Seven rifle balls had passed through his body, both of his arms were broken, and his hat and clothing were literally shot to pieces.

In the grisly aftermath, nine men were hanged, three of them loyalist officers – one accused of whipping a boy for refusing to feed his horses. Captain Patrick Carr of Georgia exclaimed, 'Would to God every tree in the wilderness have such fruit as that.' Many of the wounded died during the next few days through ill-treatment by the rebels, while the area became infested with wolves eating the partially buried dead. The 700 prisoners were marched northward, many dying on the way, 'cast down and trodden to death in the mire'. More than 100 escaped. It was a characteristically savage southern end to the worst British defeat since Saratoga.

Cornwallis was already beginning to fret at the small numbers of loyalists joining up with the British; and both the defeat and the butchery – probably intentionally – served as major new deterrents to potential recruits. The Battle of King's Mountain greatly boosted the flagging American cause, and increased Cornwallis's growing isolation in the south.

After his victory at Camden, on 8 September he had started moving slowly to Charlotte, many of his men suffering sickness in the southern heat and harrassed by irregulars along the way. After learning of the defeat at King's Mountain in October, he decided not to proceed to his original destination of Hillsboro, where he hoped to seize the main American arsenal, but withdrew tactically to Winnsboro in South Carolina by the end of October, after a gruelling march.

By this time further bad news had arrived: Thomas Sumter, the cold, ruthless, stubborn and psychotic 'Carolina gamecock', and his band of irregulars had staged two successful hit-and-run attacks against Major James Wemyss and a force of 200 on the Broad river, and against the capable Tarleton at Tyger river. Meanwhile to the east the tiny, swarthy, bow-legged Francis Marion, a guerrilla leader of humanity, genius and extraordinary mobility, virtually cut British lines of communication with Charleston. Tarleton tried to run him down, but gave up after the 'Swamp Fox's' forces disappeared into first the Pocotaligo swamp and then the Ox swamp. 'As to this damn old fox, the devil himself could not catch him,' commented Tarleton.

All this was demoralizing for Cornwallis. But he resolved to go on the offensive as soon as possible and strike back into North Carolina. He watched in satisfaction as the new American commander, Greene, performed a classic military mistake by dividing his troops into two – one force under Daniel Morgan, the effective and thoughtful veteran of Bemis Heights and Saratoga, to strike west into the border country, the remainder to cut south from Charlotte to Cheraw on the Pee Dee.

This made it much easier for Cornwallis to attack Greene's own reduced army; Tarleton's force, on the British left, could cope with Morgan. Tarleton pleaded with Cornwallis to merge both British forces to trap Morgan's contingent. But the British commander was certain of the superiority of British fighters, and anyway those under Tarleton alone outnumbered Morgan's force. On 13 January 1781 Greene wrote to Morgan, 'Colonel Tarleton is said to be on his way to pay you a visit. I doubt not that he will have a decent reception and proper dismission.' Morgan, just seven miles from fording the Broad river, decided to make a stand at Hannah's Cowpens, a stockyard, because with his heavy wagons he was certain to be overtaken by Tarleton's force.

The place could hardly have seemed a less appropriate choice. With their back to the river, Morgan's army had no escape route – something he had calculated as stiffening the resolve of his troops. The site was a wide meadow with two small hills and very little protective foliage – a disadvantage for the Americans, who preferred to fight from cover, while suiting the British, who had more cavalry, which could quickly cover the ground. Its sole attraction for the Americans was the hills.

Morgan drew up his main force of some 450 regular soldiers on the biggest of these two gentle humps. In front of them he placed around 200 militia, whom he instructed to fire two volleys and then withdraw – knowing they would probably disintegrate anyway under British attack. Some 150 riflemen crouched behind whatever cover they could find, while Morgan's small contingent of 125 cavalry waited behind the second, smaller, hill as a reserve. What followed was probably the war's most skilfully executed display of American generalship, imaginatively conceived and perfectly carried out, in which the gruff veteran Morgan, who had been with Arnold on the famous trek across the wastes of Maine in August 1775, displayed all the wisdom endowed by experience.

Tarleton, overconfident, decided to attack at first light on 17 January, to surprise the enemy with his slightly larger force of 1,100 men. Conventionally, he placed his infantry between two wings of 150 cavalry, leaving 200 more cavalry and a Highland regiment in reserve.

The British trotted steadily, unwaveringly, towards the line of American militia. Rebel sharpshooters as effectively as ever picked off British soldiers. The militia, as ordered, fired just twice, then pulled away to the left to escape around the back of the first hill.

Assuming the American line to be disintegrating, the British charged forward and caught many of the militia before they could get around the hill. But Morgan's small contingent of cavalry galloped to their aid, forcing the now outnumbered British cavalry to retreat. Meanwhile the British infantry marched steadily up the hill, only to find that the troops there, far from running away, were well-positioned regulars firing down upon them.

The now disorganized British lines had entered a trap. Tarleton, realizing this, ordered forward his reserve, which threatened to outflank the American right. Spotting them, the American officer ordered his men to wheel, but they panicked and began to retreat over the brow of the hill.

There Morgan, with great coolness, ordered them to stop and make a stand. The British, expecting a rout for the second time that day, charged up to the crest of the hill, believing the battle won – to be faced by an orderly line of Americans opening fire with deadly effectiveness just below them.

It was the British soldiers' turn to panic and run, as they were out of formation. Meanwhile the militia, reaching the back of the hill in relatively good order, now emerged from around it to cut off the British retreat, as did the small American cavalry for the second time. Within moments the tide of that fast-shifting battle had turned again, and the British were outnumbered: some 800 were taken prisoner, with 100 dead and 200 wounded. The Americans losses were just 12 killed and 60 wounded. Tarleton, who fought to the end with ferocious determination and nearly killed the American cavalry commander, Colonel William Washington, escaped with forty of his horsemen.

It had been an unprecedented defeat for the British. The redcoats had been beaten in conventional battle upon open ground – outmanoeuvred, outgeneralled, outfought – and they were even the less disciplined of the two forces.

*

Although not decisive, the defeat at Cowpens was a staggering rebuff to Cornwallis. He had been even more to blame than Tarleton for overconfidence – had he taken advantage of the divided American troops to concentrate his forces against Morgan's, the British would surely have won. Anticipating the British commander's fury, Morgan waited only two hours before moving his men as fast as possible to safety across the Broad river to the west, and then to the Catawba, before allowing them to rest.

There followed a Keystone Cops-style pursuit as the enraged Cornwallis set off after the offending Morgan with his main army – in the wrong direction from Winnsboro, through faulty intelligence. In order to move more rapidly across trails turned into quagmires by the incessant winter rain, Cornwallis abandoned his supplies – including the rum, which, to his men's dismay, he poured away.

Meanwhile Nathanael Greene, who had learned of the victory at Cowpens from his position on the Pee Dee river at Cheraw, joined the chase in an effort to link up with Morgan and create a force outnumbering the pursuing British. Taking charge of a small advance guard, he left his main army to follow behind and set off to liaise with Morgan to the north-west, marching in parallel with Cornwallis's army coming up from the south west.

The chase was on. It was vital to Cornwallis to reach Morgan before Greene could get to him with his main army – the British debacle at Cowpens had largely been caused by Cornwallis's own failure to reinforce Tarleton and create an overwhelming military strength. Unlike Howe's previous pursuit of Washington in New Jersey, this one was over a land criss-crossed with rivers, offering lethal opportunities for traps in the rain-sodden southern climate in late autumn.

The British skilfully crossed the swollen Catawba river, in spite of American attempts to stop them, encountering and killing General William Davidson of the South Carolina militia on the way. They now moved to the Yadkin, where they regrouped and the Americans 'ran away' – in fact managing to cross the river on boats hastily assembled by Tadeusz Kosciuszko with moments to spare.

Cornwallis now believed he had the Americans trapped against the Dan river. But boats were available thanks to Greene's foresighted planning and 'Light Horse' Harry Lee's skilful cavalry command. To Cornwallis's astonishment, Morgan, to his north, then turned suddenly east to meet Greene's army, which had followed slowly with its wagons and provisions behind its commander. The two divided American armies had met up at last. Cornwallis's attempt to isolate Morgan's army had failed.

Greene, newly confident, promptly decided that the joint American armies, which had met at Guilford Court House in early February 1781, should stand and fight. His fellow generals – in particular Morgan, who, despite his victory was weary and unwell – relentlessly opposed this, fearing overwhelming defeat. Greene was persuaded to send forward only a force of 700 of his best men to give the impression they would fight, while the rest crossed to safety across the Yadkin. This ruse worked brilliantly. Cornwallis pursued the force under Otho Williams, while the main American force recrossed the Yadkin further down and then the Dan. Williams himself managed to evade his pursuers and got across just in time.

An appalling massacre of Tories now ensued on 25 February 1781. Through deception, Henry Lee and the hardfaced Scots-Irish partisan leader Andrew Pickens approached a column of 400 loyalists under Colonel John Pyce: ninety were slaughtered while begging for mercy. Six prisoners were hacked to death, according to an American eyewitness. Greene declared coldly, 'It has had a very happy affect on those disaffected persons, of which there are too many in this country.'

# 24

# The British Strike back: Guilford Court House

At that stage, Cornwallis gave up the immediate chase. He was far from his home base, Camden. His men were exhausted. He was in hostile territory, and now faced the prospect of pursuing his adversary into Virginia, which was more hostile still. He had hoped to catch Morgan's army when it was separated from the main American force under Greene. But the two had joined up and, although he felt certain of defeating them, his lines of supply would be badly overstretched if he pursued them into Virginia. The British were already low on food, as an officer reported:

> Sometimes we had turnips served out for food, when we came to a turnip field; or arriving at a field of corn we converted our canteens into rasps and ground our Indian corn for bread; when we would get no Indian corn, we were compelled to eat liver as a substitute for bread, with our lean beef. In this his lordship participated, nor did he indulge himself even in the distinction of a tent; but in all things partook of our sufferings, and seemed much more to feel for us than for himself.

Cornwallis's tired men marched north east to Hillsboro, issuing a proclamation to the people of North Carolina to join them. At least he had chased Greene's army out of the state. Few, however, responded to his appeal, preferring to wait on the course of events.

Greene, after weeks of flight, was now able to persuade his officers that it was time to go on the offensive. He was in a good position to do so: his united army, reinforced by 400 Continental soldiers and 2,750 militia from Virginia and North Carolina, had swollen to 4,500, compared to the British army of just under 2,000.

After several weeks' manoeuvring for position, the heavily superior American army found the position that Greene sought. On 14 March

1781 he moved to his old bivouac at Guilford Court House, sited in a clearing surrounded by woods lining the sides of a valley. To attack him the British would have to come along the road towards the courthouse through wooded hills – classic territory for an American ambush.

To lure them on, the Americans constructed a 'defence in depth' with the American front line occupying the only cleared land on the floor of the valley. Advised by the ailing but redoubtable Morgan, Greene stationed 1,000 of his weakest men, the North Carolina militia, in the centre, and 400 snipers in the woods on either side, along with small detachments of cavalry. The North Carolina militia were ordered to fire just two volleys and then retreat, enticing the British after them – the same tactic used at Cowpens, except on much more favourable territory.

As soon as the militia disappeared into thick woods, the pursuing British would run into a second line of 1,200 Virginia militia 300 yards away entirely hidden by trees. The third line, of 1,400 regulars – the Americans' best – waited behind strongly fortified hilly ground close to the courthouse itself, about 600 yards back, again sheltered by trees. Thus the British, after chasing the fleeing front line, would meet a deadly rain of bullets from hidden snipers in the trees and, if they got through that, would then face the full American strength. It was an ingenious trap employing greater force on superior terrain using tree cover.

Cornwallis seems never to have considered not giving battle, but retraced his steps to Guilford to meet the challenge. Greene, a much more cautious general, was counting on Cornwallis to do just this. For the pursuer to become the pursued, even when his army was less than half the size of the American one, would have profoundly damaged the reputation of the British and risked the loss of their remaining loyalist supporters. It could even have signalled the collapse of the British effort in the south and the end of the war.

Besides, Cornwallis was a determined and brave commander. He believed that Britain could prevail even against superior forces, and after the defeats at King's Mountain and Cowpens. This encounter, however, was on an altogether bigger scale. Everything hung in the balance. Defeat for the British at Guilford Court House might mark American victory in the War of Independence. He believed the Americans had 10,000 men – more than double their actual strength.

In the cold first light of early morning on 15 March, Cornwallis's tired and hungry men set off for Guilford Court House. They marched in twos on either side of the road, Tarleton's cavalry acting as an advance guard, skirmishing with, and driving back, American units. As their disciplined ranks approached the American front line in the clearing, the militia let off their volleys at a distance of 150 yards.

According to one of the British officers present, 'one-half of the Highlanders dropped on the spot' – but still they marched forward in formation, and, coming into the chosen range of their own guns, loosed off a volley before charging with their bayonets. The 1,000 North Carolina militia fled in wild panic – which could hardly have surprised Greene, who had instructed them to withdraw after loosing off two volleys. One American officer reported 'Every effort was made ... to stop this unaccountable panic, for not a man of the corps had been killed or even wounded ... All was vain; so thoroughly confounded were these unhappy men that, throwing away arms, knapsacks, and even canteens, they rushed like a torrent headlong through the woods.'

Charging forward, the British found themselves caught in the first stage of the trap. On either side riflemen opened up from the shelter of the trees, while the second American line fired at them from ahead. The thick undergrowth made proper bayonet attack impossible, and, with discipline and courage under fire, the British lines regrouped, detachments on either side going in pursuit of the riflemen while the main body moved forward again.

In the confused fighting in the woods that followed, Cornwallis's horse was shot from under him. Mounting another, he was nearly captured by a party of Virginians but was rescued by a British sergeant, who guided him back to his own lines. Astonishingly, in the mêlée in the undergrowth, whose cover favoured the Americans, the British pressed forward and upward, at last gaining the clearing behind Guilford Court House. They were certain they had won.

But the third, most formidable, line – of fresh American regulars – still awaited them. At this stage Greene's men would probably have won if he had ordered them to charge the exhausted British fighters. Instead he preferred to defend his position of advantage, and the British surged forward towards what they saw to be a hole in the American line, which was soon plugged by cavalry. The British, outnumbered in ferocious hand-to-hand fighting, seemed certain to lose.

With the ruthless inspiration of a commander facing his moment of truth, Cornwallis ordered two 3-pound cannon to be brought forward to fire grapeshot ostensibly over the heads of the British before him and into American lines. Discrimination was, of course, impossible in hand-to-hand fighting, and the volley cut down both sides. The Americans, momentarily withdrawing in fear and confusion, allowed the British to regroup in disciplined lines; out on open ground with fixed bayonets, they attacked again.

Greene, seeing his men stunned and demoralized by the grapeshot, ordered a swift retreat before the British assault could begin. The cannon-fire had been a brilliant improvisation which the desperate commander's chief aide, Brigadier Charles O'Hara, had begged Cornwallis against ordering; but it had worked. Cornwallis had won a 'glorious' victory with fewer than half the men at the Americans' disposal, capturing entrenched American positions on wooded hills from below – virtually unprecedented throughout the entire campaign.

The Americans belittled the British victory, pointing out that the loyalists had suffered nearly twice as many casualties – 500 dead and wounded to the Americans' 300. But Cornwallis had avoided not only an ignominious British defeat in a trap sprung upon him by merging American armies but also probable defeat for the whole British cause in America; he could therefore draw considerable satisfaction from the outcome.

His biggest problem remained. His army, reduced to only 1,400 fit men, could not afford to be caught out in the open again by the Americans, who would be in far superior numbers once they had had a chance to regroup. If the British stayed where they were they risked running out of supplies, which had been effectively blocked by American gunboats up the Cape Fear river. He resolved for the moment to march south-east along the river to Wilmington, where his army could be supplied and he could decide what to do next.

Cornwallis believed he had secured most of the south. But the picture was disintegrating. The loyalist upsurge in both South and North Carolina had failed to materialize, and after the massacre of the loyalist column under Colonel Pyce in February the lack of Tory support for the British had become embarrassing.

Lacking local reinforcements, the British position could be strengthened only by sea from distant New York.

The British military presence in the south (North Carolina, South Carolina and Georgia) – now strung out in five bases (Wilmington, Charleston, Savannah, Fort Ninety-Six and Camden) – was still too small to be certain of prevailing in battle; and even one major defeat might be mortal. The only solution was massive reinforcement from the north. But Clinton, cowering in New York, was unwilling to deplete his army there; and the British government was unwilling to send troops across the Atlantic.

Cornwallis apparently had no alternative but to send his forces back to safety in Charleston before starting the southern campaign all over again. But this would be to admit defeat – at least for that season – and, besides, Cornwallis could not see the point. Experience had already shown that he could not secure the southern backcountry, however much he might pursue the enemy to and fro across it.

Not for the first time in the American war, a vigorous British commander decided to disobey his instructions – in this case to secure the south – and use his own initiative in a reckless and unexpected gamble. Despairing of help from Clinton, whom he detested, Cornwallis resolved upon an entirely new strategy: to charge northward into the rebel heartland of Virginia. The move superficially resembled Burgoyne's catastrophic decision to march southward from Lake Ticonderoga (although that had been rationalized by an over-rigid adherence to orders). The thoughtful modern historian Robert Middlekauf, for example, records sadly:

> These suppositions about the crucial location of the Chesapeake and the possibility of ending the Revolution with a single battle reveal once more the limitations of Cornwallis's strategic thought. Frustrated by a long, miserable, and costly campaign, he dreamed; and dreaming, he deluded himself. There was no one to stop him, and on April 25 he began the march to Virginia.

But his move was not quite as foolhardy as it seemed. Arguing in a letter in late April to Germain that to move south would be futile, Cornwallis insisted:

> The principal reasons for undertaking the winter's campaign were, the difficulty of a defensive war in South Carolina, and the hopes that our friends in North Carolina ... would make good their promises of assembling and taking an active part with us, in endeavouring to re-establish His Majesty's government. Our experience has shown that their numbers are not so great as had been represented and that their friendship was only passive; for we have received little assistance from them since our arrival in the province, and although I gave the strongest and most public assurances

that after refitting and depositing our sick and wounded, I should return
to the upper country, not above two hundred have been prevailed upon to
follow us either as provincials or militia.

If we are so unlucky as to suffer a severe blow in South Carolina, the
spirit of revolt in that province would become very general, and the
numerous rebels in this province be encouraged to be more than ever
active and violent. This might enable General Greene to hem me in
among the great rivers and by cutting off our subsistence render our arms
useless. And to remain here for transports to carry us off … would lose
our cavalry and be otherwise … ruinous and disgraceful to Britain … I
have, therefore, under so many embarrassing circumstances (but looking
upon Charleston as safe from any immediate attack from the rebels)
resolved to take advantage of General Greene's having left the back part
of Virginia open and march immediately into that province to attempt a
junction with General Phillips.

In a letter to General Phillips, his close friend, he revealed the thinking
behind his move:

Now my dear friend, what is our plan? Without one, we cannot succeed,
and I assure you that I am quite tired of marching about the country in
quest of adventures. If we mean an offensive war in America, we must
abandon New York and bring our whole force into Virginia; we then have
a stake to fight for and a successful battle may give us America. If our plan
is defensive, mixed with desultory expeditions, let us quit the Carolinas
(which cannot be held defensively while Virginia can be so easily armed
against us) and stick to our salt pork at New York, sending now and then
a detachment to steal tobacco, etc.

With every justification, Cornwallis strongly disagreed with the British
reliance on the loyalists. As he shrugged off Clinton's orders and authority, he wrote contemptuously to the commander-in-chief, offering only
the flimsiest of excuses: 'It is very disagreeable to me to decide upon
measures so very important and of such consequence to the general
conduct of the war, without an opportunity of procuring your
Excellency's directions or approbation; but the delay and difficulty of
conveying letters, and the impossibility of waiting for answers render it
indispensably necessary.'

Cornwallis's decision was bold in the extreme. Was it also insane, and
responsible for the later British defeat? Hindsight would suggest so. But,
if a return to South Carolina could be viewed as both futile and likely
to result in a collapse of the British position there, the advance into the

enemy heartland of Virginia seems to have been the only possibility open to him.

Given the paucity of loyalist support, Cornwallis wanted to fight a purely military campaign. Three other factors weighed in his decision: first, Clinton's sole offensive move since he had left the south a year before had been to send two small incursions into Virginia from the sea. Second, the evidence suggested that Washington had left his home state dangerously depleted and undefended. Finally, Cornwallis may have believed that only so bold and decisive a strike could have stirred Clinton out of his inertia in New York.

The two limited expeditions by sea, via Chesapeake Bay, had been sent by Clinton in October 1780 and March 1781. The first involved the renegade Benedict Arnold's loyalist American Legion, which was followed up by English and Hessian grenadiers and light infantry amounting to 2,500 men under General Alexander Leslie; these sailed up the James river, laying waste to Westover and Richmond. Arnold himself withdrew to winter quarters in Portsmouth.

At the end of March his legion was reinforced by 2,300 men led by Cornwallis's friend General Phillips. Washington's response had been to send his protégé Lafayette in command of 1,300 men to the Chesapeake, to link up with the small French fleet there and attempt to trap Arnold's force before Phillips's reinforcements arrived. The French, however, were driven off by a British fleet, and Lafayette was forced to withdraw, although in April he seized Richmond before the British could occupy it.

One aim of these British expeditions had been to draw General Greene away to the defence of Virginia. But Greene preferred to defend the southern states, and Cornwallis decided to move north to liaise with the British forces there.

How realistic was Cornwallis's hope of winning a decisive battle in Virginia? He may have believed that, had he induced Greene to follow him to defend the state, the combined British forces could inflict a decisive defeat upon Greene's army. If so, he was frustrated: Greene decided to continue his campaign to subdue the south, probably because he feared his men would lose an open fight with Cornwallis.

By securing Virginia, Cornwallis also hoped, as General Howe had before him in marching on Philadelphia, that the British would deal a devastating blow to enemy morale. The rebel force in the south had been supplied and encouraged from Virginia. Cornwallis's strategy was to strike across their supply lines and convince the southern loyalists that they could safely rise up on the British side. Securing Virginia would effectively cut off Greene's army from the north.

The difficulty with Cornwallis's strategy was the same one that had dogged Howe in Philadelphia: even if he secured the main population centres in the state, what then? – particularly if the rebels failed to give battle. He could only hope that the damage to American spirits, and in particular Washington's prestige, of securing the rebel commander-in-chief's home state would finally puncture the American cause.

This was, indeed, a distinct possibility. Although Cornwallis had failed to secure the south, he had not been defeated; and Washington had just come through yet another harrowing winter without achievement. If Washington himself could be drawn into battle for his home state, so much the better. Clinton would surely be forced out of his redoubt to fight as well. Cornwallis's vision of a single decisive battle for America was not as unrealistic as at first appeared.

But he had made three huge miscalculations: he had seriously underestimated Washington's ability; he, of all people, had overestimated Clinton's capacity for decisive action; and he had not allowed for French seapower. Cornwallis was right in one respect, however: he was engaged upon Britain's last throw in the War of Independence, and there was to be a decisive battle – although a very different one from that which he had in mind.

As Cornwallis prepared to march northward, his old adversary, Nathanael Greene, set off south on 8 April towards Camden, where Lord Francis Rawdon, Cornwallis's deputy, was garrisoned with 1,500 men. However, Greene's army was now severely depleted as his militia dispersed, and he had only a small advantage in regular soldiers over the British when he arrived at the strongly fortified town. Encamped outside for a few days on a pine-covered ridge, Hobkirk Hill, he presented a tempting prospect to Rawdon, who marched forward with 800 men on 25 April.

Again the British were at a disadvantage, attacking up a hill. Greene sent two regiments down to meet them, while the American cavalry galloped to surprise the British rear. But Rawdon was unfazed and continued to advance, his men's disciplined volleys causing consternation among the Maryland Regiment in the centre of the American line. The Marylanders panicked and fled, inducing the nearby Virginia militia to retreat as well. With only the unreliable North Carolina militia in reserve to plug the gap, Greene wisely chose not to proceed, retreating with the enemy in full pursuit for two miles.

Neither side had suffered heavy casualties, but the British had gained the field again. Rawdon attempted to pursue Greene's forces, but found them too strongly regrouped and decided to withdraw from his exposed position in Camden along the Santee river, ordering Colonel John Cruger to do the same from his exposed position at Fort Ninety-Six, where he commanded 500 men. Greene tried to encircle this with a force double the size, but was forced to abandon the siege as Rawdon came in pursuit.

After this Greene allowed his troops to rest in the intense summer heat in the hills along the Santee, while the British resumed their withdrawal to the coast. With the loss of two minor outposts – Fort Watson to Marion and Lee's irregulars, as well as Fort Motte – the British troops were concentrated at the coastal strongholds of Charleston and Savannah, an exhausted Rawdon handing over his command to Lieutenant Colonel Alexander Stewart.

Making a sortie, Stewart's forces were surprised on 8 September by Greene at Eutaw Springs, about thirty miles from Charleston. The British, who believed the Americans still to be in summer quarters, hastily formed their lines outside their camp as Greene attacked in three columns, the militia this time out in front. When the British nevertheless held the centre, Greene brought in regular troops who continued the advance against the hastily improvised British position. Soon they had broken through the British lines and were in the camp, where many turned to looting, particularly indulging in the rum they found.

But the British, under Major John Marjoribanks, had taken refuge at the edge of the camp near a fortified house, and after holding out there they launched a counter-attack which drove out the disorganized, tipsy Americans. It would have been a rout had not a number of Maryland regulars defied the British advance. The Americans' surprise attack had gone sour, narrowly turning into a British victory, with losses about even on each side.

In spite of these victories, the British attempt to secure the south was over. Although now left largely in peace at Charleston and Savannah, they could sally out only in strength into the countryside, which was host to patrols of rebel irregulars as well as to Greene's army. The British had won virtually every significant engagement, except the battles at King's Mountain and Cowpens. But they had lost the campaign, because the loyalists would not rally to them as expected, having been bludgeoned into submission by the American irregulars over the preceding four years. The British could never convince the populations of North and South Carolina that they had any prospect of controlling the whole territory or that they would stay on, and the cowed local population was not prepared to take the risk of joining them only to suffer American reprisals later on. The sole hope now rested on Cornwallis's campaign to gain control of Virginia, the base for many American forces in the south, and cut off Greene's army.

# 25

# *Into Virginia*

At first Cornwallis's prospects in his latest gamble seemed promising. The British commander and his column of 1,000 weary, battle-hardened men arrived in Petersburg, Virginia after a 200-mile march on 20 May 1781. He discovered that, apart from Lafayette's force, the state had been left virtually defenceless: Virginia's regulars were mostly serving with Washington and Greene. Virginia's governor, Thomas Jefferson, was desperate for help. In Petersburg, Cornwallis also found that his old friend Phillips had died of tidewater fever a few days before. But present there were some 4,000 fresh soldiers under the renegade Arnold's command. Thus encouraged, Cornwallis set off for Richmond, held by Lafayette.

The young general, with a force of militia half the British strength, abandoned the town and was pursued by Cornwallis. Meanwhile other British forces struck effectively into the state. One chased the redoubtable Baron von Steuben and his force of 500 men. Von Steuben refused to fight, and was forced to retreat. Another marauding party, up the Potomac, threatened George Washington's Mount Vernon estate, where his cousin furnished them with supplies to prevent it being sacked. Washington was furious:

> It would have been a less painful circumstance to me to have heard that in consequence of your non-compliance with their request they had burnt my house and laid my plantation in ruins. You ought to have considered yourself as my representative and should have reflected on the bad example of communicating with the enemy and making a voluntary offer of refreshments to them with a view to prevent a conflagration.

Still another party, of 230 cavalry under Tarleton, raided Charlottesville, home of the Virginia state legislature. They captured the town, and the president of the assembly, Thomas Jefferson, who had drafted the Declaration of Independence five years before, fled with just ten minutes to spare. After his estate was plundered, Jefferson bitterly claimed that twenty-seven of his slaves were deliberately infected with smallpox by the British, although this was more likely a cover for Jefferson's embarrassment at possessing slaves.

With Virginia rapidly coming under British control, Cornwallis moved to engage Lafayette's furtive army. On 10 June Lafayette crossed two small rivers in Cornwallis's direction, with a force reinforced by von Steuben's men and by militia recruits to around 5,300 men. But Cornwallis was apparently tiring of the chase. After destroying rebel supplies in Richmond he marched down towards Williamsburg to receive communications from Clinton, resupply and take stock. Lafayette grandiloquently claimed that the British were in retreat before him, writing to Washington on 28 June, 'The enemy has been so kind as to retire before us, twice I gave them a chance of fighting (taking care not to engage them farther than I pleased) but they continued their retrograde motions. Our numbers are, I think, exaggerated to them, and our seeming boldness confirms the opinion.'

He was soon disabused of this idea. On 4 July Cornwallis began to move his men out of Williamsburg towards Portsmouth, and sent an advance guard across the James river, concealing the bulk of his army down a riverbank behind a wood. Lafayette sent forward General Anthony Wayne with two brigades to ambush what he thought was the British rearguard. After skirmishing, Wayne's men were suddenly confronted with the bulk of the British army. Wayne courageously resisted the impulse to flee, which would have resulted in carnage among his men, and ordered them forward, while Lafayette hastily brought up troops to cover an orderly retreat. Some 145 Americans were killed.

It was a convincing demonstration that even Lafayette's comparatively large army was no match for the British in the field. Greene congratulated the Frenchman on his narrow escape, but chided him also: 'It gives me great pleasure to hear of the success of my friend; but be a little careful and tread softly, for depend upon it, you have a modern Hannibal to deal with in the person of Lord Cornwallis.'

Cornwallis has since been largely derided by historians, but he faced an impossible task. Although he remained dominant in Virginia, he had discovered that control of the state solved little. Greene had not been diverted from the south, and Lafayette's forces and other irregulars and militia could dodge him with relative impunity: he could never decisively get to grips with his slippery enemy.

Meanwhile Clinton, in a lather of indecision, bombarded Cornwallis with a flurry of contradictory orders. The British commander-in-chief forbade his subordinate to conduct a major campaign in Virginia, ordering him instead to construct a major naval station. Cornwallis was also ordered to dispatch nearly half his army – some 2,000 men – to New York. The clear objective of these orders was to prevent Cornwallis risking his forces to achieve a decisive victory in Virginia.

By weakening Cornwallis and tying him up with pedestrian duties on the coast, Clinton could claim more men for the defence of New York, which he always considered, without obvious reason, to be under threat. Alternatively, he could stage a rival offensive of his own, the preferred target being Philadelphia. His main motive now seemed to be jealousy of Cornwallis and a desire to pre-empt a decisive victory by his deputy – it was the same vacillating, diffident Clinton who had refused to help Burgoyne until too late, and had then done too little. But now he was commander-in-chief, and the chafing, contemptuous Cornwallis was forced to abide by this cascade of orders, which he could not ignore, as he had done when far distant.

Soon fresh instructions told Cornwallis to prepare to add his troops to the projected expedition to Philadelphia. Then he was informed they would be diverted again to New York. Meanwhile he was ordered again to fortify a naval strongpoint, possibly for use by British ships to secure the entrance to Chesapeake Bay in the event of an attack on Philadelphia, but also to ensure the possible evacuation of his forces.

Cornwallis, angry and frustrated, asked Clinton for permission to send his men down to Charleston in South Carolina – the option he had rejected before. He wanted to give up on Virginia and Pennsylvania, where Clinton was attempting to tie his hands, and at least save the position in the south. He set about reinforcing Yorktown at the southern end of Chesapeake Bay, in preparation for embarkation to the south, and refused to send any troops to New York.

Cornwallis's initial decision to attack Virginia, and then to abandon the state, the squabbling between rival British military commanders, and the abandonment of the countryside in the south have all contrived to give the impression that the British war effort was on its last legs, and that the newly confident Americans were closing in for the kill. In fact the position was one of stalemate and exhaustion, with two equally cautious commanders facing each other across the expanse of the eastern states, incapable of striking a decisive blow.

For, if Clinton was indecisive and Cornwallis frustrated, Washington's own position was if anything worse. The British had been obliged to abandon the southern backcountry for lack of support and to secure their supplies, but they had not left the region. Greene could roam around at will, but he could not dislodge them from Charleston and Savannah. Further north, Lafayette, while unprotected by a larger force, dared not tangle with Cornwallis's army. Virginia did not belong to the British, but neither did it belong to the Americans.

To the north, Washington was still in dire straits in the early spring of 1781. He had just survived another wretched winter, this time descending from the uplands to intimidate Clinton, but not daring to attack him frontally. In January there had been two serious mutinies by enlisted men entering their fourth winter in camp, long after they had expected the war to end and to be allowed to return to their families. They had originally been enlisted for three years or until the end of the war, whichever was the longer.

The first mutiny was bought off with concessions from Congress which Washington opposed for fear they would lead to another. He was right, and the second insurrection was suppressed with his customary ruthlessness in times of necessity: two ringleaders were shot. General Wayne was sympathetic to the plight of the troops –

> poorly clothed, badly fed and worse paid, some of them not having received a paper dollar for nearly twelve months; exposed to winter's piercing cold, to drifting snows and chilling blasts, with no protection but old worn-out coats, tattered linen overalls and but one blanket between three men. In this situation the enemy begin to work upon their passions and have found means to circulate some proclamations among them ...
>
> The officers in general, as well as myself, find it necessary to stand for hours every day exposed to wind and weather among the poor naked fellows while they are working at their huts and redoubts, often assisting with our own hands in order to produce a conviction to their minds we share, and more than share, every vicissitude in common with them; sometimes asking to participate in their bread and water. The good effect of this conduct is very conspicuous and prevents their murmuring in

public, but the delicate mind and eye of humanity are hurt, very much hurt, at their visible distress and private complainings.

Washington himself was bitter and realistic about the Americans' plight:

> Instead of having magazines filled with provisions, we have a scanty presence scattered here and there in the different states. Instead of having our arsenals well supplied with military stores, they are poorly provided. Instead of having the regiments completed ... scarce any state in the union has, at this hour, an eighth part of its quota in the field, and little prospect, that I can see, of ever getting more than half. In a word, instead of having everything in readiness to take the field, we have nothing; and instead of having the prospect of a glorious offensive campaign before us, we have a bewildered and gloomy defensive one, unless we should receive a powerful aid of ships, land troops, and money from our generous allies; and these, at present, are too contingent to build upon.

This hardly squares with the commonly held view that America was by now coasting towards victory. The Americans, for all their bravado, could hardly be certain that their doggedness would prevail, or that the will to win in London was fading. Gloomy and tetchy, the commander-in-chief was falling out with his closest associates including, briefly, Alexander Hamilton, and showering favours on his sycophants, especially Lafayette.

The French, increasingly sceptical about the Americans' chances, proposed a peace leaving each side in control of the territory it occupied, and there was a real prospect that this would end the conflict. But the extremists on both sides reinforced each other – Franklin, Paine and others vigorously opposing the idea, George III refusing to grant the Americans title over an inch of territory, even though they already possessed thousands of square miles.

Washington's army having dwindled to around 3,500 men huddled in West Point in March 1781, and with the 4,000-strong French standing idle and stranded at Newport, Rhode Island, for more than a year because they had little faith in their allies, American prospects seemed dismal indeed. The 11,000-strong British garrison in New York seemed impregnable, although, under Clinton's command, it was just as unemployed. In the north, elsewhere in the colonies, the rebels could point to no great upsurge in support for independence, no massive inflow of new recruits, no real control of the countryside.

The vast majority of Americans, it seemed, were no more enthusiastic about independence than about the continuation of British rule. They hankered after an end to plunder and scavenging for supplies, the return of the rule of law, and the restoration of sound finance for a land where American paper money was almost worthless, inflation raged, goods continued to be seized, and the cause itself faced bankruptcy.

The cause of independence was probably never less popular than in the spring of 1781, when most histories suggest it was gathering irresistible momentum before the devastating British defeat at Yorktown. Strategically, Washington's prospects were scarcely more encouraging than these of the wretched Clinton, and he showed only marginally more initiative. His chief fear seems to have been that Cornwallis would return south to threaten Greene. To pre-empt this, he toyed with the idea of attacking New York, while holding out no great hopes of success: but he hoped that the timorous Clinton would order Cornwallis north to support him, and their combined troops could then be pinned down. In May, Washington met Rochambeau, the commander of French forces at Newport, and wrote to Greene:

> Our affairs were very attentively considered in every point of view, and it was finally determined to make an attempt upon New York with its present garrison, in preference to a southern operation, as we had not the decided command of the water ... I hope that one of these consequences will follow: either that the enemy will be expelled from the most valuable position which they hold upon the continent, or be obliged to recall part of their force from the southward to defend it. Should the latter happen, you will be most essentially relieved by it.

He was tired and dispirited even as he prepared for the siege of New York. His appeal to Congress for support could hardly have been less stirring:

> We must not despair. The game is yet in our own hands; to play it well is all we have to do, and I trust the experience of error will enable us to act better in future. A cloud may yet pass over us, individuals may be ruined, and the country at large, or particular states, undergo temporary distress, but certain I am that it is in our power to bring the war to a happy conclusion.

Victory for both sides seemed as elusive as ever. The contest seemed likely to be determined by whichever side grew weary of the stalemate first, and it was by no means certain that the British would be the first to back down.

Then something entirely unexpected happened that dramatically scattered the pieces on the chessboard. Suddenly, briefly, the British lost control of the sea. Washington, patient, plodding, tough-minded, ruthless, cold, apparently bereft of initiative, received an opportunity which galvanized him into one of his rare displays of dynamic action. And, as at Saratoga, a succession of mistakes and bad luck delivered the British into their enemies' hands.

As late as 13 August 1781, the British still probably held the initiative in this tired war. By the following day it was handed to the Americans with the news that the Comte de Grasse, at the head of twenty-eight warships accompanied by smaller vessels, had sailed from Santo Domingo in Haiti with 3,300 French regular troops.

De Grasse had set out from France in May for the West Indies, with twenty warships to challenge Britain's domination of the region. Rodney, since his return to the Caribbean the previous December, had seized the neutral Dutch Island of St Eustatius – the main entrepôt for the rebel cause – as soon as he learned of Holland's entry into the war on France's side. In February, without a fight, he had taken 130 merchant ships and the port's bulging warehouses, seizing goods then worth some £3 million in all – perhaps the biggest treasure trove in history.

Rodney's second-in-command, Rear-Admiral Sir Samuel Hood, heavily outnumbered by de Grasse on his arrival near St Lucia, had been forced to pull back to St Eustatius. The French found the fortification at St Lucia too strong, but de Grasse dispatched a small force to take the island of Tobago. Then he took aboard 3,300 troops from Santo Domingo before calling briefly at Havana and sailing northward.

His destination was not, however, New York, where the new, American–French land offensive was being planned at that very moment, but the much closer Chesapeake Bay, where Cornwallis's smaller army was far more exposed. The choice may have been dictated by expediency: de Grasse had promised the Spanish that he would return to help them in the West Indies by November. Almost certainly he could pounce successfully – provided, first, that Cornwallis did not move out of the peninsula there beforehand; second, that American and French troops could be got there overland in time to close the trap; and, third, that the French continued to enjoy control of the sea.

None of these things was certain, or even highly likely. Cornwallis – apparently safe in the Yorktown peninsula, surrounded on three sides by

water and with a heavily defended 'neck' – had orders to construct a
naval base for the British and, refusing to send his troops north to bolster
Clinton in New York, was waiting for the opportunity to take them
south again. It seems not to have occurred to him that the British might
lose their naval superiority, although by mid-July there were strong
rumours that de Grasse might sail north. With a large fleet in the
Caribbean under Rodney, and a smaller one under Graves at New York,
the British felt ready to meet any challenge.

Nor had they apparently given much thought to the possibility of a
joint French–American expedition to Virginia. The British had inter-
cepted a letter from Washington to Lafayette saying that New York would
be the target of their proposed offensive – as indeed, at that stage, it was.
After a year of enforced idleness at Newport, the French army under
Rochambeau – a force of 4,000 men – had moved in good order to
Providence, then travelling the 220 miles to Phillipsburg in Westchester
County to meet up with the Americans at the beginning of July.

The proposed siege of New York was on schedule, and the two armies
began to manoeuvre in preparation for a long campaign. Clinton, meanwhile, remained completely inert. The joint Franco-American army was
now in a position to threaten the fortifications at Kingsbridge across
from Manhattan Island, as well as those on Long Island. A month later,
on 14 August, news arrived that de Grasse's fleet was on the way, as well
as a message from Lafayette at Portsmouth, observing with uncharacter-
istic understatement that 'Should a French fleet now come to Hampton
Roads [at the entrance to Chesapeake Bay], the British army would be
ours, I think.' With remarkable speed, Washington and Rochambeau
decided to reverse all their plans and seize the opportunity of marching
their army across the 400 miles to Chesapeake Bay. Washington alerted
Lafayette, 'By the time this reaches you, the Count de Grasse will either
be in the Chesapeake or may be looked for every moment.... you will
immediately take such a position as will best enable you to prevent [the]
sudden retreat [of the enemy] through North Carolina, which I presume
they will attempt the instant they perceive so formidable an armament.'

But Lafayette's army had already proved it was no match for
Cornwallis's force and could not have prevented a British breakout from
the Yorktown peninsula. Just four days later, on 19 August, the joint
army of 4,000 Frenchmen and 2,500 Americans set out, leaving just
3,500 defending the upper reaches of the Hudson around West Point.

*

The march itself is justly described as an epic. One of the longest in the entire war, it was an act of astonishing boldness, comparable to Washington's crossing of the Delaware in 1776 but on a much larger scale. If it were to go wrong, he had left his small force at West Point virtually unprotected from Clinton's army of 11,000, and his own army was also vulnerable to attack from the rear. He calculated, correctly, that Clinton would do nothing.

More serious was the risk that Cornwallis would slip away and the whole enterprise prove futile. To prevent this, Washington engaged in a subtle show of deceit, wheeling around after crossing the Hudson to a position opposite Staten Island and Sandy Hook, giving the impression he was preparing to attack New York from the south. Roads were improved, boats were commandeered, and a bakery was even set up to make French bread, all to reinforce this feint.

Only when Washington crossed the Raritan at New Brunswick on 30 August did even his own officers realize he was heading south. The news reached Clinton two days later. He argued plaintively:

> If I had as many reasons to believe that Mr Washington would move his army into Virginia without a covering fleet as I had to think he would not, I could not have prevented his passing the Hudson under the cover of his forts at Verplank's and Stony Points. Nor (supposing I had boats properly manned) would it have been advisable to have landed at Elizabethtown, in the face of works which he might easily have occupied, as they were only seven miles from his camp at Chatham, without subjecting my army to be beat *en detail*. Nor could I, when informed of his march toward the Delaware, have passed any army in time to have made any impression upon him before he crossed that river.

The following day Washington reached the Delaware river and Trenton, and he and Rochambeau spurred forward to enter Philadelphia, followed by the American troops on 2 September and the French on 3 September. They were received rapturously in the American capital. The French were bemused by the speed of the march: Rochambeau's chaplain complained of being woken at 2 a.m. to march until the sun rose and grew too hot, when they would rest exhausted while the baggage train caught them up, bringing provisions. One burning day, 400 men collapsed from the heat.

Admiral Rodney, correctly interpreting the news that de Grasse had left the West Indies, promptly dispatched a ship to warn Admiral Graves in New York, but it was intercepted. Meanwhile Rodney, who had fallen ill, sent Sir Samuel Hood with fourteen ships after de Grasse, who had a three days' lead. Such was Hood's seamanship that he inadvertently overtook de Grasse and reached the Chesapeake before him. Finding not even a dispatch ship from Admiral Graves there, Hood concluded that de Grasse had sailed on to New York.

It was a fatal miscalculation. Hood abandoned the bay and Cornwallis's army for the best of reasons, fearing that New York was under threat. Reaching Sandy Hook on 28 August, he met up three days later with Graves, who had been off on a reconnaissance mission to Boston. Not finding de Grasse, the two men realized what must have happened. The incompetent Graves, as senior officer, now took command of the fleet of nineteen warships, which promptly sailed for the Chesapeake, bearing the disturbing news that another French fleet had sailed from Newport under Admiral de Barras, consisting of eight warships, four frigates and transports of siege equipment and guns.

By this time Cornwallis was aware of the pincer closing in from the land, although his army was isolated and his intelligence fragmentary. He chose not to make a break for safety, still confident of Britain's ability to rule the waves, unaware of the approach or size of de Grasse's fleet.

Besides, he feared that, although he could undoubtedly overwhelm Lafayette's inferior force at Williamsburg, he would then be pursued southward by a greatly superior American force, with no effective means of supply until he reached Charleston 350 miles to the south. He had grown tired of running, and the prospect of a land victory must have seemed remote. It was safer to stay where he was and hope for evacuation from the sea.

But Clinton, dithering, had already missed the opportunity to order this, and inexplicably did nothing to relieve Cornwallis's force by land, either by creating a diversionary attack on West Point, or by going after Washington and Rochambeau: although unlikely to catch them, his force might have arrived to tilt the balance and relieve Cornwallis. The truth was that the inert Clinton had not prepared for such an expedition out of New York, and was incapable of improvising at the last moment, with the result that the biggest British army in America – some 11,000 men – was completely out of the picture as events unfolded.

When news that de Grasse's fleet had actually reached Chesapeake Bay reached Washington, who had just left Philadelphia on 5 September, one

French observer reported, 'I have never seen a man so thoroughly and openly delighted.' Back in the capital the news was announced at a banquet for French officers, which erupted into cheering. Outside, there was a carnival atmosphere in the streets. With the fleet's protection, the French and American armies could be safely embarked across the bay, and the French fleet had the advantage of being inside the immense natural harbour.

But they had not yet won control of the sea. De Grasse, who had just landed 3,000 troops under the Marquis de Saint-Simon on James Island, had positioned ships in the James river to prevent the British slipping away to the south, as well as at the entrance to the York river to the north. Meanwhile troop transports were sent to pick up the American and French armies, which had marched to Baltimore and were now waiting at Head of Elk at the top of Chesapeake Bay to be ferried across to the neck of the Yorktown peninsula.

At 8 a.m. on 5 September, the French commander sighted the British fleet, which threatened to block the troops being ferried across the bay. De Grasse's first instinct was to avoid being trapped, and he ordered his twenty-four warships out of the bay as the British fleet's nineteen warships closed in from the north-east.

As the French fleet spread out over the open sea, the British commander, Graves, adopted strictly conventional tactics, bringing his flagship, the *London*, to windward of the French fleet, which was sailing about three miles away on a parallel course. As his flagship was about halfway down the British line, running parallel with the rear of the French fleet, the seven British ships behind him were shadowing no one; but Graves gave no order that they should close up. The result was that the seven were left out of the ensuing battle altogether.

Graves ordered his flagship and the ships ahead to close with the French, who were struggling to order their lines in their haste to escape the bay. The British opened fire at about 5 p.m. The battle raged for two hours until just after sunset, when Graves belatedly ordered the redundant ships behind him to close. But it was too late: the French had peeled away from the conflict.

Despite having five ships fewer, increased to twelve through Graves's ineptitude, the British ended the battle with even honours with the French. One French ship, the *Diadème*, had lost 120 men and had received more than 20 holes in her hull, virtually knocking her out of action. A British ship, the *Terrible*, was so badly damaged she had to be set on fire. Some 90 British seamen were killed and 25 wounded. French losses were higher.

But this commendable performance could not disguise the fact that Graves had thrown away a British victory, for, backed by a favourable wind, he could have routed a confused French line. Hood, commanding the ships that were never ordered into battle, had been beside himself with fury.

The two fleets now manoeuvred for a week within sight of each other in the open sea. Graves, a stickler for the rulebook and a commander of caution bordering on cowardice, refused to fight again, on the grounds that his ships had suffered enough damage. De Grasse, similarly afraid, had realized that he had been mistaken to leave Chesapeake Bay; it was impossible to be 'trapped' in a stretch of water so large, and his ships could have concentrated their attack on British ships as they entered it. Even if the British had tried to stage a blockade, he would have had to be there for a while anyway, and the French fleet could surely have slipped out to sea after a storm, for example, or if the British had grown tired and needed to resupply.

Hood impatiently urged that the British fleet move into the bay, to allow Cornwallis's army to slip away north or south across the York or James rivers, and also possibly to intercept the republican troops being ferried across to the Yorktown peninsula.

Unlike Saratoga, there was no inevitability about Yorktown until the very last moment. Had Graves had the courage to move into the bay, de Grasse would almost certainly have stayed outside, and disaster would have been averted. But Graves was even more obsessed with not getting his ships trapped than de Grasse was, and preferred to stay in the open sea. This was madness. Mistake was piled on mistake by Graves and Clinton and to a lesser extent Cornwallis.

While the two fleets shadow-boxed, the smaller French fleet with its eight warships, military engineers and siege equipment under de Barras slipped into the bay behind them. When the wind turned favourable again, de Grasse was able to sail back. Graves arrived two days later and found a combined French fleet of thirty-six warships at anchor inside the bay.

Seeing this, this most ineffectual of all British commanders throughout the war not only chose not to engage, but gave up the struggle altogether and returned to New York, leaving Cornwallis to his doom. For, with French control of the bay, both his escape routes across the river to north and south of the Yorktown peninsula were cut off, and no supplies could reach him. Also the French and Americans were now being ferried across to the neck of the peninsula in overwhelming numbers, so there was no escape that way either.

Graves's grossly incompetent attack on de Grasse and his refusal to fight again when the odds were reasonably favourable and the survival of a British army was at stake, as well as his indecision and ineptitude in failing to follow Hood's advice to occupy Chesapeake Bay, were the biggest causes of the subsequent British disaster, which was arguably the turning point in the War of Independence (although this study will argue that even so the defeat was by no means decisive).

Of all the British commanders in the war, three were to be most responsible for the eventual British defeat – General John Burgoyne, General Sir Henry Clinton, and the elderly, irascible, cautious and panicky Admiral Sir Thomas Graves – and the worst was Graves.

# 26

# *Encirclement*

Cornwallis was trapped, and he knew it. But he was determined to make a fight of it, in the hope that Admiral Graves might return, or that Sir Henry Clinton in New York would come to his relief by land – both forlorn expectations in view of the characters of the two men concerned. Clinton made it clear in a letter on 24 September that a relief force would arrive by sea on 5 October. Graves's withdrawal, he intimated, had been no more than a tactical one to allow some 7,000 troops to be embarked from New York, while his fleet was reinforced to twenty-five ships of the line as well as two 50-gun vessels and eight frigates.

Both Clinton and Graves were men of such caution that they refused to act unless the odds were heavily in their favour. They had failed to rise to the urgency of the moment, for Cornwallis's position was now desperate, and both knew that drastic measures were called for if Britain was not to lose an entire army.

Cornwallis, believing from his letters that Clinton did indeed understand the need to evacuate his army, committed three mistakes of his own. He had made no attempt to break out of the trap on the landward side: in early September, as the American and French armies were ferried across Chesapeake Bay, he could probably have broken through Lafayette's army, even though it had been reinforced by the Marquis de Saint-Simon's 3,000.

He further failed to use the few British ships on the York river to ferry his men across to the British enclave in Gloucester, held by Tarleton and his cavalry. To do so, of course, would have brought his own army out into the open, where the French and American forces landing on the Yorktown peninsula could have been diverted to catch it. A landing on the Gloucester side would have made it difficult to escape without being caught by the allied joint armies, and with so few boats at his disposal any evacuation would take time and could leave part of his force at risk of being trapped. But he would at least have had a chance of escape.

Worst of all, he abandoned his outer defences across broken and difficult ground nearly a mile to the west of Yorktown, which could have taken several days for the Americans and French to break through. All this made sense only in the certainty that relief was close at hand. As Cornwallis put it to Clinton after the battle:

> I never saw this post in a very favourable light, but when I found I was to be attacked in it, in so unprepared state, by so powerful an army and artillery, nothing but the hopes of relief would have induced me to attempt its defence; or I would either have endeavoured to escape to New York by rapid marches from the Gloucester side immediately on the arrival of General Washington's troops at Williamsburg, or, I would, notwithstanding the disparity of numbers, have attacked them in the open field, where it might have been just possible that fortune would have favoured the gallantry of the handful of troops under my command.
>
> But, being assured by your Excellency's letter that every possible means would be tried by the navy and army to relieve us, I could not think myself at liberty to venture upon either of those desperate attempts; therefore, after remaining for two days in a strong position in front of this place, in hopes of being attacked, upon observing that the enemy were taking measures which could not fail of turning my left flank in a short time, and receiving on the second evening your letter of the 24th of September, that the relief would fall about the 5th of October, I withdrew within the works on the night of the 29th of September hoping by the valour and firmness of the soldiers to protect the defence until you could arrive.
>
> Under all these circumstances, I thought it would have been wanton and inhuman to the last degree to sacrifice the lives of this small body of gallant soldiers, who had ever behaved with so much fidelity and courage, by exposing them to an assault which, from the numbers and precautions of the enemy, could not fail to succeed.

Cornwallis had every reason to feel confident even in this dangerous situation; for the British navy was still almost equal to the French in size, having been only slightly damaged in the Battle of Chesapeake Bay, and any competent commander should have been able to force his way into the wide neck of the bay. Now spared the danger of attack on New York, Clinton would surely fulfil his promise to send most of his troops to Cornwallis's rescue. The latter even saw the approaching battle as an opportunity to trap the Americans and the French at last into a classic encounter which the British could hope to win. As long as reinforcements were likely, Cornwallis regarded it as his duty to stay at Yorktown, keeping his army behind a defensive position rather than risking an open battle against a far superior enemy force.

In this he made a gross error of judgement of his own, for he left himself no means of escape should reinforcements fail to arrive, and he was depending on two men notoriously reluctant to take action. It would not be the first time Clinton failed to arrive in time, and relations between Clinton and Graves were notoriously poor. In the event, the relief expedition did not set out until the second week of October – a week later than the arrival date promised by Clinton.

The Americans and the French, who were in position to begin the siege on 28 September, were surprised by the quick abandonment of the outer perimeter by the British, and by the comparatively restrained defence thereafter.

But Cornwallis, despite his image as a reckless general, knew the weaknesses of his position. Apart from a ravine to the west and a creek to the east of the small town, there was only a swamp to the south covering part of the approaches. All this could easily be bypassed,

With only a few weeks to fortify the surrounding area, Cornwallis had built a line of earthworks around the town, as well as six redoubts, and had placed sixty-five small guns from his few ships along them; but this system was far from complete. Beyond that was an outer line of four redoubts and virtually no earthworks. Far from being a fortress, Yorktown was defended only by a hastily built, half-constructed earth wall and trench and a handful of defensive positions. Behind this inadequate line sheltered some 7,500 soldiers and 800 militia – men with dwindling supplies now that the French were blockading Chesapeake Bay – facing a mixed force totalling some 18,000, at least ninety guns, many of them heavy, and advanced French siege equipment brought from Newport.

Yorktown has been portrayed as a classic siege of its period, against a heavily fortified position. While the British defences there barely deserved that label, the siege was certainly meticulously carried out according to the textbooks – one of the last of its kind, directed by the French. It was as if both sides had to go through the motions, though knowing that the outcome was inevitable unless relief came.

The rebel armies closing in for the siege on 28 September consisted of some 8,000 Frenchmen and 9,500 Americans, of whom around 6,000 were regulars and 3,500 militia. The Americans were drawn up in the south in three divisions under Washington's two foreign protégés, Lafayette and von Steuben, and General Benjamin Lincoln, the commander humiliated at Charleston.

The French, by contrast with the dowdy Americans, were professional regiments bedecked in spectacular uniforms under aristocratic commanders: the Bournannais, in crimson and pink, under the Baron de Viomenil; the Royal Deux-Points, in blue and yellow, under the command of the German-speaking Duc de Deux-Points; the Soissonais, with their red, blue and yellow uniforms; the Saintonge, with their distinctive green and yellow dress, under the Comte de Custine; the Lauzun Legion, under Saint-Simon's command; and the Gatinais, the Touraine and the Agenois. They took up positions to the west of the British garrison. Part of the Lauzun Legion and a detachment of Virginia militia were dispatched to cut off escape from Tarleton's enclave at Gloucester across the river.

The whole scene now settled down into the eerie ritual of an eighteenth century siege. Unless help reached them, or they escaped across the river, the 8,300 British troops would have no choice but to surrender. Cornwallis remained optimistic, but they were already running out of supplies. As one British officer put it, 'We get terrible provisions now ... putrid meat and wormy biscuits that have spoiled on the ships. Many of the men have taken sick here with dysentery or the bloody flux and diarrhoea ... Foul fever is spreading ... we have had little rest day or night.'

Washington had responded to Cornwallis's withdrawal from the outer defences by occupying the abandoned redoubts and constructing two more of his own. Time was the American commander's obsession – to close in for the kill before relief could reach the British from New York. 'A vigorous use of the means in our power cannot but ensure success,' he remarked, impatient at the caution of the French. The Americans revelled in the unfamiliar experience of having their enemy at bay.

The youthfully impulsive and arrogant Alexander Hamilton, Washington's aide, ordered his men to take the first abandoned British position in parade-ground fashion – as one of his officers recorded: 'Our next manoeuvre was rather extraordinary. We were ordered to mount the bank, front the enemy, and there by word of command go through all the ceremony of soldiery, ordering and grounding our arms; and although the enemy had been firing a little before, they did not now give us a single shot.'

The same officer accused Hamilton of 'wantonly exposing the lives of his men'. The experienced French commander, Rochambeau, more soberly ordered his men to stop beating their drums as they marched, as this drew British fire. The French set up their main batteries to the north-west of the town.

Artillery was drawn up to the south-west, and, during the dark and stormy night of 6 October, 4,300 American and French troops were brought up to the south-western corner to start work on a first parallel – a 1,000-yard trench cutting around the south of Yorktown about 400 yards away from the British positions, out of range of all but the biggest cannon. While the British guns blazed away at campfires set up as a decoy to one side, Washington himself ceremonially broke the first ground of the trench with a pickaxe.

The following morning, the earthwork and the trench were complete, and by noon on 9 October the guns and emplacements were in place along the parallel. In recognition of the work done by the 600 French artillerymen present, Washington allowed a French gun to fire the first shot at noon. With several 24-pounders in place against the smaller British guns, the contest was unequal from the first, and all Yorktown was well within range. So accurate was the French and American fire that the British were forced to use their guns only at night, when their embrasures could not be seen.

Most of the small British flotilla in the York river was destroyed in the first artillery assault. The American surgeon Dr Thacher exulted:

> The ships were enwrapped in a torrent of fire spreading with vivid brightness among the combustible rigging and running with amazing rapidity to the tops of the several masts, while all around was thunder and lightning from our numerous cannon and mortars, and in the darkness of night, presented one of the most sublime and magnificent spectacles which can be imagined. Some of our shells, overreaching the town, were seen to fall into the river and, bursting, throw up columns of water like the spouting of the monsters of the deep.

The following night some 1,000 shells landed on Yorktown.

Cornwallis had still not given up hope: the relief force was overdue, but not by much. But he had not delayed the enemy advance by maintaining the outer defence or by using raiding parties to harass the enemy camp outside Yorktown, which would have gained precious time.

On the night of 11 October, American and French positions came under intense British fire. The spectacle of red-hot shot being lobbed through the night between the two sides was almost surreal. The French and Americans displayed considerable courage, right under the British guns and within range, at only 300 yards distance.

To the right were two British redoubts which had to be taken before the second trench could be finished and artillery be safely brought up. On the night of 14 October a French party crept forward and had to fight a vicious battle to overwhelm the 120 defenders in the first redoubt; no fewer than 40 were killed and 68 wounded in the fiercest action of the entire siege. Meanwhile the smaller, less defended, redoubt was attacked by another group of Americans under Hamilton's command: 8 were killed and 30 wounded by the sixty or so defenders before it was captured.

With the second parallel completed just 300 yards from British lines, the American and French gunners were able to blast away straight into the British positions. Cornwallis was driven out of the governor's house, which had been half destroyed, into a kind of cave by the riverside at the bottom of the garden. The relief force was now more than a week overdue. He wrote, 'My situation becomes very critical. We dare not show a gun ... The safety of the place is therefore so precarious that I can not recommend that the fleet and army should run great risk in endeavouring to save us.'

The French had been surprised at the British failure to counter-attack on the night of the 14th. Cornwallis obliged them the following night, sending 350 men under General James Abercrombie to disable the American and French guns facing them. They gained control of the second parallel, killing and wounding seventeen men and driving off the rest. But they had only the time and means to jam bayonets into the touchholes of six guns instead of pouring liquid metal into them to disable them permanently before retreating.

When the Americans and French returned, the spikes were removed and the uneven bombardment resumed. The British positions were pummelled to devastating effect by superior French guns at point-blank range, the half-built British defences proving of little use. Having advised Clinton that it was now too dangerous to try to save him – which, as the commander-in-chief had not even set out from New York, was as redundant a counsel as any ever – Cornwallis tried one last throw. On the night of 16 October he began to ferry his troops, in whatever boats he could muster, across the York river to Gloucester in a last desperate bid to stage a breakout.

Surprisingly, de Grasse had not yet closed off this escape route, being wary of moving too far upriver. Perhaps more astonishingly, Cornwallis had not tried this way out before: but he had been slow to realize the impossibility of his position and the fact that help would not arrive. However, after 1,000 men had been ferried across to Tarleton's enclave, a storm blew up, and he realized that it was hopeless: there were too few successfully to break through the enemy lines outside Gloucester and escape. When the storm abated, the troops there were rowed back, to avoid unnecessary carnage.

At 10 a.m. on 17 October a lone drummer appeared on the British defences and the cannonading stopped. Washington suspended the firing for two hours as Cornwallis sent his terms. Like Burgoyne, who had surrendered on the very same day four long years before, the British commander sought a negotiated surrender which would spare his men. Washington, who had objected to the Saratoga agreement, refused, and was in a strong position to dictate terms. The surrender was to be virtually unconditional.

On 18 October representatives of both sides met to discuss the terms. Washington made them deliberately humiliating: the British were to come out with their colours folded, to give up their arms, and to be treated as prisoners of war. Their drums were to play a British march, for fear they would try to mock an American tune, as had happened before. They were given until 11 a.m. the next day to agree to these terms, or the murderous barrage would be resumed.

At 2 a.m. on 19 October the British filed out to, it is said, the tune of 'The World Turned Upside Down'. Cornwallis, however, snubbed Washington, claiming to be ill. Instead he sent his second-in-command, Brigadier Charles O'Hara, who pointedly presented his sword to General Rochambeau at Washington's side – a gesture signifying that the British had been defeated by the French, not by the Americans. Rochambeau pointed to the American commander. In cold and controlled fury, Washington passed Cornwallis's subordinate on to General Lincoln, the American general defeated at the siege of Charleston, who ordered O'Hara and his men down a gauntlet of French troops on the left and American soldiers on the right to a field, where the British threw down their arms contemptuously, according to some witnesses.

The bitterness over, O'Hara was entertained cordially at dinner by Washington. Then at last the British commander appeared at a banquet in a field tent, with a double-edged compliment: 'When the illustrious part which your Excellency has borne in the long and arduous contest becomes a matter of history, fame will gather your brightest laurels from the banks of the Delaware rather than those of the Chesapeake.'

The aristocratic French officers present were generous to the defeated foe, in the best traditions of courtly eighteenth-century warfare. Rochambeau loaned Cornwallis £10,000, while the Vicomte de Noailles lent him a popular book on tactics. None of these men could have imagined that the Revolution would have its first imitator not in Britain but across the Channel in France, where their order would be swept away by a whirlwind of class hatred far more violent than that which had swept the thirteen colonies. Meanwhile the camaraderie the French showed the British after Yorktown aroused criticism from Americans, who resented the fraternizing between officers and gentlemen of the old order.

# 27

# *Defeat*

To many, Yorktown signalled the decisive American triumph. It was certainly the turning point. Cornwallis's bitterness was not entirely ill-founded in terms of the battle itself, which had involved relatively minor casualties, with 156 killed and 326 wounded on the British side and 75 killed and 200 wounded on the French and American side. But more than 8,000 troops had surrendered – double the number at Saratoga – in a humiliation for the British army almost without parallel.

Lord North took the news 'like a bullet in his breast', exclaiming, 'It is all over.' George III, on hearing of the surrender, showed greater aplomb and sense of proportion: 'I have no doubt when men are a little recovered of the shock felt by the bad news, and feel that if we recede no one can tell to what a degree the consequence of this country will be diminished, that they will find the necessity of carrying on the war, though the mode of it may require alterations.'

North would be proved right. But at least three aspects of Yorktown made it a less straightforward conclusion to the war than it is usually portrayed.

First and foremost, it was the war's greatest strategic coup. The American and French co-ordination in moving with such precision to take advantage of the enemy's situation remains one of the greatest feats in military history. The real achievement had been the rapid march of the two allied forces across more than 400 miles of territory to trap Cornwallis; the action afterwards was an anticlimax.

Contrary to Cornwallis's view, Washington's dash to Yorktown was his most glorious military achievement, eclipsing Trenton and Princeton. Few armies have moved so far so fast – and in conjunction with another army. The culminating feat in a remarkable career, the march on Yorktown established Washington's greatness in the field. Knowing the territory well, he led the joint expedition all the way, as the French respectfully acknowledged.

The achievement showed him in his most attractive light: as in crossing the Delaware, he was capable of great feats of boldness and daring when he judged them appropriate. Washington had displayed caution bordering on inertia for year after year; then he had suddenly sprung at the decisive moment, to deliver a fatal blow to his enemy. This was leadership of the highest order, displaying self-control, patience, extraordinary good sense, and the rare ability to strike with lethal speed at exactly the right time. Moreover, to trap an enemy is arguably a greater achievement than to defeat him in open battle, which is what he achieved at Yorktown.

It was to Cornwallis's credit that he too saw no sense in unnecessary carnage and surrendered before lives were wasted – although the unpleasant precedent of Admiral Byng served to remind him how this might be regarded in Britain.

Yorktown was also a self-inflicted British defeat. In few battles (Saratoga was another) can one side have made so many mistakes in placing themselves at the mercy of the enemy. Cornwallis can be blamed for pushing up to Virginia and stopping within reach of the French and the Americans in the north, as well as for doing nothing to leave Yorktown as the danger of being trapped began to materialize. Yet it was Clinton who had first dispatched British forces to the area, under Benedict Arnold and William Phillips, and it was their armies, not Cornwallis's depleted band, that made up the bulk of the British army caught at Yorktown.

Cornwallis was also in error for submitting to Clinton's insistence that he confine himself to coastal Virginia and set up a naval base. Yet, relatively close to New York, it was difficult to disobey Clinton's orders with impunity. The choice of Yorktown was Cornwallis's, and ideal for the purpose intended.

Cornwallis also failed to display his usual initiative in not seeking to break out of the trap, relying instead on Clinton's promises and his own faith in British seapower. Perhaps exhausted by his long campaign, he for once displayed caution at just the wrong moment. But he had at least tried with energy, flair and intelligence: in marching into Virginia, his daring had been of an entirely different order from that of the swaggering Burgoyne.

Perhaps Cornwallis's finest hour was his surrender, realizing the imminence of defeat without shedding unnecessary blood. Cornwallis emerges, if not as a great commander, as humane, able, vigorous and realistic, if unlucky and flawed.

Neither of his co-commanders can escape with these qualified accolades. Graves had had the chance to rescue Cornwallis, and had flunked it. With a fleet almost as powerful as that of the French, he had thrown away his tactical superiority, and had shown excessive caution in refusing to engage the enemy thereafter, stupidity in failing to occupy Chesapeake Bay when he could, then further caution in returning to New York for reinforcements instead of going to Cornwallis's help. He abandoned a British army to its fate.

Clinton, as commander-in-chief, bears perhaps the greatest responsibility of all. Diffident, intelligent and complex, he had shown he could be a brave and resourceful leader in the field in his action on the Hudson in 1777, at the siege of Charleston, and at the Battle of Camden. But he was woefully lacking in leadership qualities, causing both Howe, his superior, and Cornwallis, his junior, to despise him for his inability to make up his own mind.

He proved hopeless at stamping his authority on the navy, incapable of persuading the independent and assertive Graves to do his bidding. Only during General William Howe's years as commander-in-chief had co-operation with the navy proved possible, because his brother Richard had then been in charge of the fleet. Graves had already made the well-meaning General Gage's life a misery, and he refused to co-operate at all with Clinton unless he chose to do so.

If courage and improvisation in an emergency are the real test of leadership, then Clinton singularly failed. His assessment of the consequences of every possible course of action was so thorough that it paralysed him almost completely. As a result he personally never lost a battle, but others were made to do so. His response to the prospect of the imminent loss of Britain's second army in America was not to rush to the rescue overland or to order Graves into an immediate maritime intervention, but to accede to the latter's cautious decision to engage only when the two sides were evenly matched, and to prepare his own men before sending them. As a result, they arrived too late.

Moreover, Clinton's jealousy had effectively paralysed Cornwallis's Virginia campaign, and ordering him to the coast had been instrumental in paving the way for the trap Cornwallis fell into. Cornwallis did what Clinton had asked, against his instincts, and was snared; and the latter failed to come to his help. So victory was delivered on a plate to the French and the Americans.

It is, of course, easy to fault individual commanders for failing to win the war they were being asked to fight, but their personal defects were exacerbated by a rush of events in which they were also victims of circumstance. Command and control remains the greatest bane in the conduct of modern warfare, where communications are virtually instant and key decision are taken at headquarters.

The tendency to centralize decision-making away from the commanders on the spot has, however, had one great benefit: co-ordination between different commanders. Its downside has been the tendency to take military decisions for political reasons. In Britain's war with the colonies, not only was there a delay of weeks before orders from London could reach the commanders; when decisions were made in Britain they were almost invariably wrong, because London had incredibly little knowledge of conditions on the ground.

Accordingly, Whitehall's role was limited to issuing general instructions and finding the men and equipment necessary to continuing the war effort – invariably too little and too late.

With London exercising no control over strategy, never mind tactics, it was up to loyal commanders to dictate both. In many ways this was a benefit, but in one conclusive respect it was disastrous – there was no co-ordination. For, if orders from Whitehall took weeks to reach the military commanders in America, it also took at least several days for intelligence and instructions to pass between the different commands. This gave the field commanders tactical authority – which was beneficial in some ways: had Cornwallis been forced to submit to Clinton's orders from New York throughout the southern campaign, this would surely have ended much sooner and even more disappointingly than it did. But it made strategic planning all but impossible. Clinton was unable to control Cornwallis until the last disastrous order to construct a naval base on the coast of Virginia, just as Howe had been unable to control Burgoyne. Worse, the navy regarded itself as independent, if not superior, to the army – which was reflected in the Admiralty's relationships with the Secretary of War back in Whitehall, and indeed with the rest of the Cabinet.

In this decentralized command structure, there was a serious danger of different commanders pursuing entirely separate campaigns and objectives – as happened in the chains of events leading both to Saratoga and to Yorktown. In addition, success depended largely on the commander in the field. Sometimes this worked out wonderfully – Generals Howe and Cornwallis at their best proved the point. Sometimes it was disastrous – as with Burgoyne, Clinton and Admiral Graves. Whatever their abilities, however, the lack of co-ordination between commanders was a major handicap.

The Americans suffered less from this problem, because Congress in Philadelphia was much closer than London, because its authority was much weaker, and above all because the commander-in-chief and the Continental Army were a much more centralized authority than the British commander in New York, with fewer American armies in the field and better internal communications.

Nevertheless, even Washington had perpetually to exert his authority, which was further challenged when the French entered the war: his allies looked on him with the paternal contempt of a major power in the Old World towards a group of disorganized rebels in the New, and initially plotted to replace him as commander-in-chief. He could win over the French only through charm and an appeal to common self-interest.

Although Washington certainly had a fatherly and mentor–protégé interest in Lafayette, it was surely more than that which led to the manner in which, on his arrival in Williamsburg just before the siege of Yorktown, this most reserved of men was embraced by the emotional young man, who 'caught the general round his body, hugged him close as it was possible, and absolutely kissed him from ear to ear once or twice … with as much ardour as ever an absent lover kissed his mistress on his return'. Modern writers might see an almost sexual attachment between the two men. More cynically, Washington sought to hold the French to the American cause in an iron grip, and his open affection for Lafayette was one way of achieving this. It was the American co-operation with the French in a rare joint operation that brought about the triumph at Yorktown.

Was Yorktown an American victory? The question at first sight seems absurd. Washington was the commander, and the majority of the troops eventually involved were American. Yet the plan to encircle Cornwallis's army at Yorktown was decided by the movement of de Grasse's fleet, not by Washington, who had been preparing to attack New York. Whether de Grasse made his choice on Rochambeau's recommendation or on his own initiative is not known. Almost certainly it was an inspired decision: a siege of New York, as Washington wanted, would probably have been a long and costly failure. Significantly, a siege of Yorktown was the policy being urged by Lafayette on the spot in Virginia.

It is not disputed that Washington decided, in close consultation with Rochambeau, to march south to Yorktown after hearing of de Grasse's intention to sail to Chesapeake Bay. But nor is it disputed that, until news of the destination of the French fleet arrived, it had been Washington's intention to besiege New York. The strategy that led to Yorktown was thus dictated by the French.

The American army that marched down from the north was slightly outnumbered (at least until reinforced in Virginia) by the French force, which was superior in terms of equipment, training, uniforms and discipline. Rochambeau, eight years older than Washington, was the more experienced officer, but both veterans had the good sense to co-operate as equals. Certainly the rapid movement of Washington's troops showed them at their best, and the French had difficulty keeping up – though in Europe the French were no strangers to rapid marches across long distances, as Napoleon's campaigns would soon show. At the Head of Elk, French transports ferried the troops across to Williamsburg, where they joined an army commanded by a Frenchman, Lafayette, reinforced by 3,000 French troops under Saint-Simon. Indeed, French regulars outnumbered American regulars at Yorktown; only the presence of Virginia's militia tipped the balance in the American's favour.

The siege equipment was French, the military engineers were largely French, the artillerymen mostly French, the artillery which wrought so much devastation largely French, and, as it happened, the French had the worst fighting in seizing the most bitterly defended British redoubt – although this was accidental, and not for want of Americans willing to do so. The siege was conducted along almost entirely classical French lines, under Rochambeau's direction; Washington, in overall charge, lacked the experience to plan it in detail and was happy to delegate, while performing ceremonial functions and always urging haste.

Most important of all, victory at Yorktown was made possible only by the French fleet which had gained control of Chesapeake Bay and sealed the fate of the British army by preventing the British fleet from lifting off Cornwallis's men or reinforcing or resupplying them. If the French sailors are added to the French land forces, Yorktown can be seen as overwhelmingly a land and sea battle between the French and the British, with the Americans playing a supporting role.

Without the Americans, the French would probably have won none-theless. Without the French, the Americans would certainly have lost – indeed, there would probably never have been a siege at all. If Yorktown was the victory that secured American independence, it was also the only battle (apart from the naval engagements) won largely by the French.

Until Yorktown, the cause of independence had been languishing. The French defeat of the British at Yorktown handed the keys of freedom to their allies, although they did not at first realize it. Thus the United States was born, five years after the Declaration of Independence, by the old-fashioned defeat of one colonial power by another. The revolutionary Americans were handed their independence from the parliamentary government of England by the absolutist mon-archy of Louis XVI.

Yorktown was the last battle between colonial powers on North American soil, and was a sweet revenge by the French for the humilia-tion inflicted by Pitt during the Seven Years War a quarter of a century earlier – although the British were to have the last laugh with the violent overthrow of the French monarchy just eight years later, owing in good measure to the expense of the war and America's revolutionary example.

The Americans had not won their independence in six long years of war. At Yorktown the French stepped in and gave it to them. Neither Rochambeau nor Washington can have missed the deliberate irony with which O'Hara had attempted to surrender to the Frenchman.

Although in retrospect the turning point, Yorktown was not itself a decisive military defeat; the war went on. But Yorktown was decisive in tipping the scales in London between a peace party that had been stead-ily gaining in strength and the war party which had so palpably failed to deliver a convincing victory in the colonies. Although they could have carried on, the British decided to give up major offensive operations after a major setback, because they foresaw no possibility of bringing the war to a successful conclusion.

This is an important distinction. They had never thrown all their resources into the American War, preferring to fight it on the cheap, and now they were unable to do so because they were engaged in a global conflict. They could hang on indefinitely – and did so for a while. But Yorktown was the deciding factor in persuading them eventually to give up.

# 28

# *The Diplomatic War*

Because the struggle in the colonies had been subsumed into a wider war between the British, the French and the Spanish, Yorktown was not in fact the end of the war, as is commonly assumed today. The British stayed on defensively in America, and the Americans could not dislodge them – particularly without major help from their French allies. The reason why the British lingered was that they believed the fate of the colonies would be determined by the outcome of the wider war: just as their gravest defeat in America had been inflicted by their old enemy, so a British defeat of the French elsewhere might enable them to keep the colonies. While realizing that they could not now subjugate all of America, the British were confident that only the French could drive them from the continent altogether, and in the past their European rival had shown a marked reluctance to contribute the necessary men and resources. So the outcome in America would have to hang on the resolution of the global battle. That at any rate was the thinking of the government in Whitehall.

Early in 1781, during the long campaign in the Carolinas, with an indefinite stalemate in prospect, France had actually tried to broker a settlement in which each side retained the territory it occupied. The French might conceivably have been able to impose this on their reluctant American allies; but George III flatly refused to contemplate any such agreement. After Yorktown the Americans would brook no agreement that did not recognize the independence of all thirteen colonies and a complete British withdrawal.

After Yorktown, the French considered they had achieved their secondary war aim of weakening Britain by depriving it of a pillar of its empire. The French gamble in going to war with Britain had been a costly mistake, as they had realized. Their unrealistic ambition of staging an invasion of the British mainland had fizzled out. In India and the West Indies, expensive campaigns had proved inconclusive. Only in America, after two frustrating years, had they achieved a dramatic success which would justify the expensive and largely fruitless conflict; they now wanted to settle, and believed that their grateful American allies should do so on French terms. But there were two major obstacles: first, their allies the Spanish did not want to make peace without acquiring major gains in north America's deep south, and without winning their great objective of Gibraltar; and, second, the Americans themselves, influenced by Yorktown, would settle only on terms overwhelmingly stacked in their favour.

The British had lost their second army in America. But the British northern army was still intact in New York; and Britain still held Wilmington, Charleston and Savannah, with around 8,000 soldiers dispersed between them. The loss of Yorktown had strategically ruled out a major offensive in Virginia and Philadelphia – but that had been unlikely anyway. Washington certainly did not regard the war as over. He wrote:

> My only apprehension (which I wish may be groundless) is lest the late important success ... should produce such a relaxation in the prosecution of the war, as will prolong the calamities ... Yorktown was an interesting event that may be productive of much good if properly improved ... My greatest fear is that Congress will fall into a state of languor and relaxation.

He dispatched his army under Benjamin Lincoln to the north, to shadow the British army in New York. The Comte de Grasse meanwhile departed with his fleet for the West Indies, leaving the British back in control of the sea, although Rochambeau remained with his troops on the American mainland, and Greene was modestly reinforced in the south. But in one sense Washington's apprehension was unfounded, for, although the British had no intention of giving up yet, they had abandoned any idea of an offensive war. The positions they held in America were valuable pawns to be traded in the diplomatic negotiations that would end the war with France and Spain, and were not to be yielded lightly.

The real impact of the defeat at Yorktown was on public opinion in Britain. The King wanted to fight on, as did his supporters. But neither Parliament nor the electorate would let him. Britain, unlike the minority revolutionary government in America, or France, run by an absolutist central monarchy, had a constitutional system under which the government was ultimately responsible to Parliament, which, for all the corruption and jobbery, was responsible to its voters and to public opinion; and the three million or so Britons who made up the influential electorate at the time were by now deeply disillusioned with the war and fed up with paying for it.

Three months after the news of Yorktown reached Britain in late November 1781, the House of Commons curbed the King by voting that anyone who sought to prosecute an offensive war with the colonies was an enemy – thus confining Britain to defence of the posts it already held. A week later Lord North was dismissed and was replaced by the great Whig grandee the Marquess of Rockingham, who had presided over the retreat from the Stamp Act – the symbol, after Chatham, of British internal opposition to the war in America. However, Rockingham, whom the King detested, was now elderly and infirm, and the real power in the new government lay with the Earl of Shelburne, the Home Secretary, whose main rival in the ministry was the brilliant and irresponsible Charles James Fox, in charge of negotiations with the French. Shelburne was a 'dove': he did not favour American independence, but he was prepared to be conciliatory, which was the best the King could hope for. Lord Germain fell in 1782, and the King was a spent force who seriously considered abdication.

Despite the fall of North, prospects for peace were anything but promising. Shelburne sent an elderly Scottish sympathizer with the American cause to Paris to meet with Benjamin Franklin and sound out the prospects for a separate peace between Britain and America, leaving the French to one side. Franklin said this was out of the question.

Soon afterwards the much more authoritative and astute Thomas Grenville, son of George Grenville, arrived in Paris as Fox's representative, bringing specific proposals which included, for the first time, the offer of independence, on borders reverting to those at the end of the Seven Years War. Franklin rejected these terms on the grounds that America should be recognized as independent before any negotiations could begin. The real reason was that the French were incensed that they were to gain no territory in exchange for their efforts on the Americans' behalf.

A complex three-sided diplomatic battle began, in which the British tried to drive a wedge between the Americans and the French, the French sought territory as a reward for helping the Americans, and the

Americans sought the best possible deal from the British while wriggling out of their obligations to the French, who had won the war for them.

Franklin wanted Canada incorporated into the United States – a prospect which horrified the French, who believed Canada had been stolen from them and who relished an overmighty United States no more than an overmighty Britain in North America. The French also wanted the rich fishing rights in the waters extending fifty yards off Newfoundland and Nova Scotia which they had kept after the Seven Years War and which the Americans now coveted. The French also sought to protect the interests of their allies the Spaniards, who, as well as gaining control of Florida and New Orleans, wanted a huge swath of territory east of the Mississippi while the Americans wanted to retain all the land up to the Mississippi.

Having delivered Yorktown to the Americans, the French were in a strong position to prevent any double-crossing by their allies. Their highly capable minister in Philadelphia, the Chevalier La Luzerne, generously bribed congressmen to secure his country's interests. John Adams, implacably uncorrupt and determined to reassert his country's interests, arrived in Paris to try to offset Franklin's overcosy relationship with the French Foreign Minister, the Comte de Vergennes, but was snubbed by the French.

After Yorktown, the Americans were overambitious and the French overpatronising and determined to make the most of their advantage, as were the Spanish. The British, while willing to concede independence, would not do so at any price. They spotted an opportunity in this falling-out between allies, and pressed both sides separately for peace. Meanwhile they showed no sign of withdrawing from America.

France's hubris was soon curbed. In early 1782 Rodney returned to command of the British fleet, to find the French and Spanish planning a giant expedition of 35 warships with 150 troop and supply ships, to seize Jamaica. Rodney set off in pursuit with 35 warships and decisively defeated the French and the Spanish, who called off the invasion. De Grasse – the man most responsible for Britain's loss of the American colonies – was taken prisoner, and was shipped back to England.

This stunning naval victory, six months after Yorktown, sobered the French, and secret negotiations with the British soon confirmed their objections to American claims on the Newfoundland fisheries and Canada. In turn the Americans, learning of these secret talks and fearing they would be abandoned by the French, became more amenable: they dropped their 'minimum demands' and insisted on the single precondition of recognition of their independence. They had become uneasily aware that Britain remained a great power and that the French were as capable of duplicity as themselves. Worse, the French were supporting exorbitant demands on the south by Spain, which still refused to recognize American independence.

John Jay, who had replaced the ailing Benjamin Franklin as America's chief negotiator, signalled America's abandonment of its commitment to make no separate peace without the French. Within ten months the alliance climaxing in the glory of the victory at Yorktown had collapsed. Jay sent a secret emissary to the new British Prime Minister, Shelburne, who had taken office in July, after Rockingham's death, and who agreed to negotiate with 'the Thirteen United States' – a compromise between the formula acceptable to George III, 'the thirteen united provinces', and the name of independent America, 'the United States'.

Once this semantic difficulty was overcome, Jay proposed a draft treaty – as always, overly ambitious, demanding control over the fisheries and a large part of Canada, although the imperialistic American claim to all of that country was dropped. But the British, while anxious to separate the Americans from the French, were no longer feeling so humble. After the naval successes in the West Indies the previous April, news had just arrived of the most stunning victory yet in the war with France and Spain, which at last permitted Britain to reach an honourable settlement with the two Continental powers.

In July 1779, after Spain had joined the war against Britain, Gibraltar had come under seige. In 1782 a massive Franco-Spanish assault on the fortress failed, and in 1783 the longest continuous siege in history was lifted. News of the failed Franco-Spanish assault reached the British just as John Jay submitted his draft treaty. The British promptly stiffened their terms, flatly refusing to cede land north of the old border with Canada and insisting that the Americans pay their national pre-war debt to the British and compensate the loyalists for their seized property. The Americans were forced to agree to these terms, and their northern frontier was established along the line of the Great Lakes. The Americans slyly gave responsibility for compensating the loyalists to the state governments, which were highly unlikely to do anything of the kind; but this satisfied the British, who in turn promised to waive the pre-war debts.

More satisfyingly, the Americans were granted the lands east of the Mississippi in the south – a British concession calculated to cheat the Spaniards – and the British and Americans also agreed to joint navigation rights down the great river at the expense of the Spaniards. Moreover, a secret protocol appended to the agreement entitled Britain to possession of Florida if it should seize the peninsula from Spain – an open invitation to do so.

The British ceded Minorca but insisted on retaining Gibraltar as well as their right to regain Florida for the moment. On 20 July 1783 the preliminary articles of peace were agreed upon, and on 3 September the final articles were signed at the Treaty of Paris. The first article began, 'His Britannic Majesty acknowledges the said United States to be free, sovereign and independent states.' The long road had ended: the United States had become a country, free at last.

Why had Britain conceded independence? There was no pressing necessity to do so. The British retained two considerable armies in America, and, with the war going favourably for them first in the Caribbean and then at Gibraltar, they might soon have been in a position to reinforce their strength in the colonies.

The answer is simple: the war had from the first been controversial, expensive, unpopular and opposed by a large section of the British establishment and public opinion. The spectacle of British troops fighting their American kin pleased very few. The war had drained British resources and, worse, had brought the country to the threshold of real danger – possible defeat by the French, taking advantage of the haemorrhage of resources across the Atlantic, and the threat of invasion.

The war had taken an appalling toll in casualties, arms and expense. With up to 100,000 men having served in America at some time over the previous eight years, and around 30,000 at the war's height, some 10,000 British soldiers had been killed and around 15,000 taken prisoner. For a country with a population of around 10 million, this was proportionately as many Americans as were to serve in Vietnam two centuries later, and a casualty rate nearly three times as high.

The British government was also increasingly conscious of the dangers of national bankruptcy. The national debt had reached a dizzying £240 million in 1783 – three times as much as a quarter of a century earlier – costing some £9.4 million annually to service.

On the American side, out of a population of 3 million, maybe as many as 120,000 had served under arms – some 30,000 at the height of the war – and maybe 15,000 were killed (8,000 in action, 7,000 as prisoners of war in appalling conditions) and a further 8,000 died of disease – a staggeringly high proportion of the population.

Several British bishops had joined the humanitarian outcry against the war, including the bishops of Peterborough, Exeter and St Asaph. In a then celebrated novel, *Emma Corbett*, published by Samuel Jackson Pratt in 1780, its heroine is torn between her brother on the American side and her lover, a British officer. Thomas Day penned protest verses – the 'Where Have All the Flowers Gone' of his day – telling of

> The cries of wretched mothers, that in vain
> Lament their fate, and mourn their children slain;
> The virgin's shriek, who trembling in the dust,
> Weeps the pollution of a ruffian's lust;
> The mangled infant's wail, that as he dies,
> Looks up in vain for pity to the skies.

The view had gained currency that the colonies had been quasi-independent before 1775, and that it was futile to seek to keep them against their wishes. Let the mother country be shot of these troublesome people, who would lose the benefits of British protection with independence, but would still have to trade with Britain. It was Britain that stood to gain from the shedding the burden of responsibility for these difficult and ungrateful cousins.

Thus, like America in Vietnam, Britain withdrew out of weariness at fighting an unwinnable war, after lingering on for more than a year and a half. In negotiating the peace, the Americans naturally sought the best possible deal for themselves without regard for principle or for their debts to others. In cutting the French out of the final deal and negotiating directly with the British, they infuriated the ally who had delivered them Yorktown. In riding roughshod over Spanish interests, they angered another powerful ally.

The British, who retained Canada, watched with wry amusement as the Americans behaved with exactly the same cussed self-interest towards their closest allies as they had towards the British themselves years before – and only shortly after the victory at Yorktown. The newly independent United States was now more than happy to treat with its fellow English-speaking Protestant enemies and dash the hopes of its Catholic Latin allies. When Vergennes bitterly protested to Franklin, the old rogue responded by apologizing for the oversight in not consulting him, and by hoping that so small a matter would not come between their two countries. As throughout the struggle, the Americans displayed a brilliant, if ruthless, understanding of the realities of power, and their own self-interest. No card player played a more skilful hand, often with very few cards.

One of the darkest and least researched corners of the American Revolution was the treatment of the loyalists, and the coercion practised against them after the war. They formed no small section of the population. The War of Independence, as we have seen, was not a great popular movement uniting the American people. The rebels were almost certainly a minority in every major city – especially in New York and Philadelphia, and even in Boston, although these were the capitals of the states with the most revolutionary sympathizers. But the rebels were probably a majority in the countryside of New England, and certainly so in Rhode Island, which was reflected in the ease with which militia could be assembled there, maddeningly undisciplined and averse to authority though they might be.

In New York and Philadelphia most rebels were essentially populist and anti-establishment, with a few well-heeled exceptions, but they were in a small minority. In Virginia, uniquely, a significant part of the gentry supported the war; but they were far from constituting a majority among their peers, and were partly motivated by resentment at the limits the British sought to impose on their prospects in the west, and by rivalry with New York.

In the southern states, the gentry were initially pro-British; but feeling themselves abandoned by the mother country during the first few years of the war, and intimidated by gangs of backwoodsmen, their consensus split, and eventually a purely survivalist ethic took over. In the west the settlers were unsurprisingly anti-British and anti-Indian, with a few exceptions.

The American War of Independence was, in many ways, a quintessentially middle-class, or in Marxist terms, 'bourgeois' revolution; the rising of a new, tough and numerous middle class against a staid propertied class (although this could hardly be described as feudal). It is hard to gauge how many were actively on the British side in the American War of Independence. Probably the great majority preferred the status quo of a settled social order, but this is very different from asserting that they actually favoured (largely nominal) British rule over rule by their own government.

What is clear is that at least 100,000 people so actively identified with the cause of American independence that they passed through the ranks as militia or regular soldiers; and that, on the loyalist side, at least 30,000 were sufficiently motivated to serve with British troops. Also a staggering 80,000–100,000 voted with their feet after the war and left their country, livelihoods and possessions for a precarious and often desperate exile in Canada, the West Indies or, for the lucky few, Britain rather than remain in rebel-dominated America.

The usual estimate of loyalist support is about 500,000 out of America's total population of 2,500,000. John Adams – hardly an independent observer – believed the true figure to be closer to 850,000 (a third of the population), while in New York Gouverneur Morris, a prominent member of the Committee of Safety and congressman, reckoned the loyalists to comprise at least half of the state's 180,000 people.

When figures such as these are added to the overwhelmingly pro-British majority of blacks and the Indian population, even by the admission of the revolutionary leaders nearly half the population was loyalist. It is probably fair to guess (without evidence) that some 200,000 Americans were strongly pro-rebel and some 200,000 strongly pro-British, with the remaining majority, whatever their subliminal sympathies, preferring not to take sides (excluding most of the blacks and the Indians, who had overwhelming reasons of self-interest to be pro-British).

One of the factors that determined loyalty was, of course, not enthusiasm but coercion, and in this the rebels had a distinct advantage. Apart from the few areas occupied by the British army, and where loyalist supporters held sway, such as New York and much of the south, in the largely unpoliticized American heartland the rebels and their guerrillas, spies and sympathizers were free to go about unchallenged, and to intimidate. From a very early stage the radicals understood the need to force ordinary people to support the American cause; their network of coercion vastly outstripped anything the British could muster.

Already in 1774, before the war, 'committees of safety and inspection' had come into being, noting the names of those who refused to serve in the militia, pay their dues to the states, or support levies, or who spoke out against the patriot cause. In New York a Committee and Commission for Detecting and Defeating Conspiracies was set up.

The Pennsylvania legislature passed a brutal measure providing extreme penalties for certain specified severe offences of helping the enemy, whereby estates could be forfeited and imprisonment imposed for 'treason, including every or any resistance to the government, stirring up tumults or opposing revolutionary acts'. No fewer than 500 people were stripped of their property in Pennsylvania alone.

Loyalists who fled as the revolution advanced had their property seized, although the families they left behind were entitled to a third of their estates after all debts had been settled. In many cases tenants were given the first right to buy from 'Tories' whose properties were seized. The threat of seizure of property was enough to drive into submission many loyalists and their families, who went in fear of expressing their opinions, let alone urging resistance or rallying to the British cause, even when the British had control of their territory. Against the threat of imprisonment or dispossession, and comparatively rarely the death penalty, the British were in no position to compete with their political opponents.

Even so, 80,000–100,000 or so carried their hatred – or fear – of the American Revolution to the extent of uprooting themselves from the land they loved and the properties they owned: the equivalent of about 8 million of today's Americans abandoning their homes in fear and resentment against their country's system of government. The exodus was a massive expression of hatred for the new dispensation.

# PART V

*Revolution and Counter-Revolution*

# 29

# The Revolution Gathers Speed

The War of Independence had been a long and terrible struggle – far more arduous and bloody than is popularly imagined. One out of every 200 Americans had perished. Every life had been disrupted. Trade with the rest of the world had mostly collapsed – although it still thrived, and relative prosperity continued, where Britain remained in control during the war. Commerce had been widely interrupted, and crops had gone unplanted for years. Food was desperately scarce. While the war raged, soldiers on both sides had pillaged, and scavengers and outlaws had followed in their wake. In the south, a savage internecine civil war and the settling of private scores had become commonplace. To the west, the aftermath of the Indian massacres still lingered, as did every kind of lawlessness.

In 1783 it seemed too that the American Revolution, suspended through the arduous years of war, was about to be resumed. Now that the foundation of the Establishment, the British Crown, had been removed, the new nation was a ragbag of competing authorities.

The first and strongest of these was Washington's Continental Army, but it could not be in more than a few places at the same time. The Continentals, the regulars, had taken control from the class warriors, the militias, earlier in the war, although this flouted the spirit of the Revolution, which had been primarily a revolt against central authority, and in particular the British professional army. But the change had been rendered inevitable by the need to win the war, although Washington was well aware of the implications of setting up a standing army in America – something barely tolerated even in Britain.

The militias, wildly fluctuating in numbers, assembled from among the hundreds of thousands of Americans who possessed guns in their backyards, represented a loose kind of local police force in an otherwise lawless land, usually at the bidding of individual states. Their members tended to return to their families in winter or to look after their crops in season, and they mostly regarded themselves as subordinate to the elected state assemblies which took the day-to-day decisions for each of the thirteen states, and also administered the system of justice there.

Under the Articles of Confederation, which were very different from the subsequent American constitution, the states had primacy over Congress. The states had provided the essential backbone of government and authority throughout the war – although parts of America, in particular the Carolinas and the West, had degenerated into near-anarchy – and they administered justice brutally and vindictively where the loyalists were concerned.

Twice conservatives in Congress had tried to draft a constitution which gave Congress real central power – first under Benjamin Franklin and Silas Deane, and then under John Dickinson. Twice Congress had rejected the proposals, and in November 1777 had approved one set of Articles of Confederation, which again rejected congressional control for that of the states: 'Each state retains its sovereignty, freedom, and independence and every power, jurisdiction and right, which is not for this confederation expressly delegated to the United States, in congress assembled.'

In all this, Congress, the supreme authority of the American Revolution, was almost impotent. Its chief function was to co-ordinate the efforts of the states and to act as a debating forum for constitutional issues. Washington's army was supposed to derive its mandate from Congress; but, although he looked to it to raise money and troops – which he considered it did appallingly – and accepted its authority to nominate commanders, he ran his command almost autonomously.

Congress, while issuing paper money in huge quantities, had no power to tax, but depended on the states to do so. The war is estimated to have cost America some $160 million. The states raised money largely for their own purposes, however, and refused to send it on to Congress, which thus simply became a major engine of inflation. Congress could not afford to pay the army, except with paper. By the end of 1779 it had committed more than $200 million. When it issued recruiting calls, it had to rely on the states to carry them out, and by the end of the war its authority was almost non-existent. Washington was effectively a warlord, taking his own decisions, and the commander-in-chief himself bitterly criticized Congress for profiteering and inertia.

The states bitterly clung to their authority to raise money and men, frustrating Congress's purpose in creating a united nation. Britain, first as ruler then as enemy, had provided the unity for thirteen colonies dispersed across a vast land, but now this binding factor was gone.

Two dangers loomed: national disintegration, in a country with barely any common sense of nationhood, or the seizure of power by the military. (Half a century later the same dangers were to face the newly independent republics of South America – and in confronting them they took a wrong turning from which they never recovered.)

At first, dictatorship and martial law seemed the bigger threat. The long-serving, hardened men who had won the War of Independence gazed with contempt upon the shambles of authority throughout America. Moreover, they had a colossal grievance. They had been lured into a long and terrible campaign on promises, and it was immediately apparent that Congress could not deliver. Most were owed some six years' back pay; they had given up the best years of their lives to creating the nascent republic, and had received little in return, with Congress even going back on its pledge to give them half pay for the rest of their lives.

It could only promise again to seek to raise the money from the states, who had no interest in subsidizing the Continental Army, which was a threat to their authority. The officer corps was accordingly in a state of near-insurrection.

In May 1782, Washington had already been urged by one of his commanders, Colonel Lewis Nicola, to seize power in place of the ineffectual Congress and the grasping and divisive states and then make himself king. Nicola in fact was part of a wide conspiracy, supported by the toughest and most influential business figure in America – Robert Morris from Philadelphia, the Superintendent of Finance for the states, a wealthy merchant of enormous drive and a habit of confusing his own interests with those of the state – and by Alexander Hamilton, Washington's headstrong, brilliant aide and, indeed, heir apparent, although one who famously on occasion fell out with his mentor. Behind them loomed the disgraced, restless, still ambitious figure of Horatio Gates. Washington slapped down the proposal indignantly:

With a mixture of surprise and astonishment I have read [your proposal] which to me seems big with the greatest mischiefs that can befall my country. If I am not deceived in myself, you could not have found a person to whom your schemes were more disagreeable ... Let me conjure you then if you have any regard for your country, for yourself, or prosperity, or respect for me to banish these thoughts from your mind, and never communicate, as from yourself, or any one else, a sentiment of like nature.

Seven months later, in the grip of winter once again, these mutterings overflowed into open mutiny. The army petitioned Congress on pay on 1 January 1783, and urged Generals Greene and Knox to move on the capital. Washington retaliated at a mass meeting in Newburgh on 15 March. He spoke with passion and eloquence, urging Americans

to rely on the lighted faith of your country, and place a full confidence in the purity of the intentions of Congress ... And let me conjure you, in the name of our common country, as you value your own sacred honor, as you respect the rights of humanity, and as you regard the military and national character of America, to express your utmost horror and detestation of the man who wishes, under any specious pretences, to overturn the liberties of our country, and who wickedly attempts to open the flood gates of civil discord, and deluge our rising empire in blood.

Finally he commented as he fumbled to put on his spectacles to read a letter, 'I have already grown grey in the service of my country, I am now going blind.'

He was rapturously received. It was a gesture of theatricality and pure statesmanship. But he had pacified the officers only momentarily.

Meanwhile, with the threat of armed revolt simmering behind him, he implored Congress to redress his men's grievances. If his men were 'to grow old in poverty, wretchedness and contempt; if they are to wade through the vile mire of dependency and owe the miserable remnant of that life to charity which has hitherto been spent in honor, then shall I have learned what ingratitude is, then I shall have realised a tale which will embitter every moment of my future life'. Congress grudgingly agreed to convert the promise of half pay for life into full pay for four years – although, without the power to tax, it remained unclear how it would obtain the funds.

Thoroughly alarmed by this confrontation, Congress insisted on disbanding the Continental Army now that the British threat had gone. Washington, fearful of plunging the country into renewed fighting, and a genuine constitutionalist at heart, reluctantly went along with this, but insisted on remaining in charge of a reduced force to shadow the British troops still in New York, Detroit and Niagara. The demobilization began in April 1783, and was completed by the end of October. However, he modified his careful respect for civilian rule with a warning. He declared in effect that Americans were on political probation:

> This is the moment when the eyes of the whole world are turned upon them; this is the moment to establish or ruin their national character forever; this is the favourable moment to give such a tone to our federal government as will enable it to answer the ends of its institution; or this may be the ill-fated moment for relaxing the powers of the union, annihilating the cement of the confederation and exposing us to become the sport of European politics, which may play one state against another, to prevent their growing importance and to serve their own interested purposes. For, according to the system of policy the states shall adopt at this moment, they will stand or fall; and by their confirmation or lapse it is yet to be decided whether the Revolution must ultimately be considered as a blessing or a curse – a blessing or a curse, not to the present age alone, for with our fate will the destiny of unborn millions be involved.

He set out his own blueprint for success:

> First, an indissoluble union of the states under one federal head. Secondly, a sacred regard to public justice (that is, the payment of debts). Thirdly, the adoption of a proper peace establishment (that is, an army, and a navy). Fourthly, the prevalence of that pacific and friendly disposition among the people of the union, which will influence them to forget their local prejudices and policies; to make those mutual concessions, which are requisite to the general prosperity; and, in some instances, to sacrifice their individual advantages to the interest of the community. These are the pillars on which the glorious future of our independency and national character must be supported.
>
> Certain I am that unless adequate powers are given to Congress for the general purposes of the federal union that we shall soon moulder into dust and become contemptible in the eyes of Europe, if we are not made the sport of her politics ... To suppose that the general concerns of this country can be directed by thirteen heads, or one head without competent powers, is a solecism, the bad effects of which every man who has had the practical knowledge to judge from that I have, is fully convinced of; though none perhaps has felt them in so forcible a degree.

\*

Little short of a personal political manifesto, this amounted to a warning that the revolution now gathering pace would not be allowed to get out of control. Just as Washington and the other moderates had seized the reins of revolution in 1775–6 and channelled them against the British, now he was signalling that the patience of the American conservative establishment which had supported independence against the now ousted loyalist gentry was not limitless.

Much of what he said was anathema to most states and to many radical congressmen. The Revolution's underlying principle had been a loose association of states, reflecting their diversity; but he was advocating a centralized system along British lines. The states' right to issue paper currency had been a central dispute with the British; yet here he was advocating sound money. His proposal for a standing army and navy was a shock for American revolutionaries whose principal argument with the British had been the dispatch of a standing army to America. His final call was a thinly veiled appeal for strong government against the rugged tradition of American individualism and the disparate self-interest of the states.

Many in Congress were furious with this 'unsolicited obtrusion of his advice', which in their eyes amounted to the substitution of an American-born tyranny for a British one, and were deeply suspicious of the motives of this new George. But the carefully considered words clearly marked an attempt by Washington to formulate a coherent, yet constitutionalist, programme which would defuse the putschist tendencies of men like Morris and Hamilton.

With the foresight and patience that had made him so effective a commander of the American army, Washington was beginning to exercise the statesmanship that made him truly great. He had channelled his officers' impatience into a coherent political programme – but he knew that it was far too early to intervene to seize power without risk of civil war and failure. The Revolution must be allowed to dash itself on the rocks before he could act decisively. He abdicated, with the well-orchestrated mixture of sobriety and panache that were his trademarks and were to establish him as a selfless American Cincinnatus.

On 25 November 1783 he presided over the departure of the last British troops from New York with a massive fireworks display on Broadway. On 4 December he entertained his old comrades-in-arms to a banquet and, with all present crying, bade them farewell. A colonel present recalled that:

Such a scene of sorrow and weeping I had never before witnessed and hope I may never be called upon to witness again ... The simple thought that we were then about to part from the man who had conducted us through a long and bloody war, and under whose conduct the glory and independence of our country had been achieved, and that we should see his face no more in this world, seemed to me utterly insupportable.

On 23 December it was the turn of an uneasy and hostile Congress to say goodbye, and Washington gave up his sword to his old enemy Thomas Mifflin, its president, an incompetent Quartermaster General whom the commander-in-chief had dismissed and who may have conspired against him with Conway years before. Trembling with emotion, Washington declared, 'Having now finished the work assigned me, I retire from the great theatre of action; and bidding an affectionate farewell to this august body under whose orders I have so long acted, I here offer my commission, and take my leave of all the employments of public life.'

Mifflin, in a cool statement prepared by Jefferson, wished him well on his retirement:

Called upon by your country to defend its invaded rights, you accepted the sacred charge before it had formed alliances and while it was without funds, or a government to support you. You have conducted the great military contest with wisdom and fortitude, invariably regarding the rights of the civil power, through all the disasters and changes. You have, by the love and confidence of your fellow citizens, enabled them to display their martial genius, and transmit their fame to posterity. You have persevered until these United States have been enabled, under a just Providence, to close the war in freedom, safety, and independence ... but the glory of your virtues will not terminate with your military command – it will continue to animate remote ages ... And for you, we address to Him our earnest prayers that a life so beloved may be fostered with all His care; that your days may be happy, as they have been illustrious; and that He will finally give you that reward which this world will not give.

With Martha, Washington left Annapolis, Maryland, where Congress was sitting, the following morning, reaching Mount Vernon at dusk on Christmas Eve.

Few were fooled. The country's saviour was holding himself in reserve; and Congress was on probation to provide effective government – or he would return. Meanwhile, with a faultless political touch, he affected a life of homespun simplicity. He wrote to George Clinton, governor of

New York, 'The scene is at last closed. I feel myself eased of a load of public care. I hope to spend the remainder of my days in cultivating the affections of good men and in the practice of the domestic virtues.'

To Lafayette he declared:

> At length, my dear Marquis, I am become a private citizen on the banks of the Potomac, and under the shadow of my own vine and my own fig tree, free from the bustle of the camp, and the busy scenes of public life. I have not only retired from all public employments, but I am retiring within myself, and shall be able to view the solitary walk and tread the paths of private life, with heartfelt satisfaction.

The new country was broke. That fact quite quickly became evident. The war had been fought on credit. In 1775 some $6 million had been issued in paper money; by 1783 some $200 million had been printed, almost all set nominally against promised state taxes. The states did indeed raise taxes – but spent the money themselves. Worse, they too printed money. Congress responded first by refusing to print more money, then by ordering the states to pay the troops themselves, and finally by repudiating the currency, declaring it to be worth one-fortieth of its old value. The states were given the job of issuing the new currency. Economic activity had fallen by nearly half in 1790 from its peak in 1772.

Robert Morris, along with two other advocates of firm central government, Alexander Hamilton and James Madison, a small, twenty-six-year-old dried-out intellectual with deep-rooted passions and a formidable intellect, now proposed a 5 per cent import duty to help stabilize public finance. The states, regarding this as an interference with their right to tax, dug in their heels so that three years after it was introduced only nine states had applied the duty, and the measure was quietly shelved.

Neither Congress's paper nor its promissory notes were worth anything to most Americans. But the states, which under the Articles of Confederation already had the sole power to tax, now had also acquired rights over monetary issue as well. Reformist governments had established themselves in both Virginia and New York. Jefferson, as governor of Virginia, had abolished primogeniture and pressed for universal public education. The radical George Clinton, who had ousted the conservative Philip Schuyler as governor of New York, fought the power of the big landlords. The composition of state legislatures changed radically: those with property of more than £5,000 now represented only around a fifth of legislators, compared with half before the war, while the number of old elite families represented had fallen by half.

Real poverty afflicted many regions. Only in the middle states of Pennsylvania, New York, New Jersey and Delaware did trade with the outside world pick up relatively quickly. In the north, trade in timber and ships collapsed with the disappearance of the British naval market, while whale oil and cod exports had also fallen off sharply; in the south, rice, indigo and tobacco exports were dramatically reduced as producers struggled to revive and export markets opened up only slowly.

In Massachusetts, birthplace of rebellion, conditions were particularly grim: the eastern merchants who controlled the legislature had imposed heavy taxes on the farmers in the interior, who had become seriously indebted. Their burden was sharper than when the British were in control, and an actual rebellion broke out in western Massachusetts when Daniel Shays, a veteran of Breed's Hill, broke up debtors courts in Worcester and Northampton and then, with 2,000 men, laid siege to Springfield, where there was a huge arsenal. There was a severe danger of such disorder spreading to other states, where the problems were as acute, if slightly different – with the collapse of currencies, creditors had lost their money while the mostly poorer debtors had benefited. The prosperous and conservative elements became convinced that the whole experiment in decentralized popular government had gone too far: the state legislators, dominated by the necessity of seeking a popular mandate, were not to be trusted with government or economic policy.

Almost as bad, the states, which had now elbowed aside the virtually impotent Congress, were quarrelling bitterly among themselves. Down south, the people living immediately east of the Mississippi threatened to join the Spanish Empire, feeling neglected by their own non-government. In Congress, the southern states continually quarrelled with the northern ones. Virginia, apparently magnanimously, agreed to give up the territories north-west of the Ohio – and then insisted that others do the same, in an obvious attempt to prepare for a new land grab in the area, angering its neighbour Maryland. However, Jefferson strongly opposed the proposal that new states be established to the west. For the most part, however, an unseemly land grab did occur as speculators and settlers rushed to seize territory from the Indians, viciously massacring or displacing those in their way. Congress feebly issued a North Carolina Ordinance to protect Indian territories, but it failed to curb these abuses.

Three years after the end of the War of Independence, populist state governments had effectively emasculated the powers of Congress and were busy levying taxes and printing money for corrupt short-term investments, while what was left of the old professional classes struggled to survive. The majority of these had seen their property confiscated and had gone into exile in a mass exodus of loyalists. A whole class had been overthrown, superseded in the states by a combination of corrupt political bosses and thrusting young business and land carpetbaggers.

The young Venezuelan political activist Francisco de Miranda, who visited the United States at this time, commented on the new mercenary spirit: 'Luxury, ostentation and a little vanity are the predominant figures in the character of those who now are called rich. Ten years ago a young man who wore silk stockings, breeches made of plain satin, and powdered his hair had not need of anything else to forfeit his "character" for ever. Today, they have all this, and more.' Property, not principle, he noted, ruled America – a bitter disappointment to a man who wanted, idealistically, to achieve the cause of the independence of his homeland.

The American Revolution was now in full swing, and the United States faced bankruptcy, poverty and fraction, just as the British had always predicted would be the case once the linchpin of their social order had been removed.

The next, inexorable, stage was to define the country's success for the next two centuries. A few clear-sighted men began to prepare for the counter-revolution. In so doing they would impose a system more centralized and efficient than anything the British had ever attempted, and which was to endure with astonishing success.

The process began in Virginia. At the controlling heart of Virginia society were some forty wealthy families, old and new, mostly deriving their fortunes from tobacco and wheat, farmed by slaves under their supervision. Born to wealth, the genteel, socially responsible Virginian elite dominated the House of Burgesses, with neither a powerful class of coastal merchants nor urban political bosses to contend with. There is no evidence that Washington was consulted, but he was inevitably closely connected to ensuing events in which the chief players were James Madison, who was one of Congress's brightest stars, and Edmund Randolph.

Their four principal non-Virginian allies were Robert Morris,

Alexander Hamilton, James Wilson from Philadelphia, a legal special-ist, and Gouverneur Morris, an eloquent and outstanding Congressman from New York. Two other non-Virginians were also to play an impor-tant role: John Adams and his cousin Samuel (who was now ailing in health) – the fathers of the original Massachusetts revolution.

The counter-revolution began quietly in 1785, when James Madison, prompted by a successful agreement over the land dispute between Maryland and Virginia reached at Mount Vernon, Washington's estate, was sent forth by the master to suggest that a meeting of the states be convened to discuss the innocuous subject of interstate commerce. This was sacrilege, since such a meeting would bypass Congress, which was supposed to be the appropriate forum. Five states – Virginia, New York, New Jersey, Pennsylvania and Delaware – attended this gathering in Annapolis, Maryland, in September 1786. (Maryland itself did not par-ticipate, out of deference to Congress.)

Less than four months later Congress itself agreed to summon a Constitutional Convention to meet in Philadelphia in May 1787. The Articles of Confederation, which had loosely guided the first few years of American self-government, desperately needed revision. With the vig-orous suppression of Shays's Rebellion in Massachusetts, brute force had become the basis of the new republic, and the founders gathered to enforce a new social order. To do this required the establishment of all the things that the supposedly uninvolved Washington had preached before his retirement in 1783: a centrally based national government with the power of taxation, a standing army, and the substitution of govern-ment by an elite for government by popular 'tyranny' – violating most of the principles for which that the Americans had nominally fought the British. The Revolution was to be unravelled, and now only the oppres-sors would be different – home-grown, as opposed to British – in a perfect example of a revolution turning full circle.

Almost certainly George Washington, with his immense authority and prestige, and his ability to raise and command an armed force if nec-essary, was the guiding spirit behind the counter-revolution. But, as a leader of immense subtlety, he preferred to leave the initiative to his sub-ordinates. He was at pains to remain behind the scenes, directing events. The constitution that emerged was to be a masterpiece of drafting, in which the elite crushed popular government behind a barrage of high-sounding and beautifully expressed sentiments proclaiming the reverse.

# 30

# *The Counter-Revolution*

The first to arrive at Philadelphia for the Convention were the Virginians, who met as a caucus before the others to draft their own plan. The witty and acerbic James Madison was the mind behind the new constitution. Washington self-deprecatingly wondered to Henry Knox 'whether my non-attendance in this convention will not be considered as dereliction to republicanism, nay more, whether other motives may not (however injuriously) be ascribed to me for not exerting myself on this occasion in support of it'. But he followed shortly afterwards, to take up his post as the venerated president of the Convention.

Thomas Jefferson, the brilliant Virginian lawyer and author of the Declaration of Independence as well as his own state's constitution – Washington's only rival on his home ground, but considered unacceptably liberal – was conveniently away in France. Edmund Randolph, the state governor, a worthy conservative, and George Mason, a close friend of Washington and another prominent conservative, also attended, as did George Wythe, a distinguished elderly lawyer and former mentor of Washington's.

Slowly the Virginians were joined by representatives from the other states. Just seven sent delegates initially, but by early June all were represented except anarchic Rhode Island and remote New Hampshire.

It was not in the interests of the radicals and the populists to have a constitution thrust upon them in their absence, for the Convention's composition was fiercely biased in favour of the new conservative elite. There were eight planters and farmers, some of them slave-owners, and some fifteen merchants or members of the commercial elite. No fewer than twenty-one were practising lawyers, and many more had legal training. There were no small farmers, no 'mechanicals', no representatives of the common people, no Indians, blacks or women. The delegates were self-appointed, not elected. The radical state leaders were not invited, their places at the Convention being taken by their opponents.

Thus in Pennsylvania Robert Morris, the self-made entrepreneur most detested by the radicals as effective leader of the opposition, was present, accommodating Washington in his splendid house and acting as his closest confidant. Benjamin Franklin, the grand old man of Pennsylvania politics – aged eighty-one, and failing at last – was also there. John Dickinson represented Delaware; his able but deeply conservative protégé James Wilson, who believed in order and the restriction of democracy, was another dominant figure. Gouverneur Morris was a powerful conservative New York ally to the Virginians.

New York, a radical heartland since the departure of the loyalist elite, sent only three delegates and, of those, only Alexander Hamilton, Washington's protégé, stayed behind after his fellow delegates walked out in disgust at the conservative slant of the Convention. Hamilton's views were so reactionary that they were largely ineffectual. Yet his influence in pressing for a national bank, for the development of industry, and for funding the national and states' debts was soon to be colossal. Massachusetts was conspicuous in sending no one of substance: Samuel Adams and John Hancock, who had started the revolution twelve long years before, ostentatiously boycotted the proceedings, and John Adams, absent in England, almost certainly shared their misgivings.

There was considerable resistance to the creeping putsch in Virginia itself – whose radical leader Patrick Henry stayed away – and in Massachusetts, New York, Pennsylvania, and North and South Carolina; there was outright hostility from both New Hampshire and Rhode Island. Only Delaware, New Jersey, Connecticut, Maryland and Georgia – all small states which had been pushed around by the bigger ones – were enthusiastic about the need for constitutional revision and a strong central government. Thus the great Convention of the founding fathers which drew up the American constitution that has endured to this day was in fact a small, tightly knit clique of self-appointed conservatives initially representing a minority of states.

The Pennsylvania radicals, who had drawn up the most populist constitution in the United States, were simply ignored. The 1776 Pennsylvania constitution had provided for only a single chamber: the general assembly was elected by all male taxpayers every year and was vastly more powerful than its president, council or the judiciary. An elected council of censors further shielded this arrangement from constitutional revision, and ordinary people were allowed to attend its meetings.

For the eighteenth century this was popular government indeed, and was even buttressed by a bill of rights. Strong opposition in the state came from a conservative Republican party in rivalry to the dominant radical Constitutionalists. In other states there was usually a second chamber, or senate, of some kind, although the popularly elected chamber predominated. Yet it was the conservatives in all states who attended the Constitutional Convention of 1787.

On 29 May Randolph had introduced to the Convention the Virginia Plan, largely drafted by Madison, almost certainly with Washington's approval if not at his instigation, based on Jefferson's constitution for Virginia. Jefferson, judged too radical to attend this assembly, had been no supporter of a senate alongside a single popularly elected second chamber: 'My observations do not enable me to say I think integrity the characteristic of wealth.'

Others preferred a senate composed of men of 'great property' chosen for life. Jefferson had written of government by popular assembly that the concentration of power 'is precisely the definition of despotic government' and that '173 despots would surely be as oppressive as one'. Afterwards, in 1781, Jefferson had also remarked gloomily:

> It can never be too often repeated, that the time for fixing every essential right on a legal basis is while our rulers are honest, and ourselves united. From the conclusion of this war we shall be going down hill. [The people of America] will be forgotten, therefore, and their rights disregarded.
>
> They will forget themselves, but in the sole faculty of making money, and will never think of uniting to effect a due respect for their rights. The shackles, therefore, which shall not be knocked off at the conclusion of this war, will remain on us long, will be made heavier and heavier, till our rights shall revive or expire in a convulsion.

Six years on, his prophecies had been borne out. Randolph, the aristocratic governor of Virginia, reflecting Madison's even more conservative thinking, set out the conservative blueprint, while ingenuously claiming he wanted only to correct and amend the existing constitution. Congress was to be divided into a two-house national legislature: a popularly elected House of Representatives, and a Senate indirectly elected by the states. Congress would in turn elect a national executive and judiciary with sweeping powers to legislate supposedly only where the states' interests were in conflict – which in practice was most of the time. The national legislature would be subordinate to a 'council of revision' consisting of the executive and senior judges.

It was a sweeping, if cumbersome and complex, proposal for centralized government – in effect reducing the powers of the states to those of local government. Clearly the executive would be powerful – more so than the British government, which for so long had ruled from far away through local state governors in practice appointed with the consent of the states.

The Virginia plan attracted two types of opposition. Most voluble were the smaller states, which stood to lose their autonomy to a government potentially dominated by the bigger ones; while the provisions for a strong government, powerful executive and indirectly elected second chamber antagonized the populist radicals.

With the latter underrepresented, the main argument at the Convention was with the small states. Most of these were natural conservatives, favouring the reimposition of authority, and hence potential allies for the Virginians. So the argument soon revolved around how the states should be represented in this more powerful central dispensation.

Both Wilson, a Scottish-born legal scholar with a taste for the good things in life, and Madison, the Convention's intellectual, were blunt in seeking to steamroller the small states. Wilson pointed out caustically that, if they had equal representation in Congress, seven states with a third of the American population could override six with two-thirds: 'Can we forget for whom we are forming? Is it for men, or for the imaginary beings called states? … The rule of suffrage ought on every principle to be the same in the second as in the first branch.'

Madison was even more acerbic. The states, he said, were only political:

> There is a gradation of power in all societies, from the lowest corporation to the highest sovereign. The states never possessed the essential rights of sovereignty. These were always vested in congress. The states are only great corporations, having the power of making by-laws, and these are effectual only if they are not contradictory to the general confederation. The states ought to be placed under the control of the general government – at least as much so as they formerly were under the King and British Parliament.

The smaller states refused to budge: Gunning Bedford of Delaware even hinted that they would seek foreign allies to defend their interests. Gouverneur Morris brutally retorted, 'The country must be united. If persuasion does not unite it, the sword will. The gallows and halter will finish the work of the sword.' This was the bluntest warning yet of the lengths to which the conservatives would go to impose their will: the counter-revolution would be imposed by force if necessary.

A compromise of sorts was proposed. The bigger states reluctantly accepted that all states should have equal representation in the upper house of Congress – the Senate. In addition, the upper house representatives would be nominated by the state legislatures, not by the lower house, as under Jefferson's constitution for Virginia. The lower house – the House of Representatives – would be elected by popular vote alone, each state being represented in proportion to its population. The bigger states would thus be dominant – with one important modification. Allowing for precedent set in the south, under which five slaves would count as three freemen for taxation purposes, the southern states' support for the new deal was bought with the unsavoury compromise that, although blacks had no rights, least of all to vote, each would count as three-fifths of a white in population terms, to bolster the standing of the southern states in the union. This bargain was agreed on 16 July by a narrow margin.

The argument now moved on to the new executive. Hamilton made a passionate speech in favour of an elective monarchy, which was clearly designed to advance the interests of his old boss, Washington. Others argued for an elected executive with a fixed term of office. The Virginia cabal argued in favour of a popularly elected president, partly because they felt this would endow the office with the necessary authority, and partly because it would strengthen the power of the populous states. Also, popular legitimacy would provide an excuse for strong government – their chief concern – and they were certain Washington would win.

On this matter, for once they were on the populist side. They lost. The president, it was at first decided, would be elected by the legislature. The advocates of a strong president argued that he should be given a veto over Congress, and secured this. The advocates of a strong legislature argued that he be liable to impeachment by Congress, and won this. The conservatives now attempted to restrict the franchise even in the lower house. Gouverneur Morris argued that, if 'mechanicals and manufacturers' had the vote, they would be bought by their employers. Only the propertied classes should be enfranchised. This proved too much even for Madison and Franklin to stomach; they feared the people would rise up in revolt.

The southern conservatives of Georgia and South Carolina even tried to write a ban on taxing the slave trade into the constitution, but this was modified into a promise that slavery would be maintained for at least thirty years. Thus were dashed the radical and egalitarian ideals on which the American Revolution had been founded.

Congress was also given virtually limitless powers over the states 'to provide, as may become necessary, from time to time, for the well managing and securing the common property and general interests and welfare of the United States in such manner as shall not interfere with the governments of individual states in matters which respect only their internal police, or for which their individual authorities may be competent'.

The Senate – the more conservative house, in which the small states were disproportionately represented – was accorded such extensive powers to originate many bills, to make treaties and to nominate Supreme Court judges and ambassadors that they had to be watered down.

The final key question was the method of electing the president, and the length of his term. Some suggested that he be chosen by popular vote, others that he be elected by Congress. The compromise reached was that he should be indirectly chosen by an electoral college of state representatives; this satisfied both the conservatives, who abhorred popular election, and the states, which were thus further empowered. If the college failed to decide, the House of Representatives would choose, with each state delegation casting one vote. The American constitution was then edited down to its succinct final version, a literary masterpiece, by a committee chaired by Gouverneur Morris, although both Hamilton and Madison were members. On 17 September 1787 the draft was signed.

It began with the preamble 'We the people of the United States' – to blur the fact that it would come into effect even if only nine of the thirteen states ratified it: 'We the states' would have been inaccurate if any had failed to do so.

The constitution was to become one of the greatest documents in human history. It was also highly conservative – and therein lay the secret of its longevity. Apparently the product of a revolution, and denounced as such by the absolute monarchs of continental Europe, it was actually a series of curbs on revolution.

It provided for strong central government; it embraced the self-interest of the smaller states, particularly in the south, as an excuse to entrench conservatism into the system; and it rendered radical action by the president, who would not now be popularly elected, or by Congress virtually impossible because of the system's inbuilt inertia. However, Washington, the first president, quickly established his right to rule by his own nominated cabinet, not the Senate – and to control foreign policy.

The debate within the Convention had been one between extreme and moderate conservatives conducted entirely in secret. To this day even major American television analyses on the subject talk of the proceedings as unknowable, achieved mysteriously by consensus.

The sole truly popular element in the new constitution was election to the House of Representatives: in order to check and balance that, there existed the Senate, a Supreme Court and a president selected indirectly. The Senate could block the decisions of the House of Representatives; the Supreme Court could modify them; the president could veto them; and, in case the president himself grew populist and tyrannical, he could be impeached and removed from office. It was a brilliant and ingenious assertion of power by the elite. America would now have a strong central government – with an authority far exceeding that of the British – a strong army, and the power to tax and legislate.

The Convention was no more than an assertion of authority by the conservative majority in America. But the states would have to ratify its decisions, and the proponents of states' rights united with the radicals in bitterly opposing the new constitution. It was denounced as 'our new king'; Washington, who had presided over the Convention, was directly attacked as the 'president-general' behind whom served a 'masked aristocracy'. There was truth in all these charges.

The authors of the original 1776 Revolution were bitter at its proposed betrayal. The new constitution's supporters became known as Federalists, and its opponents as anti-Federalists. The latter were faced with a new government structure that had replaced the Articles of Confederation of 1776 (amended in 1777 and again in 1781) which they believed they had been fighting for. The centralism, one-man rule, aristocratic government, standing army, and central taxing authority which they had battled against were all to be imposed upon them. The

Revolution had been halted in its tracks, and a new ruling class was preparing to take over. Richard Henry Lee of Virginia headed the anti-Federalist offensive, at first supported by New York, Virginia, Rhode Island, Massachusetts and New Hampshire.

In Pennsylvania, the hotbed of revolution, a fierce debate broke out at once. Robert Morris was lampooned as 'Robert the Cofferer', while the wealthy and ambitious men behind the new constitution were decried. The document was denounced for failing to promote a bill of rights and the guarantees of freedom long enjoyed under English common law, for swallowing up the rights of ordinary people; and for the small role given to the popular will, as well as for the peremptory imposition of the constitution upon the people. For, in order to hurry the process, the conservatives decided that only nine states needed to ratify the new constitution to bring it into force. The old Congress, which suggested amendments, was brusquely pushed aside.

The first key vote was in Pennsylvania, where shopkeepers, farmers and congressmen in Philadelphia swamped the assembly's radicals in a two-to-one vote in favour. Delaware (happy with the concessions made to state power), New Jersey and Georgia (then under threat from the Creek Indians and needing the support of federal troops) followed with their approval almost immediately, as did Connecticut, delighted to have an influence in the Senate equalling that of its overwhelming neighbour, New York. Of these five, only Pennsylvania was a political big hitter. Other states waited for the decision from the cradle of American independence, Massachusetts, and the big states.

In Massachusetts, conditions were dangerous and opinions bitterly divided: having started the war, the state remained in the economic doldrums and, worse, had been subjected to the profiteering and exploitation that had led to Shays's Rebellion. The Massachusetts farmers – storm troopers of the revolution outside Boston and later decisively at Saratoga – had been the worst hit by the financial exactions of the state government, dominated by the rich merchants and their followers. They hated it almost as much as they had once hated the British; yet they wondered if a strong central government, while diluting state authority, would not prove even more autocratic.

In Boston a complex power struggle had evolved, at the centre of which were the three men who had started the American Revolution: Samuel Adams, John Hancock, and John Adams. Sam Adams, the frenzied backroom manoeuvrer behind the Declaration of Independence, had been chairman of the most important congressional committee, the Board of War, as well as of the Foreign Alliance Committee and no fewer than six others. At that stage he was probably the Revolution's most powerful figure.

After the defeat of Washington at Brandywine in 1777, which many believed to be the end of the American cause, Adams had taken on the role of keeping the flame burning. He had made a memorable address to Congress at Yorktown, to which it had fled:

> Gentlemen, your spirits appear oppressed with the weight of the public calamities. Your sadness of countenance reveals your disquietude. A patriot may grieve at the distress of his country, but he will never despair of the commonwealth. Our affairs, it is said, are desperate! If this be our language, they are indeed. If we wear long faces, long faces will become fashionable. The eyes of the people are upon us. The tone of their feelings is regulated by ours. If we despond, public confidence is destroyed, the people will no longer yield their support to a hopeless contest, and American liberty is no more. But we are not driven to such narrow straits. Though fortune has been unpropitious, our condition is not desperate. Our burdens, though grievous, can be borne. Our losses, though great, can be retrieved. Through the darkness which shrouds our prospects the ark of safety is visible. Despondency becomes not the dignity of our cause, nor the character of those who are its supporters. Let us remember, always, that common adage, that 'the darkest hour was just before the dawn of day'.

When, in 1776, the British had issued a promise of amnesty for all Americans, only Sam Adams and Hancock, the original instigators of the rebellion, were excluded. Still the effective leader of Congress, when Howe entered Philadelphia in 1778 Adams had continued to blast the British with almost biblical tirades, such as this one on the conditions in which the British held prisoners (which were appalling, but no different from the American equivalents):

> We, therefore, the congress of the United States of America, do solemnly declare and proclaim that if our enemies presume to execute their threats, or persist in their present career of barbarity, we will take such exemplary vengeance as shall deter others from a like conduct. We appeal to the God who searcheth the hearts of men for the rectitude of our intentions; and in His holy presence declare that, as we are not moved by any light or hasty suggestions of anger or revenge, so through every possible change of fortune we will adhere to this our determination.

Yet by the winter of 1781 this most implacable of American revolutionaries was beginning to be exhausted and the reins of power were slipping
from his hand. He wrote to his supporters:

> When time enfeebles [a citizen's] powers, and renders him unfit for further
> service, his country, to preserve its own vigour, will wisely call upon others;
> and if he decently retreats to make room for them, he will show that he
> has not totally lost his understanding. Besides, there is a period in life
> when a man should cover the exalted pleasures of reflection in retirement.

He retired again to Massachusetts, where his hatred of the British did
not diminish. He blocked a post-war attempt there to reintegrate the
loyalists, whom he always denounced as traitors deserving 'the just punishment of the Almighty'. When someone offered to trace his ancestry,
he exploded, 'It is a subject I have not thought much about. On this side
of the water, I believe my ancestors were exemplary men and good citizens. But I have never looked much beyond that, not knowing what
scoundrels a further research might rake out.'

When the Order of Cincinnatus was founded, consisting of military
officers who wanted to retain their links after the War of Independence,
and Washington joined, Adams was scathing, suspecting, probably
rightly, that it existed to bring military pressure to bear upon the new
republic. He eventually forced it to disband – although the secret ties
remained. No respecter of persons, he wrote of Washington:

> It is a tribute due to the man who serves his country well, to esteem him
> highly and confide in him. We ought not, however, to think any man
> incapable of error. But so it is with the bulk of mankind, and even in a
> free country; they reprobate the idea of implicit faith, and at the same
> time, while the impression of gratitude is deep in their minds, they will
> not admit that of a benefactor which must be said of every man – ali-
> quando dormitat [someone is sleeping].
>
> I would never inculcate a base and envious suspicion of any man, espe-
> cially of those who have rendered signal services to their country. But
> there is a degree of watchfulness over all men possessed of power or influ-
> ence, upon which the liberties of mankind must depend. It is necessary
> to guard against the infirmities of the best as well as the wickedness of the
> worst of men. Such is the weakness of human nature, that tyranny has
> perhaps oftener sprung from that than any other source. It is this that
> unravels the mystery of millions being enslaved by the few.

In 1786 when Shays's Rebellion broke out in western Massachusetts,
staged by the very men who had launched the American Revolution and

had been Adams's diehard supporters, the veteran revolutionary turned into their most implacable opponent, believing that the very survival of independent America was at stake. With renewed vigour, Adams spurred the state government to set up a 4,000-strong militia army under Benjamin Lincoln. In a clash with the rebels, three were killed, and 150 captured after a night-long chase in a snowstorm. Sporadic fighting went on for weeks, but the insurrection of those wretched, impoverished men was at an end. Although Adams's actions made him deeply unpopular among his own former supporters, the grim old revolutionary's determination to safeguard the United States he had helped to bring into being enormously enhanced his prestige.

With only five states having so far endorsed the constitution, the attitude of Massachusetts, where the whole independence movement had begun, became crucial – and Sam Adams was known to be against the new constitution. As he explained, with devastating logic:

> I meet with a national government instead of a federal union of sovereign states. I am not able to conceive why the wisdom of the convention led them to give the preference to the former before the latter. If the several states in the union are to become one entire nation under one legislature, the powers of which shall extend to every subject of legislation, and its laws be supreme and control the whole, the idea of sovereignty in these states must be lost. Indeed, I think, upon such a supposition, those sovereignties ought to be eradicated from the mind; for they would be *imperia in imperio*, justly deemed a solecism in politics, and they would be highly dangerous and destructive of the peace, union and safety of the nation.
>
> And can this national legislature be competent to make laws for the free internal governments of one people, living in climates so remote, and whose 'habits and particular interests' are, and probably always will be, so different? Is it to be expected that general laws can be adapted to the more eastern and the more southern parts of so extensive a nation? It appears to me difficult, if practicable. Hence, then, may we not look for discontent, mistrust, disaffection to government, and frequent insurrections, which will require standing armies to suppress them in one place and another, where they may happen to arise. Or, if laws could be made, adapted to the local habits, feelings, views and interests of those distant parts, would they not cause jealousies of partiality in government which would excite envy and other malignant passions, productive of wars and fighting?
>
> But should we continue as distinct sovereign states, confederated for

the purpose of mutual safety and happiness, each contributing to the federal head such a part of its sovereignty as would render the government fully adequate to those purposes, and no more, the people would govern themselves more easily, the laws of each state being well adapted to its own genius and circumstances, and the liberties of the United States would be more secure than they can be, as I humbly conceive, under the proposed new constitution ...

The seeds of aristocracy began to spring, even before the conclusion of our struggle for the natural rights of men – seeds which, like a canker-worm, lie at the root of free governments. So great is the wickedness of some men and the stupid servility of others, that one would be almost inclined to conclude that communities cannot be free. The few haughty families think that they must govern; the body of the people tamely consent, and submit to be their slaves ...

Opinion had polarized between the Federalist men of property, supporting the new centralizing constitution, and the anti-Federalist poor farmers and workers. Perhaps many of the old waterfront gangs of mechanicals who had initiated the Revolution supported the constitution as providing a strong hand in a country desperately in need of one. If so this was almost certainly under the influence of the wealthier merchants, who tended to hire the gangs for their own purposes. Paul Revere reported to John Hancock, after a meeting at the Green Dragon Inn, that a large assembly of 'mechanicals' had voted for the new constitution. Sam Adams himself now began to waver.

Meanwhile Hancock, his old friend and rival, had been bought out with the job of presiding over the Massachusetts convention to approve the new constitution, and the hope of becoming vice-president of the new United States. He began to work on the 'old incendiary'. At length, Adams agreed to support the new constitution provided that a crucial series of amendments was introduced to protect individual rights. In a speech to the state assembly at the end of January 1788 he listed his conditions:

that the said constitution be never construed to authorise congress to infringe the just liberty of the press or the rights of conscience; or to prevent the people of the United States who are peaceable citizens from keeping their own arms; or to raise standing armies, unless when necessary for the defence of the United States, or of some one or more of them; or to prevent the people from petitioning, in a peaceable and orderly manner, the federal legislature for a redress of grievances; or to subject the people to unreasonable searches and seizures of the persons, papers, or possessions.

In Virginia his fellow radical leader Patrick Henry took the same line. A few days later the Massachusetts convention voted. Thanks to Adams's change of heart, 187 delegates ratified the constitution while 168 were opposed. If it had gone the other way, the constitution would have been dead in the water and a civil war might have loomed.

Adams explained his reasoning thus:

> I was particularly afraid that, unless great care should be taken to prevent it, the constitution, in the administration of it, would gradually, but swiftly and imperceptibly, run into a consolidated government, pervading and legislating through all the states; not for federal purposes only, as it professes, but in all cases whatsoever. Such a government would soon totally annihilate the sovereignty of the several States, so necessary to the support of the confederated commonwealth, and sink both in despotism.
>
> I mean, my friend, to let you know how deeply I am impressed with the sense of the importance of amendments; that the good people may clearly see the distinction – for there is a distinction – between the federal powers vested in Congress and the sovereign authority belonging to the several states, which is the palladium of the private and personal rights of the citizens.

The amendments were his price, and they were written into the constitution in the spring of 1789, the first ten of the twelve representing a bill of rights. Following Massachusetts's ratification, Maryland and South Carolina quickly followed suit. New Hampshire – Massachusetts's neighbour – now had the pivotal role of being the ninth state to ratify, which would make the constitution binding on all states. It narrowly voted in favour by 57 votes to 47.

In key Virginia, although the constitution was based on its own, the margin in favour was just ten votes, in June. The voting divide was almost precisely between the urban centres and the developed east. New York followed, with the pencil-thin margin of three, despite Alexander Hamilton's best efforts. North Carolina approved only in November 1789, and Rhode Island – which might well have been nicknamed Rogue Island for its maverick qualities – came aboard in May 1790.

Thus America's Lenin had been forced to bury his own revolution, which had truly come full circle: even Sam Adams had joined the new ruling class. He was to pay a price, however: when he stood for Congress, he was soundly defeated by his old working-class supporters, and Hancock, who had had the temerity to oppose Washington as the first president of the United States in February 1789, was also humiliatingly rebuffed. John Adams was elected vice-president, which was some consolation for his unbending older cousin.

Samuel Adams himself ran for lieutenant-governor of Massachusetts on a ticket headed by Hancock for governor, and this time they won. When Hancock died in office in 1793, Adams became governor, and alarmed his contemporaries with his extravagant praise for the French Revolution, which happened to be going through its most extreme phase, as a 'noble new democracy' – entirely consistent with the unbending republican's old philosophy.

Adams the governor proved as puritanical and frugal as ever. He refused to permit theatres in Boston and would rarely use the governor's carriage; when criticized for this he answered, 'The Almighty gave me two feet for the purpose of using them, sir! I have been walking through the streets of Boston for seven decades, and shall continue to do so until I can no longer walk!'

However, he had become a firm supporter of central government, and when Washington ordered 15,000 troops to put down the bloodless 'whiskey rebellion' in Pennsylvania in 1795, objecting to a tax similar to British levies imposed thirty years earlier, Adams unequivocally sided with the new federal army:

> It is with pain that I mention the insurrection which has lately taken place in a sister state. It was pointed more immediately at an act of the federal government. An act of that government as well as of the governments in the union is constitutionally an act of the people; and our constitutions provide a safe and easy method to redress any real grievances. No people can be more free than under a constitution established by their voluntary compact, and exercised by men appointed by their own frequent suffrages. If any law shall prove oppressive in its operation, the future deliberations of a freely elective representative will afford a constitutional remedy. But the measures adopted by the President of the United States, supported by the virtue of every citizen of every description in that and the adjacent states, have prevailed, and there is an end to the insurrection.

Having thus completed this obeisance to authority, America's greatest revolutionary and the real founding father of the United States died in October 1803, aged eighty-one.

Meanwhile George Washington had been inaugurated president of the United States on 20 April 1789, amid a hero worship that appeared almost idolatrous. A young lady gushed, 'I never saw a human being that looked so grave and noble as he does. I could fall down on my knees before him.' Washington himself, to his credit, complained of 'feelings not unlike those of a culprit who is going to the place of his execution'. John Adams had spoken of 'this dangerous enthusiasm' for Washington. Another contemporary writer declared, 'We have given him the powers and prerogatives of a King.' He left office wounded by criticism eight years later – a new George III to his critics.

He was soon reinvented as a saintly incarnation of modesty, rectitude, duty and wisdom – an image that persists to this day, only tarnished a little. But perhaps it is the real George Washington – stubborn, tough, often mean-minded, acutely self-conscious, hot-tempered beneath a reserved exterior, often harsh, ruthless with his competitors, and yes, intensely patriotic, resilient, dutiful and aware of his own failings – who best embodies the spirit of America today.

# Select Bibliography

Adair, Douglas, *Frame and Founding Fathers* ed. Trevor Colbourn (New York, 1974)

Adams, James Truslow, *Revolutionary New England, 1691–1716* (Boston, 1923)

——*The Adams Family* (Boston, 1930)

Adams, John, *Works* (Boston, 1819, 3 vols)

Adams, Randolph, *Political Ideas of the American Revolution* (New York, 1958)

Adams, Samuel, *Writings*, ed. Harry A. Cushing (New York, 1904, 4 vols)

Agar, Herbert, *Land of the Free* (Boston, 1935)

Alden, John R. *The American Revolution, 1775–1783* (New York, 1954)

——*The South in the Revolution* (Baton Rouge, Louisiana, 1957)

Allen, Herbert, *John Hancock, Patriot in Purple* (New York, 1948)

Anburey, Lieutenant T., *With Burgoyne from Quebec* (S. Jackman, 1963)

Anderson, Fred, *A People's Army: Massachusetts Soldiers and Society in the Seven Years' War* (Chapel Hill, North Carolina, 1984)

Anderson, Troyer, *The Command of the Howe Brother* (New York, 1936)

Andrews, Charles, *The Colonial Period of American History* (New Haven, Connecticut, 1934–8, 4 vols)

Aptheker, Herbert, *The Negro in the American Revolution* (New York, 1940)

Bailyn, Bernard, *The Ideological Origins of the America Revolution* (Cambridge, Massachusetts, 1967)

——*The Ordeal of Thomas Hutchinson* (Cambridge, Massachusetts, 1974)

Bass, Robert, *The Swamp Fox* (New York, 1949)

Becker, Carl, *The Eve of the Revolution* (New York, 1920)

——*The Declaration of Independence* (New York, 1922)

Belcher, Henry, *The First American Civil War, 1775–1778* (New York, 1911, 2 vols)

Bemis, Samuel, *The Diplomacy of the American Revolution* (Washington, 1935)

Bernière, Ensign Henry de, *Narrative of Occurrences, 1775* (Boston, 1779)

Boatner, Mark, *Encyclopedia of the American Revolution* (New York, 1976)

Bobrick, Benson, *Angel in the Whirlwind* (New York, 1997)

Bowler, R. Arthur, *Logistics and the Failure of the British Army in America, 1775–1783* (Princeton, New Jersey, 1975)

Bowman, Allen, *The Morale of the American Revolutionary Army* (Washington, DC, 1943)

Brinton, Crane, *The Anatomy of Revolution* (New York, 1938)

Buell, Augustus, *Paul Jones, Founder of the American Navy* (New York, 1900, 2 vols)

Bullock, Charles, *The Finances of the United States from 1775 to 1789* (Madison, 1895)

Burgoyne, *The Dramatic and Poetical Works of Lt.-Gen. J. Burgoyne* (London, 1808, 2 vols)

Butterfield, L. H., ed., *Adams Family Correspondence* (Cambridge, Massachusetts, 1963–73, 4 vols)

Calhoon, Robert, *The Loyalist Perception* (New York, 1989)

Callahan, North, *Henry Knox* (New York, 1958)

Calloway, Colin *The American Revolution in Indian Country* (Cambridge, Massachusetts, 1998)

Carter, Clarence, ed., *The Correspondence of General Thomas Gage* (New Haven, Connecticut, 1933, 2 vols)

Chinar, Gilbert, *Honest John Adams* (Boston, 1933)

Clinton, General Sir Henry, *The American Rebellion*, ed. William Willcox (New Haven, Connecticut, 1954)

Coleman, Kenneth, *The American Revolution in Georgia, 1763–1789* (Athens, Georgia, 1958)

Commager, Henry Steels, *Documents of American History* (New York, 1934, 2 vols.)

——and Richard Morris, *The Spirit of '76* (Indianapolis, Indiana, 1958)

Coupland, Reginald, *The American Revolution and the British Empire* (New York, 1930)

Curtis, Edward, *The Organisation of the British Army in the American Revolution* (New Haven, Connecticut 1926)

Davidson, Philip, *Propaganda and the American Revolution, 1763–1783* (Chapel Hill, North Carolina, 1941)

Donne, Bodham, ed., *Correspondence of King George III with Lord North* (London, 1867, 2 vols)

Dull, Jonathan, *The French Navy and American Independence* (Princeton, New Jersey, 1975)

Egerton, Hugh, *Causes and Character of the American Revolution* (Oxford, 1923)

Ferrie, Richard, *The World Turned Upside Down* (New York, 1988)

Fischer, David Hackett, *Paul Revere's Ride* (New York, 1994)

Fisher, Sydney, *The Struggle for American Independence* (Philadelphia, 1908, 2 vols)

Forbes, Esther, *Paul Revere and the World he Lived in* (Boston, 1942)

Fortescue, Sir John, *A History of the British Army, Vols. Two and Three* (London, 1910–11)

Franklin, Benjamin, *Writings*, ed. Albert Smyth (New York, 1905–7, 10 vols)

Freeman, Douglas, *George Washington: A Biography* (New York, 1948–54, 6 vols)

Frey, Sylvia, *The British Soldier in America* (Austin, Texas, 1981)

Freidenwald, Herbert, *The Declaration of Independence* (New York, 1904)

Fuller, J.F.C. *Decisive Battles of the USA* (1942)

Galvin, John, *The Minute Men* (New York, 1967)

Glover, Michael, *General Burgoyne* (London, 1976)

Goss, Elbridge, *The Life of Colonel Paul Revere* (Boston, 1891, 2 vols)

Gottschalk, Louis, *Lafayette and the Close of the American Revolution* (Chicago, 1942)

Granger, Bruce, *Political Satire in the American Revolution* (New York, 1960)

Graymont, Barbara, *The Iroquois in the American Revolution* (Syracuse, New York, 1972)

Greene, Evarts, *The Provincial Governor in the English Colonies of North America* (New York, 1898)

Greene, Nathanael, *Papers*, ed. Dennis Conrad (Ann Arbor, Michigan, 1971–2001, 9 vols)

Gruber, Ira, *The Howe Brothers and the American Revolution* (New York, 1972)

Hacker, Louis, 'The First American Revolution', *Columbia University Quarterly*, 1935

Haiman, Miecislaus, *Kosciuszko in the American Revolution* (New York, 1943)

Headley, W.T., *Washington and his Generals* (New York, 1848, 2 vols)

Hibbert, Christopher, *Redcoats and Rebels: The War for America, 1770–1781* (London, 1990)

Hutchinson, Thomas, *Diary and Letters* (Boston, 1884, 2 vols)

Jackson, Luther, *Virginia Negro Soldiers and Sailors in the Revolutionary War* (Norfolk, Virginia, 1994)

James, William, *A sketch of the life of Brigadier General Francis Marion* (Marietta, 1948)

Jefferson, Thomas, *Papers*, ed. Julian Boyd (Princeton, New Jersey, 1950, Vols. 1 and 2)

——*Writings*, ed. Albert Bergh (Washington, 1904–5, 20 vols)

Jensen, Merrill, *The Founding of a Nation: A History of the American Revolution 1763–1774* (New York, 1968)

Johnson, Curt, *The Battles of the Revolutionary War* (New York, 1879, 2 vols)

Kettner, James, *The Development of American Citizenship 1608–1870* (Chapel Hill, North Carolina, 1978)

Lafayette, *Memoires* (Leipzig, 1838)

Lee, Henry, *Memoirs of the War* (New York, 1870)

Lewis, Paul, *The Grand Incendiary* (New York, 1973)

Livermore, George, *An Historical Research Respecting the Opinions of the Founders of the Republic on Negroes as Slaves, as Citizens and as Soldiers* (Boston, 1862)

Lowell, Edward, *The Hessians in the American Revolution* (New York, 1884)

McCrady, Edward, *The History of South Carolina in the Revolution, 1780–1783* (New York, 1902)

McDonald, Forrest, *The Economic Origins of the Constitution* (Chicago, 1958)

Madison, James, *Papers* (Washington, 1840, 3 vols)

Main, Jackson, *The Antifederalists* (Chapel Hill, North Carolina, 1961)

—— *The Social Structure of Revolutionary America* (Princeton, New Jersey, 1966)

Malone, Dumas, *The Story of the Declaration of Independence* (New York, 1954)

May, Robin, *The British Army in North America, 1775–1783* (London, 1998)

Mazyck, Walter, *George Washington and the Negro* (Washington, 1932)

Merriam, Charles, *A History of American Political Theories* (New York, 1903)

Middlekauf, Robert, *The Glorious Cause* (New York, 1982)

Miller, John, *Sam Adams: Pioneer in Propaganda* (Boston, 1936)

—— *Origins of the American Revolution* (Boston, 1943)

Mintz, Max, *Gouverneur Morris and the American Revolution* (Norman, Oklahoma, 1970)

Morgan, Edmund and Helen, *The Stamp Act Crisis* (Chapel Hill, North Carolina, 1953)

Morison, Samuel Eliot, *John Paul Jones* (New York, 1959)

Morris, Richard, *The Peacemakers: The Great Powers and American Independence* (New York, 1965)

Moultrie, William, *Memoirs* (New York, 1802, 2 vols)

Namier, Sir Lewis, *The Structure of Politics at the Accession of George III* (London, 1965)

—— *England in the Age of the American Revolution* (London, 1966)

Nevins, Allan, *The American States during and after the Revolution, 1775–1789* (New York, 1925)

Nickerson, Hoffman, *The Turning Point of the Revolution* (New York, 1928)

O'Donnell, James, *Southern Indians in the American Revolution* (Knoxville, Tennessee, 1973)

Paine, Thomas, *Writings* (New York, 1894–6, 3 vols)

Percy, Colonel Hugh, *Letters* (Boston, 1902)

Perkins, James, *France in the American Revolution* (Boston, 1911)

Pitt, William, *Correspondence of William Pitt, Earl Chatham*, ed. Taylor and Prince (London, 1840)

Poole, William, *Anti-Slavery Opinions before the Year 1800* (Cincinnati, Ohio, 1873)

Quarles, Benjamin, *The Negro in the American Revolution* (Chapel Hill, North Carolina, 1961)

Ramsay, David, *A History of the American Revolution* (London, 1793, 2 vols)

Randall, Henry, *The Life of Thomas Jefferson* (New York, 1858, 3 vols)

Randall, Willard, *Benedict Arnold: Patriot and Traitor* (New York, 1990)

Riedesel, Baroness von, *Letters and Journals relating to the War of the American Revolution and the Capture of the German Troops at Saratoga* (Albany, New York, 1867)

Ritcheson, Charles, *British Politics and the American Revolution* (Norman, 1954)

Robson, Eric, *The American Revolution in its Political and Military Aspects* (London, 1955)

Rochambeau, Marshal Comte de, *Mémoires* (Paris, 1838)

Rockingham, *Memoirs*, ed. George Thomas (London, 1852, 2 vols)

Royster, Charles, *A Revolutionary People at War* (Chapel Hill, North Carolina, 1976)

Rush, Benjamin, *Letters* (Princeton, New Jersey, 1951, 2 vols)

Sabine, Lorenzo, *The American Loyalists* (Boston, 1847)

Sandwich, Earl of, *Private Papers* (London, 1932–8, 3 vols)

Schwartz, Barry, *George Washington* (London, 1987)

Sellers, Charles, *Benedict Arnold* (New York, 1930)

Shaw, Peter, *The Character of John Adams* (Chapel Hill, North Carolina, 1976)

Shlesinger, Arthur, *The Colonial Merchants and the American Revolution* (New York, 1917)

Silverman, Kenneth, *A Cultural History of the American Revolution* (New York, 1987)

Simms, William, *Nathanael Greene* (New York, 1858)

Smith, Page, *A New Age Now Begins: A People's History of the American Revolution* (New York, 1976, 2 vols)

——*The Causes of the American Revolution*

Smith, Paul, *Loyalists and Redcoats* (Chapel Hill, North Carolina, 1964)

Sullivan, General John, *Letters and Papers* (Concord, New Hampshire, 1930–9, 3 vols)

Syrett, Harold (ed.), *The Papers of Alexander Hamilton 26 vols* (New York 1961–79)

Tarleton, Banastre, *A History of the Campaign in the Southern Provinces* (Dublin, 1787)

Thacher, James, *Military Journal of the American Revolution* (Hartford, Connecticut, 1827)

Thane, Elswyth, *The Fighting Quaker: Nathanael Greene* (New York, 1972)

Thayer, Theodore, *Nathanael Greene, Strategist of the American Revolution* (New York, 1960)

Treacy, M.F., *Prelude to Yorktown* (Chapel Hill, New Carolina, 1963)

Trevelyan, Sir George, *The American Revolution* (New York, 1899–1907, 4 vols)

Tuckerman, Bayard, *Lafayette* (New York, 1889, 2 vols)

Tyler, Moses, *Patrick Henry* (Boston, 1898)

Van Tyne, Claude, *The Loyalists in the American Revolution* (New York, 1922)

Wahike, John, *The Causes of the American Revolution* (Lexington, Massachusetts, 1973)

Walpole, Horace, *Letters* (London, 1906)

Warren, Mercy, *History of the American Revolution* (Boston, 1805, 3 vols)

Washington, George, *Writings* (Washington, 1937–44, 39 vols)

Weems, Mason, *A History of the Life and Death, Virtues and Exploits of General George Washington* (Georgetown, DC, 1800)

Wheatley, Phillis, *Poems and Letters* (New York, 1915)

Wheeler, Richard, *Voices of 1776* (New York, 1972)

Wiecek, William, *The Source of Antislavery Constitutionalism in America, 1760–1848* (New York, 1977)

Williams, George Washington, *History of the Negro Race in America* (New York, 1885)

Willcox, William, *Portrait of a General: Sir Henry Clinton in the War of Independence* (New York, 1964)

Will Garry, *Cincinnatus: George Washington and the Enlightenment* (New York, 1984)

Wood, Gordon, 'Mobs in the American Revolution', *William and Mary Quarterly*, October 1966

——*The Creation of the American Republic, 1776–1787* (New York, 1969)

Woodward, W.E., *Lafayette* (New York, 1938)

Wright, Esmond, ed., *Causes and Consequences of the American Revolution* (Chicago, 1966)

# Index